W9-BCQ-514

America's
TEST KITCHEN

"Ideal as a reference for the bookshelf and as a book to curl up and get lost in, this volume will be turned to time and again for definitive instruction on just about any food-related matter."

PUBLISHERS WEEKLY ON *THE SCIENCE OF GOOD COOKING*

"A one-volume kitchen seminar, addressing in one smart chapter after another the sometimes surprising whys behind a cook's best practices.... You get the myth, the theory, the science and the proof, all rigorously interrogated as only America's Test Kitchen can do."

NPR ON *THE SCIENCE OF GOOD COOKING*

"*The Cook's Illustrated Cookbook* is the perfect kitchen home companion."

THE WALL STREET JOURNAL ON *THE COOK'S ILLUSTRATED COOKBOOK*

"A wonderfully comprehensive guide for budding chefs.... Throughout are the helpful tips and exacting illustrations that make ATK a peerless source for culinary wisdom."

PUBLISHERS WEEKLY ON *THE COOK'S ILLUSTRATED COOKBOOK*

"If this were the only cookbook you owned, you would cook well, be everyone's favorite host, have a well-run kitchen, and eat happily every day."

THECITYCOOK.COM ON *THE AMERICA'S TEST KITCHEN MENU COOKBOOK*

"America's Test Kitchen spent two years reimagining cooking for the 21st century. The result is an exhaustive collection offering a fresh approach to quick cooking."

THE DETROIT NEWS ON *THE AMERICA'S TEST KITCHEN QUICK FAMILY COOKBOOK*

"This comprehensive collection of 800-plus family and global favorites helps put healthy eating in an everyday context, from meatloaf to Indian curry with chicken."

COOKING LIGHT ON *THE AMERICA'S TEST KITCHEN HEALTHY FAMILY COOKBOOK*

"This book upgrades slow cooking for discriminating, 21st-century palates—that is indeed revolutionary."

THE DALLAS MORNING NEWS ON *SLOW COOKER REVOLUTION*

"Forget about marketing hype, designer labels and pretentious entrées: This is an unblinking, unbedazzled guide to the Beardian good-cooking ideal."

THE WALL STREET JOURNAL ON *THE BEST OF AMERICA'S TEST KITCHEN 2009*

"Expert bakers and novices scared of baking's requisite exactitude can all learn something from this hefty, all-purpose home baking volume."

PUBLISHERS WEEKLY ON *THE AMERICA'S TEST KITCHEN FAMILY BAKING BOOK*

"Scrupulously tested regional and heirloom recipes."

THE NEW YORK TIMES ON *THE COOK'S COUNTRY COOKBOOK*

"If you're hankering for old-fashioned pleasures, look no further."

PEOPLE MAGAZINE ON *AMERICA'S BEST LOST RECIPES*

"This tome definitely raises the bar for all-in-one, basic, must-have cookbooks.... Kimball and his company have scored another hit."

PORTLAND OREGONIAN ON *THE AMERICA'S TEST KITCHEN FAMILY COOKBOOK*

"A foolproof, go-to resource for everyday cooking."

PUBLISHERS WEEKLY ON *THE AMERICA'S TEST KITCHEN FAMILY COOKBOOK*

"The strength of the Best Recipe series lies in the sheer thoughtfulness and details of the recipes."

PUBLISHERS WEEKLY ON *THE BEST RECIPE SERIES*

"Further proof that practice makes perfect, if not transcendent.... If an intermediate cook follows the directions exactly, the results will be better than takeout or mom's."

THE NEW YORK TIMES ON *THE NEW BEST RECIPE*

"The best instructional book on baking this reviewer has seen."

LIBRARY JOURNAL (STARRED REVIEW) ON *BAKING ILLUSTRATED*

THE TV COMPANION
COOKBOOK

2014

THE TV COMPANION COOKBOOK

2014

BY THE EDITORS AT
AMERICA'S TEST KITCHEN

PHOTOGRAPHY BY
DANIEL J. VAN ACKERE
CARL TREMBLAY
STEVE KLISE

AMERICA'S TEST KITCHEN
BROOKLINE, MASSACHUSETTS

AMERICA'S TEST KITCHEN
17 Station Street, Brookline, MA 02445

AMERICA'S TEST KITCHEN: THE TV COMPANION COOKBOOK 2014
1st Edition

ISBN-13: 978-1-936493-59-3   ISBN-10: 1-936493-59-4
ISSN 2161-6671
Hardcover: $34.95 US

Manufactured in the United States of America

10 9 8 7 6 5 4 3 2 1

Distributed by America's Test Kitchen
17 Station Street, Brookline, MA 02445

EDITORIAL DIRECTOR: Jack Bishop
EDITORIAL DIRECTOR, BOOKS: Elizabeth Carduff
EXECUTIVE EDITOR: Lori Galvin
ASSOCIATE EDITORS: Kate Hartke, Debra Hudak, and Alyssa King
EDITORIAL ASSISTANT: Melissa Herrick
DESIGN DIRECTOR: Amy Klee
ART DIRECTOR, BOOKS: Greg Galvan
DESIGNERS: Taylor Argenzio, Sarah Horwitch Dailey, and Allison Pfiffner
STAFF PHOTOGRAPHER: Daniel J. van Ackere
PHOTO EDITOR: Steve Klise
ADDITIONAL PHOTOGRAPHY: Steve Klise and Carl Tremblay
FOOD STYLIST: Marie Piraino
PRODUCTION DIRECTOR: Guy Rochford
SENIOR PRODUCTION MANAGER: Jessica Lindheimer Quirk
PROJECT MANAGEMENT DIRECTOR: Alice Carpenter
ASSISTANT PROJECT MANAGER: Brittany Allen
WORKFLOW AND DIGITAL ASSET MANAGER: Andrew Mannone
SENIOR COLOR AND IMAGING SPECIALIST: Lauren Pettapiece
PRODUCTION AND IMAGING SPECIALISTS: Heather Dube and Lauren Robbins
COPY EDITOR: Cheryl Redmond
PROOFREADER: Christine Corcoran Cox
INDEXER: Elizabeth Parson

CONTENTS

PREFACE

EVERY YEAR, THE MEDIA DOES "YEAR IN REVIEW" stories: the headlines, the fashion mistakes, the best and worst movies, the winners and the losers. Here at America's Test Kitchen, we do the same thing when we film 26 episodes of our public television show. Standing next to Julia or Bridget, I get to relive the best recipes from the year, to watch them being made, and, best of all, to actually taste them one more time.

The 2014 lineup is our best yet. A simple recipe—Grown-Up Grilled Cheese—was an eye-opener since it transforms a formerly pedestrian dish into a recipe that is more for adults than kids. Creamy Cauliflower Soup (OK, it sounds boring) is also revolutionary. The cauliflower is cooked in two separate batches so that part is smooth and part fresh-tasting. Plus, we use not a drop of cream but the soup is extra-creamy. We also came up with a way to braise potatoes (why didn't someone else think of this?) that turns out super-smooth red potatoes with lots of flavor, and it's easy to do. And along the way, I got to retaste the world's best Fresh Peach Pie, Oatmeal Muffins, Butterscotch Pudding, and Grilled Beef Kofte. The masterpiece recipe this year was Chocolate-Espresso Dacquoise. It takes time and effort but it will be on my Christmas menu every year from now on.

There are a lot of cooking shows out there—contest shows, travel shows, and celebrity shows—but *America's Test Kitchen* is a bit different. Although I did dress up as a shrimp, Henry IV, a court jester, and an "uncommon" beet this year, we are here to help you become a better cook. We do that by starting with a failed recipe and then explaining how we turned it into a foolproof one. All of this results, we hope, in recipes that really work and home cooks who end up truly understanding what is important, and what is not, when making a pie, a cake, a roast, or a stew. You are part of the process.

I own a 1969 Citroën DS. They started making them in 1956 and the last cars rolled out of the factory in the 1970s. Every year, I invite a mechanic friend of mine, Dave, over to the farm for lunch. This year the Citroën would start up just fine but then, after running for a bit, would not restart. I watched as he diagnosed the problem, going through his mechanic's checklist. Were the plugs getting spark? Was the fuel pump delivering fuel? His system was step-by-step and thorough. He finally replaced some ignition parts and the car now runs just fine.

We do the same thing in the kitchen. A cookie is too cakey. A roast is too tough. A soup is too bland. We go through our checklist in the kitchen as we do on the television show and you get to see the process unveiled.

But, most of all, our show is about all of you who watch it. Young kids, great-grandmothers, and everyone else in between have told us that they enjoy visiting our kitchen every week through public television. It's like going over to help a neighbor make dinner except that we now have millions of neighbors.

Many people ask which are my favorite recipes. I could say the French-Style Chicken and Stuffing in a Pot or perhaps the Foolproof Spaghetti Carbonara or the Summer Berry Trifle. But this reminds me, of course, of an old Vermont story about recommending recipes. At a church supper, one of the waiters was a 14-year-old boy. A lady summer visitor had finished the main course and was asked by the boy if she'd like some dessert. She said that she might and inquired what they were offering for dessert. "Pie," said the young man, "apple and quince." She looked up at him and asked, "What do you recommend?" Following good native practice and cautions, he replied, "I don't."

Enjoy the show and enjoy this year's crop of new recipes. I recommend every one!

Christopher Kimball
Founder and Editor, *Cook's Illustrated* and *Cook's Country*
Host, *America's Test Kitchen* and
Cook's Country from America's Test Kitchen

WELCOME TO AMERICA'S TEST KITCHEN

THIS BOOK HAS BEEN TESTED, WRITTEN, AND EDITED by the folks at America's Test Kitchen, a very real 2,500-square-foot kitchen located just outside of Boston. It is the home of *Cook's Illustrated* and *Cook's Country* magazines and is the Monday-through-Friday destination for more than three dozen test cooks, editors, food scientists, tasters, and cookware specialists. Our mission is to test recipes over and over again until we understand how and why they work and until we arrive at the "best" version.

Our television show highlights the best recipes developed in the test kitchen during the past year—those recipes that our test kitchen staff makes at home time and time again. These recipes are accompanied by our most exhaustive equipment tests and our most interesting food tastings.

Christopher Kimball, the founder and editor of *Cook's Illustrated* magazine, is host of the show and asks the questions you might ask. It's the job of our chefs, Julia Collin Davison, Bridget Lancaster, Becky Hays, Bryan Roof, and Dan Souza, to demonstrate our recipes. The chefs show Chris what works and what doesn't, and they explain why. In the process, they discuss (and show you) the best examples from our development process as well as the worst.

Adam Ried, our equipment expert, and Lisa McManus, our gadget guru, share the highlights from our detailed testing process in equipment corner segments. They bring with them our favorite (and least favorite) gadgets and tools. Jack Bishop is our ingredient expert. He has Chris taste our favorite (and least favorite) brands of common food products. Chris may not always enjoy these exercises (hot sauce isn't exactly as fun to taste as mozzarella or cocoa powder), but he usually learns something as Jack explains what makes one brand superior to another.

Although just 10 cooks and editors appear on the television show, another 50 people worked to make the show a reality. Executive Producer Melissa Baldino conceived and developed each episode with help from Co-Executive Producer Stephanie Stender and Lead Production Assistant Kaitlin Hammond. Meg Ragland

and Debby Paddock assisted with all the historical recipe and photo research. Guy Crosby, our science expert, researched the science behind the recipes. Along with the on-air crew, executive chefs Erin McMurrer and Keith Dresser helped plan and organize the 26 television episodes shot in April and May 2013 and ran the "back kitchen," where all the food that appeared on camera originated. Taizeth Sierra, Hannah Crowley, and Amy Graves organized the tasting and equipment segments.

During filming, chefs Andrea Geary, Nick Iverson, Andrew Janjigian, Cecelia Jenkins, Lan Lam, Rebeccah Marsters, Suzannah McFerran, Christie Morrison, Chris O'Connor, Diane Unger, and Cristin Walsh and interns Liz Sullivan and Amy Young cooked all the food needed on set. Cooks Sarah Gabriel, Danielle Desiato-Hallman, David Pazmiño, and Dan Souza and interns Allison Graham, Brandon Roffis, Marysol Varela, Kayla Vowell, and Nicole Wihowski worked on-set developing recipes for our magazines and books. Assistant Test Kitchen

Director Leah Rovner and Senior Kitchen Assistants Michelle Blodget and Meryl MacCormack were charged with making sure all the ingredients and kitchen equipment we needed were on hand. Kitchen assistants Maria Elena Delgado, Ena Gudiel, Shane Drips, and Eliot Carduff also worked long hours. Chefs Dan Cellucci, Sara Mayer, Ashley Moore, Stephanie Pixley, Lainey Seyler, Meaghen Walsh, and Dan Zuccarello helped coordinate the efforts of the kitchen with the television set by readying props, equipment, and food. Shannon Hatch, Kate May, and Christine Gordon led all tours of the test kitchen during filming.

Special thanks to director and editor Herb Sevush and director of photography Jan Maliszewski.

We also appreciate the hard work of the video production team, including Stephen Hussar, Michael McEachern, Peter Dingle, Roger Macie, Gilles Morin, Brenda Coffey, Ken Fraser, Joe Christofori, James Hirsch, Bob Hirsch, Jeremy Bond, Mark Scheffler, Ken Bauer, Kelly Emerson, Eric Joslin, Jill Nevins, and Christina Ng. Thanks also to Nick Dakoulas, the second unit videographer.

We also would like to thank Nancy Bocchino, Bara Levin, and Victoria Yuen at WGBH Station Relations, and the team at American Public Television that presents the show: Cynthia Fenneman, Chris Funkhouser, Judy Barlow, and Tom Davison. Thanks also for production support from Elena Battista Malcom and DGA Productions, Boston, and Zebra Productions, New York.

DCS by Fisher & Paykel, Kohler, Diamond Crystal Salt, Cooking.com, Wente Vineyards, and Lee Kum Kee helped underwrite the show, and we thank them for their support. We also thank Anne Traficante, Kate May, and Morgan Ryan for handling underwriter relations and Deborah Broide for managing publicity.

Meat was provided by Ronnie Savenor at Savenor's Market of Boston, Massachusetts. Fish was supplied by Ian Davison of Constitution Seafoods of Boston, Massachusetts. Live plants and garden items for the show were furnished by Mahoney's Garden Center of Brighton, Massachusetts. Aprons for Christopher Kimball were made by Nicole Romano and staff aprons were made by Crooked Brook.

AMERICA'S TEST KITCHEN

THE TV COMPANION COOKBOOK 2014

Let's Start with Soup

*For our cauliflower soup,
we cook the cauliflower in
stages to turn it nutty and
sweet. Then Bryan whirs the
mixture in a blender for a
thick, creamy texture.*

IT'S A POPULAR MISCONCEPTION THAT VEGETABLE SOUPS CAN SIMPLY be thrown together in a slapdash manner and yield something anyone would want to make again. Though they tend to follow a straightforward formula—most start by sautéing aromatics, adding broth and hearty vegetables, and then simmering until done—recipes invariably go astray by tossing in way too much from the crisper drawer or going overboard with seasonings and thickeners. We looked at two classic soups, determined to get them back on track by keeping the focus on the main ingredients.

Creamy cauliflower soup should actually taste of cauliflower—yet most iterations taste purely of cream or a plethora of seasonings that are intended to enrich or liven up this simple soup, but end up interfering with its flavor. With a little research into the composition of cauliflower, and lots of experimentation, we found that we could get away with ditching the cream altogether and cutting back extras to just flavor accents, for an ultrasmooth, rich soup rife with the sweet, nutty flavor of cauliflower.

Wild rice and mushroom soup rarely tastes like either one of its namesake ingredients. Instead of a satisfying soup brimming over with earthy, nutty flavor and boasting a substantial texture, many versions are watery, with a one-note flavor. We wanted a hearty, warming soup perfect for a cold winter's day—and it had to offer the rich, complex flavor and texture we expected. We found that a few well-chosen additions were key to intensifying the earthy, deep notes inherent in the main ingredients, resulting in a soup that truly tasted like its name.

CREAMY CAULIFLOWER SOUP

✔ WHY THIS RECIPE WORKS: For a creamy cauliflower soup that tasted first and foremost of cauliflower, we did away with the distractions—no cream, flour, or overpowering seasonings. Cauliflower, simmered until tender, produced a creamy, velvety smooth puree, without the aid of any cream, due to its low insoluble fiber content. For the purest flavor, we cooked it in salted water (instead of broth), skipped the spice rack entirely, and bolstered it with sautéed onion and leek. We added the cauliflower to the simmering water in two stages so our soup offered the grassy flavor of just-cooked cauliflower and the sweeter, nuttier flavor of long-cooked cauliflower. Finally, we fried a portion of the florets in butter until both the cauliflower and butter were golden brown and used each as a separate, richly flavored garnish.

IF YOU JUDGED CAULIFLOWER BY CAULIFLOWER SOUP, you might think of it as a characterless white vegetable with no flavor of its own. This is because most classic cauliflower soups go overboard on the heavy cream; thicken with flour; or incorporate ingredients like bacon, tomatoes, or curry powder, whose potent flavors smother this vegetable's more delicate ones. But if you've ever experienced the full spectrum of cauliflower's flavors, which can range from bright and cabbagelike to nutty and even sweet, you know cauliflower to be imminently worthy of being the real focal point of the recipe. We set out to create a soup that was everything such a dish should be: creamy without being stodgy and highlighting, not covering up, the flavors of this often mistreated vegetable.

To get our bearings, we started by stripping down the soup to just cauliflower and water. We cut a 2-pound head of cauliflower into ½-inch-thick slices (slices cook more evenly than florets, which are hard to cut into same-size pieces) and simmered the vegetable in salted water for 20 minutes before pureeing it in a blender. We

were immediately struck by its texture. The soup was supremely silky and smooth. We literally couldn't detect any of the graininess that would be evident in a puree of, say, cooked peas or any of the glueyness you'd get when pureeing potatoes. We called a few colleagues over to try it, and they were all as astonished as we were. How could a soup with no cream be so creamy?

As we began to do research, we learned that how much a vegetable breaks down when it is cooked and pureed depends largely on one thing: fiber. Vegetables have two kinds: soluble and insoluble. When subjected to heat and liquid, soluble fiber readily breaks down, providing viscosity, while insoluble fiber remains stable even when pureed. Cream's lubricating effect goes a long way toward mitigating the graininess of insoluble fiber, which is why it is so often included in pureed vegetable soups. Cauliflower, however, is remarkably low in overall fiber—and especially in insoluble fiber, with just ½ gram per ½-cup serving. (This is about one third as much insoluble fiber as found in green peas.) No wonder we discovered that cauliflower could be blended to an ultra-smooth creamy consistency—no cream needed.

Next we looked for additions that would complement the cauliflower flavor rather than compete with or overwhelm it. We started by swapping in chicken and vegetable broth for the water. Each added more flavor, but we found that this wasn't necessarily a good thing. The chicken broth was too dominant, while the vegetable broth just muddied the flavor. We stuck with water alone and headed next to the allium bin.

We tested onion, shallot, leek, and garlic, which we softened in the pot with a few tablespoons of butter before adding the cauliflower. Garlic proved pungent and out of place, and the flavor of mild shallots simply disappeared. Onion, however, provided pleasant background sweetness while leek lent a welcome grassiness, so we chose both. In the name of due diligence, we also tested a range of spices, but tasters thought that they all distracted from the cauliflower's flavor.

We were wondering what to try next when we stumbled upon a cauliflower soup recipe from chef and restaurateur Thomas Keller that calls for cooking the vegetable for almost an hour. The recipe (from his book *Ad Hoc*

CREAMY CAULIFLOWER SOUP

at Home) also calls for a lot of cream, so when we tried the soup, it was hard to tell what impact longer cooking was having. But our curiosity was piqued, so we tried simmering the cauliflower in our working recipe for 30 minutes (roughly twice as long as we had been doing up to this point). Even when we added back a little water to the pot to make up for the liquid that had evaporated over the longer cooking time, we were surprised by how much sweeter and nuttier-tasting this vegetable had become compared with our previous efforts. Everything else being equal, was it possible that mere cooking time could so greatly affect flavor?

We ran a simple experiment: We simmered six batches of cauliflower, each in 2 cups of water, cooking the first batch for 10 minutes and each subsequent batch for 10 minutes more so that the last pot cooked for 60 minutes. We called over our colleagues to sample all the batches side by side. The cauliflower that cooked for 10 minutes had a pronounced grassy, cabbagelike

flavor that reminded some tasters of cooked broccoli. By 20 minutes, this sulfurous bite was starting to fade, and by 30 minutes, it had transformed into a sweet nuttiness, which the cauliflower held on to through 40 minutes of cooking. Continued cooking, however, led to a vegetable so tasteless that it was hard to identify it as cauliflower at all. Intrigued by this transformation, we contacted our science editor.

It turns out that cauliflower, like all cruciferous vegetables (including cabbage, Brussels sprouts, kale, and arugula), contains a host of odorless compounds that convert to volatile aromatic ones first during cutting and then during cooking. One such compound is carbon disulfide, which becomes a gas at cooking temperatures. Anyone who's walked into a kitchen where cauliflower is on the stove is familiar with its sulfurous, cabbagelike scent. For the first 15 minutes of cooking, the concentration of carbon disulfide is relatively high. Over time it dissipates, allowing the sweeter, nuttier flavors of other compounds known as thioureas to come to the fore. But by the hour mark, both types of compounds have disappeared so that the vegetable has almost no flavor at all.

So at what point in the cooking process does cauliflower taste best? Most tasters remarked that they liked the punchy, cabbagey flavor of the cauliflower cooked for 10 and 20 minutes as well as the nuttier, cleaner, sweeter flavor of 30-minute-cooked cauliflower. Could we get all these flavors in our soup? For our next batch, we sliced the head into ½-inch-thick slices as usual and simmered half (along with the tougher core, which is edible so long as it's cooked until tender) for 30 minutes, adding the remaining half of the cauliflower after 15 minutes (we decided to split the difference between 10 and 20 minutes of cooking, to get a flavor profile somewhere in between). It was a simple adjustment to the recipe, but the results were dramatic. Not only did this soup taste more intrinsically of cauliflower than any of its predecessors but its flavors were also more complex. It was at once grassy, pleasantly sulfurous, sweet, and nutty. We turned our focus to a few final touches.

We're big fans of the intense nuttiness of roasted cauliflower and wondered if there was a way to bring some of that intensity to the soup. We cut a cup of ½-inch florets from the cauliflower before slicing up the rest for the soup. We melted a few more tablespoons of butter in a small skillet and fried the florets to a golden-brown color. Tossed with a little sherry vinegar and sprinkled over the soup, they served as the ideal complement to our clean-tasting puree. But during frying, the cauliflower wasn't the only thing that was cooking—the butter also turned a rich golden brown. This gave us an idea. Why not cook the florets in extra butter and use a drizzle of it as a second garnish? Just a teaspoon or two of browned butter brought an almost-surprising richness to each bowl of soup. A shower of minced chives and some fresh black pepper finished the job.

We like to think our recipes often get accolades from those who try them, but tasters' raves went beyond anything we'd ever experienced for such a simple recipe. And we have to say, with its magnificently creamy texture and complex palette of flavors, our soup was indeed killer.

SCIENCE DESK

COAXING DIFFERENT FLAVORS FROM CAULIFLOWER
While developing our recipe for cauliflower soup, we discovered that cauliflower's flavor changes dramatically depending on how long you cook it. Shorter cook times bring out its cabbagelike flavors, while longer cook times turn it nuttier and sweet. Too much cooking leaches out all of its flavor. To bring the full spectrum of possible flavors into our soup, we cooked some of the cauliflower in our soup for 15 minutes and the remainder for 30 minutes.

15 MINUTES
The punchy, cabbagelike taste and sulfurous odor of a compound known as carbon disulfide are dominant.

30 MINUTES
Carbon disulfide dissipates, allowing the sweeter, nuttier flavors of other substances known as thioureas to break through.

60 MINUTES
After an hour, nearly all of the flavor has dissipated, leaving the cauliflower bland and flavorless.

Creamy Cauliflower Soup

SERVES 4 TO 6

White wine vinegar may be substituted for the sherry vinegar. For best flavor and texture, trim core thoroughly of green leaves and leaf stems, which can be fibrous and contribute to a grainy texture in the soup.

1 head cauliflower (2 pounds)

8 tablespoons unsalted butter, cut into 8 pieces

1 leek, white and light green parts only, halved lengthwise, sliced thin, and washed thoroughly

1 small onion, halved and sliced thin

Salt and pepper

4½ cups water

½ teaspoon sherry vinegar

3 tablespoons minced fresh chives

1. Pull off outer leaves of cauliflower and trim stem. Using paring knife, cut around core to remove; thinly slice core and reserve. Cut heaping 1 cup of ½-inch florets from head of cauliflower; set aside. Cut remaining cauliflower crosswise into ½-inch-thick slices.

2. Melt 3 tablespoons butter in large saucepan over medium-low heat. Add leek, onion, and 1½ teaspoons salt; cook, stirring frequently, until onion is softened but not browned, about 7 minutes.

3. Increase heat to medium-high; add water, sliced core, and half of sliced cauliflower; and bring to simmer. Reduce heat to medium-low and simmer gently for 15 minutes. Add remaining sliced cauliflower, return to simmer, and continue to cook until cauliflower is tender and crumbles easily, 15 to 20 minutes longer.

4. While soup simmers, melt remaining 5 tablespoons butter in 8-inch skillet over medium heat. Add reserved florets and cook, stirring frequently, until florets are golden brown and butter is browned, 6 to 8 minutes. Remove skillet from heat and use slotted spoon to transfer florets to small bowl. Toss florets with vinegar and season with salt to taste. Pour browned butter in skillet into small bowl and reserve for garnishing.

5. Process soup in blender until smooth, about 45 seconds. Rinse out pan. Return pureed soup to pan and return to simmer over medium heat, adjusting consistency with up to ½ cup water as needed (soup should have thick, velvety texture, but should be thin enough to settle with a flat surface after being stirred) and seasoning with salt to taste. Serve, garnishing individual bowls with browned florets, drizzles of browned butter, and chives and seasoning with pepper to taste.

WILD RICE AND MUSHROOM SOUP

✔ WHY THIS RECIPE WORKS: For a rich, earthy, nutty-tasting soup, we had to figure out how to make the wild rice and mushrooms do more than just add bulk. Fresh cremini mushrooms provided a meaty texture, and dried shiitakes, ground into a powder and added to the broth, ensured full-bodied mushroom flavor. Simmering the wild rice with baking soda decreased the cooking time and brought out its complex flavor. Cooking the rice in the oven, instead of on the stovetop, made it tender with a pleasant chew. To infuse the entire soup with wild rice flavor, we replaced some of the water for the soup with the rice's leftover cooking liquid. Including tomato paste and soy sauce amplified the nutty, earthy flavor profile. A final addition of cornstarch helped suspend the rice in the broth to give our soup a velvety texture.

WHEN WILD RICE APPEARS ON THE DINNER TABLE, it's almost always in the form of a salad or stuffing for the Thanksgiving bird. The long smooth grains, which were first harvested from lake grasses by several Great Lakes–area Native American tribes and are now largely cultivated in artificial paddies, have remarkably nutty, savory depth, not to mention a distinct chew that makes them an ideal base for hearty side dishes.

But that profile also lends itself to another popular wild rice application—soups—and we've come across quite a few recipes that pair the grain with mushrooms. The combination makes sense: Together, the two should produce a soup that's substantial, but not heavy, and full of earthy depth. Just the kind of food we want to tuck into in the dead of winter.

However, we've never had a wild rice and mushroom soup fitting this description—including the handful we tried when we set out to make our own version. Whether they were minimalist broths or stewlike concoctions, all the soups we made shared a common flaw: The namesake ingredients didn't play a starring role.

WILD RICE AND MUSHROOM SOUP

We knew we could do better, so we decided to develop this soup with a clear objective in mind: Namely, keep the focus on the nutty wild rice and meaty mushrooms, and limit any additions to ingredients that could amplify their earthy, *umami*-rich flavor.

For the sake of establishing a working recipe, we tabled all testing of wild rice cooking methods and simply boiled the grains separately until they were firm-tender, which took a good hour. In the meantime, we built our soup base from an entire pound of sliced cremini mushrooms (a test kitchen favorite for their meaty flavor and texture and wide availability) sautéed in a Dutch oven with aromatic foundations like onion, garlic, and tomato paste. By the time the mushrooms had taken on color, we were left with a dark fond at the bottom of the pot that we easily liberated with a generous pour of sherry. A few minutes of reduction left us with a fortified mushroom concentrate to which we added chicken stock (for savory depth) and water before stirring in the cooked rice.

SCIENCE DESK

USING BAKING SODA TO BROWN WILD RICE

We brown meat, baked goods, and many other foods as a matter of course, since the deeper color is an indication of the Maillard reaction, the process triggered by heat that causes a food's proteins and sugars to recombine into hundreds of new flavor compounds that boost complexity. To achieve richer browned flavor in ordinary rice, we often toast the raw grains in the pan before adding liquid. But toasting doesn't work as well with wild rice, since it is technically a grass with a hard pectin-rich coating that must break down before the proteins and sugars on the inside can brown. However, we stumbled upon another way to achieve browning: adding baking soda to the cooking water. Baking soda not only breaks down the pectin seed coat to speed cooking (our original goal) but also lowers the temperature necessary for browning to occur—from at least 300 degrees to below water's boiling point of 212 degrees. Another factor in our favor: Wild rice is high in the amino acids lysine and glycine, proteins that are particularly sensitive to browning. Baking soda added to the pot led to nuttier-tasting wild rice and a savory, deep-brown stock that enriched the soup.

This early iteration was several steps in the right direction, but we still had a ways to go. The most glaring issue was the mushroom flavor, which was subtler than we'd hoped. Replacing some of the salt with soy sauce boosted savoriness, but the earthy quality we were after hadn't come through yet.

The thing was, the soup was already brimming with mushrooms. We considered trading inexpensive cremini for more costly portobellos, oysters, or shiitakes, but when we did, none of the other varieties provided significant flavor improvement. Instead, we opted to supplement the cremini with an alternative that packed the intense mushroom flavor we wanted without the bulk: dried shiitakes. We stock these umami-loaded pantry staples for just such applications, but rather than tease out their flavor using the usual steeping and chopping method, we ground the pieces into a powder that we stirred into the broth. Just ¼ ounce, pulverized in a spice grinder (or in a blender), infused the soup with full-bodied mushroom flavor.

Flavorwise, we were making strides, but so far these versions didn't have enough body. Without it, the liquid was not only unsatisfying but also too thin to support the heftier mushrooms and rice. We hoped that a flour-based roux might be an easy way to thicken the pot—and it was, but we needed a full ½ cup to get the consistency we wanted, which dulled the flavor we'd worked so hard to build. Thankfully, there was an easy substitute: cornstarch. Unlike flour, cornstarch is a pure starch and a more powerful thickener, which meant we could get away with just ¼ cup.

Robust mushroom flavor? Check. Hearty body? Check. Now our soup just needed to earn the other half of its title.

We could have just dumped the boiled rice into the soup and called it a day, but marrying the liquid and rice at the last minute wouldn't allow much time for a flavor transfer. As it was, the rice needed an hour of cooking time on its own, so waiting to simmer it in the soup base would really drag out the overall cooking time. Thinking there had to be a better way, we read up on wild rice cookery and ran some tests. Turns out we were right.

Each grain of wild rice is enveloped in a thick pectin-rich coat that hardens further when the rice is dried during processing. Wild rice is properly cooked when this black seed coat splits and the grains are tender yet still chewy. But stovetop simmering—we were using the pasta method, cooking the rice in an excess of water and then draining it—was not only a long process but an inconsistent one as well, unless we constantly fiddled with the heat to make sure the pot wasn't bubbling too slowly or too quickly. The other problem: Using the pasta method meant that we were discarding the cooking liquid—literally pouring some of the flavor from the wild rice down the drain. Thinking we'd keep all that flavorful liquid in the pot, we tried the absorption method—cooking the rice in a measured amount of water that the grains completely soak up—but that method required even more babysitting to prevent the liquid from evaporating too quickly. No thanks.

Instead, we abandoned stovetop simmering altogether and turned to a more even heat source: the oven. After setting the dial to 375, we switched back to the pasta method and brought the water to a boil on the burner, added the rice, covered the pot, and transferred the vessel to the oven. Just as we'd hoped, the rice cooked—babysitter-free—at an even simmer and emerged firm yet tender with pleasant chew.

We were about to reluctantly pitch the leftover cooking liquid when an obvious thought occurred to us: Why not strain the flavorful liquid and substitute it for some of the water in the soup? One test proved that it was an easy way to ensure that the flavor of the wild rice permeated the broth.

The good news: We finally had a foolproof cooking method and rich wild rice flavor throughout our soup. The bad: It was still costing us an hour. We weren't sure how we could speed things along until a colleague reminded us that we had solved a similar dilemma in our recipe for polenta by adding a pinch of baking soda to the pot. The more basic environment facilitated the breakdown of the pectin and shaved 15 minutes off the cooking time, and this approach worked beautifully with the rice, too. When we added just ¼ teaspoon, the seed coat broke down faster, cutting down the rice's cooking time to about 45 minutes.

There was also a side benefit to our baking soda trick that we didn't realize until we took a closer look at the strained cooking liquid. Unlike prior batches, which were straw-colored, this wild rice stock was deep brown. A spoonful surprised us with its savory nuttiness—it was far richer and more complex than the prior baking soda–free batches.

brightened things up nicely. We also stirred in ½ cup of cream, which enriched the earthy broth.

Robustly flavored with its namesake ingredients, this soup had finally earned its title, not to mention a permanent spot in our collection of staple soups.

Wild Rice and Mushroom Soup

SERVES 6 TO 8

White mushrooms can be substituted for the cremini mushrooms. We use a spice grinder to process the dried shiitake mushrooms, but a blender also works.

¼	ounce dried shiitake mushrooms, rinsed
4¼	cups water
1	sprig fresh thyme
1	bay leaf
5	garlic cloves, peeled (1 whole, 4 minced)
	Salt and pepper
¼	teaspoon baking soda
1	cup wild rice
4	tablespoons unsalted butter
1	pound cremini mushrooms, trimmed and sliced ¼ inch thick
1	onion, chopped fine
1	teaspoon tomato paste
⅔	cup dry sherry
4	cups chicken broth
1	tablespoon soy sauce
¼	cup cornstarch
½	cup heavy cream
¼	cup minced fresh chives
¼	teaspoon finely grated lemon zest

Our science editor explained that baking soda not only helps break down the pectin in the seed coat but also lowers the temperature necessary for Maillard reaction–induced browning to occur. Though most commonly associated with the browning of meat or baked goods, Maillard reactions occur when heated proteins and sugars undergo chemical changes, resulting in entirely new flavors. Typically these reactions require much higher temperatures (at least 300 degrees) than a simmering pot can achieve, but alkaline baking soda effectively lowers this temperature barrier and allows the reactions to occur below the boiling point of water (212 degrees). Also working in our favor: Wild rice is especially well suited for the Maillard reaction, as it contains high concentrations of amino acids (lysine and glycine) that are particularly reactive.

Deeper, more complex flavor as a result of a faster cooking method? We'd take it. In fact, this soup was so full of earthy depth that our tasters suggested we balance it out with some fresher flavors. Chives and lemon zest

1. Adjust oven rack to middle position and heat oven to 375 degrees. Grind shiitake mushrooms in spice grinder until finely ground (you should have about 3 tablespoons).

2. Bring 4 cups water, thyme, bay leaf, garlic clove, ¾ teaspoon salt, and baking soda to boil in medium saucepan over high heat. Add rice and return to boil. Cover saucepan, transfer to oven, and bake until rice is tender, 35 to 50 minutes. Strain rice through fine-mesh strainer set in 4-cup liquid measuring cup; discard thyme, bay leaf, and garlic. Add enough water to reserved cooking liquid to measure 3 cups.

3. Melt butter in Dutch oven over high heat. Add cremini mushrooms, onion, minced garlic, tomato paste, ¾ teaspoon salt, and 1 teaspoon pepper. Cook, stirring occasionally, until vegetables are browned and dark fond develops on bottom of pot, 15 minutes. Add sherry, scraping up any browned bits, and cook until reduced and pot is almost dry, about 2 minutes. Add ground shiitake mushrooms, reserved rice cooking liquid, broth, and soy sauce and bring to boil. Reduce heat to low and simmer, covered, until onion and mushrooms are tender, about 20 minutes.

4. Whisk cornstarch and remaining ¼ cup water in small bowl. Stir cornstarch slurry into soup, return to simmer, and cook until thickened, about 2 minutes. Remove pot from heat and stir in cooked rice, cream, chives, and lemon zest. Cover and let stand for 20 minutes. Season with salt and pepper to taste and serve.

RATING WILD RICE

Although it's usually stocked in the supermarket with long-grain, brown, and basmati, wild rice is actually an aquatic grass. (Wild rice is North America's only native grain. It grows naturally in lakes and is cultivated in man-made paddies in Minnesota, California, and Canada.) When we tasted five brands both plain and in our Wild Rice and Mushroom Soup, textural differences stood out the most; our top three cooked up springy and firm, while the other two blew out. What accounted for the difference? Processing. To create a shelf-stable product, manufacturers heat the grains, which gelatinizes their starches and drives out moisture, according to one of two methods: parching (the traditional approach) or parboiling. To parch, manufacturers load rice into cylinders, which spin over a fire—an inexact process that produces "crumbly," "less toothsome" results. Parboiling, a newer method, steams the grains in a controlled pressurized environment, resulting in more uniform and complete gelatinization, which translates into rice that cooks more evenly. Brands are listed in order of preference. See AmericasTestKitchen.com for updates and further information on this tasting.

RECOMMENDED

GOOSE VALLEY Wild Rice
PRICE: $4.69 for 5 oz ($0.94 per oz)
PROCESSING: Parboiled
COMMENTS: Our favorite product benefited from the parboiling method: It retained a "bouncy pop" and the grains had a "crunchy exterior, yet were tender inside." An added boon: Its flavor was "woodsy" and "pecan-y."

BOB'S RED MILL Wild Rice
PRICE: $7.85 for 8 oz ($0.98 per oz)
PROCESSING: Parboiled
COMMENTS: This wild rice had a "sweet, grassy flavor" that our tasters called "nutty," "earthy," and "smoky." Its "hearty," "nubby" texture "held its shape without being stiff."

REESE Wild Rice (also sold as Gourmet House Wild Rice)
PRICE: $3.99 for 4 oz ($1.00 per oz)
PROCESSING: Parboiled
COMMENTS: This wild rice was fairly "neutral," with a "light woody aroma" that was "slightly sweet." It tasted "faintly wheaty," with "background nuttiness." Tasters appreciated its "fairly firm, crunchy texture" and its "nice pop."

RECOMMENDED WITH RESERVATIONS

LUNDBERG Organic Wild Rice
PRICE: $7.39 for 8 oz ($0.92 per oz)
PROCESSING: Parched
COMMENTS: This rice had a decent flavor—it had "delicate nuttiness" and was "slightly buttery"—but it lost points because the grains were "really starchy and messy-looking" and "broken and crumbly," likely a result of the parching method.

NOT RECOMMENDED

EDEN Wild Rice
PRICE: $7.02 for 7 oz ($1.00 per oz)
PROCESSING: Parched
COMMENTS: This dank, pale-green rice is the only one that is still parched over a traditional wood fire. The process yields rice that tasted like "mold," "dirt," and "burnt veggies," with roasted notes of "campfire," "smoke," and "ash." "Clumpy" grains were "blown out," even when cooked according to package instructions.

Hearty Spanish & Italian Soups Revamped

CHAPTER 2

THE RECIPES

Hearty Spanish-Style Lentil and Chorizo Soup

Hearty Spanish-Style Lentil and Chorizo Soup with Kale

Italian Wedding Soup

TASTING LAB

Chicken Broth

For Italian wedding soup, Chris and Bridget shape mini meatballs, which include pork, beef, and a secret ingredient—baking powder—for lightness.

WHEN MOST OF US THINK OF LENTIL SOUP, WE THINK OF A BROTHY or creamy dish that's simply seasoned and comforting, but not all that exciting. Enter Spanish-style lentil soup, which adds garlicky chorizo, smoky paprika, and sherry vinegar for big, bold flavor. In this version of lentil soup, the lentils don't break down but rather remain intact, for a soup that's heartier and more satisfying. To bring this Spanish dish to the American table, figuring out the best way to cook our lentils was key. But so was figuring out how to build robust, complex flavor. And for that, we looked to another cuisine where lentils are a staple.

Italian wedding soup, dotted with tiny meatballs, small pasta, and greens, is a familiar dish, too—and if you've ever prepared an authentic recipe, we're sure it made quite an impression. Traditional versions start with from-scratch broth and include labor-of-love meatballs made with multiple cuts of meat, some of which can be hard to find. On the other hand, there are the streamlined Americanized versions, which disappoint in more ways than one. Not only is the mild, barely there flavor a letdown, but so is the texture and lack of richness, with dry meatballs (which are sometimes just chunks of sausage). We wanted the best of both worlds: a richly flavored soup with an ultrasavory broth and tender, meaty bites, and it had to be easy and quick, so we wouldn't have to spend all day at the stovetop.

HEARTY SPANISH-STYLE LENTIL AND CHORIZO SOUP

SPANISH-STYLE LENTIL AND CHORIZO SOUP

✔ **WHY THIS RECIPE WORKS:** For our own version of Spain's thick and smoky lentil soup, we started with the lentils. Soaking them in a warm brine for 30 minutes before cooking prevented blowouts and ensured they were well seasoned. Browning links of Spanish chorizo and then simmering them in the soup ensured a juicy texture. Slowly sweating finely chopped aromatics in the chorizo's fat gave our soup incredible depth of flavor. For more intensity, we finished the soup with an Indian preparation called a *tarka*, which is a mixture of spices (smoked paprika ramped up the smoky notes) and finely minced aromatics (we used onion and garlic) bloomed in oil. Adding a little flour helped thicken the soup and some sherry vinegar brightened its flavors.

SPANIARDS HAVE A LONG TRADITION OF TAKING *la comida*, their largest meal of the day, in the early afternoon. Hearty, sustaining soups and stews, many of which economically pair dried beans with some form of flavor-packed pork such as ham, bacon, or sausage, are typically on the table. A particularly intriguing example is *sopa de lentejas con chorizo* (lentil and chorizo soup). It's a standout not just for its robust taste—provided by rich, garlicky chorizo, heady smoked paprika (*pimentón*), and the bright depth of sherry vinegar—but also for its unique texture: Neither entirely brothy nor creamy, the soup features whole lentils suspended in a thick broth.

To come up with our own recipe, we started by evaluating different types of lentils. Spaniards are fond of *lentejas pardinas* (*pardo* means brownish or darkish) from *Castilla y León*. We mail-ordered a bag and found that they cooked up with a nutty, buttery flavor. But since pardinas are difficult to locate, we also simmered a few more common varieties, finding that they were all similar though not without unique subtleties. French green *lentilles du Puy* were earthy; black beluga lentils, meaty; and standard brown lentils, vegetal. The du Puy type had the best tender-firm texture, so we would use them for our remaining tests.

There was just one problem: keeping them intact. The "meat" of a lentil swells as it cooks, all too easily slipping out of its shell (which is called a blowout) and creating a mushy, split pea soup–like texture. Over the years, we have found two ways to address this issue. Both methods make use of salt and/or acid to weaken the pectin and soften the shell, leading to fewer blowouts. The first approach involves cooking the lentils with salt and vinegar before adding liquid and fully cooking them; the second requires soaking the beans in a warm saltwater brine for an hour prior to cooking. We tried the salt and acid method first, sautéing some chopped onion in olive oil and then adding the lentils along with a bit of salt and sherry vinegar. We covered the pot and let the lentils cook for a few minutes before adding water, bay leaves, smoked paprika, and cloves and simmering until the beans were fully cooked. While the shape of these lentils was somewhat retained, many did still slip out of their skins and form mush. We got much better results when we combined the approaches by brining the lentils (using boiling water cut the soaking time to 30 minutes) before sweating them with the salt and vinegar. Now each and every bean emerged fully intact and beautifully creamy.

With the lentils up to par, we focused on the chorizo. The word chorizo covers many versions of pork sausage made in Spain. The kind typically available in the United States is a cured sausage with a strong garlicky flavor, colored a distinctive red by pimentón. It is important not to confuse it with Mexican chorizo, which combines fresh ground pork or beef with chili powder and vinegar. To keep the links as moist as possible, we left them whole and browned them in olive oil, transferred them to a plate while we sweated the lentils, and then plopped them back into the pot along with the water to simmer (we would cut them into bite-size pieces toward the end of cooking). Prepared this way, the chorizo cooked up with a dense, juicy texture. But as good as the sausage was, the flavor of the soup itself wasn't nearly as complex as we wanted it to be. (Its consistency was also too thin, but we'd deal with that later.)

Our first idea for creating depth was to swap chicken broth for some of the water, but that only seemed to cloud the soup's overall flavor. Next, we tried caramelizing the aromatics, but the profound sweetness that developed only obscured the smoky chorizo and tart vinegar. But all was not lost. The failed caramelized vegetable test got us thinking about an entirely different technique for enhancing the flavor of aromatics: sweating. This approach, used by cooks around the world, involves slowly cooking aromatics in a small amount of fat in a covered pot. The vegetables are kept just this side of browning, and during the process they develop a distinctive yet subtle flavor that is said to improve almost any dish.

It was certainly worth a try. We prepared another batch of soup, first browning the chorizo and removing it from the pot and then slowly cooking the onion (plus carrots and parsley for a vegetal boost) in the rendered fat on low heat, all while the lentils brined. After 30 minutes, we dipped our spoons in for a sample and discovered that a real transformation had occurred: The unbrowned vegetables boasted a clean, pure, sweet flavor that was altogether different from the sweet, roasted taste produced via caramelization. In the finished soup, the effect was equally impressive: The slow-cooked aromatics turned out to be an extremely well-balanced base that highlighted the main flavors of the dish.

We were really getting somewhere, but the soup still didn't have that elusive "wow" factor. As we mulled over ideas, a rather unorthodox thought came to mind: Since lentils are not only a staple of Mediterranean cooking but also of Indian cuisine, why not consult Indian cookbooks? Thumbing through classic sources, we found a technique that Indian cooks use to bolster flavor in all sorts of dishes: stirring in a so-called tarka, a mixture of spices and finely minced aromatics quickly bloomed in oil. Since the test kitchen recently discovered that a brief exposure to hot oil can boost the flavor of spices tenfold, we knew that the technique held a lot of promise.

Inspired, we whipped up a Spanish tarka for our next batch of soup: Instead of adding the smoked paprika to the simmering lentils, we sizzled it in olive oil along with black pepper, minced garlic, and finely grated onion (the small pieces ensured that it would soften quickly). This was potent stuff. Thinking that it might overwhelm the

soup as a garnish, we decided to drizzle it into the broth for a few more minutes of simmering. While we were at it, we addressed the thickness of our soup (or, more accurately, the lack thereof) by adding flour. We stirred some into the oil in the tarka to make a sort of roux, finding that just 1 tablespoon was enough to develop the signature spoon-coating consistency. With our first taste, we knew we'd hit the jackpot with our multicultural approach. The soup had a lush consistency, not to mention tons of flavor: sweet, savory, and smoky, with a hint of acidity.

Hearty Spanish-Style Lentil and Chorizo Soup
SERVES 6 TO 8

We prefer French green lentils, or lentilles du Puy, for this recipe, but it will work with any type of lentil except red or yellow. Grate the onion on the large holes of a box grater. If Spanish-style chorizo is not available, kielbasa sausage can be substituted. Red wine vinegar can be substituted for the sherry vinegar. Smoked paprika comes in three varieties: sweet (*dulce*), bittersweet or medium hot (*agridulce*), and hot (*picante*). For this recipe, we prefer the sweet kind.

1 pound (2¼ cups) lentils, picked over and rinsed
  Salt and pepper
1 large onion
5 tablespoons extra-virgin olive oil
1½ pounds Spanish-style chorizo sausage, pricked with fork several times
3 carrots, peeled and cut into ¼-inch pieces
3 tablespoons minced fresh parsley
7 cups water, plus extra as needed
3 tablespoons sherry vinegar, plus extra for seasoning
2 bay leaves
⅛ teaspoon ground cloves
2 tablespoons sweet smoked paprika
3 garlic cloves, minced
1 tablespoon all-purpose flour

1. Place lentils and 2 teaspoons salt in heatproof container. Cover with 4 cups boiling water and let soak for 30 minutes. Drain well.

2. Meanwhile, finely chop three-quarters of onion (you should have about 1 cup) and grate remaining quarter (you should have about 3 tablespoons). Heat 2 tablespoons oil in Dutch oven over medium heat until shimmering. Add chorizo and cook until browned on all sides, 6 to 8 minutes. Transfer chorizo to large plate. Reduce heat to low and add chopped onion, carrots, 1 tablespoon parsley, and 1 teaspoon salt. Cover and cook, stirring occasionally, until vegetables are very soft but not brown, 25 to 30 minutes. If vegetables begin to brown, add 1 tablespoon water to pot.

3. Add lentils and sherry vinegar to vegetables; increase heat to medium-high; and cook, stirring frequently, until vinegar starts to evaporate, 3 to 4 minutes. Add 7 cups water, chorizo, bay leaves, and cloves; bring to simmer. Reduce heat to low; cover; and cook until lentils are tender, about 30 minutes.

4. Heat remaining 3 tablespoons oil in small saucepan over medium heat until shimmering. Add paprika, grated onion, garlic, and ½ teaspoon pepper; cook, stirring constantly, until fragrant, 2 minutes. Add flour and cook, stirring constantly, 1 minute longer. Remove chorizo and bay leaves from lentils. Stir paprika mixture into lentils and continue to cook until flavors have blended and soup has thickened, 10 to 15 minutes. When chorizo is cool enough to handle, cut in half lengthwise, then cut each half into ¼-inch-thick slices. Return chorizo to soup along with remaining 2 tablespoons parsley and heat through, about 1 minute. Season with salt, pepper, and up to 2 teaspoons sherry vinegar to taste, and serve. (Soup can be made up to 3 days in advance.)

VARIATION

Hearty Spanish-Style Lentil and Chorizo Soup with Kale

Add 12 ounces kale, stemmed and cut into ½-inch pieces, to simmering soup after 15 minutes in step 3. Continue to simmer until lentils and kale are tender, about 15 minutes.

NOTES FROM THE TEST KITCHEN

BUILDING AUTHENTIC SPANISH FLAVOR

Three quintessential ingredients provide our soup with authentic Spanish flavor.

SMOKED PAPRIKA
Pimentón, made by drying red peppers over an oak fire, offers a distinctive rich and smoky taste.

SHERRY VINEGAR
Lightly sweet sherry vinegar boasts assertive yet balanced acidity.

SPANISH CHORIZO
This heady sausage combines coarsely ground, dry-cured pork with a hit of pimentón.

ITALIAN WEDDING SOUP

✔ **WHY THIS RECIPE WORKS:** Traditional recipes for this hearty soup featuring meatballs, tender greens, and pasta require an afternoon-long stint on the stovetop, which starts with building the *brodo*, a long-cooked broth made from the bones of meat and poultry. Wanting a quicker path to this richly flavored soup, we created a speedy yet ultrasavory broth by simmering ground beef and pork in a mixture of chicken and beef broth. Dried porcini mushrooms and Worcestershire sauce further boosted the meaty flavor. For the meatballs, we nixed the hard-to-find ground veal and stuck with ground beef and ground pork. To make up for the loss in texture from omitting the veal, we added baking powder and whipped the pork in a stand mixer to ensure the meatballs remained light, juicy, and supple. Chopped kale and ditalini, stirred in toward the end of the cooking time, became perfectly tender in a matter of minutes.

WE'VE NEVER BEEN TO A WEDDING BANQUET IN MILAN, Venice, or Palermo, but we'd hazard a guess that Italian wedding soup would not have been on the menu. Its Italian name, *minestra maritata* ("married soup"), refers not to actual nuptials but to the marriage of hearty greens to a savory mixture of meats against the backdrop of a rich broth. The Italian-American rendition takes this pairing even further by transforming the meats into tender miniature meatballs and adding bits of wheaty pasta.

But over the years, Italian wedding soup has lost touch with its roots, sliding into the dodgy territory of convenience food. Most recipes seem to call for nothing more than simmering a few cans of broth, adding some ersatz "meatballs" in the form of dollops of Italian sausage, dumping in a bag of greens, and dusting it all with grated Parmesan before slapping the soup on the table. We didn't want a project that took an entire afternoon at the stove, but surely there was a middle ground that

would bring back the deeper, more complex flavors of the old-fashioned version.

Traditionally, Italian wedding soup is built from a base of meaty brodo, brewed from cured meats and the bits, bobs, and bones of animals both hoofed and winged, for a broth that doesn't taste strongly of any one particular kind of meat. Beyond gathering the requisite odd parts and specialty meats, cooks must spend hours simmering traditional brodo to fully develop its flavor—not to mention the constant skimming to remove foam and the tedious work of separating out the fat. Overall, this is more time and attention than most of us want to devote to a soup. But we hoped that with the right collection of meats, aromatics, and flavorings we could render store-bought broth into something resembling a classic brodo in the 30-odd minutes it would take to prepare meatballs.

Since we wanted a base with a well-rounded meaty taste, it made sense to use both chicken and beef broths. After a bit of experimentation, we found that a 2:1 ratio of chicken broth to beef broth, cut with a little water, tasted the most balanced. Some basic aromatics, like sautéed onion and a few smashed cloves of garlic, nudged the broth in the right direction, especially with a sharpening splash of dry white wine. To further enrich the broth, we tried adding carrots and celery but found the sweetness of the former too cloying while the metallic taste of the latter came on too strong. A fennel bulb turned out to be a better choice, lending a pleasant anise note and mild warmth.

With convenience in mind, we eschewed the gnarly cuts used in traditional brodo in favor of easy-to-find, bone-in pieces. We tried out chicken wings, country-style pork ribs, and beef short ribs. They all contributed terrific flavor but made the broth too fatty, and our half-hour time frame was not enough to extract maximum flavor from the bones. Then it occurred to us: Since we would be using ground meat to make the meatballs, why not enlist some of it to lend flavor to the broth as well? After the meat had contributed its richness to the broth, we could strain out the nubbly bits—an easy enough step. We took a few ounces of the ground beef and pork that

ITALIAN WEDDING SOUP

we'd bought to make the meatballs and lightly browned them along with the aromatics before adding the broth. The ground meats cooked quickly and the broth's meatiness was clearly amplified—another step in the right direction. But our soup base still tasted too thin, lacking the full-throated savor of a long-simmered stock.

Several traditional recipes that we'd consulted called for the leftover bone and scraps from a leg of prosciutto. Ever looked for a prosciutto bone? It's easier to find hens' teeth. Chopped and blended in with the ground meats, a few thin slices of the salt-cured pork, which is packed with the glutamates that contribute savory richness to food, did help matters. But we couldn't tolerate discarding $10 worth of top-shelf charcuterie when we strained the broth. We tried out a few other Italianate flavor enhancers, both traditional and non. A Parmesan rind proved that it's easy to be too cheesy, sun-dried tomatoes tasted

too sour and dyed the stock a ruddy color, and anchovies took the broth into overly salty territory.

Continuing our search for flavor-boosting ingredients, we borrowed an idea from an earlier recipe for vegetable and barley soup: the combo of dried porcini mushrooms and soy sauce. We loved the deep earthiness that the mushrooms provided, but soy sauce in the amount necessary to detect any real difference made the broth too salty. We experimented with—and quickly ruled out—other *umami* boosters, including fish sauce and miso. They all added flavor but also muddied the primal meatiness that our brodo required. Then we remembered a condiment that tends to get pushed to the back of our pantry: Worcestershire sauce. This dark, old-fashioned liquid was bringing a jolt of savory flavor to meats and Bloody Marys long before umami became a household word. We added a dash of the stuff and noted that the broth's flavor was now somewhat deeper. A full tablespoon galvanized that flavor, highlighting the beef and pork alike. With just 30 minutes and a well-edited handful of ingredients, we now had a full afternoon's worth of flavor in our pot.

Italian meatballs are often rolled from a blend of ground beef, pork, and veal and bound with a panade, a mixture of bread and dairy (and sometimes eggs) that moisturizes the meats and prevents their proteins from binding too tightly and growing tough. Why the blend of meats? Each brings something to the party: Beef packs big flavor; pork adds sweetness and richness; and veal's high concentration of gelatin gives the meatballs body while keeping them tender and light. Ground veal, though, can be hard to find. What happens if you simply skip it? Our veal-less meatballs were a bit chewy and bland.

We wondered if we needed a substitute for veal, or if a cooking method could compensate for its missing attributes. Drawing on test kitchen experience, we ended up turning to both approaches. When we tackled Swedish meatballs (another meatball typically made from a beef-pork-veal blend), we found success using ground beef and pork alone by adding a secret ingredient: baking powder. Just 1 teaspoon ensured that the meatballs remained light once cooked. We'd also borrowed a technique from sausage making, whipping the ground pork

in a stand mixer until it formed a smooth emulsion before adding the panade, seasonings, and ground beef. This step evenly distributes the pork's fat and moisture and traps them both within the meat's protein structure so that the meatballs remain juicy and pleasingly supple. (Pork has a lower proportion of muscle fibers than beef and can be whipped without risk of toughening.) Both of these tricks brought the same great results to our mini meatballs.

Some Italian wedding soup recipes instruct you to pan-fry the meatballs before adding them to the brodo, but our tasters disliked the crisp exterior of browned meatballs in soup, plus the extra step was a hassle. But when we cooked the meatballs directly in the broth, the egg in the panade made the meatballs turn out rubbery (the proteins in eggs and meat bind to form an elastic structure, which grows more resilient when cooked in liquid). Out went the egg—with no ill effect. We also learned that batches with a high ratio of panade to meat produced lighter, almost dumpling-like meatballs that paired really well with the tender greens and pasta.

With the texture of the meatballs perfected, we just needed to fine-tune their flavor. Finely grated onion was a must, and a little Parmesan, blended into the panade, brought a subtle nuttiness. Dried herbs added little, but fresh oregano tied everything together and tempered the meatballs' richness.

All manner of greens find their way into this soup. We started our testing with spinach, a popular choice, but were disappointed by the way it quickly turned limp and slimy. Sturdier chard, cabbage, escarole, and kale were more successful, with kale's meaty texture and assertive flavor trumping the rest. Thinly sliced into a chiffonade, kale strands wove themselves into an unwieldy clump; chopped bits worked better. The small pieces kept to themselves, fit tidily on a spoon, and softened in the time it took the pasta to cook.

And what about that pasta? Tiny bite-size shapes, like ditalini, worked best. To avoid mushy pasta, we added it at the last minute, testing it frequently. In just less than an hour in the kitchen, we had an elegant, satisfying soup tasting of far more work than we had invested—a successful compromise between tradition and convenience.

Italian Wedding Soup

SERVES 6 TO 8

Use a rasp-style grater to process the onion and garlic for the meatballs. Tubettini or orzo can be used in place of the ditalini.

BROTH

- 1 onion, chopped
- 1 fennel bulb, stalks discarded, bulb halved, cored, and chopped
- 4 garlic cloves, peeled and smashed
- ¼ ounce dried porcini mushrooms, rinsed
- 4 ounces ground pork
- 4 ounces 85 percent lean ground beef
- 1 bay leaf
- ½ cup dry white wine
- 1 tablespoon Worcestershire sauce
- 4 cups chicken broth
- 2 cups beef broth
- 2 cups water

MEATBALLS

    1   slice hearty white sandwich bread, crusts
        removed, torn into 1-inch pieces
    5   tablespoons heavy cream
    ¼   cup grated Parmesan cheese
    4   teaspoons finely grated onion
    ½   teaspoon finely grated garlic
        Salt and pepper
    6   ounces ground pork
    1   teaspoon baking powder
    6   ounces 85 percent lean ground beef
    2   teaspoons minced fresh oregano
    1   cup ditalini pasta
   12   ounces kale, stemmed and cut into
        ½-inch pieces (6 cups)

1. FOR THE BROTH: Heat onion, fennel, garlic, porcini, pork, beef, and bay leaf in Dutch oven over medium-high heat; cook, stirring frequently, until meats are no longer pink, about 5 minutes. Add wine and Worcestershire; cook for 1 minute. Add chicken broth, beef broth, and water; bring to simmer. Reduce heat to low, cover, and simmer for 30 minutes.

2. FOR THE MEATBALLS: While broth simmers, combine bread, cream, Parmesan, onion, garlic, and pepper to taste in bowl; using fork, mash mixture to uniform paste. Using stand mixer fitted with paddle, beat pork, baking powder, and ½ teaspoon salt on high speed until smooth and pale, 1 to 2 minutes, scraping down bowl as needed. Add bread mixture, beef, and oregano; mix on medium-low speed until just incorporated, 1 to 2 minutes, scraping down bowl as needed. Using moistened hands, form heaping teaspoons of meat mixture into smooth, round meatballs; you should have 30 to 35 meatballs. Cover and refrigerate for up to 1 day.

3. Strain broth through fine-mesh strainer set over large bowl or container, pressing on solids to extract as much liquid as possible. Wipe out Dutch oven and return broth to pot. (Broth can be refrigerated for up to 3 days. Skim off fat before reheating.)

4. Return broth to simmer over medium-high heat. Add pasta and kale; cook, stirring occasionally, for 5 minutes. Add meatballs; return to simmer and cook, stirring occasionally, until meatballs are cooked through and pasta is tender, 3 to 5 minutes. Season with salt and pepper to taste and serve.

NOTES FROM THE TEST KITCHEN

MAKING FLAVORFUL SOUP STOCK IN 30 MINUTES

Skipping the fuss of a typical brodo doesn't have to mean sacrificing flavor. By doctoring commercial chicken broth, we got comparably rich-tasting results in under an hour.

ATYPICAL AROMATIC
We rejected the standard carrots and celery for the anise notes of fennel. Onion and garlic, though, were musts.

TWO MEATS
No need to seek out meat scraps and bones for depth. A broth simmered with ground pork and beef is plenty savory.

TWO BROTHS
In addition to chicken broth, we use beef broth to mimic the flavor of traditional brodo.

UMAMI BOOSTERS
Umami-packed porcini mushrooms and Worcestershire sauce amp up the broth's meaty flavor.

RATING CHICKEN BROTH

In the test kitchen, we rarely go a day without reaching for chicken broth. We use it as a base for soups and stews; for simmering pilafs and risottos; and to moisten braises, pan sauces, and gravies. But supermarket shelves are teeming with options—besides canned and boxed liquid broths, there are also granulated powders, cubes, concentrates, and liquids, plus there's an array of sodium levels to choose from—so what should you buy? To find the one that offered the richest, most chicken-y flavor, we sampled 10 broths—eight liquids and two concentrates that are reconstituted with water—plain, in a simple risotto, and reduced in gravy. Several samples tasted awful, with wan chicken flavor, but two (one a liquid, the other a concentrate) clearly stood apart. We thought protein levels might have something to do with the results; our top-rated brand had a relatively high amount of protein, but the brand with the most protein in our lineup scored poorly. Examining the labels more closely, we learned that our top two broths both included glutamates, forms of an amino acid that enhance a food's meaty flavor. Our runner-up also included nucleotides, flavor-enhancing compounds, to achieve its "savory" depth, though it lost points for its high sodium content. Brands are listed in order of preference. See AmericasTestKitchen. com for updates and complete tasting results.

RECOMMENDED

SWANSON Chicken Stock
PRICE: $3.19 for 3 cups ($1.06 per cup)
SODIUM: 510 mg **PROTEIN:** 4 g
INGREDIENTS: Chicken stock; contains less than 2%: sea salt, dextrose, carrots, cabbage, onions, celery, celery leaves, salt, parsley
COMMENTS: This liquid broth achieved "rich," "meaty" flavor the old-fashioned way—with a relatively high percentage of meat-based protein. The only problem: Some tasters thought it came across as "beefy" or even "mushroomy," not chicken-y.

BETTER THAN BOUILLON Chicken Base `BEST BUY`
PRICE: $5.99 for 8-oz jar that makes 38 cups ($0.16 per cup)
SODIUM: 680 mg **PROTEIN:** 1 g
INGREDIENTS: Chicken meat including natural chicken juices, salt, sugar, corn syrup solids, chicken fat, hydrolyzed soy protein, dried whey (milk), flavoring, disodium inosinate, guanylate, turmeric
COMMENTS: By adding nucleotides to its glutamate-rich base, this brand produced a remarkably "savory" broth, despite very little protein. The cheapest broth we tasted, once opened it lasts for two years in the fridge. Its high sodium content made us dial back the company's prescribed ratio of concentrate to water.

RECOMMENDED WITH RESERVATIONS

KNORR Homestyle Stock Reduced Sodium Chicken
PRICE: $3.99 for 4 tubs that make 3.5 cups each, 14 cups total ($0.29 per cup)
SODIUM: 600 mg **PROTEIN:** 0 g
INGREDIENTS: Water, maltodextrin (corn), salt, palm oil, autolyzed yeast extract, sea salt, sugar, carrots, lactic acid, chicken fat, leeks, potato starch, xanthan gum, garlic, chicken powder (with rosemary extract to protect quality), parsley, natural flavor, malic acid, locust bean gum, thiamin hydrochloride, disodium guanylate, disodium inosinate, disodium phosphate, glycerin, ascorbic acid, caramel color, succinic acid, spice, mustard oil, beta carotene (for color), coconut oil, sulfur dioxide (used to protect quality)
COMMENTS: This concentrate fared well as straight broth. But 32 ingredients later, it fell short on actual chicken flavor. It was sweet like "canned pumpkin" when reduced.

RECOMMENDED WITH RESERVATIONS *(cont.)*

SWANSON Natural Goodness Chicken Broth
PRICE: $2.99 for 4 cups ($0.75 per cup)
SODIUM: 570 mg **PROTEIN:** 2 g
INGREDIENTS: Chicken stock; contains less than 2%: salt, flavoring, yeast extract, carrot juice concentrate, celery juice concentrate, onion juice concentrate
COMMENTS: This broth was "not super-meaty"; it was like "sweet squash" when reduced in gravy. No surprise: It was average for salt and contains the most sugar per serving, carrot juice being the likely culprit.

IMAGINE Chicken Cooking Stock
PRICE: $4.29 for 4 cups ($1.07 per cup)
SODIUM: 500 mg **PROTEIN:** Less than 1 g
INGREDIENTS: Organic chicken stock (filtered water, organic chicken broth concentrate), sea salt, natural flavors, organic evaporated cane juice, organic chicken flavor, organic turmeric
COMMENTS: Despite only natural ingredients, this broth tasted artificial—like "ramen" or "powdered seasoning packets," tasters said. With less than 1 gram of protein, it's likely that this product contains very little actual chicken.

PROGRESSO Reduced Sodium Chicken Broth
PRICE: $2.79 for 4 cups ($0.70 per cup)
SODIUM: 560 mg **PROTEIN:** 3 g
INGREDIENTS: Chicken broth, salt, sugar, natural flavor, carrot puree, yeast extract
COMMENTS: Off-notes detracted from the otherwise "good chicken flavor" of this broth. Some of us called out a "sour" lemony taste, while others identified "sweet," "floral," "gingery," and even "minty" flavors that were out of place in chicken broth.

It's Pasta Night

Cooking the pasta in half the amount of water gives us a starchier liquid to use to make a creamy, but not prohibitively rich, sauce for spaghetti carbonara.

JUDGING BY THE NUMBER OF JARRED SAUCE OPTIONS AT THE supermarket, a lot of home cooks are slacking off when it comes to pasta night. It's a shame, really, especially since it doesn't take that long, or that many ingredients, to get a truly flavorful from-scratch pasta dinner on the table.

Spaghetti carbonara, with its silky, velvety texture, subtle, eggy flavor, and rich, meaty notes, satisfies on many levels—yet it still doesn't take more than half an hour to prepare, nor does it require any special items or a terribly complicated procedure. But don't be fooled into thinking this favorite can be made with a blindfold. The egg-based sauce can be quite finicky, often becoming overly thick and turning gluey in a matter of seconds. Many recipes add loads of butter or cream to ward off these problems, but this only results in a dish so heavy, it's hard to finish a plateful. We wanted to find a way to deliver a light yet lush and creamy sauce every time, for a foolproof and fuss-free pasta dinner that would be easy to make any night of the week.

Classic pasta puttanesca is another dish that comes together quickly. It's built from staples found in most pantries, including anchovies, olives, capers, and red pepper flakes, which impart a bold, briny character to the dish. But one of those staples—canned tomatoes—tends to lead to a sauce with an overly cooked, heavy flavor (similar to what might be found in those jars at the store). We hoped swapping in fresh tomatoes, easy to come by whether in the produce aisle or at a farmers' market, would help us ramp up the bright, fresh notes of this simple, yet robustly flavored, sauce.

FOOLPROOF SPAGHETTI CARBONARA

✔ **WHY THIS RECIPE WORKS:** Spaghetti carbonara should be luxurious and ultracreamy, but often the rich egg-based sauce becomes thick and gluey when tossed with hot pasta. We wanted a carbonara that retained its velvety texture, but without adding tons of cream, butter, or bacon fat, which could weigh our dish down. First we combined three whole eggs and one extra yolk (which provided plenty of body and eggy flavor) with a good amount of Pecorino Romano cheese. To give the sauce a smooth, silky consistency and ensure that it wouldn't get gluey after being tossed with the pasta, we thinned it with pasta cooking water. Boiling the pasta in half the usual amount of water gave us extra starchy water to coat the proteins and fats in the cheese, preventing them from separating or clumping. Tossing the spaghetti with the sauce in a warm serving bowl allowed the warm pasta to gently "cook" the carbonara sauce without overcooking the eggs. Stirring crisp chopped bacon plus 1 tablespoon of bacon fat into the sauce gave it lots of meaty flavor throughout.

THERE'S A REASON THAT *SPAGHETTI ALLA CARBONARA* is wildly popular not just in Rome but here in the United States, too. It's one of those minimalist Roman pastas made from a handful of pantry staples—pasta, eggs, some form of cured pork, Pecorino Romano, garlic, and black pepper—that add up to something incredibly satisfying and delicious. But don't be fooled by its short ingredient list: The dish is devilishly hard to get right. The finicky egg-based sauce (made from either whole eggs or just yolks, plus finely grated cheese) relies on the heat of the warm pasta to become lush and glossy, but that rarely happens. Instead, the egg either scrambles from too much heat or, as the pasta cools, the sauce thickens and turns gluey. Often the cheese clumps, too. The few recipes that do produce a creamy, velvety sauce succeed by adding tons of fat. Case in point: The silky-smooth carbonara

recipe from British chef Jamie Oliver that's built on five egg yolks, nearly ½ cup of heavy cream, and a goodly amount of rendered bacon fat. Delicious as it was, we couldn't handle more than a couple of forkfuls.

That, we realized, was precisely the problem we had to solve as we set out to perfect our own version: how to make a classic carbonara that was foolproof but not so rich that eating a full serving was impossible.

The ingredient list for carbonara is already short, but to isolate what makes or (literally) breaks the sauce, we started our testing with an even more pared-down recipe: two whole eggs, a couple of ounces of finely grated Pecorino Romano, and 8 ounces of cooked bacon pieces drained of all their rendered fat. (In Italy, *guanciale*, or cured pork jowl, is a more typical choice than bacon in this dish, but we wanted to stick with an ingredient that's a pantry staple here.) We boiled 1 pound of spaghetti, set it aside briefly, and created the sauce by thoroughly whisking the eggs and finely grated cheese in a serving bowl before tossing the mixture with the hot pasta and crisp bacon pieces. The final product? Dry, thin, and, thanks to the cheese, a little gritty. Things went even further downhill after just a few minutes. The longer the sauced pasta sat the pastier it became. Also, our tasters complained that it lacked the eggy richness they were expecting and that the pork flavor was a little faint.

We figured that adding a third egg would help with the dryness and the thinness. (We'd circle back to boosting porkiness later.) And it did—at least for a couple of minutes. But just as with our first batch of carbonara, the light, glossy sauce we started with quickly dried up and left the pasta coated with a thin, pasty residue; those who caught the tail end of the tasting were left with a bowl of dry, stuck-together spaghetti strands.

Since a sauce made with whole eggs didn't seem to have much staying power (or rich flavor), we decided to try changing course. We'd ditch the whites and revisit the idea of an entirely yolk-based sauce, minus all the extra fat in the Oliver recipe. We cooked another pound of spaghetti, mixed up a new batch of sauce with six yolks and the same amount of cheese, and for a few moments things looked better: The fat and emulsifiers in the yolks

FOOLPROOF SPAGHETTI CARBONARA

made for a sauce with velvety body, not to mention superbly eggy flavor. But once again our success was short-lived, as that same combination of fat and emulsifiers—and the fact that the sauce was drier without the moisture contributed by the whites (which are about 90 percent water)—quickly caused the sauce to tighten up into a tacky glue.

Lessons learned: Yolks—plenty of them—were a must for flavor and richness, but without enough water in the mix, there was no hope for producing a fluid sauce. The challenge would be making a sauce that was loose enough to gloss the pasta strands but creamy and viscous enough to cling nicely—and would stay that way through most of a meal.

We were about to go back to testing whole eggs when we realized that we had another liquid source we could use: the pasta cooking water. Reserving some of the starchy liquid after draining spaghetti and adding it to dressed spaghetti is a common trick that Italians use to loosen overthickened sauces. Taking this approach, we thinned out our all-yolk mixture with ¾ cup of cooking

water and once again met with initial success: The sauce was rich and creamy and, as expected, looser than the all-yolk sauce made without the added water. But maddeningly, the dressed noodles turned gluey moments later and continued to tighten up no matter how much extra cooking liquid we added.

The only scenario left was to make a sauce with whole eggs and try using the cooking water to moisten that. We circled back to the one we'd made with three whole eggs, to which we added the cheese and a little less of the starchy cooking liquid to account for the extra water introduced by the whites. This time something had changed: The sauce wasn't as velvety as we wanted, but it was surprisingly stable, holding creamy and fluid for a good 10 minutes without need for further water adjustment. The gritty bits of cheese were gone, too.

Pleased as we were with our success, we were also baffled. Why would a combination of whole eggs and pasta water create a smoother, more stable sauce than yolks and pasta water? The key turned out to be the relationship between the starch and ovomucin, one of 148 different proteins in egg whites. When ovomucin and the starch from the cooking water interact, they form a network that not only contributes viscosity but is also fairly stable and less responsive to temperature decline than a sauce made with just egg yolks. The starch was also coating both the egg and the cheese proteins, preventing the eggs from curdling and the cheese from clumping.

This information was encouraging and also gave us an idea about how to further boost the viscosity of the sauce—add more starch. We decided to try a trick we discovered when developing our recipe for *cacio e pepe*, another of those minimalist Roman pasta dishes: cooking pasta in less water (just 2 quarts per pound of pasta rather than the typical 4) to produce a starchier liquid that in turn leads to a "creamier" sauce when tossed with the spaghetti. We did the same here, halving the amount of water that we used to cook the spaghetti and then whisking ½ cup of this super-starchy liquid into the eggs and cheese before combining the sauce with the pasta. It was a huge success. The sauce was

SCIENCE DESK

LESS FAT = MORE STABLE SAUCE

The hardest part about making carbonara isn't coming up with the right ratio of egg whites to yolks to make a creamy, rich sauce; it's figuring out how to make a sauce that doesn't curdle, turn gritty, or tighten up into a glue—the usual problems as the pasta cools down. Some recipes get around the issues by adding lots of fat, which boosts the viscosity of the sauce and makes it more stable. We came up with a better, less cloying alternative: starchy pasta cooking water. Starch performs two functions. First, it coats the proteins in the eggs and the cheese, preventing them from curdling in the heat and clumping, respectively. Second, it combines with ovomucin, a protein in the egg whites, to form a network that is relatively resistant to temperature change, which means the sauce does not tighten up as it cools.

To take full advantage of the starch's effect, we concentrate it by cooking the pasta in half the usual amount of water and then add up to 1 cup of the starchy water to the sauce. The dressed pasta stays silky for a good 15 minutes.

rich and glossy and, what's more, held that consistency for a record 15 minutes. To ensure that the egg mixture thickened properly, we also made two small (but critical) tweaks to our technique. First, we warmed the empty serving bowl with the drained cooking water—another classic Italian pasta trick—to be sure that there was enough heat to "cook" the sauce. Second, we let the sauced pasta rest briefly and tossed it several times before serving; as the pasta cooled, the sauce reached just the right consistency.

This carbonara sauce was already the best we'd had to date: stable and creamy but not cloyingly rich. What it lacked was the true egg flavor of the all-yolk sauce, so we made that our next goal. And while we were at it, our tasters reminded us, could we please amp up and even out the meaty pork flavor?

Since yolks were the key to eggy richness, we tried adding an extra one to our three-whole-egg formula, not knowing if the flavor of just one would suffice or how it would affect the holding time of the sauce. Fifteen minutes later, we were pleasantly surprised to see that the sauce was just as glossy and loose as the batch without the extra yolk. And the flavor? Custardy rich but not heavy.

As for the bacon, we were sure the ½ pound we were using was plenty, but our tasters were right: Tossing bacon bits into the pasta didn't make for well-rounded pork flavor. The carbonara traditionalists among us also wished that the texture of the bacon could more closely mimic the satisfying chew of guanciale. We had ideas for addressing both issues. First, we cooked the bacon with a little water, which we recently discovered produces tender-chewy—not crumbly—pieces. Second, we caved on our resolution not to add extra fat—but just a little. Whisking a mere tablespoon of bacon fat into the sauce before tossing it with the pasta brought bacon flavor to every bite.

Finally, we'd nailed it: carbonara that was lush and rich with egg, bacon, and cheese but still light enough that our tasters didn't just eat a full bowl: They went back for seconds.

NOTES FROM THE TEST KITCHEN

WARM THE BOWL
To help the sauced pasta stay creamy longer, we warm the mixing bowl (and the serving bowls).

Drain the cooked spaghetti in a colander set in a large serving bowl. The water will heat the bowl, and some of it can be reserved for the sauce.

Foolproof Spaghetti Carbonara

SERVES 4

It's important to work quickly in steps 2 and 3. The heat from the cooking water and the hot spaghetti will "cook" the sauce only if used immediately. Warming the mixing and serving bowls helps the sauce stay creamy. Use a high-quality bacon for this dish; our favorites are Farmland Hickory Smoked Bacon and Vande Rose Farms Artisan Dry Cured Bacon, Applewood Smoked.

 8 slices bacon, cut into ½-inch pieces
 ½ cup water
 3 garlic cloves, minced
 2½ ounces Pecorino Romano, grated (1¼ cups)
 3 large eggs plus 1 large yolk
 1 teaspoon pepper
 1 pound spaghetti
 1 teaspoon salt

1. Bring bacon and water to simmer in 10-inch nonstick skillet over medium heat; cook until water evaporates and bacon begins to sizzle, about 8 minutes. Reduce heat to medium-low and continue to cook until fat renders and bacon browns, 5 to 8 minutes longer. Add garlic and cook, stirring constantly, until fragrant, about 30 seconds. Strain bacon mixture through fine-mesh strainer set in bowl. Set aside bacon mixture. Measure out 1 tablespoon fat and place in medium bowl. Whisk Pecorino, eggs and yolk, and pepper into fat until combined.

2. Meanwhile, bring 2 quarts water to boil in Dutch oven. Set colander in large bowl. Add spaghetti and salt to pot; cook, stirring frequently, until al dente. Drain spaghetti in colander set in bowl, reserving cooking water. Pour 1 cup cooking water into liquid measuring cup and discard remainder. Return spaghetti to now-empty bowl.

3. Slowly whisk ½ cup reserved cooking water into Pecorino mixture. Gradually pour Pecorino mixture over spaghetti, tossing to coat. Add bacon mixture and toss to combine. Let spaghetti rest, tossing frequently, until sauce has thickened slightly and coats spaghetti, 2 to 4 minutes, adjusting consistency with remaining reserved cooking water if needed. Serve immediately.

SUMMER PASTA PUTTANESCA

✔ WHY THIS RECIPE WORKS: We wanted a pasta puttanesca that balanced the big, potent flavors of garlic, anchovies, olives, and capers with the clean, sweet notes of fresh tomatoes. Fancy heirloom varieties and larger specimens of tomatoes required a longer cooking time, resulting in a less flavorful sauce, so we opted for cherry or grape tomatoes, which needed just a short stint over the heat and provided a bright, sweet flavor. After separating the tomato juices from the pulp by pureeing and draining them, we reduced the juices to intensify their flavor and added the pulp at the end to boost the brightness of the sauce. Sautéing the anchovies with the other ingredients tamed their assertive flavor. We bypassed the usual strand pasta and opted for campanelle, which trapped all the bits of the sauce nicely.

COME THE END OF SUMMER, WE INEVITABLY FIND ourselves with a glut of beautiful garden tomatoes and are always searching for ways to use them beyond salads. Puttanesca is one of our favorite tomato-based sauces, as we love the clash of flavors it presents: salty anchovies, olives, and capers; spicy pepper flakes; and pungent garlic meet clean-tasting fresh herbs and tangy-sweet tomatoes. Putting our harvest to use in this quick sauce would also address the "cooked," generic "red sauce" quality that stems from using canned tomatoes (the traditional choice). We wanted a fresher puttanesca— one that retained the fruits' clean-tasting sweetness alongside the richer, more assertive flavors that are the dish's essence.

We knew that not just any old tomato would suffice, so we started by gently sautéing the base of the sauce— minced garlic, red pepper flakes, chopped kalamata olives, anchovies, and whole capers—in olive oil and trying out every variety of tomato we could obtain.

Many of them lost much of their distinctiveness once cooked down to a saucy consistency. If bright

SUMMER PASTA PUTTANESCA

With the tomatoes in place, we could concentrate on taming their rowdier siblings in the sauce. Up to this point, we'd been adding the anchovies along with the olives, capers, and tomato pulp, and their fishiness stood out in the sauce a little too assertively. We tried lowering the amount we used, but then the sauce lost complexity. We found a better approach was to cook them in the oil along with the garlic and pepper flakes, which tamed their pungency while still retaining the meaty depth they brought to the sauce.

The olives are an equally important player in puttanesca sauce, and deserved special attention, so we tried using a few different common varieties. Salt-cured Moroccan olives had a nice creamy texture, but they were far too salty to use as is, and we weren't about to soak them to remove the excess. Brine-cured black olives such as Gaeta (from Naples itself) with their fruity flavor and yielding texture, were excellent, as was the larger but otherwise similar kalamata variety. Size mattered, too: we all preferred them coarsely rather than finely chopped, since the latter tended to leave the sauce with a muddy brown color. (The capers, on the other hand, benefited from being finely chopped, because that way their flavor permeated every bite.)

As for herbs, we liked the grassy flavor and bright color that a generous amount of fresh parsley gave to the sauce, along with a pinch of dried oregano. The final flourish that brought the recipe together was entirely nontraditional: In one test—fresh out of the standard pasta choices, spaghetti or linguine—we reached instead for a box of campanelle. Surprisingly, we all preferred the compact size and shape of this convoluted, flower-shaped pasta, since it did a far better job of trapping the coarse sauce.

tomato flavor was what we were after, it was key that the tomatoes not contain so much moisture that they needed long cooking. The best of the bunch were cherry tomatoes, which shed the least amount of moisture in the pan.

The one problem with the cherry tomatoes was that the chewiness of their skins marred the texture of the final sauce. It was easy to remove the skins from the larger varieties with a quick dunk in boiling water, but cherry tomatoes are far too small and too numerous to skin. Instead, we gave the tomatoes a quick blitz in a blender, which pulverized the thin skins completely.

But doing so also caused them to release much more moisture into the sauce, requiring longer cooking to thicken it up, by which time most of their fresh flavor was long gone. To prevent this, we let the puréed tomatoes drain briefly in a sieve before using them. At first, we simply discarded the excess water, but, realizing it contained loads of flavor, opted to cook it down before adding the pulp. To further boost the brightness of the sauce, we began adding the pulp right at the very end of cooking, so that the bulk of the tomatoes were hot but barely cooked upon serving.

Summer Pasta Puttanesca

SERVES 4

Our preference is to make this dish with campanelle pasta, but fusilli and orecchiette also work. Very finely mashed anchovy fillets (rinsed and dried before mashing) can be used instead of anchovy paste. Use a high-quality black olive such as Gaeta, Alfonso, or kalamata.

3 tablespoons extra-virgin olive oil

4 garlic cloves, minced

1 tablespoon anchovy paste

¼ teaspoon red pepper flakes

¼ teaspoon dried oregano

1½ pounds grape or cherry tomatoes

1 pound campanelle

Salt

3 tablespoons capers, rinsed and minced

½ cup chopped pitted kalamata olives

½ cup minced fresh parsley

1. Combine oil, garlic, anchovy paste, pepper flakes, and oregano in bowl. Process tomatoes in blender until finely chopped but not pureed, 15 to 45 seconds. Transfer to fine-mesh sieve set in large bowl and let drain for 5 minutes, pressing gently on solids with rubber spatula occasionally to extract liquid (it should yield about ¾ cup). Reserve tomato liquid and tomato pulp in strainer.

2. Bring 4 quarts water to boil in large pot. Add pasta and 1 tablespoon salt and cook, stirring often, until al dente. Reserve 1 cup pasta water, then drain pasta and return it to pot.

3. While pasta is cooking, cook anchovy mixture in 12-inch skillet over medium heat, stirring frequently, until garlic is fragrant but not brown, 2 to 3 minutes. Add tomato liquid and simmer until reduced to ⅓ cup, 2 to 3 minutes. Add tomato pulp, capers, and olives; cook until just heated through, 2 to 3 minutes. Stir in parsley.

4. Pour sauce over pasta and toss to combine, adding reserved pasta water as needed to adjust consistency. Season with salt to taste. Serve immediately.

RATING PIMENTO-STUFFED GREEN OLIVES

Pimento-stuffed green olives aren't just for martinis. They should also deliver a snappy bite and briny (but balanced) jolt of flavor to vinaigrettes, relishes, and other dishes. But after tasting the best-selling olive varieties from four nationally available brands, both straight from the jar and chopped up in our Cuban-Style Picadillo (page 63), we discovered that a good olive is mostly about the other ingredients in the jar. Brines spiked with vermouth and vinegar make olives taste "mouth-puckering" (though cooking mellows the sharpness). Calcium chloride is a good thing, as it helps to strengthen the flesh-firming pectin in the olives. Salt is good, too—tasters panned the product with the least amount of salt as "bland." As for varietals, larger Spanish Queen and Sevillano olives were preferred for their "meaty" and "juicy" textures—pluses when snacking that predictably mattered less once the fruit was cut into pieces. Brands are listed in order of preference; sodium is per 14-gram serving. See AmericasTestKitchen.com for updates and further information on this tasting.

RECOMMENDED

MEZZETTA Super Colossal Spanish Queen Pimiento Stuffed Olives
PRICE: $4.99 for 10 oz
SODIUM: 255 mg
VARIETY: Spanish Queen
COMMENTS: The "meaty, firm flesh" of these jumbo olives reminded tasters of "a ripe piece of fruit" and remained "crisp and firm" with a "bright" taste when cooked into picadillo.

SANTA BARBARA OLIVE CO. Pimento Martini Olives
PRICE: $4.59 for 5 oz
SODIUM: 240 mg
VARIETY: Sevillano
COMMENTS: Large Sevillano olives were "juicier" than others, with a pleasing "snappy texture." The vermouth-and vinegar-spiked brine rendered the fruit a bit too "mouth-puckering" from the jar, but it cooked off in picadillo.

RECOMMENDED (*cont.*)

PEARLS Pimiento Stuffed Manzanilla Olives
PRICE: $2.19 for 5.75 oz
SODIUM: 310 mg
VARIETY: Manzanilla
COMMENTS: Midsize Manzanillas made for "bright," "sweet" snacking olives but lost some of their oomph when simmered: Though the olives were still "briny," a few tasters found them "one-dimensional."

RECOMMENDED WITH RESERVATIONS

GOYA Manzanilla Spanish Olives Stuffed with Minced Pimientos
PRICE: $3.09 for 9.5 oz
SODIUM: 210 mg
VARIETY: Manzanilla
COMMENTS: Though "buttery," these smaller Manzanillas had a few strikes against them: lower sodium and, most important, no texture-preserving calcium chloride in the brine. As a result, they were "bland" and "mushy" and "got lost" in picadillo.

French-Style Dutch-Oven Dinners

Chicken broth and water, added by chef Suzannah McFerran, provide plenty of flavorful liquid in which to simmer the bite-size chunks of meat and vegetables for a French-style pork stew.

THE FRENCH MIGHT BE KNOWN FOR *BOEUF BOURGUIGNON* AND *coq au vin*, but we thought it was time to shine the spotlight on two lesser-known dishes prepared in the French countryside that deliver the same hearty qualities and appealing textures.

In *poule au pot*, a specialty from southwest France, cooks put a spin on the usual roast chicken dinner by stuffing the bird with bread crumbs and pork and braising it in a pot with a mix of vegetables. Diners are served bowls of carved chicken and tender stuffing and vegetables, all moistened with a ladle's worth of the richly flavored broth. With all the elements gently cooked together in a covered pot, this dish promises to deliver ultratender meat, moist stuffing, and deeply flavored vegetables—taking the standard chicken dinner to new heights. But the lid and long cooking time can present some problems, namely dried-out meat and a watery, tasteless broth. To bring this French dish to the American table, we'd have to figure out how to avoid these missteps.

Potée is a boiled peasant dinner that combines multiple cuts of pork with sausage, cabbage, and root vegetables and lets it all simmer for hours until the meat and vegetables practically fall apart. We thought this satisfying dish would be the perfect antidote to chilly fall or winter nights. But for a more casual meal, we wanted to transform it from a roast to a simple stew with fork-friendly bites, and the same robust, smoky flavors as the authentic French dish. Determining the right cuts of meat to guarantee intense, complex flavor, but keep our grocery list manageable, was the first step in developing our recipe for potée.

FRENCH-STYLE CHICKEN AND STUFFING IN A POT

FRENCH-STYLE CHICKEN AND STUFFING IN A POT

✔ **WHY THIS RECIPE WORKS:** The French classic poule au pot is a rather unique take on stuffed chicken: Instead of being roasted, the stuffed bird is braised with vegetables in a Dutch oven to make a satisfying and hearty one-pot meal. Our first attempts gave us wan flavor and dry chicken. To ensure the pork and bread-crumb stuffing would cook through before the chicken was overdone, we skipped stuffing the bird and instead patted the stuffing into logs, wrapped them in parchment paper, and nestled them into the pot. To make room for the chicken and vegetables, we swapped out the whole bird for parts and browned them first to give the broth rich flavor. We layered them on top of the vegetables with just enough broth to cover the vegetables so the delicate breast meat could cook more gently raised above the simmering liquid. A simple herb sauce flavored with the traditional cornichons and mustard rounds out this rustic meal.

IN AMERICA, WE TEND TO ROAST WHOLE CHICKENS, but French cooks like to put them in a pot, add vegetables and a little broth, and simmer them until tender and juicy. The poule au pot that intrigues us most hails from southwest France. For this traditional Sunday dinner, cooks stuff the bird with bread crumbs and some form of pork before cooking it in the pot with vegetables. To serve, the stuffing is removed from the cavity, the bird is carved, and both components are placed in bowls with the vegetables, a ladle of the rich broth, and accompaniments like crusty bread, cornichons, and mustard.

The dish's hearty profile appealed to us, but the handful of recipes we tried produced dismal results: Most of the birds were dry, the broths washed-out, and the stuffings loose and damp. Still we decided to refine poule au pot, with the following goals: juicy chicken, tender vegetables, a hearty stuffing, and a clean, concentrated jus.

We stuffed and stewed several birds according to various methods, but no matter what approach we took, the white meat had cooked up dry and stringy by the time the stuffing was cooked through. Plus, cramming the stuffing inside the bird and then extracting it was a pain. It was time to separate the two components.

The idea wasn't entirely ours. A recipe from Linda Arnaud's *The Artful Chicken* skips the stuffed-bird route and instead calls for forming the bread-sausage mixture into cylinders, wrapping them in foil or parchment paper, and steaming the packages in the pot until the meat had cooked through. The stuffing cylinders came out lightly springy, sliceable, and much tidier than inside-the-bird stuffing. This seemed promising.

The only problem was where to fit the stuffing "logs" in an already-crowded Dutch oven. But then we had an idea: Since we no longer needed the chicken's cavity, why not work with chicken parts instead? That way we could arrange the chicken pieces, vegetables, and stuffing logs as needed. Using parts would also speed up the cooking time, and save us the trouble of carving.

We gave it a try, seasoning two leg quarters and two breasts with salt and pepper and placing them in the pot, nestling the vegetables and stuffing logs around the chicken. We poured in just enough chicken broth to partially submerge the meat and vegetables, brought the liquid to a simmer, and transferred the vessel to a low (300-degree) oven, hoping the gentle heat would help prevent the white meat from drying out.

Now the chicken and stuffing were done in about an hour, but the flavor was thin and the white meat was still dry. We recalled a similar problem for red wine–braised pork chops. We had propped the chops on top of meat scraps and vegetables, which allowed them to cook more gently. With that in mind, we rearranged the pot's contents and came up with the following stacking order (from the bottom up): vegetables, leg quarters, stuffing logs (on either side of the dark meat), and breasts. We added just enough broth to partially submerge the vegetables, making sure that the white meat sat above the liquid, and then slid the pot into the oven.

After about an hour, we pulled the lid off the pot and sampled both the white and dark meat, which were, just as we'd hoped, equally tender and juicy. Now all we had to do was tune up the flavors.

Our original stuffing was bread-heavy, so we upped the sausage from 12 ounces to a full pound to help build savory depth, and we mixed in whole-grain mustard, garlic, and shallot. This meatier batch was also juicier and firmer and thus easier to form into sturdy logs.

The broth, however, was still weak, so though it went against tradition, we browned the chicken pieces before adding the liquid, which considerably boosted the savory flavor. (We removed the skin before serving, since it lost its appealing crispness as it simmered.) Some recipes called for adding a bouquet garni (herbs and aromatics tied together with twine) to flavor the pot, so we did the same. And to insert some fresh sweetness, we turned to a classic sausage mate: fennel. The quartered bulb went in with the other vegetables, the minced fronds into the stuffing.

Serving the mustard and cornichons alongside was fine, but the dish came together nicely when we mixed those bold-flavored accoutrements (along with more aromatics) into an olive oil–based dressing.

As we set out our final batch of poule au pot, we found ourselves thinking that, although we'd strayed from the classic recipes, we couldn't be more pleased by this package of juicy meat, savory stuffing, tender vegetables, and rich-tasting jus.

NOTES FROM THE TEST KITCHEN

SLICEABLE STUFFING

Many poule au pot recipes call for cramming the stuffing inside a whole chicken; we made an easier compact, sliceable stuffing by rolling the bread-sausage mixture in parchment and cooking it right alongside the chicken and vegetables.

French-Style Chicken and Stuffing in a Pot
SERVES 4 TO 6

A neutral bulk sausage is best, but breakfast or sweet Italian sausage can be used. You'll need a Dutch oven with at least a 7¼-quart capacity. Use small red potatoes, measuring 1 to 2 inches in diameter. Serve this dish with crusty bread and cornichons and Dijon mustard or Herb Sauce (recipe follows).

SAUSAGE STUFFING

- 2 slices hearty white sandwich bread, crusts removed, torn into quarters
- 1 large egg
- 1 shallot, minced
- 2 garlic cloves, minced
- 2 tablespoons minced fresh parsley
- 2 tablespoons minced fennel fronds
- 2 teaspoons whole-grain mustard
- 1 teaspoon minced fresh marjoram
- ¼ teaspoon pepper
- 1 pound bulk pork sausage

CHICKEN

- 2 celery ribs, halved crosswise
- 8 sprigs plus 1 tablespoon minced fresh parsley
- 6 sprigs fresh marjoram
- 1 bay leaf
- 2 teaspoons vegetable oil
- 2 (12-ounce) bone-in split chicken breasts, trimmed
- 2 (12-ounce) bone-in chicken leg quarters, trimmed
     Salt and pepper
- 1½ pounds small red potatoes, unpeeled
- 2 carrots, peeled and cut into ½-inch lengths
- 1 fennel bulb, stalks trimmed, bulb quartered
- 8 whole peppercorns
- 2 garlic cloves, peeled
- 3-3½ cups low-sodium chicken broth

1. FOR THE SAUSAGE STUFFING: Adjust oven rack to middle position and heat oven to 300 degrees. Pulse bread in food processor until finely ground, 10 to 15 pulses. Add egg, shallot, garlic, parsley, fennel fronds, mustard, marjoram, and pepper to processor and pulse to combine,

6 to 8 pulses, scraping down sides of bowl as needed. Add sausage and pulse to combine, 3 to 5 pulses, scraping down sides of bowl as needed.

2. Place 18 by 12-inch piece of parchment paper on counter, with longer edge parallel to edge of counter. Place half of stuffing onto lower third of parchment, shaping it into rough 8 by 2-inch rectangle. Roll up sausage in parchment; gently but firmly twist both ends to compact mixture into 6- to 7-inch-long cylinder, approximately 2 inches in diameter. Repeat with second piece of parchment and remaining stuffing.

3. FOR THE CHICKEN: Using kitchen twine, tie together celery, parsley sprigs, marjoram, and bay leaf. Heat oil in large Dutch oven over medium-high heat until just smoking. Pat chicken breasts and leg quarters dry with paper towels, sprinkle with ½ teaspoon salt, and season with pepper. Add chicken, skin side down, and cook without moving it until browned, 4 to 7 minutes. Transfer chicken to large plate. Pour off and discard any fat in pot.

4. Remove Dutch oven from heat and carefully arrange celery bundle, potatoes, carrots, and fennel in even layer over bottom of pot. Sprinkle peppercorns, garlic, and ¼ teaspoon salt over vegetables. Add enough broth so that top ½ inch of vegetables is above surface of liquid. Place leg quarters on top of vegetables in center of pot. Place stuffing cylinders on either side of leg quarters. Arrange breasts on top of leg quarters. Place pot over high heat and bring to simmer. Cover, transfer to oven, and cook until breasts register 160 degrees, 60 to 75 minutes.

5. Transfer chicken and stuffing cylinders to carving board. Using slotted spoon, transfer vegetables to serving platter, discarding celery bundle. Pour broth through fine-mesh strainer into fat separator; discard solids. Let stand for 5 minutes.

6. Unwrap stuffing cylinders and slice into ½-inch-thick disks; transfer slices to platter with vegetables. Remove skin from chicken pieces and discard. Carve breasts from bone and slice into ½-inch-thick pieces. Separate thigh from leg by cutting through joint. Transfer chicken to platter with stuffing and vegetables. Pour ½ cup defatted broth over chicken and stuffing to moisten. Sprinkle with minced parsley. Serve, ladling remaining broth over individual servings.

Herb Sauce
MAKES ABOUT ½ CUP

⅓ **cup extra-virgin olive oil**
6 **cornichons, minced**
2 **tablespoons minced fresh parsley**
1 **tablespoon minced fennel fronds**
2 **teaspoons minced shallot**
2 **teaspoons whole-grain mustard**
1 **teaspoon minced fresh marjoram**
½ **teaspoon finely grated lemon zest plus**
   2 tablespoons juice
¼ **teaspoon pepper**

Whisk all ingredients together in bowl. Let stand for 15 minutes before serving.

FRENCH-STYLE PORK STEW

✓ WHY THIS RECIPE WORKS: In the French-style boiled dinner known as *potée*, multiple cuts of pork, sausages, and vegetables are simmered until tender, then served with their flavorful cooking liquid. We set out to turn this dish into a fork-friendly stew that was robust and satisfying, but not heavy. Pork butt, cut into chunks, became succulent and tender with the long cooking time. Supplementing it with a smoked ham shank and kielbasa gave our stew the delicate smokiness and intense porky notes found in authentic versions, plus it provided such meaty flavor and complexity that we could skip the extra step of browning the pork. Chicken broth cut with water provided a subtle flavor base that kept the flavor clean; simmering it with aromatics and seasonings added depth. For ease, we limited the traditional roster of vegetables to just three—carrots, potatoes, and cabbage—which we added toward the end of cooking so they would retain their texture. Finally, moving our stew to the oven allowed it to cook through gently and evenly.

IN THE REALM OF STEWS, BEEF DOMINATES. PORK STEWS are harder to come by, and when you do find them, the meat often gets lost in the shadows of more assertive or distinctive ingredients. Consider Mexican chili verde, boldly flavored with tomatillos and spicy green chiles, or Hungarian pork stew, loaded with sweet paprika. As pork lovers we wanted to find a stew that put the spotlight on the headlining ingredient. But we also wanted a stew that, while robust and satisfying, wouldn't be heavy.

We did a little research on pork dishes and discovered a recipe close to what we had in mind: *potée* (pronounced poh-TAY). This French peasant recipe varies from region to region, but most versions take the form of an old-fashioned boiled dinner. They combine multiple cuts from almost any part of the pig (but always including one smoked cut); sausages; and a mix of cabbage, onions, and sturdy root vegetables. The ingredients are simmered together in liquid (usually water) until tender, and then

the pork and sausages are sliced and served with the vegetables—the whole lot moistened with some of the cooking liquid. The dish is plenty porky, and because it's typically not thickened with anything, the broth has the clean taste we were looking for.

That said, a couple of things didn't suit: With the meat and vegetables served in big pieces in only the barest suggestion of broth, potée is typically more of a knife-and-fork affair that requires plating. We wanted a true stew: in other words, bite-size chunks, swimming in lots of broth. And since we'd be using more of it, we wanted that broth to have as complex a flavor as possible. With these goals in mind, we got cooking.

Determining which cuts of pork to use was first on our agenda. Many potée recipes that we found called for large, tough whole roasts that required several hours of cooking to turn tender. We knew that we wanted to keep the stew somewhat light, we kicked off the testing process by simmering cubes of pork loin and tenderloin (which also had the benefit of cooking much faster) in separate pots of water. Both cuts are ultralean, so it was not much of a surprise that they cooked up dry and stringy, plus neither contributed much toward our goal of a broth that, while not overly rich, was still meaty. We moved on to try pork butt, which we first cut into 1½-inch chunks and browned before simmering. With its mix of lean and fat, the butt (which actually comes from the shoulder of the pig), contributed solid pork flavor to the broth, making the 2 hours it took to become succulent and fork-tender worth it. We settled on 3 pounds, which netted about 2 pounds of meat once the fat was trimmed.

Next up: choosing some kind of smoked pork; potée usually includes pork belly and/or ham hocks or shanks. Since pork belly—the cut used to make bacon—can be tricky to find, we tried the latter instead, along with the hocks and shanks. Bacon, even when cut into bite-size pieces and browned before simmering, became limp and rubbery and left an oil slick on the surface of the broth. Smoked hocks weren't greasy, but this bony cut contributed very little meat that could be shredded and added back to the pot. A smoked shank was by far the best choice because of its size and meatiness—just one yielded well over a cup of shredded pork that was a nice

FRENCH-STYLE PORK STEW

supplement to the shoulder—and it infused the broth with a delicate smokiness. The shank was tender after about 1½ hours of simmering. We removed it and allowed it to cool so that we could shred the meat.

Sausage (usually a regional variety) is the final meaty component. Our options were limited by availability, and the most widely available types, chorizo and Italian sausage, contained seasonings that seemed out of place in the stew. We opted for the firm bite and more straightforward smoked pork flavor of kielbasa. But unlike the butt and hock, the sausage did not take well to long cooking—it wound up bland and dry, having released its seasoning and fat into the simmering liquid. Adding the slices during the final 15 minutes or so of cooking heated them through and kept them moist.

We had one more tweak to investigate: Following typical stew-making protocol, we had been browning the pork butt before simmering it. Browning creates caramelized bits of fond in the pot and on the meat that contribute flavor compounds to the finished dish, but it's a step that takes time and makes a mess. With so much smoke flavor in the pot from the shank and the sausage, we wondered if browning was really necessary. When we made side-by-side batches, we were glad to find that

any additional flavor benefit from browning was barely discernible. Browning was officially out.

We'd finally produced deeply meaty-tasting broth; now it was time to add more layers of flavor. Up to this point, we had been using water as the cooking liquid, as almost all potée recipes do, but we wanted to see if we could improve the stew with chicken broth. Using all broth made the stew too reminiscent of chicken soup. Diluted with water, however, the chicken broth added a subtle flavor base that didn't compete with the pork. For even more depth, we added halved onions plus parsley, thyme, bay leaves, garlic, peppercorns, and a couple of whole cloves to the pot as the meat simmered—a step that many potées don't bother with.

The last elements to consider were the vegetables. Literally anything goes in traditional potée, and six different vegetables is not uncommon. We wanted a nice mixture in the stew, but to simplify shopping and prep, we had to make careful selections.

One common addition, turnip, was eliminated when some tasters objected to its bitter taste. With onions flavoring the broth, leeks were redundant, so they were also out. We settled on shredded cabbage (we used savoy because it has a more delicate texture than regular green cabbage) and chunks of carrots and potatoes—a manageable lot. Tasters were happy with this core group—it offered a balance of sweet, earthy flavor; nice texture; and appealing color. And we made sure to include enough of them to balance out the meat in the stew.

As for the best way to incorporate the vegetables, some potée recipes call for simply combining all of the meat and vegetables in the pot, adding liquid, and simmering for hours until the meat is done. Others start with the meat and introduce the vegetables near the end of the cooking time. We knew that the latter method was superior, since vegetables cooked for too long would end up lifeless and limp. After testing various times, we ended up adding the carrots and potatoes to the pot for the last 40 minutes of cooking, and found that the cabbage wilted nicely into the broth if cooked for just the final 15 minutes.

Next, we considered transferring the operation to the oven after bringing the stew to a simmer on the stovetop. Because the heat of the oven is steady, constant, and all-encompassing, we often prefer it for stews and braises. Indeed, 325 degrees was ideal for keeping the liquid at a gentle simmer and eliminated the need for frequent burner adjustments.

A sprinkle of chopped fresh parsley, and our stew was done. Besides meeting our goal of a meaty yet light dish, we'd never created a dish so satisfying with so little hands-on work.

French-Style Pork Stew

SERVES 8 TO 10

Pork butt roast, often labeled Boston butt in the supermarket, is a very fatty cut, so don't be surprised if you lose a pound or even a little more in the trimming process (the weight called for in the recipe takes this loss into account). Serve with crusty bread.

  6 **sprigs fresh parsley**
  3 **large sprigs fresh thyme**
  5 **garlic cloves, unpeeled**
  2 **bay leaves**
  1 **tablespoon black peppercorns**
  2 **whole cloves**
  5 **cups water**
  4 **cups chicken broth**
  3 **pounds boneless pork butt roast, trimmed and cut into 1- to 1½-inch pieces**
  1 **meaty smoked ham shank or 2–3 smoked ham hocks (1¼ pounds)**
  2 **onions, halved through root end, root end left intact**
  4 **carrots, peeled, narrow end cut crosswise into ½-inch pieces, wide end halved lengthwise and cut into ½-inch pieces**
  1 **pound Yukon Gold potatoes, unpeeled, cut into ¾-inch pieces**
 12 **ounces kielbasa sausage, halved lengthwise and sliced ½ inch thick**
  8 **cups shredded savoy cabbage**
     Salt and pepper
 ¼ **cup chopped fresh parsley**

1. Adjust oven rack to middle position and heat oven to 325 degrees. Cut 10-inch square of triple-thickness cheesecloth. Place parsley sprigs (fold or break to fit), thyme sprigs, garlic, bay leaves, peppercorns, and cloves in center of cheesecloth and tie into bundle with kitchen twine.

2. Bring water, chicken broth, pork butt, ham shank, onions, and herb bundle to simmer in large Dutch oven over medium-high heat, skimming off scum that rises to surface. Cover pot and place in oven. Cook until pork chunks are tender and skewer inserted into meat meets little resistance, 1¼ to 1½ hours.

3. Using slotted spoon, discard cheesecloth bundle and onion halves. Transfer shank to plate. Add carrots and potatoes to pot and stir to combine. Cover pot and return to oven. Cook until vegetables are almost tender, 20 to 25 minutes. When cool enough to handle, using two forks, remove meat from shank and shred into bite-size pieces; discard skin and bones.

4. Add shredded shank meat, kielbasa, and cabbage to pot. Stir to combine, cover, and return to oven. Cook until kielbasa is heated through and cabbage is wilted and tender, 15 to 20 minutes. Season with salt and pepper to taste, then stir in parsley. Ladle into bowls and serve.

NOTES FROM THE TEST KITCHEN

THREE CUTS OF PORK, NO BROWNING
Three types of pork give our stew contrasting textures and so much complex flavor that browning any of it (a typical step in stew) is unnecessary.

PORK BUTT
The fat-streaked shoulder of the pig turns succulent during cooking.

SMOKED SHANK
The collagen-rich front leg imparts a silky consistency and smoky flavor.

KIELBASA
Smoked sausage provides a snappy texture and heady flavor.

Classic Italian Fare

A combination of bread crumbs and grated Parmesan keeps the coating on chicken cutlets crunchy and flavorful.

DIG INTO A PLATE OF CHICKEN PARMESAN, AND YOU MIGHT BE disappointed. Sure, an ultracrisp exterior, tender chicken, and gooey, cheesy layer is the gold standard—but most of the time, you're met with a soggy coating of bread crumbs, dried-out, flavorless meat, and a chewy blanket of mozzarella that slides off the chicken with one slice of the knife. In our efforts to revitalize this dish, we tried a variety of fixes. Fortunately, achieving juicy cutlets that kept their crunch under the sauce didn't involve shopping for any oddball ingredients, and it wasn't just a matter of nailing the breading—how we handled the chicken before coating it played a huge role, too.

Less familiar, but no less satisfying when done well, *pasta alla norcina* coats al dente pasta with a light, creamy sauce dotted with crumbles of tender sausage. However, making an authentic-tasting, richly flavored version of this Umbrian classic was a challenge before we even set foot in the test kitchen because we were missing one key ingredient: the garlicky, rosemary-spiked sausage from the village of Norcia. Store-bought Italian sausage was a poor imposter, loaded up with spices and seasonings that just weren't right in our recipe. The solution? Making our own. Join us as we figure out how to bring this creamy pasta dish with homemade sausage to the dinner table—minus the airplane ticket.

BEST CHICKEN PARMESAN

BEST CHICKEN PARMESAN

✔ **WHY THIS RECIPE WORKS:** Classic chicken Parmesan should feature juicy chicken cutlets with a crisp pan-fried breaded coating, complemented by creamy mozzarella and a bright, zesty marinara sauce. But more often it ends up dry and overcooked, with a soggy crust and a chewy mass of cheese. To prevent the cutlets from overcooking, we halved them horizontally and pounded only the fatter halves thin. Then we salted them for 20 minutes to help them hold on to their moisture. To keep the crust crunchy, we replaced more than half of the sogginess-prone bread crumbs with flavorful grated Parmesan cheese. For a cheese topping that didn't turn chewy, we added some creamy fontina to the usual shredded mozzarella and ran it under the broiler for just 2 minutes to melt and brown. Melting the cheese directly on the fried cutlet formed a barrier between the crispy crust and the tomato sauce.

IT'S SURPRISING THAT CHICKEN PARMESAN EVER became so popular. True, at its best it's a wonderful combination of juicy chicken, crisp crust, and rich cheesy flavor offset by zippy tomato sauce, but the classic cooking method makes it difficult for the home cook to achieve such results with any degree of regularity.

In the traditional recipe, boneless, skinless chicken breasts are pounded until thin and then coated in breading and fried until crispy and golden—so far so good. But then those fully cooked cutlets are blanketed with tomato sauce, mozzarella, and a token dusting of Parmesan and baked in the oven. During baking, the sauce saturates and softens the crust, the chicken overcooks, and the cheeses meld into a thick mass that turns tarpaulin-tough soon after being removed from the oven. After all that work, what should be a delicious indulgence is all too often a soupy, soggy, chewy disappointment.

Contrary to popular belief, chicken Parmesan is a fairly recent American invention, not a sacred recipe with a noble and distinguished old-world provenance. That was good news for us; not beholden to any tradition, we were free to create a version that delivered the best features every time. Only then would it earn a place in our collection of classic recipes.

First, we wondered if we could avoid the usual frying step by coating the chicken with precrisped crumbs and a bit of fat and then baking it—an approach that could potentially simplify the dish and make it a bit lighter at the same time. No such luck. The coating wasn't as crunchy or cohesive as we would have liked, and it sogged out the second it came in contact with the sauce. Shallow frying it would have to be.

Following the usual method, we pounded four boneless, skinless chicken breasts with a rubber mallet until they were ¼ inch thick. Their surface area increased almost threefold, so maneuvering the wide pieces through the breading treatment (flour, then beaten egg, and then seasoned bread crumbs) was unwieldy, but we consoled ourselves with the thought that more surface area would mean more crunch.

We shallow-fried the cutlets in batches in several table-spoons of oil until they were crispy, drained them on paper towels, shingled them in a baking dish covered with a simple tomato sauce, and then topped it all with a layer of mozzarella and Parmesan. After 20 minutes in a 375-degree oven, the cheese was bubbly and starting to brown in spots.

This test turned out to be a successful demonstration of everything that can possibly go wrong. The cutlets were overcooked and tough, while the delicate crust that frying had wrought was soft and soggy. And the cheese? It quickly coagulated into a sheet so unyielding that we had difficulty getting our knives through it.

We flirted with the idea of subbing chicken thighs for the usual breasts, thinking that they would stay moister, but we tried it and the flavor was all wrong. Chicken Parmesan relies on the clean, neutral flavor of white meat to balance the fried coating, zesty sauce, and creamy cheese—the slight gaminess of dark meat just didn't work. Breasts it would be, but we'd have to find a way to keep them moist and tender.

We realized that pounding the chicken very thin increased the likelihood of overcooking, but taking the breasts straight from the packaging to the breading didn't work either. The thick breasts didn't cook through in the quick skillet fry, so they had to spend more time in the oven, which gave the crust even more time to get soggy.

Eventually, we settled on slicing two large breasts horizontally and pounding only the thick end of each piece to achieve a consistent ½-inch thickness from end to end. We salted the cutlets for 20 minutes, knowing that the salt would penetrate the surface of the meat and alter the proteins in such a way as to help them hold on to more of their moisture. These two changes gave us the moistest, most tender, most well-seasoned cutlets yet—but the crust still had no chance against the sauce.

There are three parts to the crust problem. The first and biggest issue is that bread crumbs are starch, and starch readily absorbs liquid and turns soft. Second, completely covering the crusted cutlets in a very wet sauce exposes the most crust to the most liquid. And third, waiting around for the cheese to melt in the oven gives the sauce plenty of time to saturate and soften the crust.

We turned our attention to the sauce and began by cooking the combination of canned tomatoes, garlic, and seasonings longer so that it thickened—and then brightened it with red pepper flakes and fresh basil. Rather than cover the entire surface of the chicken, we put just a small amount on top of each cutlet, figuring we could pass more at the table. And we radically limited the time the two components spent together. Because the dish was going into the oven only to melt the cheese, we swapped the moderate oven for the fiercer heat of the broiler and took the 20 minutes of "together time" down to 2.

A more reduced sauce and less oven time helped the situation, but they didn't fix it completely. The breading would still need to be reengineered. And how do you get around the problem that breading is, well, bread? It occurred to us that there was one recipe we'd come across in our research that actually didn't have a breaded coating. Instead, it featured a coating so outlandish that we'd rejected it outright: crushed pork rinds. (Confession: The recipe was from a low-carb cookbook.) But why not give it a shot? After all, since pork rinds are simply rendered pig skin and composed of nothing more than proteins and fat, in theory they wouldn't be prone to the sogginess of a starch-based breading. However, our hopes were quickly dashed. Pulverized pork rinds had a light, fluffy texture, and when used in place of breading, they gave the cutlets an oddly puffy, delicate exterior, nothing like the crunch we sought. And the flavor was noticeably porcine.

But this got us thinking about what else is mostly protein and fat and contains no starch . . . perhaps the most obvious choice of all: Parmesan cheese. Replacing more than half of the bread crumbs with grated Parmesan not only made the crust on our cutlets more moisture-proof but also meant that our chicken Parmesan was starting to earn its surname.

Unfortunately, our cheese problems were not completely solved. The mozzarella continued to mar the dish by forming a leathery layer on top. Recalling a test kitchen recipe for macaroni and cheese in which the solution to a texture problem was using a combination of cheeses, we considered possible creamy, tenderizing companions for the rubbery mozzarella. Cream cheese and heavy cream were too liquid, and cheddar and Monterey Jack (the solution to the mac and cheese) had the wrong flavors. Mozzarella's ideal accomplice turned out to be creamy, nutty fontina. Used in equal parts, the two cheeses provided the perfect combination of authentic Italian flavor and tender, soft texture.

Our chicken Parmesan required a few final adjustments, the first of which concerned the tedious and messy three-step breading procedure. For some recipes each step of the process is vital: The initial coat of flour helps the egg stick, and the egg helps the crumbs stick. Not in this case. We found that we could simply mix a bit of flour into the egg; coat the cutlets with the mixture; and proceed straight to crumbs with cleaner fingers, one less dish to wash, and no decrease in crumb adherence.

The soggy crust problem had lessened, but it was not completely solved—not until we began to play with the order in which the components of the dish were assembled. Instead of putting the cheese combo on top

of the sauce, we placed it between the crust and the sauce so it melted to form a cheesy raincoat that protected the cutlet. Sogginess? Gone.

Every bite of our revamped chicken Parmesan offered crispy, juicy chicken; wispy strands of creamy mozzarella and fontina cheeses; fresh, bright tomato sauce; and nutty Parmesan flavor. Finally it was worth the indulgence.

Best Chicken Parmesan

SERVES 4

Our preferred brands of crushed tomatoes are Tuttorosso and Muir Glen. This recipe makes enough sauce to top the cutlets as well as four servings of pasta. Serve with pasta and a simple green salad.

SAUCE

- 2 **tablespoons extra-virgin olive oil**
- 2 **garlic cloves, minced**
- **Kosher salt and pepper**
- ¼ **teaspoon dried oregano**
- **Pinch red pepper flakes**
- 1 **(28-ounce) can crushed tomatoes**
- ¼ **teaspoon sugar**
- 2 **tablespoons coarsely chopped fresh basil**

CHICKEN

- 2 **(6- to 8-ounce) boneless, skinless chicken breasts, trimmed, halved horizontally, and pounded ½ inch thick**
- 1 **teaspoon kosher salt**
- 2 **ounces whole-milk mozzarella cheese, shredded (½ cup)**
- 2 **ounces fontina cheese, shredded (½ cup)**
- 1 **large egg**
- 1 **tablespoon all-purpose flour**
- 1½ **ounces Parmesan cheese, grated (¾ cup)**
- ½ **cup panko bread crumbs**
- ½ **teaspoon garlic powder**
- ¼ **teaspoon dried oregano**
- ¼ **teaspoon pepper**
- ⅓ **cup vegetable oil**
- ¼ **cup torn fresh basil**

1. FOR THE SAUCE: Heat 1 tablespoon oil in medium saucepan over medium heat until just shimmering. Add garlic, ¾ teaspoon salt, oregano, and pepper flakes; cook, stirring occasionally, until fragrant, about 30 seconds. Stir in tomatoes and sugar; increase heat to high and bring to simmer. Reduce heat to medium-low and simmer until thickened, about 20 minutes. Off heat, stir in basil and remaining 1 tablespoon oil; season with salt and pepper to taste. Cover and keep warm.

2. FOR THE CHICKEN: Sprinkle each side of each cutlet with ⅛ teaspoon salt and let stand at room temperature for 20 minutes. Combine mozzarella and fontina in bowl; set aside.

3. Adjust oven rack 4 inches from broiler element and heat broiler. Whisk egg and flour together in shallow dish or pie plate until smooth. Combine Parmesan, panko, garlic powder, oregano, and pepper in second shallow dish or pie plate. Pat chicken dry with paper towels. Working with 1 cutlet at a time, dredge cutlet in egg mixture, allowing excess to drip off. Coat all sides in Parmesan mixture, pressing gently so crumbs adhere. Transfer cutlet to large plate and repeat with remaining cutlets.

4. Heat oil in 10-inch nonstick skillet over medium-high heat until shimmering. Carefully place 2 cutlets in skillet and cook without moving them until bottoms are crispy and deep golden brown, 1½ to 2 minutes. Using tongs, carefully flip cutlets and cook on second side until deep golden brown, 1½ to 2 minutes. Transfer cutlets to paper towel–lined plate and repeat with remaining cutlets.

5. Place cutlets on rimmed baking sheet and sprinkle cheese mixture evenly over cutlets, covering as much surface area as possible. Broil until cheese is melted and beginning to brown, 2 to 4 minutes. Transfer chicken to serving platter and top each cutlet with 2 tablespoons sauce. Sprinkle with basil and serve immediately, passing remaining sauce separately.

NOTES FROM THE TEST KITCHEN

CREATING THIN, EVEN CUTLETS

Slice cutlets horizontally (freeze them first for 15 minutes to help with slicing), then pound only fat ends to achieve an even ½-inch thickness.

PASTA ALLA NORCINA

✔ **WHY THIS RECIPE WORKS:** *Pasta alla norcina*, from an Italian village in Umbria, features tender pasta and richly flavored pork sausage in a light cream sauce. To bring an authentic-tasting version of this dish to the American dinner table, we bypassed store-bought Italian sausage—the size of the grind and the fat levels varied too much, and the seasonings were out of place in this dish—and made our own. Brining ground pork and mixing it briefly with a spatula ensured it had a sausagelike snappy texture; rosemary, nutmeg, and garlic offered robust flavor. Adding baking soda and searing our sausage in patty form before chopping it into small pieces helped it stay juicy and tender when it finished cooking in the cream sauce. Finely chopped mushrooms provided earthy background notes, and a splash of wine balanced the richness of the dish. For the pasta, we preferred orecchiette, which cradled the chunky sauce nicely.

IN THE MIDDLE AGES, BUTCHERS IN THE UMBRIAN village of Norcia became so adept at cutting, salting, and curing pork that the products they produced—sausage, bacon, prosciutto, and capocollo salami, to name a few—became legendary. Still named after the small town to this day, most butcher shops throughout Italy are called *norcinerie*, and master butchers bear the title of *norcino*. It's no surprise, then, that pasta alla norcina—featuring fresh sausage—is widely considered to be the ultimate pasta and sausage dish.

On a recent trip to the region, we sampled many versions, the best of which featured crumbles of fresh sausage (juicy and tender as could be) napped with cream and tossed with a small, chunky pasta. While some plates were fancied up with black truffles or other garnishes, sausage was always the focus. It tasted first and foremost of rich pork (Umbrian black pigs are prized for their meat) with background hints of garlic and sometimes rosemary. We typically avoid trying to replicate dishes so deeply connected to their birthplace for fear that we won't do them justice, but our persistent cravings for this pasta won out. Our goal was to come up with a version possessing all the virtues of the ones we'd savored abroad.

Whipping up a simple cream-based sauce would be relatively easy, so we first focused our efforts on getting the sausage just right. And here we (predictably) ran into a big obstacle: Store-bought Italian sausage didn't even come close as a substitute for the true handmade Italian stuff. Depending on the brand, we found that the grind size and fat and salt contents varied considerably. Even more problematic was that the overwhelming majority of mild Italian sausage in this country is the fennel-spiked type, which was all wrong for this recipe. Undeterred, we decided to simply follow Norcian tradition: We would make our own sausage.

Making fresh sausage at home may sound daunting, but it's actually pretty easy. At its simplest, sausage is nothing more than a humble mixture of chopped or ground meat (in this case pork), fat, and salt. The typical procedure is to rub pork shoulder with salt and allow it to sit for at least a few hours, during which time the salt pulls water from the meat. The water then mixes with the salt and forms a shallow brine on the meat's surface. The brine is then reabsorbed by the flesh, and it starts to dissolve some of the protein fibers. Finally, the salted meat is ground with fat and then kneaded by hand or by machine. During kneading, the proteins cross-link and bind together, and a strong protein network develops—much like the gluten network that is created when bread dough is kneaded. This network traps moisture and fat and produces the satisfying snappy texture of a good sausage. Easy enough, but we wanted to find a way around the extended salting time, which seemed beyond the pale for what was ultimately a weeknight pasta dish.

Grinding our own meat was too much trouble, so we jumped straight to an 8-ounce package of preground pork. Luckily, store-bought ground pork already has the 80:20 ratio of meat to fat typically used for pork sausage. We mixed kosher salt into several different batches and let them sit for various lengths of time. We had hoped that the greater surface area of the preground pork

PASTA ALLA NORCINA

would significantly reduce the salting time (from hours to just minutes) and allow us to start kneading right away. Unfortunately, it took a full 30 minutes for the salt to dissolve, form a brine, and reabsorb. We needed to speed up the salting process. What if, instead of waiting for the salt to dissolve in the pork juices, we made the brine ourselves?

We did just that for our next batch, dissolving the salt in a spoonful of water and folding the solution into the ground pork. After just 10 minutes, we could see the surface of the meat darken to a deeper shade of red, a sure sign that the proteins were dissolving (as proteins dissolve they reflect light differently, causing a color shift). To this base, we added the simple flavorings we recalled from the sausage back in Norcia: minced garlic, ground black pepper, and chopped fresh rosemary. The pork was also quite soft; 10 seconds of mixing with a spatula efficiently brought the meat together into a thick, sticky mass, which meant that a strong protein network had developed.

We eagerly fried a small patty to check for seasoning. This stuff had the springy texture of well-made sausage, and it also tasted pretty good. Our colleagues suggested adding a warm background spice, and a few tests proved that a little grated nutmeg accented the garlic and rosemary nicely. Still, for our imitation to compete with the real Umbrian sausage, we'd need to brown it well to develop as much meaty complexity as possible. And here we ran into another common problem: Thoroughly browning crumbled sausage deepens its flavor, but it practically guarantees tough, dry, meat. Was there a way to produce sausage that was well browned yet still moist?

Since ground pork sausage, like ground beef, has a tendency to dry out when crumbled and seared in a hot skillet, perhaps we needed to stop breaking it apart; instead, we'd try cooking it in one big piece, as we would a hamburger. We gave this approach a shot, pressing the sausage into a 6-inch disk and frying it in a hot skillet slicked with oil. About 3 minutes per side was all it took to develop a crusty, well-browned exterior, at which point the interior was still pink. We transferred the patty to a cutting board, chopped it into ⅛- to ¼-inch pieces, added

EQUIPMENT CORNER

PAPER STORAGE AND COOKING BAGS

The typical paper and plastic shopping bags are old news. Nowadays, some companies are branching out, with useful products that are meant to do more than help you get your groceries home. **Formaticum's Cheese Bags**, $9 for 15 bags, and **Cheese Paper**, $9 for 15 sheets with stickers, promise to help keep your cheese fresh in the refrigerator. As cheese releases moisture, tight wrappings encourage mold; loose ones let it dry out and harden. But these bags and papers use a two-ply material (wax-coated paper lined with thin, porous polyethylene plastic) that allows moisture to wick off the cheese but not escape entirely. We tested them out, wrapping cheddar, Brie, and goat cheese in both the bags and the paper, refrigerating them, and checking on them every other day for a month. Both products kept all cheese types pristine for two weeks longer than identical samples that we double-wrapped with parchment and aluminum foil. Slightly more convenient to use than the cheese paper, the bags didn't need to be sealed with stickers: Just fold over the ends a few times to close.

In the past, when we've wanted to cook *en papillote*—the traditional French method that uses parchment paper as a packet in which to bake and serve fish, chicken, meat, or vegetables—we've become frustrated with the cumbersome task of folding parchment and substituted aluminum foil. Luckily, we've found a new product, **PaperChef Culinary Parchment Cooking Bags**, $3.79 for 10 bags, that promises to eliminate the fuss. We prepared chicken, fish, and vegetables in the bags (you simply slide the food in and fold the open end over three times to seal) and compared them with foil pouches and traditionally crimped parchment. Food cooked similarly in each wrapper, but the PaperChef bags sped up preparation. Though they cost a little more than parchment paper or foil, they do eliminate the need for scissors and a ruler and taming unruly sheets of curling parchment. See AmericasTestKitchen.com for updates and further information on these testings.

the pieces back to the skillet, poured in some cream, and gently cooked them through. The good news: This sausage had terrific meaty flavor. The bad: It was still a bit drier than we would have liked. Could we do even better?

The test kitchen recently discovered the powerful effect that baking soda can have on moisture retention in meat, putting it to good use in everything from pork stir-fries to turkey burgers. The alkaline soda raises the pH of the meat and dramatically improves its water-holding capacity by tenderizing its muscle fibers and giving them a looser structure. It was worth giving it a try in our sausage. We mixed up a few more batches of our recipe with increasing amounts of baking soda added to the brine. We then seared each batch on both sides, chopped them into rough bites, and simmered them for a few minutes in cream until they were no longer pink. With ¼ teaspoon of soda in the mix, the meat stayed incredibly juicy and tender—finally, our American-made sausage was a reasonable facsimile of the Italian stuff.

With the sausage squared away, we focused on adding complementary flavors to the sauce. After chopping the browned sausage patty, we transferred it to a bowl with cream where it could infuse its flavor while we built the rest of the sauce; we would add the sausage-cream mixture back to the skillet later to cook the meat through. Super-pricey black truffles were out of the question, but we thought that a little background flavor from a much more common (and affordable) variety of fungi—cremini mushrooms—would be nice.

We roughly chopped 8 ounces of cremini mushrooms and sautéed them in the skillet until they were nicely browned. Tasters liked the flavor but felt that the pieces of mushroom competed for attention with the sausage. Easy enough to fix: A quick spin in the food processor reduced them to a fine consistency that blended discreetly into the dish. To mirror the flavors in the sausage, we added garlic, black pepper, and rosemary to the mushrooms. Then, to balance the richness of the dish, we deglazed the skillet with white wine and stirred in the sausage and cream to finish cooking. As is tradition, we also stirred in a handful of grated Pecorino Romano.

After tossing the sausage-speckled sauce with al dente orecchiette—this cupped, ear-shaped pasta cradled the chunky sauce nicely—we sprinkled it with chopped parsley and a squeeze of lemon juice for a fresh-tasting finish. We'd finally met our objective: a true tribute to the dish we'd eaten abroad, complete with the requisite homemade sausage.

Pasta alla Norcina

SERVES 6

White mushrooms may be substituted for the cremini mushrooms. Short tubular or molded pastas such as mezze rigatoni or shells may be substituted for the orecchiette.

    Kosher salt and pepper
¼ teaspoon baking soda
4 teaspoons water
8 ounces ground pork
3 garlic cloves, minced
1¼ teaspoons minced fresh rosemary
⅛ teaspoon ground nutmeg
8 ounces cremini mushrooms, trimmed
7 teaspoons vegetable oil
¾ cup heavy cream
1 pound orecchiette
½ cup dry white wine
1½ ounces Pecorino Romano, grated (¾ cup)
3 tablespoons minced fresh parsley
1 tablespoon lemon juice

1. Spray large dinner plate with vegetable oil spray. Dissolve 1⅛ teaspoons salt and baking soda in water in medium bowl. Add pork and fold gently to combine; let stand for 10 minutes.

2. Add 1 teaspoon garlic, ¾ teaspoon rosemary, nutmeg, and ¾ teaspoon pepper to pork and stir and smear with rubber spatula until well combined and tacky, 10 to 15 seconds. Transfer pork mixture to greased plate and form into rough 6-inch patty. Pulse mushrooms in food processor until finely chopped, 10 to 12 pulses.

3. Heat 2 teaspoons oil in 12-inch skillet over medium-high heat until just smoking. Add patty and cook without moving it until bottom is well browned, 2 to 3 minutes. Flip patty and continue to cook until second side is well browned, 2 to 3 minutes longer (very center of patty will be raw). Remove pan from heat and transfer patty to cutting board. Using tongs to steady patty, roughly chop into ⅛- to ¼-inch pieces. Transfer meat to bowl and add cream; set aside.

4. Bring 4 quarts water to boil in large Dutch oven. Stir in orecchiette and 2 tablespoons salt and cook, stirring often, until al dente. Reserve 1½ cups cooking water, then drain orecchiette and return it to pot.

5. While orecchiette cooks, return now-empty skillet to medium heat. Add 1 tablespoon oil, mushrooms, and ⅛ teaspoon salt; cook, stirring frequently, until mushrooms are browned, 5 to 7 minutes. Stir in remaining 2 teaspoons oil, remaining 2 teaspoons garlic, remaining ½ teaspoon rosemary, and ½ teaspoon pepper; cook until fragrant, about 30 seconds. Stir in wine, scraping up any browned bits, and cook until completely evaporated, 1 to 2 minutes. Stir in meat-cream mixture and ¾ cup reserved cooking water and simmer until meat is no longer pink, 1 to 3 minutes. Remove pan from heat and stir in Pecorino until smooth.

6. Add sauce, parsley, and lemon juice to orecchiette and toss well to coat, adjusting consistency with remaining cooking water as needed. Season with salt and pepper to taste, and serve.

Spiced-up Cuban Cuisine

*Chris observes as Julia
pan-fries shreds of simmered
beef so their edges crisp and
develop a deep crust.*

THERE'S A LOT TO RECOMMEND THE SWEET, SAVORY, BRIGHT, AND boldly spiced flavors of Cuban cooking. Black beans and rice might come to mind first when considering dishes from this Caribbean island, but there's so much more to the menu than that. Consider *picadillo*, which is like a hearty meat chili ramped up with warm spice notes, olives, and raisins. Served atop a bed of rice and garnished with toasted nuts and hard-cooked eggs, this dish is undoubtedly satisfying and hearty. Yet for such a rustic, casual dinner, authentic recipes start out with a good amount of work—like chopping a beef roast into tiny pieces before stewing the meat with a homemade *sofrito* (a sautéed base of onion, bell pepper, and garlic), and that's on top of prepping all the other ingredients. We wanted to re-create this lively dish at home for a quick, yet flavor-packed, weeknight dinner.

Enlivened with lime juice and garlic, *vaca frita* (meaning "fried cow") is another Cuban classic featuring beef, but this is beef that's been cooked twice: boiled first to tenderize it, then pan-fried in shreds to achieve a deep crust on the exterior. Sounds amazing, but often the meat ends up overly crisped and dry. Could we find a way to ensure bites of meat with both a nice crust and a succulent, juicy interior? Swapping out the typical flank steak for a more marbled and collagen-rich chuck roast was a good start, but we had a few other tricks up our sleeve to ensure vaca frita with more than just a "frita" texture.

CUBAN-STYLE PICADILLO

✔ **WHY THIS RECIPE WORKS:** Authentic recipes for this Cuban dish of spiced ground meat, sweet raisins, and briny olives call for hand-chopping or grinding the beef, but we wanted our version to be a quick weeknight option. Store-bought ground beef provided a convenient substitute, and supplementing it with ground pork added a subtle sweetness and complexity. Browning the meat made it tough, so we skipped the extra step and soaked the meat in a mixture of baking soda and water to ensure it remained tender. Pinching it off into sizable 2-inch chunks before adding it to the pot to simmer also kept it moist. For the spices, we pared the possibilities down to just oregano, cumin, and cinnamon, then bloomed them to heighten their flavor. Beef broth added a savory boost, while drained canned whole tomatoes and white wine provided brightness. Raisins and chopped green olives were a given, but we also liked the bright, briny notes contributed by capers and a splash of red wine vinegar.

BACK IN COLLEGE, ONE OF OUR COLLEAGUES HAD A Cuban American roommate whose mother ("Mama Estelle") used to visit and make big batches of picadillo. This Latin staple varies widely depending on the region, the country, and indeed the very household (picadillo is more of a home-cooked dish than restaurant fare). Mama Estelle's take involved chopping a beef roast into tiny pieces and then stewing the meat with tomatoes and her homemade sofrito—a flavor base of cooked onion, green bell pepper, and garlic. Along the way, she stirred in spices like cumin and cinnamon, and for the dish's trademark sweet-sour balance, she finished it with raisins and chopped pimento-stuffed olives. The result was tangy, sweet, and satisfying, and it came together in about an hour. The spread of traditional accompaniments that she made—rice, black beans, and sometimes fried plantains or potatoes—turned it into a complete meal.

We wish we'd been there when Mama Estelle was cooking, but coming up with our own picadillo recipe couldn't be too hard, we figured. The ingredients are easily accessible and the whole dish comes together in one pot. We just had some experimenting to do.

Per tradition, we started by sautéing chopped aromatic vegetables for the aforementioned sofrito in a Dutch oven. But we had to forgo tradition when it came to the meat. Many of the oldest and most authentic picadillo recipes call for hand-chopping or grinding beef (the Spanish verb *picar* means "to mince" or "to grind") as Mama Estelle did, but we wanted our picadillo to be a quick weeknight option, which meant switching to the convenience of preground beef. We swapped in a couple of pounds for the roast and browned it. Then we chopped up a can's worth of tomatoes, added it to the pot with spices, and let it simmer down. When the mixture had thickened a little, we added handfuls of chopped green olives and raisins for punchy, briny, and sweet flavors.

This first attempt was . . . OK. While the savory-sweet profile was appealing, it tasted off-balance, more like beef chili with olives and raisins tossed in at the last minute. Worse, we'd paid dearly for the convenience of switching to ground beef, which was chalky, dry, and dull rather than tender and juicy.

Going back to chopping up a roast wasn't an option, but we had another idea. While doing research, we'd come across a number of recipes that supplemented the beef with ground pork or chorizo. When we tried it, there was no question that the sausage was a mistake. Its heat overwhelmed the other flavors—even when we added just a small amount. The ground pork was a good move, though: With a full pound of it, the meat mixture was juicier and more supple. It also tasted a touch sweeter than beef alone—something we've noticed in other dishes when we've added pork. We did some investigating and learned that as it cooks, pork develops a relatively high concentration of glycine, an amino acid formed by the breakdown of proteins. It's the glycine that lends a subtle sweetness that helps boost complexity whenever pork makes its way into a recipe. With that mystery solved, we turned our attention to texture: Neither the beef nor the pork was as tender as we wanted it to be.

Fortunately, we had a couple of ground-meat-tenderizing tricks to fall back on. In other recipes, we've briefly treated the raw meat with baking soda. Just a pinch

CUBAN-STYLE PICADILLO

(mixed with a little water to dissolve it, plus salt and pepper for seasoning) raises the beef's pH, which prevents it from toughening during cooking. Second, since browning and simmering the ground beef was causing it to dry out, we skipped the sear, pinched the meat into 2-inch chunks (the larger the pieces the moister the meat would stay), and added them directly to the simmering sauce. Sure enough, these changes rendered the meat tender and juicy. The problem was that since meat develops its deepest, most savory flavor when it browns (during a process called the Maillard reaction), doing away with that step was a blow to the dish's meaty depth. Still, we weren't about to undo the textural progress we'd made, so we moved on to tinkering with the flavors, hoping that the right combination of spices, acidity, and sweetness would boost the dish's complexity.

While onion, grassy green bell pepper, and lots of garlic were picadillo mainstays, we had some play in the choice of spices. Ground cumin was a given, but many recipes use various combinations of thyme, oregano, bay leaf, clove, allspice, and cinnamon—and several call for all of the above. We tried various combinations and amounts of spices until we pared down the list to a judicious tablespoon each of oregano and cumin, three bay leaves, and ½ teaspoon of ground cinnamon. We also switched up our order of operations and sautéed the spices along with the onion and bell pepper (the bay was left for adding later) in a little oil—standard practice for drawing out their fat-soluble flavor compounds.

Next we turned to the acid sources, which were twofold, since most recipes call for both tomatoes and a dry wine called *vino seco*. But tomatoes must walk a fine line in picadillo: While they are almost always included, the finished dish should not taste tomato-based. We reached for a small can of whole tomatoes (fresh ones are inevitably bad for a good part of the year). After a few rough chops, into the pan they went. As for the vino seco, we weren't impressed with either the red or the white versions that we tried, and we weren't surprised. The product, which is treated with salt as a preservative, is salty and acidic—more akin to the seasoning liquid known as cooking wine than to drinking wine. Switching to a dry white (such as

SCIENCE DESK

MAKING GROUND BEEF BETTER
Using ground beef (rather than chopping up a roast) turned this dish into a quick weeknight supper, but the convenience came with a couple of drawbacks—namely, the beef's one-note flavor and dry, chalky texture. Here's what we did to fix these problems.

ADD GROUND PORK FOR SWEETNESS
Cooked pork contains relatively high levels of an amino acid called glycine, which lends the meat a faint sweetness.

TREAT WITH BAKING SODA FOR TENDERNESS
Tossing the ground meats with baking soda (dissolved in a little water) tenderizes their texture by raising their pH.

Sauvignon Blanc) balanced out the picadillo's spices and provided the punch that it needed. And yet neither the tomatoes nor the wine had compensated enough for the missing meatiness, so we reached for a more direct source: beef broth. Just ½ cup gave the meat the rich, savory boost it needed.

Finally, we went back to the traditional last-minute additions. Raisins and coarsely chopped green olives were givens, but we were also intrigued by other possibilities we'd read about—namely, capers, vinegar, and chopped almonds. A couple of spoonfuls of the capers plus a last-minute splash of red wine vinegar cut the spiced meat. But the pleasant crunch of the almonds quickly softened when we stirred them into the meat mixture. They were much better sprinkled on each dish at the table.

The sauce was now perfect—at least the bites with the raisins were perfect. But since we'd been stirring them into the pot in the last minutes of cooking, they remained sporadically scattered throughout the mixture. We wanted each bite to have some of that jammy grape flavor, so we added the raisins earlier, along with the broth and bay leaves. Allowed to simmer, the fruit's sweet flavor diffused through the dish and evened out the recipe's other strong flavors.

Savory, sweet, and briny, the ground beef mixture was now a showpiece, but it was a truly impressive spread when partnered with all the trimmings: rice and beans on the side and fresh parsley, toasted almonds, and chopped hard-cooked egg sprinkled over the top. The dish was a snap to throw together, too. Who knows? Maybe one day we will be bringing this satisfying meal to our kids when they're in college.

Cuban-Style Picadillo

SERVES 6

We prefer this dish prepared with raisins, but they can be replaced with 2 tablespoons of brown sugar added with the broth in step 2. Picadillo is traditionally served with rice and black beans. It can also be topped with chopped parsley, toasted almonds, and/or chopped hard-cooked egg.

- 1 pound 85 percent lean ground beef
- 1 pound ground pork
- 2 tablespoons water
- ½ teaspoon baking soda
    Salt and pepper
- 1 green bell pepper, stemmed, seeded, and cut into 2-inch pieces
- 1 onion, halved and cut into 2-inch pieces
- 2 tablespoons vegetable oil
- 1 tablespoon dried oregano
- 1 tablespoon ground cumin
- ½ teaspoon ground cinnamon
- 6 garlic cloves, minced
- 1 (14.5-ounce) can whole tomatoes, drained and chopped coarse
- ¾ cup dry white wine
- ½ cup beef broth
- ½ cup raisins
- 3 bay leaves
- ½ cup pimento-stuffed green olives, chopped coarse
- 2 tablespoons capers, rinsed
- 1 tablespoon red wine vinegar, plus extra for seasoning

1. Toss beef and pork with water, baking soda, ½ teaspoon salt, and ¼ teaspoon pepper in bowl until thoroughly combined. Set aside for 20 minutes. Meanwhile, pulse bell pepper and onion in food processor until chopped into ¼-inch pieces, about 12 pulses.

2. Heat oil in large Dutch oven over medium-high heat until shimmering. Add chopped vegetables, oregano, cumin, cinnamon, and ¼ teaspoon salt; cook, stirring frequently, until vegetables are softened and beginning to brown, 6 to 8 minutes. Add garlic and cook, stirring constantly, until fragrant, about 30 seconds. Add tomatoes and wine and cook, scraping up any browned bits, until pot is almost dry, 3 to 5 minutes. Stir in broth, raisins, and bay leaves and bring to simmer.

3. Reduce heat to medium-low, add meat mixture in 2-inch chunks to pot, and bring to gentle simmer. Cover and cook, stirring occasionally with 2 forks to break meat chunks into ¼- to ½-inch pieces, until meat is cooked through, about 10 minutes.

4. Discard bay leaves. Stir in olives and capers. Increase heat to medium-high and cook, stirring occasionally, until

NOTES FROM THE TEST KITCHEN

PUTTING THE PUNCH IN PICADILLO
Picadillo may be humble fare, but thanks to its mix of warm spices and sweet and tart elements, the flavors of this dish are anything but ho-hum.

SWEET
Adding jammy raisins early in the cooking process allows their sweetness to diffuse evenly.

BRINY AND BRIGHT
Chopped green olives, capers, and a last-minute splash of red wine vinegar add piquant flavors.

SPICED
Warm spices like cinnamon and cumin bring out the meats' rounder, more complex flavors.

sauce is thickened and coats meat, about 5 minutes. Stir in vinegar and season with salt, pepper, and extra vinegar to taste. Serve.

VARIATION

Cuban-Style Picadillo with Fried Potatoes

After pulsing vegetables in food processor, toss 1 pound russet potatoes, peeled and cut into ½-inch pieces, with 1 tablespoon vegetable oil in medium bowl. Cover and microwave until potatoes are just tender, 4 to 7 minutes, tossing halfway through microwaving. Line surface of large plate with double layer of coffee filters and lightly spray with vegetable oil spray. Drain potatoes well, transfer to coffee filters, and spread in even layer. Let cool for 10 minutes; proceed with recipe from step 2. After step 3, heat 1 cup vegetable oil in large saucepan over medium-high heat until shimmering. Add cooled potatoes and cook, stirring constantly until deep golden brown, 3 to 5 minutes. Using slotted spoon, transfer potatoes to paper towel–lined plate and set aside. Add potatoes to pot with vinegar in step 4.

CUBAN SHREDDED BEEF

✔ **WHY THIS RECIPE WORKS:** *Vaca frita* is a Cuban classic that features beef (usually flank steak) that's been boiled, shredded, and fried so that the exterior develops a deep crust; a bit of lime juice and garlic contribute the bright, tart, and robust flavors typical of Caribbean cuisine. For our recipe, we were after meat with some textural contrast—we wanted a good exterior crust, plus a moister, more tender interior. We started with a collagen-rich chuck-eye roast and cut it into 1½-inch cubes to reduce the cooking time. Gently simmering it rather than boiling it helped keep it moist. Pounding the meat flat was much more efficient than shredding the pieces by hand. To reinforce the beefy flavor, we fried it, along with some thin-sliced onion (a classic element of vaca frita), in its own fat before finishing everything with a mixture of garlic, cumin, oil, and citrus juices (lime as well as orange, to mellow the lime's acidity but maintain brightness).

CITRUSY, GARLICKY PORK ROASTS ARE A HALLMARK OF Cuban cuisine, but the country is also home to a lesser-known beef dish with similarly bold, bright flavors. Vaca frita, which literally translates as "fried cow," consists of an evenly grained flat cut such as flank or skirt steak (in Latin America, these cuts might be called "*falda real*" and "*arrachera*," respectively) that's cooked twice: first boiled to tenderize it and then pulled into meaty shreds and pan-fried until the exterior develops a deep crust. Along the way, the meat is seasoned with liberal doses of garlic and fresh lime as well as a touch of ground cumin, and an onion is sliced thin, fried in the same pan, and stirred together with the beef. Extra lime wedges are often passed at the table, and the mixture is usually accompanied by generous helpings of rice and beans.

We're addicted to the combination of lime, garlic, and beef—especially when the beef comes with crispy edges—so vaca frita is almost always the first thing we

CUBAN SHREDDED BEEF

order at Cuban restaurants. That said, sometimes the dish isn't perfect. The beef can be so much about crispiness that after a few bites it starts to seem a little dry and stringy. Our ideal version would showcase the dish's tangy, garlicky aspect while offering shreds of beef that were crispy and richly flavored at the edges but moist and succulent inside.

We figured that cuts more marbled and collagen-rich than flank steak might not dry out as much. When heated, collagen breaks down into gelatin, which retains water, while fat bastes the cooked meat and increases its perceived juiciness. So we rounded up flap meat, boneless short ribs, and a chuck roast, all of which are streaked with fat and collagen, and we prepared them according to a typical vaca frita recipe—but we made one notable change from the get-go. Instead of boiling the meats, we lowered the temperature of the cooking water to a simmer, knowing that the amount of moisture that meat loses during cooking is directly related to the temperature at which it cooks. To the water in the Dutch ovens we added the beef cuts, a halved onion, several garlic cloves, and a couple of bay leaves, all per tradition, and we let the pots bubble until the meats were tender. Once they'd cooled, we shredded the meats with two forks and tossed the strips with minced garlic, lime juice, ground cumin, salt, and pepper. While those flavors were absorbed, we thinly sliced another onion for each batch, grabbed some large skillets, and fried the pieces in about 1 tablespoon of oil per batch oil each until they'd softened but still retained a little crunch. We removed the onions from the pan, added more oil, and seared the various cuts of beef, letting them sizzle until their edges were crispy and deeply brown.

Compared with the flank steak vaca frita that we'd tasted, all three alternatives cooked up moister, and we favored chuck for its bigger beef flavor. But there were a number of problems left to solve. The most glaring was the amount of time that it took to prepare the dish. Simmering the whole roast had taken almost 3 hours, so we cut it into 1½-inch cubes; that reduced the simmering time to less than 2 hours, making the extra knife work worth the time and effort. Cooking the beef in smaller chunks also allowed us to easily remove

any large pockets of fat and connective tissue while we shredded the meat.

Our other substantial cooking issue was rather obvious: If you fry uniformly shredded meat, you're going to have uniformly dry (albeit crispy) strips because the moisture evaporates so easily. We certainly wanted those crispy, delicate filigrees of beef, but some of the beef also needed to stay fairly intact if it was going to hang on to any moisture. In other words, we needed to shred the beef into different-size pieces.

That thought reminded us of a timesaving technique that we'd come across in a recipe from a food blog called Cuban in the Midwest: Rather than pull apart the beef with two forks, the blogger placed the cooked meat on a rimmed baking sheet, covered it with plastic wrap, and pounded it with a mallet. Turns out that flattening, not shredding, the beef is a brilliant shortcut. (We used heat-safe aluminum foil and a rolling pin since we didn't have a mallet.) Not only was this method faster, but it also generated irregular pieces—some fine threads and some broken but intact chunks. Once they hit the hot oil, these now-flattened chunks needed less than 5 minutes to form a crispy crust, and the abbreviated frying time ensured that their insides remained moist and tender. Meanwhile, the finer threads contributed more fine shards of pure crispiness.

Having made progress with the meat's texture, we turned our focus to brightening the citrus flavor. Stripping zest off the lime and adding it to the juice didn't do enough, so we added more juice—which took the acidic bite too far and overwhelmed the beefy flavor. It wasn't until we thought about the flavors in Cuban roast pork that we realized we could supplement the lime juice with orange for bright (but not sharp) citrus flavor. Two tablespoons rounded out the fruity taste nicely and more subtly.

At the same time, the garlic element needed work, too. Three tablespoons of raw minced garlic wasn't just strong—it bit back. Instead, we treated it (and the cumin) as we would the aromatics in any sauté, pushing the browned meat to the sides of the skillet and quickly cooking the aromatics (with a little oil) in the center; after 30 seconds, the garlic's harshness had softened and the cumin's flavor had bloomed. It was also time to test whether adding aromatics to the cooking water actually infused the meat with any noticeable flavor. We compared our working recipe with one in which we simmered the meat in plain salted water. It was impossible to tell which batch was which. Aromatics in the cooking water were out.

This change made us wonder whether we could make yet another one: Instead of simmering the meat in a big pot of water (which took a good chunk of time to heat), what if we simply cooked it in a smaller amount of water in the skillet that we would then use to fry the beef? This way we could save time and reduce our dirty dish count. We threw a lid on the skillet while the beef simmered over low heat; when it was fully tender, we uncovered the pan and cranked the heat to medium so that any excess liquid would cook off. Once it had, only the beef fat was left—which gave us yet another idea. Rather than fry the onion and meat in vegetable oil, we'd reserve and reuse some of the rendered beef fat. One tablespoon turned out to be plenty. The trick ended up being more than thrifty; cooking in beef fat amped up the savory quality of the whole dish.

About the onion slices: We hadn't fiddled much with them, since our tasters liked how their faint crunch complemented the richer flavor and chew of the meat, but they were a tad on the sharp side. For due diligence, we tried bringing one batch to a caramelized stage, but their creamy, soft texture and deep sweetness just didn't mesh with the garlicky, tangy beef. Instead, we softened their sharp edge just a bit by deglazing the sautéed onion with a little dry sherry and water, knowing that the nutty fortified wine pairs naturally with onion.

The dish was finished when we added the onion slices back to the pan with the beef and tossed the whole mixture in the tangy citrus juices. Bright, garlicky, savory, and addictively crispy yet tender, vaca frita was well on its way to becoming one of our favorite beef preparations. And once we had scooped some beans and rice onto our plates, it turned into one of the most satisfying meals we'd ever made.

NOTES FROM THE TEST KITCHEN

PICK THE RIGHT CUT TO SHRED
Before we fine-tuned our vaca frita cooking method, we chose a cut of beef that would stay moist and tender during the two-part process. Flank steak is traditional, but we opted for chuck roast, which is streaked with fat and collagen—both of which increase the beef's perceived succulence.

CHOOSE CHUCK
For moist, tender meat, we ditched the traditional lean flank steak and used fattier, collagen-rich chuck roast instead.

Cuban Shredded Beef

SERVES 4 TO 6

Use a well-marbled chuck-eye roast in this recipe. When trimming the beef, don't remove all visible fat—some of it will be used in lieu of oil later in the recipe. If you don't have enough reserved fat in step 3, use vegetable oil. This dish pairs well with rice and beans, or it can be used as a filling for tacos, empanadas, or sandwiches.

2   **pounds boneless beef chuck-eye roast, pulled apart at seams, trimmed, and cut into 1½-inch cubes**
Kosher salt and pepper

3   **garlic cloves, minced**

1   **teaspoon vegetable oil**

¼   **teaspoon ground cumin**

2   **tablespoons orange juice**

1½   **teaspoons grated lime zest plus 1 tablespoon juice**

1   **onion, halved and sliced thin**

2   **tablespoons dry sherry**
Lime wedges

1. Bring beef, 2 cups water, and 1¼ teaspoons salt to boil in 12-inch nonstick skillet over medium-high heat. Reduce heat to low, cover, and gently simmer until beef is very tender, about 1 hour 45 minutes. (Check beef every 30 minutes, adding water so that bottom third of beef is submerged.) While beef simmers, combine garlic, oil, and cumin in bowl. Combine orange juice and lime zest and juice in second bowl.

2. Remove lid from skillet, increase heat to medium, and simmer until water evaporates and beef starts to sizzle, 3 to 8 minutes. Using slotted spoon, transfer beef to rimmed baking sheet. Pour off and reserve fat from skillet. Rinse skillet clean and dry with paper towels. Place sheet of aluminum foil over beef and, using meat pounder or heavy sauté pan, pound to flatten beef into ⅛-inch-thick pieces, discarding any large pieces of fat or connective tissue. (Some of beef should separate into shreds. Larger pieces that do not separate can be torn in half.)

3. Heat 1½ teaspoons reserved fat in now-empty skillet over high heat. When fat begins to sizzle, add onion and ¼ teaspoon salt. Cook, stirring occasionally, until onion is golden brown and charred in spots, 5 to 8 minutes. Add sherry and ¼ cup water and cook until liquid is absorbed, about 2 minutes. Transfer onion to bowl. Return skillet to high heat, add 1½ teaspoons reserved fat, and heat until it begins to sizzle. Add beef and cook, stirring frequently, until dark golden brown and crusty, 2 to 4 minutes.

4. Reduce heat to low and push beef to sides of skillet. Add garlic mixture to center and cook, stirring frequently, until fragrant and golden brown, about 30 seconds. Remove pan from heat, add orange juice mixture and onion, and toss to combine. Season with pepper to taste. Serve immediately with lime wedges.

RATING TORTILLA PRESSES

Corn tortillas are easy to make at home, especially if you use a tortilla press (instead of a rolling pin) to flatten the balls of masa, or dough, into disks. (Tortilla presses are only for corn, not flour, tortillas, as the gluten in the wheat flour is too elastic and would not work in a press. Flour tortillas must be shaped with a rolling pin.) We tested four brands, made of wood, cast iron, cast aluminum, and plastic and priced from $14 to $65, pressing a dozen tortillas in each and then browning them in a skillet. We noted the amount of force required with each press, the diameter of the pressing surface, and the thickness of the tortillas. The biggest differences were in the evenness of the tortillas and the amount of effort required to press them. The heavy cast-iron and wood models practically flattened the tortillas for us, while the lighter-weight cast-aluminum and plastic models required more muscle. We preferred presses with a large pressing surface; on smaller presses dough sometimes squeezed out the sides if the dough ball wasn't perfectly centered. Some presses lent themselves to overpressing, making the sides of the tortillas too thin and liable to tear. Brands are listed in order of preference. See AmericasTestKitchen.com for updates and further information on this testing.

HIGHLY RECOMMENDED

LA MEXICANA Tortilladora de Madera Barnizada/Mesquite Tortilla Press
MODEL: M134
PRICE: $64.95
MATERIAL: Mesquite wood
WEIGHT: 11.75 lb
WORKING SURFACE: 8¹⁄₁₆ in by 8⅛ in
DESIGN: ★★★
TORTILLAS: ★★★
COMMENTS: By far the largest press, this wooden behemoth caught the eye of every cook in the kitchen. Lovely appearance aside, this machine was easy to work, though its heavy plates can be a bit intimidating at first. A wooden sliver on the top plate keeps tortillas from getting too thin and also keeps thickness consistent. The 14-inch arm on this press gives great leverage, but it arrives detached and requires some assembly.

RECOMMENDED

IMUSA VICTORIA Cast Iron Tortilla Press
MODEL: SKU VICTORIA 85008
PRICE: $23.99
MATERIAL: Cast iron
WEIGHT: 7.5 lb
WORKING SURFACE: 7⅞ in (diameter)
DESIGN: ★★
TORTILLAS: ★★★
COMMENTS: This product is lighter and more compact than our winner but still has sufficient heft to make pressing easy. The handle arrives detached, so there is some assembly required (though the instructions are clear and easy to follow). At first, the handle was a bit stiff, but it loosened with use, and the ample surface area kept dough from squeezing out the sides.

RECOMMENDED *(cont.)*

NORPRO Cast Aluminum Tortilla Press
MODEL: 1063
PRICE: $15.20
MATERIAL: Cast aluminum
WEIGHT: 1.2 lb
WORKING SURFACE: 6¼ in (diameter)
DESIGN: ★★
TORTILLAS: ★★½
COMMENTS: Compact and lightweight, this press required more finesse when pressing since the user applies all the pressure with little to no help from the weight of the plate. At first it's easy to under- or overpress the tortillas, but most testers got the hang of it after only a few tries. If you are willing to put up with a bit of a learning curve, this model is a fine choice. It comes preassembled and is easy to store.

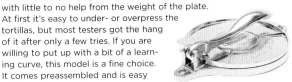

NOT RECOMMENDED

THE LATIN PRODUCTS Plastic Tortilla Press
MODEL: SKU 48610868
PRICE: $13.99
MATERIAL: Plastic
WEIGHT: 2 lb
WORKING SURFACE: 7¼ in (diameter)
DESIGN: ★
TORTILLAS: ★
COMMENTS: Both copies of this model that we tested were warped and produced uneven tortillas. When stacked, these tortillas wobbled, with their centers clearly thicker than the sides and ranging from 0.82 to 3.01 millimeters thick across a single tortilla. While this product was easy to use and came preassembled, the poor quality of the tortillas canceled out any redeeming qualities.

A Modern Take on Pizza & Grilled Cheese

GOOEY MELTED CHEESE IS IRRESISTIBLE, WHETHER IT'S SCATTERED over a pizza or grilled between two slices of bread. In this chapter, we set out to put a fresh spin on a pair of cheesy favorites.

Nowadays, pizza is featured on many a bistro menu, topped with a variety of fancy cheeses and gourmet ingredients. But it's not only the toppings that have been revamped—the dough itself has been getting a whole-wheat makeover. Yet simply swapping in some whole-wheat flour for the white flour in traditional dough recipes often leads to pizza with a dense, heavy texture and an overwhelmingly wheaty taste. To overcome these common pitfalls, we'd have to review the basics of bread making and figure out how to tame the robust flavor of whole-wheat flour.

When we think of grilled cheese sandwiches, most of us envision two thin slices of bread with a layer of orange cheese oozing out the middle. While the gooey texture is good, what isn't good is the flavor—because there's none of it! But substitute a nutty-tasting aged cheese for the slice of American, and the improvement in flavor is offset by an inferior texture, which tends to be so greasy that a single napkin won't cut it. Developing a grilled cheese sandwich with both intense flavor and a smooth, creamy texture would take some work and a clear understanding of how the composition of cheese affects its ability to melt well.

The right mix of whole-wheat and bread flours makes our pizza dough nutty and light.

THIN-CRUST WHOLE-WHEAT PIZZA

✔ **WHY THIS RECIPE WORKS:** For a whole-wheat pizza that was as crisp and chewy as traditional pizza and that offered a good, but not overwhelming, wheat flavor, we used a combination of 60 percent whole-wheat flour and 40 percent bread flour. To ensure that this higher-than-normal ratio of whole-wheat to bread flour still produced a great crust, we increased the hydration, which resulted in better gluten development and chew. To compensate for the added moisture, we employed the broiler to speed the baking process and guarantee a crisp crust and a moist, tender interior. Finally, we threw out the traditional pizza toppings, which tended to clash with the whole-wheat flavor, and opted instead for oil- and cream-based sauces and bold ingredients like blue cheese, pesto, and wine-braised onion.

A QUICK SURVEY OF PIZZA PARLOR MENUS SUGGESTS that pies are going the way of rustic bread: They're no longer a white flour–only affair. Even most supermarkets offer a partial whole-wheat-flour dough alongside their standard white. In theory, this is good news, since whole wheat can lend rich, nutty flavor and satisfying depth to most kinds of baked goods. But we often find the marriage of whole wheat and pizza crust to be strained.

Most recipes seem to fear commitment to the style, casually throwing a scant amount of whole-wheat flour into a white-flour formula. At the other end of the spectrum, we've tried following pizza dough recipes with a high ratio of whole-wheat flour (some with as much as 100 percent), and we've found that for the most part they produce dense pies devoid of satisfying chew or crisp crust. Not to mention that these crusts have an overly wheaty flavor that competes for attention with even the most potent toppings. We decided to rethink whole-wheat pizza, examining it through the lens of a bread baker in order to formulate a dough (and a cooking technique) that would give us a crust with it

all: good—but not overwhelming—wheat flavor; a crisp bottom; and a moist, chewy interior.

We started our journey by deciding exactly what style of crust we wanted. After all, whole-wheat pizza crusts run the same gamut as white-flour ones: from thin and crispy to thick, deep-dish-style pies. We wanted a crust that could withstand some full-flavored toppings, but not one that would overwhelm with its wheaty heft. A thin-crust pizza like the one we recently developed seemed a good model: Its crust is thin and crisp with perfect spots of char alongside a tender, chewy interior. We would start there, tailoring the ingredient ratio and baking techniques to withstand the challenges of whole wheat.

This pizza uses high-protein bread flour and the food processor for fast kneading. The use of bread flour would be particularly important. Why? Bread flour contains more of the proteins (glutenin and gliadin) that form gluten—the network of proteins that gives dough structure and chew—than all-purpose flour. We would use King Arthur brand bread flour, which features a particularly high protein content of 12.7 percent. And while high in protein, whole-wheat flour has less gluten potential than does white flour for two reasons. One is the type of proteins in the mix. The second is that whole-wheat flour, ground from the wheat berry, includes both the germ and the bran. These constituents provide great flavor, but the bran physically inhibits gluten development by cutting gluten strands with its sharp edges. We would therefore need to punch up the gluten potential in other ways; bread flour would be a great start.

But the thin-crust pizza recipe also used an overnight rise in the refrigerator to allow for better flavor development and an easier-to-stretch dough. We wondered if we could skip that step. The nutty flavor of the whole wheat, we figured, would make up for any other flavor benefits of letting the dough sit overnight.

We started our testing by swapping in varying proportions of whole-wheat flour in our thin-crust pizza dough recipe. Our goal was to determine the ideal amount of whole-wheat flour from a flavor perspective and then deal with textural issues. For each test dough, we pulsed the flours, water, yeast, and a sweetener to

THIN-CRUST WHOLE-WHEAT PIZZA WITH GARLIC OIL, THREE CHEESES, AND BASIL

PIZZA TOOLS

All you really need to make pizza at home is a ripping-hot oven and a pizza wheel to slice it, but we've found a couple of other tools that can make the job much easier. See AmericasTestKitchen.com for updates and further information on these testings.

Baking stones simulate a brick oven in your home, absorbing and radiating intense, consistent heat to produce pizza with a super-crisp, golden-brown crust. While we have an established favorite, the **Old Stone Oven Pizza Baking Stone**, $39.99, we were intrigued by a baking "stone" made not of ceramic or clay, but of steel. The **Baking Steel by Stoughton Steel**, $72, produced a crust that was slightly more crisp and airy and more deeply browned than the stone-baked crust. But when we followed the method for our whole-wheat crust (superheating the baking stone using the oven, then broiler, and switching back to the oven to bake the pizza), the steel transferred heat so quickly that the pizza bottom scorched before the top browned. We found that leaving the broiler on to cook the pizza worked best and produced a crisp pizza quickly, although we had to pay constant attention to avoid scorching. The Baking Steel's heft was also an issue: 15 pounds with no handles. So while we prefer our old favorite, the Baking Steel is a worthwhile splurge for avid pizza bakers.

To get your pizza dough into the oven, a pizza peel is a must-have. It makes sliding a perfectly topped pie onto a baking stone a snap (although in a pinch, you could use an upside-down baking sheet in place of the peel). We recently tested several peels, both metal and wood, to find the best one. We prefer models with a 14- to 16-inch surface, spacious enough for pizza and free-form bread loaves, and a handle length of at least 8 inches, to keep our hands a safe distance from the hot baking stone. After baking lots of pizzas, we found our favorite in the **EXOProducts Super-Peel**, $55.95, which is a wooden peel with an innovative twist: It has a pastry cloth wrapped around the end. Once floured, the cloth, which is on a roller, works like a conveyor belt to help move the pizza onto and off of the peel, making baking pizza at home that much easier.

promote browning (we opted for honey to complement the wheat flavor) until they were just combined, and then we allowed the doughs to sit for 10 minutes. During this brief respite, called an autolyse, gluten formation gets a jump start. We then added salt and oil and processed the doughs for a minute, until they were smooth and satiny. After a final rise, we shaped, topped, and baked the pizzas on a preheated 500-degree pizza

stone. These test batches confirmed that tasters preferred a dough with 60 percent whole-wheat (and the remainder white) flour. This ratio provided a distinct, pleasant wheatiness. We were happy with the flavor of our pizza, but the texture was still lacking. The flour choice was important, but now we looked to the second key ingredient: water.

We knew that dough with more water produces chewier breads, as the added hydration allows for a stronger, more stretchable gluten network. You can see water's impact by comparing tender, fine-crumb sandwich bread with chewy rustic bread. The former is often in the range of 55 to 60 percent hydrated (this number represents the weight of the water compared with that of the flour), whereas rustic bread's hydration starts in the low 60s and can creep up to nearly 100 percent. This was of relevance to our dough because whole-wheat flour absorbs more water than does white flour. At about 64 percent hydration, our initial formula sat in the midrange of white-flour doughs. With this in mind, we started increasing the water in batches and tracking the results.

Sure enough, more water led to a pizza with better chew and larger, slightly more irregular holes—something that bakers refer to as a more open crumb structure. It also made the dough easier to work with and stretch thin—at least to a point. We found that dough with a hydration of 80 percent and up was too soft and sticky to reliably form into a 13-inch disk, and the resulting pies had a tendency to stick to the pizza peel when we attempted to slide them into the oven. In the end, we found the sweet spot with 10 ounces of water for 13¾ ounces of flour, or roughly 73 percent hydration. But even this ratio could cause trouble when it came to stretching our dough out nice and thin with ease. We found ourselves doubling back to the overnight rise: The long rest in the fridge did greatly improve the extensibility of our white-flour thin-crust pizza. Would it do the same here? One try and we knew: Yes. This dough was a pleasure to handle and stretch, and it baked into a pizza with satisfying chew and a thin but airy interior.

The increased hydration helped gluten development and chew, but if we let our pizzas bake long enough for them to really crisp on the bottom, they overbaked and dried out. It turns out that browning and crisping the bottom of a pizza is much like trying to get a good sear on a steak. A wet steak takes much longer to sear than a dry one and by the time you achieve a good crust on the former, much of the interior is overcooked. This holds true for pizza as well: A wetter dough will take longer to brown and crisp because more of the oven's energy is going into driving off the extra moisture, leaving less available for crisping. We scrambled for a solution.

Up to this point, we'd been following our established pizza baking protocol, cooking our pies in a 500-degree oven on a preheated pizza stone set on the oven rack's second-highest position. By keeping the stone near the top of the oven, we create a smaller oven space where reflected heat is trapped around the pizza. This means the top and bottom of the pizza bake at a more even rate. This was good, but how could we speed up that rate?

Again, if we were dealing with a steak in a skillet, we'd simply turn up the heat. Our oven was already set to 500 degrees, but we did have a super-hot broiler. Yet given that we were trying to get the bottom of the pizza to cook faster, we weren't quite sure how to put it to use. After some failed experiments resulting in seriously burnt toppings, we hit on a winning solution. After preheating the stone in a 500-degree oven to ensure that it was fully saturated with heat, we turned on the broiler for 10 minutes. Then, when we slid in the pizza, we switched the oven back to bake. The brief blast from the broiler served two purposes: It increased the stone's exterior temperature by about 10 to 15 degrees, leading to better oven spring and faster evaporation of moisture from the bottom of the crust, and also boosted the air temperature above the stone. The upshot? We were pulling a finished pizza out of the oven after just 8 minutes—an almost 50 percent reduction in baking time. This pizza featured a crisp bottom and a super-moist interior.

One problem remained. We had great crust, but it didn't quite fit with the flavor of the topping: an uncooked tomato sauce and some shredded mozzarella cheese. The sweetly acidic tomato sauce wasn't a perfect match with the slightly sweet whole-wheat flavor of the crust. Our job was not yet done.

We began experimenting with a range of ingredients. We found that garlicky oil, rich and nutty cheeses, and punchy ingredients like pesto and anchovies are a better match for the earthy flavor of whole-wheat crust than tomato sauce is. For one variation, we briefly heated garlic, anchovies, oregano, and red pepper flakes in extra-virgin olive oil, which we then brushed on the dough as a primer coat. Next, we added a layer of fresh basil leaves, grated Pecorino Romano, and shredded mozzarella. After the pie emerged from the oven, we dotted it with small dollops of fresh ricotta. This combination added richness and complexity without overpowering the flavorful crust. Another crowd-pleaser was an even simpler rendition: We spread a garlicky basil pesto over the pie and sprinkled it with a generous handful of crumbled goat cheese. For a third option, we braised onions in red wine, then paired them with blue cheese, crème fraîche, and nuts, for a more sophisticated flavor profile.

As taster after taster gave our pizza rave reviews, we realized why the pies were such a success: They didn't represent mere tweaks to traditional pizza. We'd invented an entirely new concept: truly good whole-wheat pizza meant to be enjoyed on its own terms.

Thin-Crust Whole-Wheat Pizza with Garlic Oil, Three Cheeses, and Basil

MAKES TWO 13-INCH PIZZAS

We recommend King Arthur brand bread flour for this recipe. Some baking stones, especially thinner ones, can crack under the intense heat of the broiler. Our recommended stone, by Old Stone Oven, is fine if you're using this technique. If you use another stone, you might want to check the manufacturer's website for guidance.

DOUGH

1½ cups (8¼ ounces) whole-wheat flour
1 cup (5½ ounces) bread flour
2 teaspoons honey
¾ teaspoon instant or rapid-rise yeast
1¼ cups ice water
2 tablespoons extra-virgin olive oil
1¾ teaspoons salt

GARLIC OIL

¼ cup extra-virgin olive oil
2 garlic cloves, minced
2 anchovy fillets, rinsed, patted dry, and minced (optional)
½ teaspoon pepper
½ teaspoon dried oregano
⅛ teaspoon red pepper flakes
⅛ teaspoon salt

1 cup fresh basil leaves
1 ounce Pecorino Romano cheese, grated (½ cup)
8 ounces whole-milk mozzarella cheese, shredded (2 cups)
6 ounces (¾ cup) whole-milk ricotta cheese

1. FOR THE DOUGH: Process whole-wheat flour, bread flour, honey, and yeast in food processor until combined, about 2 seconds. With processor running, add water and process until dough is just combined and no dry flour remains, about 10 seconds. Let dough stand for 10 minutes.

2. Add oil and salt to dough and process until it forms satiny, sticky ball that clears sides of workbowl, 45 to 60 seconds. Remove from bowl and knead on oiled countertop until smooth, about 1 minute. Shape dough into tight ball and place in large, lightly oiled bowl. Cover tightly with plastic wrap and refrigerate for at least 18 hours or up to 2 days.

3. FOR THE GARLIC OIL: Heat oil in 8-inch skillet over medium-low heat until shimmering. Add garlic; anchovies, if using; pepper; oregano; pepper flakes; and salt. Cook, stirring constantly, until fragrant, about 30 seconds. Transfer to bowl and let cool completely before using.

4. One hour before baking pizza, adjust oven rack 4½ inches from broiler element, set pizza stone on rack, and heat oven to 500 degrees. Divide dough in half. Shape each half into smooth, tight ball. Place balls on lightly oiled baking sheet, spacing them at least 3 inches apart. Cover loosely with plastic coated with vegetable oil spray; let stand for 1 hour.

5. Heat broiler for 10 minutes. Meanwhile, coat 1 ball of dough generously with flour and place on well-floured countertop. Using your fingertips, gently flatten into 8-inch disk, leaving 1 inch of outer edge slightly thicker than center. Lift edge of dough and, using back of your hands and knuckles, gently stretch disk into 12-inch

---

SCIENCE DESK

WHY WHOLE WHEAT CAN SABOTAGE TEXTURE
Whole-wheat pizza is generally so dusty and leaden that it bears little resemblance to a crust made with all-purpose flour. But why should this be so? In a nutshell: It's more difficult for whole-wheat flour to form the network of proteins, or gluten, that gives a traditional pizza dough structure and leads to a moist, puffy crumb with great chew. While whole-wheat flour is higher in protein overall than all-purpose (or even bread) flour, it has less of the proteins we're looking for when making pizza (or any other kind of dough). Wheat contains four types of proteins, but only two of them—glutenin and gliadin—are responsible for creating gluten. Ninety percent of the proteins in all-purpose flour are capable of producing gluten; only 78 percent of the proteins in whole-wheat flour can do so. The other 22 percent of whole-wheat flour is made up of the proteins albumin and globulin, which are incapable of creating structure within dough. There's one more reason that whole-wheat flour sabotages texture: It includes both the bran and the germ. The former has sharp edges that literally chop down gluten strands, while the latter contains glutathione, which retards gluten formation.

round, working along edges and giving disk quarter turns as you stretch. Transfer dough to well-floured peel and stretch into 13-inch round. Using back of spoon, spread half of garlic oil over surface of dough, leaving ¼-inch border. Layer ½ cup basil leaves over pizza. Sprinkle with ¼ cup Pecorino, followed by 1 cup mozzarella. Slide pizza carefully onto stone and return oven to 500 degrees. Bake until crust is well browned and cheese is bubbly and partially browned, 8 to 10 minutes, rotating pizza halfway through baking. Remove pizza and place on wire rack. Dollop half of ricotta over surface of pizza. Let pizza rest for 5 minutes, slice, and serve.

6. Heat broiler for 10 minutes. Repeat process of stretching, topping, and baking with remaining dough and toppings, returning oven to 500 degrees when pizza is placed on stone.

VARIATIONS

Thin-Crust Whole-Wheat Pizza with Pesto and Goat Cheese

Process 2 cups basil leaves, 7 tablespoons extra-virgin olive oil, ¼ cup pine nuts, 3 minced garlic cloves, and ½ teaspoon salt in food processor until smooth, about 1 minute. Stir in ¼ cup finely grated Parmesan or Pecorino Romano and season with salt and pepper to taste. Substitute pesto for garlic oil. In step 5, omit basil leaves, Pecorino Romano, mozzarella, and ricotta. Top pizza with ½ cup crumbled goat cheese before baking.

Thin-Crust Whole-Wheat Pizza with Wine-Braised Onion and Blue Cheese

Bring 1 onion, halved through root end and sliced ⅛ inch thick, 1½ cups water, ¾ cup dry red wine, 3 tablespoons sugar, and ¼ teaspoon salt to simmer over medium-high heat in 10-inch skillet. Reduce heat to medium and simmer, stirring often, until liquid evaporates and onion is crisp-tender, about 30 minutes. Stir in 2 teaspoons red wine vinegar, transfer to bowl, and let cool completely before using. In step 5, omit garlic oil, basil leaves, Pecorino Romano, mozzarella, and ricotta. Spread ⅓ cup crème fraîche over each dough round. Top each with half of onion mixture, ½ cup coarsely chopped walnuts, and ½ cup crumbled blue cheese before baking. After letting pizza rest, top each with 2 tablespoons shredded fresh basil.

SECRETS TO WHOLE-WHEAT PIZZA WORTH MAKING

We transform whole-wheat flour into a crust that's wonderfully chewy and crisp, with an earthy complexity.

ADD BREAD FLOUR
Using both whole-wheat flour and white bread flour (which has more structure-building proteins than all-purpose flour does) increases chewiness.

USE LOTS OF (ICE) WATER
Our highly hydrated dough helps strengthen the gluten network; ice water keeps the dough from overheating as it kneads in the food processor.

REST IT OVERNIGHT
This gives enzymes in the dough time to slightly weaken gluten strands, increasing extensibility; it also allows more flavor-boosting fermentation.

USE THE BROILER
Because our dough is so wet, preheating the pizza stone under the broiler's high heat (after an hour at 500 degrees) is key to a nicely browned crust.

NO TOMATOES!
The sweet-tart flavors of tomato sauce clash with earthy whole wheat. Instead, we top our pizza with three cheeses, garlicky oil, and basil.

RATING GOAT CHEESE

It's not hard to see why fresh goat cheese is so popular: With its unmistakable tang, it can be eaten on crackers, enliven a simple salad or pasta dish, and enhance pizza toppings. And while it was once produced primarily in France, goat cheese is now made domestically. With so many choices, which one is best? We gathered nine brands and tasted them on plain crackers and rolled in bread crumbs and baked; we also tossed our top- and bottom-ranked brands with hot pasta. Sampled straight from the fridge, many brands were creamy and smooth with a distinctly tangy, grassy taste, which is just what we want in goat cheese. Those that were chalky and pasty or tasted neutral or overly gamy were downgraded. Once baked, the flavors mellowed a bit but texture remained a problem in some brands. Cheeses that were chalky straight out of the package didn't improve; others that had been creamy baked up crumbly and grainy. A bit of research revealed that while flavor differences could be attributed to the goats' diets and their hormone levels, textural differences were due to varying salt levels; the brands with the least salt were crumbly, while the ones with more salt stayed smooth and cohesive. Brands are listed in order of preference; salt and fat are per 100-gram serving. See AmericasTestKitchen.com for updates and complete tasting results.

RECOMMENDED

LAURA CHENEL'S CHÈVRE Fresh Chèvre Log
PRICE: $6.99 for 8 oz ($0.87 per oz)   MADE IN: California
SALT: 1,053 mg in 100 g   pH: 4.05
FAT: 21.20 g in 100 g (6 g in 1-oz serving)
COMMENTS: "Rich-tasting," "grassy," and "tangy," our favorite goat cheese was "smooth" and "creamy" both unheated and baked, and it kept its "lemony, bright flavor" in both iterations. A high salt content helped: Salt not only enhances flavor but also contributes to keeping the cheese creamy when heated.

VERMONT CREAMERY Fresh Goat Cheese, Classic Chèvre
PRICE: $4.99 for 4 oz ($1.25 per oz)   MADE IN: Vermont
SALT: 784 mg in 100 g   pH: 3.95
FAT: 20.96 g in 100 g (5.9 g in 1-oz serving)
COMMENTS: "Smooth and creamy" and with a "slightly citrusy," "clean, lactic" taste, this was one of our favorites sampled straight from the package. Its moderate salt content allowed it to turn slightly "mealy" when baked, but its "grassy," "citruslike" flavors continued to earn raves from tasters.

CHEVRION Plain Goat Cheese
PRICE: $4.29 for 4 oz ($1.07 per oz)   MADE IN: France
SALT: 1,200 mg in 100 g   pH: 3.91
FAT: 16.89 g in 100 g (4.8 g in 1-oz serving)
COMMENTS: This "tangy," "creamy" sample was "very strong" and "goaty" eaten unheated, but mellowed to "bright, tangy, and sweet" when baked, retaining a "luscious" texture thanks to its high salt content.

CYPRESS GROVE CHÈVRE
Ms. Natural Goat Milk Cheese
PRICE: $6.50 for 4 oz ($1.63 per oz)   MADE IN: California
SALT: 955 mg in 100 g   pH: 4.04
FAT: 21.55 g in 100 g (6.1 g in 1-oz serving)
COMMENTS: Unheated, this cheese wowed us with "lemony," "grassy" flavors and a "smooth," "melts-in-your-mouth" texture. Though baking dried out its texture a bit, tasters were still enthusiastic.

RECOMMENDED (cont.)

SIERRA NEVADA CHEESE CO.
Bella Capra Chèvre
PRICE: $7.99 for 8 oz ($1.00 per oz)   MADE IN: California
SALT: 882 mg in 100 g   pH: 3.86
FAT: 25.56 g in 100 g (7.2 g in 1-oz serving)
COMMENTS: "Fresh" and "tangy" and with a "creamy" texture when sampled unheated, this cheese with a moderate salt content turned a little "crumbly" when baked but still offered "tang" and "good goat flavor."

CHAVRIE Fresh Goat Cheese
PRICE: $8.99 for 11 oz ($0.82 per oz)   MADE IN: Pennsylvania
SALT: 1,078 mg in 100 g   pH: 4.66
FAT: 22.86 g in 100 g (6.5 g in 1-oz serving)
COMMENTS: Though it had some fans, the "barnyard" and "gamy" flavor of this cheese reminded some tasters of "lamb fat." These flavors dissipated in baking, when this sample shone with a "tasty tang and milky flavor" and a "nice creamy texture."

RECOMMENDED WITH RESERVATIONS

MONTCHÈVRE Fresh Goat Cheese
PRICE: $3.99 for 4 oz ($1.00 per oz)   MADE IN: Wisconsin
SALT: 686 mg in 100 g   pH: 4.27
FAT: 24.49 g in 100 g (6.9 g in 1-oz serving)
COMMENTS: Though "very creamy" with a "nice smooth consistency" when unheated, without much salt it was "neutral" to many and just "mildly tangy." Too little salt also left it "watery and crumbly" when baked.

ILE DE FRANCE Chèvre Fresh Goat Cheese
PRICE: $10.99 for 10.5 oz ($1.05 per oz)   MADE IN: France
SALT: 637 mg in 100 g   pH: 3.96
FAT: 22.95 g in 100 g (6.5 g in 1-oz serving)
COMMENTS: Also low in salt, this sample had a pleasant but "mild-mannered" taste and "slightly chalky" texture when eaten from the package. Baking turned it "crumbly," a flaw that was offset by its "subtle herb" flavor notes.

GROWN-UP GRILLED CHEESE SANDWICH

✔️ **WHY THIS RECIPE WORKS:** American cheese is fine when making sandwiches for the kids, but we wanted a grilled cheese for adults that offered robust flavor. Aged cheddar gave us the complexity we were after, but it made for a greasy sandwich with a grainy filling. Adding a splash of wine and some Brie helped the aged cheddar melt evenly without separating or becoming greasy. Using a food processor to combine the ingredients ensured our cheese-and-wine mixture was easy to spread. A little bit of shallot ramped up the flavor without detracting from the cheese, and a smear of mustard butter livened up the bread.

THE FIRST BITE OF A GRILLED CHEESE IS ALWAYS THE best one. The aroma of toasted butter is a familiar prelude to the crunch of crisp bread, which gives way to warm, gooey cheese. But the mystique fades quickly, mainly because the American cheese that is typically slapped between the slices of bread has no taste. We crave a grilled cheese with potent flavor, which means taking several steps up from American. But whenever we try to make a sandwich with, say, aged cheddar and a white sandwich loaf (its delicate crust and fine crumb make it ideal for grilled cheese), we end up disappointed, since upscale cheeses tend to become grainy and leak fat as they melt.

Before attempting a fix, we did some reading and learned that how well a cheese melts depends partly on its moisture level, which decreases with age. When a young, moist cheese (like American) is heated, its casein matrix— casein is the primary protein in cheese—remains intact and holds on to fat. But as a cheese ages and dries out, its casein binds more tightly together, making it more difficult to liquefy. When the clumpy bonded structure finally does break down, it is unable to contain the fat, so it leaks out.

When we started thinking about ways to coax our cheddar into melting smoothly, restoring moisture was an obvious move. We decided to try wine as our moisture of choice. After all, wine is a key ingredient in fondue, which is basically just melted cheese. We cubed 10 ounces of cheddar, pulled out a food processor, and whizzed the pieces along with 2 tablespoons of white wine. After smearing the cheese mixture onto bread coated with softened butter, we heated a nonstick skillet and slowly toasted the sandwich until the cheese melted and the bread browned (6 to 9 minutes per side). The good news: The wine in the cheese tasted terrific (no surprise there) and the added liquid meant that the cheese was not nearly as broken as our previous attempts. The bad news: It was still a little greasy.

We thought back to fondue, which also contains flour. Could the addition of starch absorb some of the fat in the cheddar? Yes, but at a cost: If we added enough flour, we could produce a nongreasy filling, but the starch muted the taste of the cheese. Our next strategy: Instead of trying to soak up the cheddar's excess oil, how about cutting back on the cheddar itself and replacing it with a moist, easy-melting cheese? We bought a block of Monterey Jack and a wedge of supermarket Brie and made batches of spread containing 8 ounces of cheddar and 2 ounces of one of these "melty" cheese. That turned out to be the key to success. Using less cheddar and processing it with a smooth melter eliminated any trace of grease. We chose Brie over Jack since its buttery notes paired best with the sharp, earthy cheddar.

Now we were happy with the texture of our grilled cheese, but we wanted a little more depth of flavor. Just a few teaspoons of minced shallot did the trick, accenting the cheese with savory complexity.

If only the bread tasted as good. To spice it up, we mixed a dollop of Dijon into the softened butter we had been slathering on the exterior of the sandwich. The result was a hit, smelling and tasting subtly of mustard. Emboldened by these results, we experimented and found that Gruyère and chives on rye, Asiago and dates on oatmeal bread, Comté and cornichon on rye, and Robiola and chipotle chiles on oatmeal bread are fantastic combinations as well. Finally: We had a host of grilled cheese sandwiches engineered for adult tastes and good to the last bite.

GROWN-UP GRILLED CHEESE SANDWICHES

Grown-Up Grilled Cheese Sandwiches with Cheddar and Shallot
SERVES 4

For the best flavor, look for a cheddar aged for about one year (avoid cheddar aged for longer; it won't melt well in this recipe). To quickly bring the cheese to room temperature, microwave the pieces until warm, about 30 seconds. The first two sandwiches can be held in a 200-degree oven on a wire rack set in a baking sheet while the second batch cooks.

- 7 ounces aged cheddar cheese, cut into 24 equal pieces, room temperature
- 2 ounces Brie cheese, rind removed
- 2 tablespoons dry white wine or vermouth
- 4 teaspoons minced shallot
- 3 tablespoons unsalted butter, softened
- 1 teaspoon Dijon mustard
- 8 slices hearty white sandwich bread

1. Process cheddar, Brie, and wine in food processor until smooth paste is formed, 20 to 30 seconds. Add shallot and pulse to combine, 3 to 5 pulses. Combine butter and mustard in small bowl.

2. Working on parchment paper–lined counter, divide mustard butter evenly among slices of bread. Spread butter evenly over surface of bread. Flip 4 slices of bread over and spread cheese mixture evenly over slices. Top with remaining 4 slices of bread, buttered sides up.

3. Preheat 12-inch nonstick skillet over medium heat for 2 minutes. (Droplets of water should just sizzle when flicked onto pan.) Place 2 sandwiches in skillet, reduce heat to medium-low, and cook until both sides are crisp and golden brown, 6 to 9 minutes per side, moving sandwiches to ensure even browning. Remove sandwiches from skillet and let stand for 2 minutes before serving. Repeat with remaining 2 sandwiches.

VARIATIONS

Grown-Up Grilled Cheese Sandwiches with Gruyère and Chives
Substitute Gruyère cheese for cheddar, chives for shallot, and rye sandwich bread for white sandwich bread.

Grown-Up Grilled Cheese Sandwiches with Asiago and Dates
Substitute Asiago cheese for cheddar, finely chopped pitted dates for shallot, and oatmeal sandwich bread for white sandwich bread.

Grown-Up Grilled Cheese Sandwiches with Comté and Cornichon
Substitute Comté cheese for cheddar, minced cornichon for shallot, and rye sandwich bread for white sandwich bread.

Grown-Up Grilled Cheese Sandwiches with Robiola and Chipotle
Substitute Robiola cheese, rind removed, for cheddar; ¼ teaspoon minced canned chipotle chile in adobo sauce for shallot; and oatmeal sandwich bread for white sandwich bread.

Great American Sandwiches

Adam explains the pros and cons of heavy-duty handled scrub brushes.

THERE ARE FEW SANDWICHES WORTH WRITING HOME ABOUT, BUT cooks in New England and Philadelphia have created a couple that are featured on many menus for a reason. With their rich flavors and hearty bites, the lobster roll and Philly cheesesteak are utterly satisfying. We wanted to master preparing these American classics at home so we could enjoy them anytime and anywhere.

Sweet, succulent lobster tossed in a bit of tangy mayo and piled high into a buttery bun define the classic Yankee lobster roll. But putting the sandwich together is the easy part—it's dealing with the fidgety crustacean that can be a hassle. We wanted to find a fuss-free method for cooking the starring ingredient, and it had to guarantee perfectly tender meat every time.

Likewise, the Philly cheesesteak is one of those dishes that tourists seek out while they're in town. With its strips of meat coated in a cheesy sauce, this dish elevates the humble sub to new heights. Local delis and sandwich shops make the most of their griddles, which get super-hot and have a wide, flat cooking surface, to achieve beef shavings with well-browned, super-crisp edges. But try to re-create the cheesesteak sandwich at home, minus the griddle, and you're out of luck. Our goal was to make this popular sub—without the pricey equipment. Grab some napkins as the test kitchen brings all-star American sandwiches home.

NEW ENGLAND LOBSTER ROLL

✔ **WHY THIS RECIPE WORKS:** We wanted to bring home a true New England–style lobster roll, complete with tender meat coated in a light dressing and tucked into a buttery toasted bun, but first we had to deal with the lobster. To make things easier, we sedated the lobster by placing it in the freezer for 30 minutes. Boiling was the easiest way to cook it, and removing it from the water when the tail registered 175 degrees ensured it was perfectly tender. For the lobster roll, we adhered mostly to tradition, tossing our lobster with just a bit of mayonnaise and adding a hint of crunch with lettuce leaves and a small amount of minced celery. Onion and shallot were overpowering, but minced chives offered bright herb flavor. Lemon juice and a pinch of cayenne provided a nice counterpoint to the rich lobster and mayo.

VISITORS TO NEW ENGLAND INITIALLY REGARD OUR beloved lobster roll with skepticism, and that's understandable. After all, we're talking about coating pricey lobster meat with mayonnaise, piling it into a supermarket hot dog bun, and serving it with pickles and potato chips. The usual venue for this meal—a weathered picnic table outside a roadside seafood stand—does little to dispel visitors' incredulity. It seems like a strangely cavalier treatment of a luxury foodstuff.

Such doubts vanish with the first bite. The simple mayo complements the richly flavored lobster without obscuring it, and the squishy bun molds like a custom-made cradle around the tender chunks of meat. The grilled sides of the top-loading bun provide a crisp, buttery frame for the cool salad within.

Because great seafood places are ubiquitous in these parts, New Englanders rarely make lobster rolls at home. But what if you live hundreds of miles from the Maine shore? Or what if it's January and all the lobster shacks are shut? Is it possible to re-create the New England lobster roll in your own kitchen? Sure. But first you have to figure out a safe and foolproof way to cook a live and kicking lobster.

Lobsters are cooked alive for two reasons: First, the instant a lobster dies, enzymes within its body begin to break down the flesh and cause it to turn mushy. Second, like other shellfish, deceased lobsters are vulnerable to bacterial contamination that can cause food poisoning. These days, many supermarkets cook live lobsters to order, but we wanted to control every part of our lobster roll, so we were determined to do the deed ourselves.

First decision: Would we be roasting, steaming, or boiling? Roasted lobster can be difficult to prepare because the slow heat of the oven causes proteins in the meat to adhere to the shell. We tried briefly boiling the lobster (which provides rapid heat transfer) to pull the meat away from the shell before roasting, but we found the two-step process awkward and with no apparent flavor or texture benefits. Steaming required a steamer or a rack, and it left the lobsters slightly underseasoned.

Boiling in salt water was the way to go, but there was a problem: Every time we tried to maneuver a lobster into the pot, it spread its claws wide and thrashed its muscular tail in protest, often sending a wave of boiling water across the stovetop. Surely there was an easier way—at least for the cook.

Many cooks advocate anesthetizing lobsters before cooking them. Some believe it is more humane, while others argue that gently handled lobsters are tastier and more tender. Mostly we hoped it would make the little guys more manageable. We tested several methods of desensitizing lobsters, and we tasted each supposedly desensitized lobster against one that was summarily tossed into the boiling water. The first few methods ranged from grisly to quirky, and—since they didn't sedate the lobster, didn't produce better flavor or texture, were too labor intensive, or all of the above—we quickly moved on.

In Harold McGee's *On Food and Cooking*, we discovered the most successful technique for sedating a lobster yet: immersing the lobster in an ice bath for 30 minutes

NEW ENGLAND LOBSTER ROLL

REMOVING LOBSTER MEAT FROM THE SHELL

There's a lot more meat in a lobster than just the tail and claws—if you know how to get it. Here's our tried-and-true approach to extracting every last bit, no special tools needed. The method works for both hard- and soft-shell lobsters.

1. SEPARATE TAIL
Once cooked lobster is cool enough to handle, set it on cutting board. Grasp tail with your hand and grab body with your other hand and twist to separate.

4. MOVE TO KNUCKLES
Twist "arms" to remove both claws and attached "knuckles". Twist knuckles to remove them from claw. Break knuckles at joint using back of chef's knife or lobster-cracking tool. Use handle of teaspoon to push out meat.

2. FLATTEN TAIL
Lay tail on its side on counter and use both hands to press down on tail until shell cracks.

5. REMOVE CLAW MEAT
Wiggle hinged portion of each claw to separate. If meat is stuck inside small part, remove it with skewer. Break open claws, cracking 1 side and then flipping them to crack other side, and remove meat.

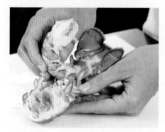

3. TAKE OUT TAIL MEAT
Hold tail, flippers facing you and shell facing down. Pull back on sides to crack open shell and remove meat. Rinse meat under water to remove green tomalley if you wish; pat meat dry with paper towels and remove dark vein.

6. FINISH WITH LEGS
Twist legs to remove them. Lay legs flat on counter. Using rolling pin, start from claw end and roll toward open end, pushing out meat. Stop rolling before reaching end of legs; open tip of leg can crack and release pieces of shell.

before cooking. The chilled lobster seemed comatose as we transferred it from ice bath to pot, and its meat was properly cooked. However, chilling a single lobster in this manner required a 6-quart container and 2 quarts of ice, and chilling additional lobsters would have required more space and more ice, making it impractical for preparing multiple lobsters simultaneously.

Wondering if a simpler method might work, we placed four wriggling lobsters in a large bowl, which we then placed in the freezer while we brought a stockpot of salted water to a boil. After 30 minutes, we nudged them gently: nary a twitch. When we transferred the chilled lobsters to the pot, they were limp and unresponsive, and they sank to the bottom with just a few reassuring flutters that indicated that they were still alive. We had found the safest, easiest way to get the lobsters into the pot. Now to make the cooking method foolproof.

Most lobster recipes are accompanied by intimidating charts that tell you how long to boil based on your lobster's weight, whether it has a hard or soft shell, and how many are being cooked in the same pot. But what if your lobsters are different sizes? What if you're unsure about the comparative firmness of their shells? Why can't we simply take the temperature of a lobster the same way we do with other kinds of meat?

We discovered that we can do just that—but the target temperature turned out to be much higher than we expected. We usually cook fish to an internal temperature of 130 to 140 degrees, but when we pulled a lobster out at 135 (determined by a digital thermometer poked into the underside of the meaty tail), the meat was undercooked, translucent, and floppy. At 160 degrees it was still too soft. Eventually we landed at a tail temperature of 175 (after about 12 minutes of cooking), which guaranteed tender claws and knuckles and a pleasantly resilient tail.

Why the higher temperature? Because lobsters aren't just fish with snazzy red armor. Fish muscle is composed of very short muscle fibers that require only mild heat to shrink them so that they firm up and turn from translucent to opaque. The muscle fibers in lobsters are much longer, especially in the tail section, so they require a higher temperature to attain that desirably firm, snappy texture. Now we were ready to build our roll.

Want to watch a Yankee's cool, unemotional facade crumble? Lure him into a conversation about what constitutes the perfect lobster roll. A discussion of seemingly innocuous subjects, like the size of the lobster pieces and the inclusion of things like lettuce, herbs, and onions, quickly escalates into an impassioned debate. Luckily, we're not afraid of a little controversy: Our roll, our rules.

Traditionalists like to leave the lobster meat in generous hunks, and the effect is one of impressive opulence, but it's darn hard to eat. Chunks are fine for the claws and knuckles because they're tender and, being smaller, well seasoned by the salted cooking water. But the tail is so meaty and dense that large pieces can seem undersalted and tough. So we bucked tradition and cut the tail into smaller pieces, making it easier to eat and giving it more surface area for the seasoned dressing to cling to.

As for the contentious vegetable additions, we opted for a single soft lettuce leaf to line each roll and a couple

of tablespoons of minced celery for unobtrusive crunch. Chopped onions and even milder shallots were nixed as too overwhelming, but a mere teaspoon of chives gave our salad a hint of bright herb flavor. A splash of lemon juice and a tiny pinch of cayenne pepper made a perfect counterpoint to the richly flavored meat and the buttery bun.

This was a New England lobster roll that would convince any skeptic. And now that we had a safe and foolproof way to cook lobster, we could enjoy it anytime.

EQUIPMENT CORNER

KNIFE SHARPENERS

Even the most expensive, well-made knives lose their sharpness quickly when used regularly. And it doesn't take months, or even weeks: A knife can go dull in just a few minutes, especially if you're cutting through tough materials, such as bone. Over the years, we've learned a few things about what to look for when selecting a knife sharpener. We prefer models that start with a coarse material and progress through stages of finer material to polish the edge; the final and hardest material should be diamond, for the sharpest edge. Also, we like sharpeners that are easy and comfortable to use, with clear instructions. Our favorite electric sharpener is the **Chef's Choice Model 130 Professional Sharpening Station**, $149.95. This quiet model has spring-loaded blade guides to make sharpening foolproof. One slot works like a sharpening steel but removes all guesswork from the usual steeling motion. For a less expensive alternative, we recommend the **AccuSharp Knife and Tool Sharpener**, $11.99. This manual hand-held model establishes a sharp edge both quickly and easily and has a plastic guard to protect hands while sharpening. See AmericasTestKitchen.com for updates and further information on this testing.

CHEF'S CHOICE MODEL 130 PROFESSIONAL SHARPENING STATION

ACCUSHARP KNIFE AND TOOL SHARPENER

New England Lobster Roll
SERVES 6

This recipe is best when made with lobster you've cooked yourself. Use a very small pinch of cayenne pepper, as it should not make the dressing spicy. We prefer New England–style top-loading hot dog buns, as they provide maximum surface on the sides for toasting. If using other buns, butter, salt, and toast the interior of each bun instead of the exterior.

  2 **tablespoons mayonnaise**
  2 **tablespoons minced celery**
1½ **teaspoons lemon juice**
  1 **teaspoon minced fresh chives**
    Salt
    Pinch cayenne pepper
  1 **pound lobster meat, tail meat cut into ½-inch pieces and claw meat cut into 1-inch pieces**
  2 **tablespoons unsalted butter, softened**
  6 **New England–style hot dog buns**
  6 **leaves Boston lettuce**

1. Whisk mayonnaise, celery, lemon juice, chives, ⅛ teaspoon salt, and cayenne together in large bowl. Add lobster and gently toss to combine.

2. Place 12-inch nonstick skillet over low heat. Butter both sides of hot dog buns and sprinkle lightly with salt. Place buns in skillet, with 1 buttered side down; increase heat to medium-low; and cook until crisp and brown, 2 to 3 minutes. Flip and cook second side until crisp and brown, 2 to 3 minutes longer. Transfer buns to large platter. Line each bun with lettuce leaf. Spoon lobster salad into buns and serve immediately.

Boiled Lobster

SERVES 4; YIELDS 1 POUND MEAT

To cook four lobsters at once, you will need a pot with a capacity of at least 3 gallons. If your pot is smaller, boil the lobsters in batches. Start timing the lobsters from the moment they go into the pot.

  4 **(1¼-pound) live lobsters**

  ⅓ **cup salt**

1. Place lobsters in large bowl and freeze for 30 minutes. Meanwhile, bring 2 gallons water to boil in large pot over high heat.

2. Add lobsters and salt to pot, arranging with tongs so that all lobsters are submerged. Cover pot, leaving lid slightly ajar, and adjust heat to maintain gentle boil. Cook for 12 minutes, until thickest part of tail registers 175 degrees (insert thermometer into underside of tail to take temperature). If temperature registers lower than 175 degrees, return lobster to pot for 2 minutes longer, until tail registers 175 degrees, using tongs to transfer lobster in and out of pot.

3. Serve immediately or transfer lobsters to rimmed baking sheet and set aside until cool enough to remove meat, about 10 minutes. (Lobster meat can be refrigerated in airtight container for up to 24 hours.)

PHILLY CHEESESTEAKS

✔ **WHY THIS RECIPE WORKS:** Authentic Philly cheesesteak recipes start with a rib eye and require use of a meat slicer and flat-top griddle to achieve ultrathin slices with crisp edges. To make this satisfying sandwich in our own kitchens, we'd need to find a stand-in for the meat and a way to slice the meat thin and get it super-crisp, without any fancy equipment. We started by looking for a more economical cut of meat and landed on skirt steak. When partially frozen, skirt steak's thin profile and open-grained texture made for easy slicing, and its flavor was nearest to rib eye, without the sticker shock. To best approximate the wide griddle typically used in Philadelphia, we cooked the meat in two batches, letting any excess moisture drain off before giving it a final sear. Finally, to bind it all together, we let slices of American cheese melt into the meat; a bit of grated Parmesan boosted the flavor.

YOU CAN GET A STEAK SUB JUST ABOUT ANYWHERE, but a real cheesesteak comes from only one place: Philadelphia. Fancy steakhouse interpretations aside, the meat is always sliced paper-thin and presented in one of two forms: cooked as is so that the wide swaths wrinkle from the griddle's heat or chopped with the edge of a metal spatula as it sizzles on the flattop, producing fine bits that fry and crisp in their own rendered fat. Either way, the meat is generously heaped into a soft-crumbed, crisp-crusted torpedo roll along with your cheese of choice: provolone, American, or, most famously, a ladle of "Whiz." It's an unapologetically decadent, classically American behemoth of a sandwich.

We're fans of the hashed style, in which the well-browned bits are especially savory and the cheese is folded in with the meat, acting just as much like a velvety binder as like a rich, salty flavor booster. Unfortunately, we don't get to Philly as often as we'd like, and our craving for the sandwich made us so bold

PHILLY CHEESESTEAKS

as to wonder if we couldn't pull off a close replica in the test kitchen.

Admittedly, it was a tall order—particularly the texture of the meat, which relied on two kitchen appliances that most home cooks don't own: a meat slicer to shave the steak super-thin and a griddle to cook it in a single layer and maximize browning. What's more, many steak shops use rib eye as their sandwich meat—beautifully marbled and flavorful but, for most of us, prohibitively expensive ($15 to $20 per pound). We'd need substitutes for all three.

We thought about asking a butcher to slice the meat for us but soon realized that would be a dead end; even if he or she were willing to indulge our odd request, the raw meat would first have to be frozen overnight to make this even possible. Our other supermarket shortcut idea was to buy thin-sliced deli roast beef and fry it, but this, too, was a bust. Even when it was cooked in a generous amount of fat, the lean, bland roast tasted unmistakably like lunchmeat. We had no choice: We'd have to slice the meat ourselves.

Without a meat slicer, we had three options available: a mandoline, a food processor, or a steady hand and a sharp knife. Using fat-streaked blade steaks as a placeholder, we ran the meat through both appliances but had little luck with either. Though the mandoline produced properly thin sheets, it was slow-going—not to mention knuckle-jeopardizing—work. The food processor seemed like a better, faster alternative at first but not once the chunks of meat got caught between the slicing blade and the lid, turning swiftly to paste. We'd have to go with hand slicing.

But shaving 2 pounds of meat by hand would require more than a steady hand and a sharp knife. We also needed the right cut of meat, one that was marbled, tender, and reasonably priced as well as a cut that we could easily slice against the grain, so that it would readily break apart into chewy-tender bits as it cooked. Blade steaks were one option, as were top round, flap meat (known as sirloin tips), boneless short ribs, and skirt steak. We cut each into 3-inch-wide strips and then, before slicing, froze the pieces for about an hour. It's a preslicing trick we frequently turn to in the test kitchen; firming up the meat makes it easier to slice cleanly.

The options dwindled quickly: Short ribs, though well marbled like rib eye, developed an unpleasant liver-y flavor, while top round and blade steak were both difficult to slice across the grain and chewy and tough when cooked. Flap meat and skirt steak, meanwhile, boasted big beefy flavor, not to mention a long grain that made them easy to slice thinly. Of the two, skirt steak was the clear winner: In addition to being easily sliceable, its extremely loose grain helped it break down. Then, to further mimic the way cheesesteak slingers hash the meat with the edges of metal spatulas, we coarsely chopped it before cooking.

That left just one more substitution: finding a viable alternative to the griddle. The advantage of the roomy flattop is that moisture evaporates almost instantly, allowing the meat to crisp up nicely. Unfortunately, it was impossible to brown 2 pounds of meat in the confines of a 12-inch nonstick skillet; with so little surface area and 2-inch walls, the meat stewed in its own juices. But the fix wasn't a hard one: We simply cooked the meat in two stages, letting each batch drain in a colander before returning it to the pan to mix with the cheese.

But the cheese was a dilemma of its own. While tasters liked the smoky tang of provolone, they decided the gooey, melty quality of American was essential. (Cheez Whiz appealed to no one.) Our nontraditional solution: Sharpening up the flavor of the smooth-melting American stuff with a little grated Parmesan.

Topped with traditional fixin's like pickled hot peppers and sautéed onions, this sandwich was as close to the real deal as we'd ever had, plus it didn't require a trip to Philly.

Philly Cheesesteaks

SERVES 4

If skirt steak is unavailable, substitute sirloin steak tips (also called flap meat). Top these sandwiches with chopped pickled hot peppers, sautéed onions or bell peppers, sweet relish, or hot sauce.

- 2 **pounds skirt steak, trimmed and sliced with grain into 3-inch-wide strips**
- 4 **(8-inch) Italian sub rolls, split lengthwise**
- 2 **tablespoons vegetable oil**
- ½ **teaspoon salt**
- ⅛ **teaspoon pepper**
- ¼ **cup grated Parmesan cheese**
- 8 **slices white American cheese (8 ounces)**

1. Place steak pieces on large plate or baking sheet and freeze until very firm, about 1 hour.

2. Meanwhile, adjust oven rack to middle position and heat oven to 400 degrees. Spread split rolls on baking sheet and toast until lightly browned, 5 to 10 minutes.

3. Using sharp knife, shave steak pieces as thinly as possible against grain. Mound meat on cutting board and chop coarsely with knife 10 to 20 times.

4. Heat 1 tablespoon oil in 12-inch nonstick skillet over high heat until smoking. Add half of meat in even layer and cook without stirring until well browned on 1 side, 4 to 5 minutes. Stir and continue to cook until meat is no longer pink, 1 to 2 minutes. Transfer meat to colander set in large bowl. Wipe out skillet with paper towel. Repeat with remaining 1 tablespoon oil and sliced meat.

5. Return now-empty skillet to medium heat. Drain excess moisture from meat. Return meat to skillet (discard any liquid in bowl) and add salt and pepper. Heat, stirring constantly, until meat is warmed through, 1 to 2 minutes. Reduce heat to low, sprinkle with Parmesan, and shingle slices of American cheese over meat. Allow cheeses to melt, about 2 minutes. Using heatproof spatula or wooden spoon, fold melted cheese into meat thoroughly. Divide mixture evenly among toasted rolls. Serve immediately.

RATING HEAVY-DUTY HANDLED SCRUB BRUSHES

It takes a serious cleaning tool to tackle seriously dirty pots and pans. Enter the heavy-duty scrub brush, which promises to take care of all kinds of crusty, caked-on messes. We gathered six models (priced from $5 to $7.99) made of plastic or wood with natural or synthetic bristles. After scraping away stuck-on scrambled eggs from cast-iron skillets, glazed salmon residue from the ridges of grill pans, and a burned-on mixture of tomato paste, mustard, and molasses from casserole dishes, we concluded that long, soft bristles are poor scrubbers. Some scrubbers also trapped food and odors as well as stained or bent after just a few uses. We preferred models with shorter, stiff bristles, which made quick work of even the toughest jobs, and which released food easily (even without a trip through the dishwasher). Brands are listed in order of preference. See AmericasTestKitchen.com for updates and further information on this testing.

RECOMMENDED

OXO Grill Pan Brush

MODEL: 1312580   **PRICE:** $7.99   **OVERALL LENGTH:** 6 in
PERFORMANCE: ★★★   **EASE OF USE:** ★★½   **DURABILITY:** ★★★
CLEANUP: ★★★   **DISHWASHER-SAFE:** Yes
COMMENTS: The only improvement that we could make to this tough little brush would be a slightly longer handle, though its compact size provides great leverage for hard scrubbing. Well-spaced bunches of short nylon bristles scoured effectively and rinsed clean without becoming stained or holding odors. The built-in scraper really dug between the ridges of a grill pan or along the rim of a baking dish, and its grippy, round handle was very comfortable.

CALDREA Dishwashing Brush

MODEL: 22011   **PRICE:** $5   **OVERALL LENGTH:** 9 in
PERFORMANCE: ★★★   **EASE OF USE:** ★★★   **DURABILITY:** ★★★½
CLEANUP: ★★   **DISHWASHER-SAFE:** Yes, but will shorten life span of brush
COMMENTS: Although it looks delicate, the natural bristles on this beechwood brush have more friction than do synthetic bristles, making them more effective cleaners. Its handle kept our hands well out of hot water. The only downside: Food gets stuck in the base of the thick bristles. You can put this brush through the dishwasher from time to time for deep cleaning, but regular dishwashing will dry it out and degrade it.

NOT RECOMMENDED

FULL CIRCLE Laid Back Dish Brush

MODEL: FLC004   **PRICE:** $7.99   **OVERALL LENGTH:** 10 in
PERFORMANCE: ★   **EASE OF USE:** ★★½   **DURABILITY:** ★★½
CLEANUP: ★   **DISHWASHER-SAFE:** Head only
COMMENTS: The bamboo handle on this natural-bristle brush was comfortable, and once we got used to the bent-back angle of the head, it was mostly easy to use. We also liked the ridge on top of the head for scraping. Too bad the soft bristles often bent and sloshed around the pan, food got trapped at their base, and odors clung. We like that the head is replaceable and can be popped off to go in the dishwasher because the handle is not dishwasher-safe.

NOT RECOMMENDED (cont.)

LODGE Cast-Iron Scrubber

MODEL: K11BRSH   **PRICE:** $5.50   **OVERALL LENGTH:** 11 in
PERFORMANCE: ★   **EASE OF USE:** ★   **DURABILITY:** ★
CLEANUP: ★★   **DISHWASHER-SAFE:** Yes
COMMENTS: The long synthetic bristles on this brush often bent and flexed when we scrubbed, making us work a little too hard to get jobs done, especially along ridges and lips of pans—we had to resort to using a fingernail to scrape a few spots. The bristles stained and splayed, making us fear for its longevity, though we like that it can go through the dishwasher.

LIBMAN Big Job Kitchen Brush

MODEL: 01042   **PRICE:** $7.04   **OVERALL LENGTH:** 10 in
PERFORMANCE: ★   **EASE OF USE:** ★   **DURABILITY:** ★★
CLEANUP: ★   **DISHWASHER-SAFE:** Yes
COMMENTS: Very sturdy and comfortable to hold, this brush easily removed stuck-on eggs, but that's about it. It couldn't dislodge glaze burned onto the grill pan's ridges, becoming greasy, stained, and blackened; it didn't come clean until a few trips through the dishwasher (but still smelled of fish). Scrubbing the casserole dish took a lot of elbow grease, and the brush struggled to remove food stuck along the rim.

FULL CIRCLE Be Good Dish Brush

MODEL: FC10108   **PRICE:** $4.99   **OVERALL LENGTH:** 9¼ in
PERFORMANCE: ★   **EASE OF USE:** ★   **DURABILITY:** ★★
CLEANUP: ½   **DISHWASHER-SAFE:** No
COMMENTS: While its rounded bamboo handle was remarkably comfortable to hold, this brush's soft, squashy bristles were ineffective at serious scrubbing; they also held on to odors. Because it's not dishwasher-safe, you have to take the time to scrub this brush by hand after finishing the dishes.

At the Seafood Counter

Before the cameras roll, chef Dan Cellucci rushes oven-steamed mussels to the set.

SWEET, BRINY, AND SUCCULENT, SHRIMP AND MUSSELS ADD SOMEthing special to the dinner hour, bringing a little more panache and flavor to the table than the typical chicken breasts or pork chops. Plus, they require very little in the way of gussying up. To make the most of their mild, sweet flavor, they need just a bit of enhancement in the form of a few spices, minced garlic, and fresh herbs. Add in the fact that both take very little time to prepare and cook, and visiting the seafood counter looks even more appealing.

Yet while both shrimp and mussels come together in a flash—making them the ideal choice for any hectic weeknight—this speed, and their leanness, tends to shrink the window of doneness, meaning that they can go from moist and tender to tough and rubbery in a matter of seconds. Our goal was to develop foolproof techniques for preparing both types of shellfish. Shrimp are often roasted, but the high heat can dry out the tender flesh in the blink of an eye. We wanted to refine this method so it yielded crustaceans with both a juicy interior and golden-brown exterior. And for our mussels, we looked to perfect the steaming method typically employed to cook them so that even if they weren't all the exact same size, they would all open at the same time to reveal the plump, juicy meat inside.

GARLICKY ROASTED SHRIMP

✔ WHY THIS RECIPE WORKS: We loved the idea of an easy weeknight meal of juicy roasted shrimp, but getting the lean, quick-cooking shrimp to develop color and roasted flavor before they turned rubbery required a few tricks. First we chose jumbo-size shrimp, which were the least likely to dry out and overcook. Butterflying the shrimp increased their surface area, giving us more room to add flavor. After brining the shrimp briefly to help them hold on to more moisture, we tossed them in a potent mixture of aromatic spices, garlic, herbs, butter, and oil. Then we roasted them under the broiler to get lots of color as quickly as possible, elevating them on a wire rack so they'd brown all over. To further protect them as they cooked and to produce a more deeply roasted flavor, we left their shells on; the sugar- and protein-rich shells browned quickly in the heat of the oven and transferred flavor to the shrimp itself.

WHEN WE SET OUT TO FIND THE BEST WAY TO MAKE roasted shrimp, we thought we'd hit the jackpot. Quick-cooking shrimp make an easy weeknight dinner, and the idea of roasting them until they develop deep, flavorful browning seemed so natural that we figured there were plenty of good recipes out there to learn from.

Imagine our surprise, then, when the handful we tried produced pale, insipid shrimp that looked as though they'd been baked, not roasted. Some of the missteps seemed obvious, such as crowding lots of small shrimp (tossed with oil and aromatics) on a sheet pan or in a baking dish, where their exuded moisture caused them to steam and prevented browning. Some of the oven temperatures were also strangely low—around 300 degrees. We were sure we could do better, while keeping the technique simple enough for an easy weeknight meal.

Our challenge was clear from the start: The goals of roasting—a juicy interior and a thoroughly browned exterior—were impeded by the fact that lean shrimp cook through very quickly. Knowing that, we made two immediate decisions: First, we would crank the oven temperature very high to get good browning on the exterior of the shrimp—500 degrees seemed like a fine place to start. Second, we would use the biggest shrimp we could get. That meant skipping right past even the extra-large size and reaching for the jumbo (16 to 20 per pound) shrimp, which would be the least likely to dry out in the heat. Using larger shrimp would also mean that there would be fewer pieces crowding the pan, and their smaller total amount of surface area would mean that less steam would be created—therefore making browning possible. As a test run, we oiled and seasoned 2 pounds of peeled shrimp with nothing more than a little salt and pepper (we'd explore flavorings once we'd nailed down a cooking method) and slid them into the oven on a sheet pan.

We thought the 500-degree blast would get the shrimp good and brown in a hurry, so we hovered around the oven and checked on their color every couple of minutes. Trouble was, the color never came—and while we waited and waited for the browning to kick in, the shrimp turned from tender and slightly translucent to fully opaque. We knew before we plunged a fork into them that they were overcooked. Clearly, high heat alone wasn't going to cut it, so we started experimenting. "Searing" them by preheating the baking sheet in the 500-degree oven helped, but only a little, since the pan's temperature plummeted as soon as the shrimp hit. Blasting the next batch under the broiler finally delivered some decent browning to the top sides of the shrimp, but their undersides were still damp and utterly pale.

Part of the problem was air circulation. When we roast beef or pork, we often elevate the meat on a rack so that hot air can surround it, drying out and browning even the underside. With that in mind, we tried broiling our next batch of shrimp on a wire rack set in the baking sheet—and finally started to see some real progress.

But the approach wasn't perfect. The heat of our broiler, as with all broilers, was uneven, which meant that we had to rotate the baking sheet halfway through cooking to prevent the shrimp from scorching under the element's hot spots, and even then we got a few desiccated pieces. In addition to using jumbo shrimp, the situation demanded a foolproof buffer against the heat, and the obvious answer was to brine the shrimp. The

GARLICKY ROASTED SHRIMP

natural protective coating and roasted them in their shells? Surely their "jackets" would prevent the surface of the meat from shriveling and, being drier than the meat, would probably brown quickly, too. The downside would be that shell-on shrimp are messier to eat, but if the results were good, having to peel them at the table would be worth it.

To make deveining and (later) peeling the shrimp easier, we used a pair of kitchen shears to split their shells from end to end without removing them from the flesh, and then we proceeded with our brine-and-broil technique. The results were stunning: shrimp that were moist and plump inside and evenly browned outside. In fact, the depth of the shrimp's "roasted" flavor exceeded our expectations and prompted us to mention the results to our science editor, who replied with some surprising intel. Turns out that the shells were doing much more than protecting the crustaceans' flesh: They are loaded with sugars, proteins, and other flavor-boosting compounds that amplify the rich seafood flavor.

Juicy, deeply browned shrimp complete, we moved on to tackle flavorings. We were already splitting the shells across the back and deveining the shrimp, so we took the technique one step further and butterflied the exposed flesh, cutting through the meat just short of severing it into two pieces. Then, to jazz up the oil-salt-pepper base, we added spices (anise seeds and red pepper flakes), six cloves of garlic, parsley, and melted butter (a natural pairing with briny seafood) and worked the flavorful mixture deep into the meat before broiling. Just as brining had seasoned the shrimp throughout, butterflying the pieces and thoroughly coating them with the oil-spice mixture made for seriously bold flavor. And since our tasters instantly gobbled up the shrimp—some of them shell and all—we developed two equally quick, flavorful variations: a Peruvian-style version with cilantro and lime and an Asian-inspired one with cumin, ginger, and sesame.

A great-tasting dish that requires almost no prep work and goes from the oven to the table in fewer than 10 minutes? We knew we'd be making this one year-round.

extra moisture that gets pulled into the lean flesh with the salt helps it stay moist even in a hot oven. Thanks to the shrimp's relatively small size, just a 15-minute soak in brine ensured that inside they stayed nice and plump—not to mention well seasoned throughout. Outside, however, they still shriveled under the broiler's heat before they had a chance to develop deep, "roasted" color and flavor.

We hoped that a thorough coat of olive oil (we'd been lightly glossing our shrimp) might stave off evaporation, but while the extra fat did keep the shrimp a bit more moist, it did nothing to even out browning. The idea of giving the shrimp a protective layer inspired another idea, though: What if we took advantage of the shrimp's

Garlicky Roasted Shrimp with Parsley and Anise

SERVES 4 TO 6

Don't be tempted to use smaller shrimp with this cooking technique; they will be overseasoned and prone to overcook.

¼ cup salt

2 pounds shell-on jumbo shrimp (16 to 20 per pound)

4 tablespoons unsalted butter, melted

¼ cup vegetable oil

6 garlic cloves, minced

1 teaspoon anise seeds

½ teaspoon red pepper flakes

¼ teaspoon pepper

2 tablespoons minced fresh parsley

   Lemon wedges

1. Dissolve salt in 1 quart cold water in large container. Using kitchen shears or sharp paring knife, cut through shell of shrimp and devein but do not remove shell. Using paring knife, continue to cut shrimp ½ inch deep, taking care not to cut in half completely. Submerge shrimp in brine, cover, and refrigerate for 15 minutes.

2. Adjust oven rack 4 inches from broiler element and heat broiler. Combine melted butter, oil, garlic, anise seeds, pepper flakes, and pepper in large bowl. Remove shrimp from brine and pat dry with paper towels. Add shrimp and parsley to butter mixture; toss well, making sure butter mixture gets into interior of shrimp. Arrange shrimp in single layer on wire rack set in rimmed baking sheet.

3. Broil shrimp until opaque and shells are beginning to brown, 2 to 4 minutes, rotating sheet halfway through broiling. Flip shrimp and continue to broil until second side is opaque and shells are beginning to brown, 2 to 4 minutes longer, rotating sheet halfway through broiling. Transfer shrimp to serving platter and serve immediately, passing lemon wedges separately.

VARIATIONS

Garlicky Roasted Shrimp with Cilantro and Lime

Annatto powder, also called achiote, can be found with the Latin American foods at your supermarket. An equal amount of paprika can be substituted.

Omit butter and increase vegetable oil to ½ cup. Omit anise seeds and pepper. Add 2 teaspoons lightly crushed coriander seeds, 2 teaspoons grated lime zest, and 1 teaspoon annatto powder to oil mixture in step 2. Substitute ¼ cup minced fresh cilantro for parsley and lime wedges for lemon wedges.

Garlicky Roasted Shrimp with Cumin, Ginger, and Sesame

Omit butter and increase vegetable oil to ½ cup. Decrease garlic to 2 cloves and omit anise seeds and pepper. Add 2 teaspoons toasted sesame oil, 1½ teaspoons grated fresh ginger, and 1 teaspoon cumin seeds to oil mixture in step 2. Substitute 2 thinly sliced scallion greens for parsley and omit lemon wedges.

SCIENCE DESK

THE SURPRISING POWER OF SHRIMP SHELLS

We found that cooking shrimp in their shells kept them juicier, but our shell-on roasted shrimp boast such savory depth that we wondered if there wasn't more to this outer layer than we thought. Our science editor confirmed our suspicions. First, shrimp shells contain water-soluble flavor compounds that will get absorbed by the shrimp flesh during cooking. Second, the shells are loaded with proteins and sugars—almost as much as the flesh itself. When they brown, they undergo the flavor-enhancing Maillard reaction just as roasted meats do, which gives the shells even more flavor to pass along to the flesh. Third, like the flesh, the shells contain healthy amounts of glutamates and nucleotides, compounds that dramatically enhance savory *umami* flavor when present together in food. These compounds also get transferred to the meat during cooking, amplifying the effect of its own glutamates and nucleotides. Bottom line: Shrimp shells not only protect the meat during cooking but also significantly enhance its flavor. This also proves that those of us who enjoy eating the roasted shell along with the meat are onto something.

RATING INNOVATIVE DUTCH OVENS

The Dutch oven is a kitchen workhorse. This piece of equipment is ideal for braises, pot roasts, soups, and stews, plus its tall sides make it useful for deep frying, and many cooks press Dutch ovens into service for jobs like boiling pasta. Our favorite brand is the Le Creuset 7¼-Quart Round French Oven, which we find to be the gold standard of Dutch ovens thanks to its heavy (but not excessive) weight and wide surface area. But we've seen a number of new models on the market that boast innovative features like a lid that locks into place for straining, a silicone oil chamber in the base that promises to build heat slowly, or aluminum ridges on the bottom to help speed up cooking. We tested three of these models by browning meat and making it into stew, deep-frying frozen French fries, steaming rice, and timing how long it took to boil water. Though two models disappointed when it came to the effectiveness of their innovations, we did find one model that delivered on its promise. However, its unwieldy size kept it a notch below our winner. Brands are listed in order of preference. See AmericasTestKitchen.com for updates and further information on this testing.

TEST KITCHEN FAVORITE (DUTCH OVEN)

LE CREUSET 7¼-Quart Round French Oven
MODEL: LS2501-28 **PRICE:** $249.95
COMMENTS: This gold standard Dutch oven puts a "gorgeous, golden crust" on meat and creates great fond. Stews, braises, and rice cook up perfectly (though cleanup requires long soaking for rice).

RECOMMENDED

PAULI COOKWARE Never Burn Sauce Pot, 10 Quart
MODEL: 1001 **PRICE:** $229.99
COOKING SURFACE: 10.5 in **WEIGHT:** 11.9 lb
INNOVATION: Silicone oil chamber in base to provide slow, even heating and prevent scorching
DOES INNOVATION WORK? Yes
STEW: ★★★ **FRIES:** ★★ **RICE:** ★★★
COMMENTS: This large, sturdy pot has a thick, multilayer base that encloses a silicone oil chamber designed to spread heat slowly and evenly. It browned meat uniformly and helped reduce stew to the ideal velvety thickness. It also retained heat well, producing fluffy rice. We let a big batch of chili bubble away for an hour without stirring, and it didn't scorch at all. The only drawback was its mammoth size. Heavy and broad, it needed well over 3 quarts of oil to get sufficient depth for cooking French fries; its tall sides got in the way when we scooped out fries, and its temperature recovery was a bit slow.

NOT RECOMMENDED

TURBO POT BY ENERON Stainless 7⅝-Quart SaucePot
MODEL: TPS4001 **PRICE:** $76.39
COOKING SURFACE: 8.75 in **WEIGHT:** 6.3 lb
INNOVATION: Aluminum ridges on bottom to channel heat and speed cooking (but only on gas stoves)
DOES INNOVATION WORK? Partly
STEW: ★ **FRIES:** ★★★ **RICE:** ★
COMMENTS: This steel stockpot features ½-inch-tall aluminum ridges across its base. They're designed to spread the heat of a gas flame more quickly across the base, and they do help: This pot was a brilliant French fry cooker, since the oil temperature recovered more quickly than it did with all the other innovators (and at about the same pace as the Le Creuset). Three quarts of water boiled in 10 minutes, shaving 2½ minutes off the time of the Le Creuset. But it was prone to overheat and scorch unless we lowered the flame substantially: Fond scorched and burned on when we browned meat for stew. The grooves don't work on electric or induction stoves.

TWIZTT BY JOAN LUNDEN 5-Quart Cook, Strain, and Serve 3-Piece Set
MODEL: CW0004777 **PRICE:** $79.99
COOKING SURFACE: 7.5 in **WEIGHT:** 5.6 lb
INNOVATION: Integrated strainer, keep-warm bowl
DOES INNOVATION WORK? Partly
STEW: ★ **FRIES:** ★ **RICE:** ★★
COMMENTS: This flimsy pot scorched any food that touched its thin walls, which bulged out from its small 7.5-inch base. The small diameter of its cooking surface meant browning stew meat in five tedious batches. Rice came out mushy and unevenly cooked. As for the locking lid designed for safe straining, it worked adequately for straining pasta and egg noodles, but chunkier foods like butternut squash blocked the opening. The melamine keep-warm bowl worked, but it was hard to care about that when the pot itself was this poor.

OVEN-STEAMED MUSSELS

✔ WHY THIS RECIPE WORKS: We wanted to figure out a foolproof way to guarantee that our mussels cooked through at the same rate, so they were all wide open and perfectly tender, even if they were different sizes. First, we moved them from the stovetop to the oven, where the even heat ensured they cooked through more gently, and we traded the Dutch oven for a large roasting pan so they weren't crowded. Covering the pan with aluminum foil trapped the moisture so the mussels didn't dry out. For a flavorful cooking liquid, we reduced white wine to concentrate its flavor and added thyme, garlic, and red pepper flakes for aromatic complexity. To avoid dirtying another pan, we simply cooked the aromatics and wine on the stovetop in the roasting pan before tossing in our mussels and transferring the pan to the oven. A few pats of butter, stirred in at the end, gave the sauce richness and body.

WE'RE ALWAYS AMAZED WHEN WE ASK FRIENDS HOW often they make mussels—and their answer is: Never. We love cooking mussels. They're cheap and quick to prepare, with tender flesh and a briny-sweet, built-in broth created by the merging of the mussels and their steaming liquid. Their flavor is distinct but still tame enough to pair with a wide variety of aromatic ingredients.

So why don't more people make them? Our friends all cite the same reasons: Mussels are hard to clean, and it seems a little dicey trying to figure out if they're fine to eat. Fortunately, these misconceptions are easy to dispel. Most mussels these days need very little cleaning. The vast majority are farmed, which leads to less sand and grit and fewer beards. As for figuring out whether a mussel is safe to cook, this couldn't be more straightforward. Your first clue is smell: A dead mussel smells very bad, whereas a live mussel should smell pleasantly briny, and its shell (if open) should close when tapped. That's it. If a mussel is alive before you cook it, it will be safe to eat when it's done.

The real problem with mussels, especially if you're a perfectionist like we are, is that they come in all different sizes. They run from pinky-finger small to almost palm-size large, and buying them en masse—they're usually sold in multipound bags—makes it virtually impossible to select a group that are all the same size and, therefore, all cook at the same rate. This means that when steamed, a solid number of mussels will turn out perfectly—with shells open and the meat within plump, juicy, and easy to extract—but inevitably some will remain closed (a sign that they're undercooked). If cooked until every last one has opened wide, however, an equal number of mussels will turn out overdone—shriveled, mealy, and tough. Could we figure out a way to get more of them to cook at the same rate?

First we needed a basic recipe. Most recipes for the classic French method of steaming mussels, or *moules marinières*, follow this simple model: Sauté garlic and other aromatics in a Dutch oven, add wine and bring it to a boil, add the mussels, cover the pot, and cook for 10 minutes or so, until all the mussels have opened. Toss in a handful of herbs, stir, and serve with crusty bread to sop up the broth.

There were differences in the recipes we tried, of course. The more successful ones had you boil down the wine a while before adding the mussels to take the edge off the alcohol and round out the flavors of the finished broth. Ditto for those recipes that added some sort of dairy as a thickener at the end of cooking to give the sauce body and help it cling to the mussels. Butter worked wonderfully, though cream and crème fraîche both served admirably as well (we saved these two ingredients to use in variations). Finally, though you don't want to overpower the mussels' own flavors, a little aromatic complexity is a plus. In the end, we decided that red pepper flakes, thyme sprigs, and bay leaves (along with a generous amount of parsley) were just the right combination.

With a good basic recipe in hand, we moved on to the mussel-cooking conundrum itself. We wondered if a more gentle approach than steaming would prevent from drying out those mussels that opened before their

OVEN-STEAMED MUSSELS

fellow bivalves caught up. We cooked two batches of mussels in big pots on the stove—one at a simmer and the other at a rolling boil. Not surprisingly, those cooked at a simmer took longer, and tasters found them a bit more moist and tender, but overall there wasn't a huge difference between the two approaches. If we waited for virtually every mussel to open, we were left with a fair number of tough, overcooked specimens.

But it was during this test that we realized another problem inherent in the traditional method of cooking mussels: the use of a big pot on the stove. With a relatively large number of mussels (at least a pound per person, so we could serve them as an entrée), our pot was nearly full to the brim, which made stirring once or twice to redistribute the mussels unwieldy. Shaking the pot, as other recipes have you do, was not effective at moving the mussels around at all. And if the mussels stay put, this only exacerbates the problem of uneven cooking, since the mussels at the bottom of the pot, whether small or large, are exposed to more heat. We tried cutting the amount of mussels in half so we could stir them more easily to see if that made more of them cook at the same rate. And sure enough, far more mussels opened at the same time so that fewer were overcooked. But how could we mimic this result and still cook the quantity of mussels we wanted? A bigger pot or pan? A large roasting pan, perhaps?

One way we've achieved more even cooking in recipes is to use the oven rather than the stove. In the oven, heat surrounds the food on all sides, leading to more even (and gentle) cooking than is possible on the stove, where the heat can't help but be more aggressive at the bottom of the pan. So for our next test, we preheated the oven to its highest setting. We placed 4 pounds of mussels in a large roasting pan, covered it tightly with foil, set it on the middle rack of the oven—and waited, fingers crossed. These mussels took a bit longer to cook (even at 500 degrees, the oven is more gentle than a direct flame), but when they were done, we breathed a sigh of relief. At last we had cause for celebration: Only one or two hadn't opened and the others were moist and plump.

NOTES FROM THE TEST KITCHEN

DEBEARDING MUSSELS

Because of the way they're cultivated, most mussels are free of the fibrous strands, or "beards," that wild mussels use to adhere to surfaces. If your mussel has a beard, hold it and use the back of a paring knife to remove it with a stern yank.

It was time to create a few variations. In one version, we added tomatoes and chorizo. In another, we paired the mussels with leeks and Pernod. In the last one, we substituted hard dry cider for the wine, and added smoky bacon to temper its sweetness.

Now all that was left was to convince our friends to get past their objections to cooking mussels. Once they discovered how unfounded their fears were and tried our method for oven-steaming, we knew they'd be as hooked as we were on cooking mussels at home.

Oven-Steamed Mussels

SERVES 2 TO 4

Serve these mussels with crusty bread to sop up the flavorful broth.

- 1 tablespoon extra-virgin olive oil
- 3 garlic cloves, minced
- Pinch red pepper flakes
- 1 cup dry white wine
- 3 sprigs fresh thyme
- 2 bay leaves
- 4 pounds mussels, scrubbed and debearded
- ¼ teaspoon salt
- 2 tablespoons unsalted butter, cut into 4 pieces
- 2 tablespoons minced fresh parsley

1. Adjust oven rack to lowest position and heat oven to 500 degrees. Heat oil, garlic, and pepper flakes in large roasting pan over medium heat; cook, stirring constantly, until fragrant, about 30 seconds. Add wine, thyme sprigs, and bay leaves and bring to boil. Cook until wine is slightly reduced, about 1 minute. Add mussels and salt. Cover pan tightly with aluminum foil and transfer to oven. Cook until most mussels have opened (a few may remain closed), 15 to 18 minutes.

2. Remove pan from oven. Push mussels to sides of pan. Add butter to center and whisk until melted. Discard thyme sprigs and bay leaves, sprinkle parsley over mussels, and toss to combine. Serve immediately.

VARIATIONS

Oven-Steamed Mussels with Tomato and Chorizo
Omit red pepper flakes and increase oil to 3 tablespoons. Heat oil and 12 ounces Spanish-style chorizo sausage, cut into ½-inch pieces, in roasting pan until chorizo starts to brown, about 5 minutes. Add garlic and cook until fragrant, about 30 seconds. Proceed with recipe as directed, adding 1 (28-ounce) can crushed tomatoes to roasting pan before adding mussels and increasing butter to 3 tablespoons.

Oven-Steamed Mussels with Leeks and Pernod
Omit red pepper flakes and increase oil to 3 tablespoons. Heat oil; 1 pound leeks, white and light green parts only, halved lengthwise, sliced thin, and washed thoroughly; and garlic in roasting pan until leeks are wilted, about 3 minutes. Proceed with recipe as directed, omitting thyme sprigs and substituting ½ cup Pernod and ¼ cup water for wine, ¼ cup crème fraîche for butter, and chives for parsley.

Oven-Steamed Mussels with Hard Cider and Bacon
Omit garlic and red pepper flakes. Heat oil and 4 slices thick-cut bacon, cut into ½-inch pieces, in roasting pan until bacon has rendered and is starting to crisp, about 5 minutes. Proceed with recipe as directed, substituting dry hard cider for wine and ¼ cup heavy cream for butter.

RATING LIGHTWEIGHT CAST-IRON SKILLETS

Traditional cast-iron skillets are heavy and solid, which gives them excellent heat retention for high-heat cooking techniques such as frying and searing. Our favorite, the Lodge Logic 12-Inch skillet, weighs in at a hefty 7 pounds. But we wanted to know if a lighter pan, made with considerably less cast iron, would have the same ability to retain heat and produce perfectly seared steak and golden-brown fried foods. We tested three lightweight cast-iron skillets, comparing them with our favorite model, by shallow-frying breaded chicken cutlets, searing steaks and making pan sauce with acidic tomatoes and capers to see if they would react with the iron surface, baking cornbread, cooking crêpes to check browning patterns, and scrambling batches of eggs in each pan before and after our other cooking tests to see if they became more or less nonstick as we used them. All of the pans were indeed lighter than a traditional cast-iron skillet, even if they still felt relatively weighty; two weighed in at 4 pounds, while the other was 2.65 pounds. But that's about all they had going for them. One had a nonstick surface and two were preseasoned, but none released foods as we hoped they would—especially by the end of our testing. Also, all three were more sensitive to heat and cooked much less evenly than the thicker traditional cast iron. In the end, the only pan that gave us truly even browning and long-term durability was our traditional heavyweight favorite, the Lodge. Brands are listed in order of preference. See AmericasTestKitchen.com for updates and further information on this testing.

TEST KITCHEN FAVORITE CAST-IRON SKILLET

LODGE LOGIC 12-Inch Cast-Iron Skillet

PRICE: $33.95 **WEIGHT:** 7 lb
COMMENTS: This preseasoned skillet has a classic design—with straight (rather than sloped) sides, thick bottom, and a roomy interior with a cooking surface of 9¼ inches. It performed well in all our cooking tests, its surface gained seasoning in the course of testing, and it will last for generations.

NOT RECOMMENDED

EXCELSTEEL BY COOK PRO 12-Inch Super Lightweight Cast Iron Fry Pan

PRICE: $29.99 **WEIGHT:** 3.75 lb
DESIGN: ★½ **COATING DURABILITY:** ★★★
COMMENTS: It took a lot of cooking, but this preseasoned pan gradually built up a shiny, reliably nonstick surface that redeemed it a bit in the end. The pan quickly recovered after food was added, but it sometimes raced and we risked burning food, especially around the perimeter. The hollow metal handle burned us several times. Also, this pan is not much lighter than regular cast iron.

NOT RECOMMENDED *(cont.)*

STARFRIT Light Cast Iron Fry Pan

PRICE: $49.95 **WEIGHT:** 2.95 lb
DESIGN: ½ **COATING DURABILITY:** ½
COMMENTS: Much lighter than traditional cast iron, this pan initially gave us hope. Its ceramic nonstick interior released foods perfectly at first but then lost most of its nonstick capability by the end of testing. (We tried the manufacturer's suggestion of wiping the pan with oil to restore it, which worked briefly and then promptly stopped working.) The pan was responsive to heat changes, the handle stayed cool, and the pan was very maneuverable. But we can't justify spending more than the price of the Lodge Logic on a pan that doesn't stay nonstick and that can't be reseasoned.

GUY FIERI 12-Inch Pre-seasoned Light Weight Cast Iron Fry Pan

PRICE: $36.59 **WEIGHT:** 4.3 lb
DESIGN: ★ **COATING DURABILITY:** ½
COMMENTS: Still fairly weighty, this preseasoned pan released a powerful plastic smell when we first cooked in it, despite the manufacturer's directions for cleaning. Browning was uneven and it took a while to recover heat. Rather than gaining seasoning through use, this pan lost all its nonstick properties.

Salmon & Latkes

Bridget explains that the key to crisp latkes is using shredded starchy russets and making sure to wring the excess moisture from the spuds before frying.

THE SIMPLEST DISHES ARE OFTEN THE HARDEST ONES TO GET RIGHT. Case in point: herb-crusted salmon. Preparing this dish is almost effortless: top salmon fillets with an herb-laced bread-crumb topping and bake or broil. But rarely does this dish deliver the light crunch, moist, tender salmon, and lively herb flavor it promises. Often, the herb and bread-crumb topping is at fault, forming a coating so thick it falls off in one fell swoop when cut into with a fork. But it's not always the herby crust that's at fault—sometimes the salmon is overcooked and dry, or it hasn't picked up much in the way of flavor from the other ingredients. We wanted a recipe that kept the ease but ramped up the flavor, so we could taste all the ingredients in the dish, and guaranteed a pleasing mix of textures.

Likewise, potato latkes require little legwork and call for just a few ingredients—potatoes, oil, and eggs are the basis for most recipes—yet what results is often far from the ideal of light, crispy cakes made from well-seasoned shredded potatoes. Most of the latkes we've sampled were heavy and greasy, leaving an unappealing oil slick in their wake. It turns out that achieving a super-crisp texture, minus the greasy feel, in our latkes would require a bit of ingenuity. We sometimes like to serve gravlax, salmon cured with sugar and salt, with our latkes so instead of going the store-bought route, we tried our hand at making it ourselves.

Join us as we look at these classics in a new way and bring them up to par, while still staying true to their simple, easy nature.

HERB-CRUSTED SALMON

HERB-CRUSTED SALMON

☑ **WHY THIS RECIPE WORKS:** Herb-crusted salmon rarely lives up to its name; it most often sports a dusty, bland sprinkling of bread crumbs and hardly any herb flavor. To make this dish the best it could be, we first brined the salmon to keep it moist (brining also inhibits the formation of the white protein albumin that appears on the fish when heated). For the herb, we thought the sweet, woodsy notes of tarragon paired especially well with our salmon. To protect its delicate flavor in the oven, we mixed the herb with mustard and mayonnaise, layered it on the fish, then sprinkled bread crumbs, which we'd seasoned with thyme, over the top. Toasting the bread crumbs in butter gave them some color and flavor. A little beaten egg helped them adhere, and a low oven kept the crust from scorching while the salmon cooked through.

HERB-CRUSTED SALMON ALWAYS SOUNDS LIKE A GOOD idea. Its very name suggests so much: fresh herb flavor and a crunchy coating that contrasts nicely with the silky salmon. It also sounds simple: Just sprinkle bread crumbs mixed with chopped herbs on a fish fillet and stick the whole thing under the broiler. An easy weeknight meal, served. But as soon as we began our testing, we knew we were in for a challenge. Our first attempts were neither herby nor well crusted. The fresh herb flavor vanished under the intense heat of the broiler, and the oily, overcharred smattering of bread crumbs fell off with the touch of a feather. We set out to make a quick herb-crusted salmon that not only was herby but also had a crust that both stayed in place and delivered a substantial crunch.

We decided to focus first on the crust and worry about incorporating herb flavor later. Our earlier tests proved that coarse, Japanese-style panko bread crumbs were a must. We seasoned them with salt and pepper; then, to moisten the mix and increase its cohesion, we tried adding small amounts of mayonnaise, mustard, melted butter, and olive oil, respectively, to four different batches. We applied the mixture to the fish and then cooked the fillets on a rack in a 325-degree oven. (We dismissed the char-inducing broiler from the get-go.) Though the added fats helped the crumbs brown evenly and the mustard increased the crust's flavor, none of these additions did much to help it all hold together.

We would need something stickier. We tried 2 tablespoons of beaten egg along with some mayo and mustard. This simple combination yielded a crust that held together but wasn't at all tough and could easily be cut with a fork. On to the crust's flavor.

One of our favorite herbs to pair with salmon is tarragon, so we started with that. The tarragon certainly smelled delicious as it baked on the fish, but by the time the crust was browned and the salmon had cooked, its delicate leaves had lost all their fragrance and flavor. It turns out that herbs can be divided into two categories: The major aromatic compounds in hardy herbs like thyme and rosemary are chemically stable and so do not dissipate when heated. Delicate herbs like tarragon, basil, and dill, however, contain unstable aromatic compounds that do not fare well at high temperatures. To protect the tarragon from the heat of the oven, we would need a shield.

What about a bread-crumb shield? We combined tarragon, mayo, and mustard, which we then spread over the top of each salmon fillet. We mixed the egg and panko separately before pressing them on top of the herb spread and baking our fish. The first time we opened the oven door, we smelled success. Instead of the familiar waft of tarragon, we smelled cooked salmon, which implied that the herb flavor was still contained beneath its crusty shield. Happily, the tarragon flavor was clear and fresh.

But since it didn't contain fat, the crust itself was pale blond in color and a bit bland. We didn't want to lose fresh tarragon flavor by upping the oven temperature. Instead, we browned the panko in a pan with some butter and then added just a bit of thyme to the mix. We knew that this hardy herb's flavor compounds could handle the heat.

The last issue was that the salmon occasionally sported a splotchy white layer of albumin, a protein in fish and other foods that congeals when heated. We've previously found that brining helps prevent some of the albumin formation: The salt in the brine keeps the surface proteins from contracting as they cook and therefore prevents the albumin from being squeezed out of the fish. A quick 15-minute brine worked wonders. This batch had very little of the unsightly white film; plus, it was perfectly seasoned and far moister. It turns out that brining fish works in a similar fashion to brining proteins like chicken and pork. The salt is drawn into the flesh, followed by water, leading to juicier fish. And because muscles in fish are shorter and looser than in meat, the salt penetrates more rapidly, leading to shorter brining times. Now we could celebrate success: Our redesigned herb-crusted salmon was silky, well seasoned, and both herby and crusty.

SCIENCE DESK

WHY YOU SHOULD BRINE FISH

In the test kitchen, we brine meats like turkey, chicken, pork, and lamb to improve both flavor and texture. But brining fish can be beneficial, too. We set up a series of tests using different brine concentrations (3, 6, and 9 percent salt-to-water solutions by weight) and types of fish (tuna, salmon, swordfish, and halibut). We found that, for up to six 1-inch-thick steaks or fillets, the optimum concentration was a 6 percent brine (5 tablespoons of salt dissolved in 2 quarts of water) and the ideal time was 15 minutes. It worked no matter the species, improving the texture of the fish without overseasoning.

As it does with meat, brining fish serves two purposes: One, it helps season the flesh, which improves flavor, and two, by partially dissolving muscle fibers to form a water-retaining gel, it helps prevent the protein from drying out. And brining works a lot faster on fish because the structure of muscle in fish is different than that in meat: Instead of long, thin fibers (as long as 10 centimeters in meat), fish is constructed of very short (up to 10 times shorter) bundles of fibers.

In addition, we seared each species of fish to see if using a wet brine would inhibit browning. Luckily, it did not, so long as the fish was dried well with paper towels just before cooking. Finally, we've found that brining helps reduce the presence of albumin, a protein that can congeal into an unappealing white mass on the surface of the fish when heated.

Herb-Crusted Salmon

SERVES 4

For the fillets to cook at the same rate, they must be the same size and shape. To ensure uniformity, we prefer to purchase a 1½- to 2-pound center-cut salmon fillet and cut it into four pieces. Dill or basil can be substituted for the tarragon.

    Salt and pepper
  4 (6- to 8-ounce) skin-on salmon fillets
  2 tablespoons unsalted butter
  ½ cup panko bread crumbs
  2 tablespoons beaten egg
  2 teaspoons minced fresh thyme
  ¼ cup chopped fresh tarragon
  1 tablespoon whole-grain mustard
1½ teaspoons mayonnaise
    Lemon wedges

1. Adjust oven rack to middle position and heat oven to 325 degrees. Dissolve 5 tablespoons salt in 2 quarts water in large container. Submerge salmon in brine and let stand at room temperature for 15 minutes. Remove salmon from brine, pat dry, and set aside.

2. Meanwhile, melt butter in 10-inch skillet over medium heat. Add panko and ⅛ teaspoon salt and season with pepper; cook, stirring frequently, until panko is golden brown, 4 to 5 minutes. Transfer to bowl and let cool completely. Stir in egg and thyme until thoroughly combined. Stir tarragon, mustard, and mayonnaise together in second bowl.

3. Set wire rack in rimmed baking sheet. Place 12 by 8-inch piece of aluminum foil on wire rack and lightly coat with vegetable oil spray. Evenly space fillets, skin side down, on foil. Using spoon, spread tarragon mixture evenly over top of each fillet. Sprinkle panko mixture evenly over top of each fillet, pressing with your fingers to adhere. Bake until center is still translucent when checked with tip of paring knife and registers 125 degrees (for medium-rare), 18 to 25 minutes. Transfer salmon to serving platter and let rest for 5 minutes before serving with lemon wedges.

RATING STOVETOP SMOKERS

Stovetop smokers promise to bring rich, smoky flavor to the dinner table year-round by making it possible to smoke meat and other foods indoors. Less complicated than the traditional versions, these smokers are essentially metal vessels fitted with a wire rack set over a drip tray and covered with a lid. To see how they compare with outdoor smokers, we cooked salmon fillets and whole chickens on four models (priced from roughly $40 to $100), evaluating the smokers on the quality of the foods' smoky flavor and how easy they were to use and clean. Smoke flavor and cook times were more or less equal across the board; the difference mainly boiled down to ease of use. On the plus side, indoor smokers use special fine wood chips (sold separately) that don't require soaking. Size, though a manageable obstacle, is where they came up short. All four smokers (designed to rest over a single burner) fit just four fish fillets, and only those with domed (versus flat) lids could house a whole bird. For the others, we crimped aluminum foil over the chickens per the manufacturers' instructions, which worked fine. Cleanup was a challenge with some smokers. All were somewhat discolored after the first use (think of the inside of a grill), but one model needed much more scrubbing than the others to remove baked-on soot. When it came to the racks, we preferred those that had parallel—rather than gridlike—wires because grids trapped food. Overall, we preferred smokers with flat lids, which ensured clean smoke flavor, moist meat, and easy cleanup and storage. Brands are listed in order of preference. See AmericasTestKitchen.com for updates and further information on this testing.

RECOMMENDED

CAMERONS Stovetop Smoker
MODEL: SMKW PRICE: $54.95
DESIGN: ★★ COOKING: ★★★
COMMENTS: This smoker performed admirably in cooking tests, producing moist, smoky salmon and chicken. The snug, flat metal lid slides on and seals in the smoke for smaller foods; whole chicken has to be covered with foil. The handles stayed cool on the stovetop and easily folded onto the sides of the smoker to fit in the oven or for storage. The rack and large drip tray were easy to clean.

MAX BURTON Stovetop Smoker
MODEL: 6300 PRICE: $39.99
DESIGN: ★★ COOKING: ★★
COMMENTS: Similar in shape and size to our winning model, this smoker produced food with a slightly less pronounced smoke flavor, probably because the instructions call for adding ¼ cup of liquid to the chips, causing food to steam a little before the chips started smoking. This product was easy to use, clean, and store.

NOT RECOMMENDED

NORDIC WARE Indoor and Outdoor Smoker
MODEL: 36550 PRICE: $79.99
DESIGN: ★★ COOKING: ★
COMMENTS: This smoker, which resembles a mini kettle grill, has an adjustable vent, a handy thermometer, and a nonstick "rack" (a metal plate with perforations). It cooked salmon perfectly, but chicken was another story. We kept the smoking temperature between 190 and 210 degrees, as instructed, but fat that dripped from the chicken vaporized inside the drip pan, creating a sooty flavor. By the end of testing, the smoker's nonstick coating sported several scratches.

DEMEYERE Stovetop Smoking Set
MODEL: REF SET80828 S PRICE: $99.95
DESIGN: ★ COOKING: ★
COMMENTS: The most expensive, this smoker was hardest to clean. The wire rack trapped the salmon flesh, causing it to stick. The manufacturer's instructions call for heating the chips until they begin to smoke before adding food; this strong smoke flavor was overpowering when we were cooking salmon, although was acceptable with chicken.

CRISPY POTATO LATKES

WHY THIS RECIPE WORKS: We wanted latkes that were light, not greasy, with buttery soft interiors and crisp outer crusts. We started with high-starch russets, shredded them, mixed them with some grated onion, then wrung the mixture out in a dish towel to rid it of excess moisture, which would prevent the latkes from crisping. To ensure that the latkes' centers were cooked before their crusts were too dark, we parcooked the potato-onion mixture in the microwave. This step also caused the starches in the potatoes to coalesce, further inhibiting the release of the potatoes' moisture when frying. We tossed the mixture with beaten egg to help bind the cakes and pan-fried them in just ¼ inch of oil. With the excess water taken care of, our latkes crisped up beautifully and absorbed minimal oil.

LATKES COME IN ALL SHAPES AND SIZES. BUT THE AIM for best texture is always the same: delicate and light throughout, with a creamy, buttery-soft interior surrounded by a shatteringly crisp outer shell. Unfortunately, many recipes produce latkes that soak up oil like a sponge, leaving them greasy and soft inside and out. Others are crisp outside but gluey and starchy within. Still others are simply undercooked and tough, with the texture and flavor of raw potato. Determined to produce a crispy specimen with real contrast between the crust and the center, we stockpiled potatoes and got to work.

Most latke recipes consist of the same core elements and a simple formula: Combine raw potatoes and onions and toss them with beaten egg, starch, salt, and pepper. Shallow-fry mounds of the thick batter until the disks are crisp and golden brown.

Trouble is, raw potatoes exude tons of moisture when their cells are broken, and excess water is the enemy of crispiness; more moisture leads to a wetter interior, and water that seeps out of the pancake during frying drags down the temperature of the oil, leading to a soggier, greasier result. That meant both the variety of potato and how we processed it would greatly affect the latkes' texture.

One quick test settled the spud question: Russets, with their high concentration of moisture-absorbing starch, produced the driest and crispiest pancakes. As for the cutting method, shredded (versus ground or chopped) potatoes yielded superior texture, the fine threads forming a lacy, weblike matrix.

That said, even floury russets gave up a tremendous amount of water, so we defaulted to the test kitchen's favorite potato-drying method: wringing out the shreds in a dry dish towel. After a few good squeezes, we mixed the dried shreds with grated onion (a fine pulp gave the latkes good flavor without adding any noticeable texture of its own), a couple of eggs, and potato starch that we'd drained from the exuded potato liquid and added back to the batter. Then we fried up another batch. Without all that water, these pancakes were on the right track—crispier for sure but also a bit raw-tasting and still oily.

The tricky thing was that these two problems presented something of a Catch-22: If we fried the latkes long enough to ensure a fully cooked interior, the crust became too dark. But if we lowered the oil temperature so that they cooked more slowly, they absorbed too much of the oil.

Precooking the potatoes seemed like a good way to deal with this, but when we quickly blanched the spuds, they turned mushy and bland, the water literally washing away their potato flavor. Forget that.

Could the microwave do a better job? We placed the shredded, squeezed potatoes in a covered bowl and zapped them for a couple of minutes before mixing them with the other ingredients. Sure enough, the batch of latkes they produced was the best yet: tender inside and shatteringly crisp outside. And the greasiness? Nowhere to be found.

Wondering if there was more to the microwave than we'd thought, we did some research and uncovered an interesting explanation. A potato's starch granules begin to absorb water at temperatures as low as 137 degrees. Briefly

CRISPY POTATO LATKES

heating the shreds in the microwave causes the starches to corral the water they contain into a gel, preventing it from leaching into the batter and lowering the oil temperature. In other words, the microwave had solved the greasiness problem, too. Latke mission accomplished.

Crispy Potato Latkes

SERVES 4 TO 6 AS A SIDE DISH

We prefer shredding the potatoes on the large holes of a box grater, but you can also use the large shredding disk of a food processor; cut the potatoes into 2-inch lengths first so you are left with short shreds. Serve with apple-sauce, sour cream, or gravlax (recipe follows).

2   **pounds russet potatoes, unpeeled, scrubbed, and shredded**
½   **cup grated onion**
    Salt and pepper
2   **large eggs, lightly beaten**
2   **teaspoons minced fresh parsley**
    Vegetable oil

1. Adjust oven rack to middle position, place rimmed baking sheet on rack, and heat oven to 200 degrees. Toss potatoes, onion, and 1 teaspoon salt in bowl. Place half of potato mixture in center of clean dish towel. Gather ends together and twist tightly to drain as much liquid as possible, reserving liquid in liquid measuring cup. Transfer drained potato mixture to second bowl and repeat process with remaining potato mixture. Set potato liquid aside and let stand so starch settles to bottom, at least 5 minutes.

2. Cover potato mixture and microwave until just warmed through but not hot, 1 to 2 minutes, stirring mixture with fork every 30 seconds. Spread potato mixture evenly over second rimmed baking sheet and let cool for 10 minutes. Don't wash out bowl.

3. Pour off water from reserved potato liquid, leaving potato starch in measuring cup. Add eggs and stir until smooth. Return cooled potato mixture to bowl. Add parsley, ¼ teaspoon pepper, and potato starch mixture and toss until evenly combined.

4. Set wire rack in clean rimmed baking sheet and line with triple layer of paper towels. Heat ¼-inch depth of oil in 12-inch skillet over medium-high heat until shimmering but not smoking (350 degrees). Place ¼-cup mound of potato mixture in oil and press with nonstick spatula into ⅓-inch-thick disk. Repeat until 5 latkes are in pan. Cook, adjusting heat so fat bubbles around latke edges, until golden brown on bottom, about 3 minutes. Turn and continue cooking until golden brown on second side, about 3 minutes longer. Drain on paper towels and transfer to baking sheet in oven. Repeat with remaining potato mixture, adding oil to maintain ¼-inch depth and returning oil to 350 degrees between batches. Season with salt and pepper to taste and serve immediately.

TO MAKE AHEAD: Cooled latkes can be covered loosely with plastic wrap and held at room temperature for up to 4 hours. Alternatively, they can be frozen on baking sheet until firm, transferred to zipper-lock bag, and frozen for up to 1 month. Reheat latkes in 375-degree oven until crisp and hot, 3 minutes per side for room-temperature latkes and 6 minutes per side for frozen latkes.

Gravlax

MAKES ABOUT 1 POUND

Gravlax is simply salmon cured with salt and sugar, and it's incredibly easy to make. The sugar and salt mixture works to draw out the moisture from the salmon and firm up its flesh. We prefer brandy for its delicate sweet notes and brown sugar imparts a deeper, more complex flavor. Note that the gravlax will require three days in the refrigerator before it is ready to serve. To serve, slice the salmon thin on the bias using a long, sharp knife. For the optimum texture, slice the gravlax just before serving.

⅓ **cup packed light brown sugar**

¼ **cup kosher salt**

1 **(1-pound) skin-on salmon fillet**

3 **tablespoons brandy**

1 **cup coarsely chopped fresh dill**

1. Combine sugar and salt. Place salmon, skin side down, in 13 by 9-inch glass baking dish. Drizzle with brandy, making sure to cover entire surface. Rub salmon evenly with sugar mixture, pressing firmly on mixture to adhere. Cover with dill, pressing firmly to adhere.

2. Cover salmon loosely with plastic wrap, top with square baking dish or pie plate, and weight with several large heavy cans. Refrigerate until salmon feels firm, about 3 days, basting salmon with liquid released into baking dish once a day.

3. Scrape dill off salmon. Remove fillet from dish and pat dry with paper towels. Slice and serve. (Gravlax can be wrapped tightly in plastic and refrigerated for up to 1 week.)

Revisiting Julia Child's Roast Turkey

Chris easily carves a deboned turkey thigh stuffed and roasted Julia Child's way.

THOUGH WE LOOK FORWARD TO THANKSGIVING DINNER ALL YEAR long, the main course is often a letdown, which is a shame given the effort and time behind it. And even when the bird is out of the oven, the work isn't over—there's still the carving to tackle while your hungry crowd awaits. After years of hosting the big meal, many cooks find their own ways of dealing with these challenges. Take Julia Child. Never one to let a cooking challenge get the best of her, she had her own method for turning out a holiday bird that boasted perfectly cooked meat and addressed the carving situation by breaking down the turkey prior to roasting. Yet like many of Julia's recipes, this one called for an inordinate amount of work and knife skills that only a Michelin-star chef would possess. Could we find a way to adapt her recipe for the modern-day home cook?

To complete our turkey dinner, we set out to create a side dish of roasted root vegetables. Given their different shapes and varying moisture levels (which means that they cook through at different rates), it's not a shock that most attempts at this simple dish result in some bites that are still crunchy and others that are burnt. We wanted a medley of vegetables that were tender throughout and offered complex, subtly sweet flavor.

JULIA CHILD'S THANKSGIVING TURKEY

✔ **WHY THIS RECIPE WORKS:** In her 1989 cookbook, *The Way to Cook*, Julia Child separates a raw turkey into legs and breast to ensure that both white and dark meat are roasted to perfection. Other benefits include a quicker cook time and a small mound of rich sausage stuffing that tastes as though it has been roasted inside the bird. We loved this idea, but saw a couple of opportunities for improvement. In our version, we brined the breast to keep it juicy and flavorful. Jump-starting the cooking of the breast at 425 degrees decreased the overall cooking time, which also helped the meat to retain moisture. To make even more stuffing, we increased the amount of bread, and we swapped the sausage for the brighter flavor of dried cranberries.

WE'RE ALL FAMILIAR WITH THE PROBLEM POSED BY A holiday turkey; namely, it takes forever to cook. What's more, the breast and leg quarters cook at different rates, making it close to impossible to deliver both perfectly cooked white and dark meat. In the past, we've tackled these problems by buying and roasting separate turkey parts rather than the whole bird. After all, parts do cook more quickly and evenly, mostly because we are able to control the exact placement and timing of each piece when roasting. But in the end, roasted turkey parts look like roasted turkey parts and don't have the celebratory feel of a whole bird. Is it possible to have it both ways: a turkey that is perfectly cooked *and* a showstopping centerpiece? We weren't so sure—that is, until we picked up a copy of Julia Child's 1989 cookbook, *The Way to Cook*. In it, she offers an alternative.

Julia starts with a whole turkey. But then she turns it to parts—first by using a cleaver and a rubber mallet to remove the turkey's backbone, then by lopping off the legs with a chef's knife. Next she debones the thighs and seasons their interiors with salt, pepper, and fresh sage.

This way, the parts can be roasted separately—giving the breast a head start in a 325-degree oven before following with the leg quarters, which require less oven time. As we've also found, this means the bird cooks in about half the time of a traditional roast turkey—especially without the impediment of the backbone, a poor conductor of heat—and is roasted to perfection.

There are three major differences between Julia's deconstructed turkey and our recipes for roasted turkey parts. First, she roasts her turkey breast atop a pile of stuffing—meaning that the stuffing is enriched with flavorful turkey juice and tastes like it has been cooked right in the bird. (Because this stuffing has greater exposure to heat than traditional cooked-in-the-cavity stuffing does, it reaches a safe 185 degrees by the time the breast is cooked.) Second, her step of deboning the thighs is a boon for carving: Since many cooks take out the thighbone during carving in order to slice the meat against the grain for a more pleasing texture, this eases things up by getting this out of the way before serving time. Third, and most important, is the assembly. Julia's recipe mounds the stuffing on a platter, props the breast on top, and rests a leg quarter on each side, cleverly camouflaging any gaps with garnishes so it looks like a whole, intact (and celebratory!) bird.

Quick, even cooking, idiot-proof carving, and rich stuffing, all endorsed by Julia Child? We were sold.

We started by following Julia's recipe to a T. Our first lesson? It turns out that dismantling a turkey with a cleaver and mallet isn't quite the carefree affair that Julia suggests, at least not for us. But with some experimenting, we figured out a way to accomplish the task with just kitchen shears and a chef's knife: We followed the vertical line of fat where the breast meets the back with our knife and then, using two hands, bent back the breast to pop the shoulder joint and cut the back away (see "Deconstructed Turkey"). Happily, removing the legs and boning the thighs was a surprisingly simple operation.

Turkey prep set, we continued to follow Julia's lead by whipping up a mound of her sausage and bread stuffing, which contains eggs, celery, and onions along with its healthy dose of white sandwich bread and sausage. We placed the breast over the stuffing and roasted it at 325 degrees, then put the seasoned leg quarters in the

JULIA CHILD'S STUFFED TURKEY, UPDATED

TURKEY RACK

Julia Child's recipe for perfectly roasted turkey doesn't require a rack, but our traditional recipe does. To give slower-cooking dark meat a head start, it calls for roasting poultry breast side down and flipping midway through. But flipping the bird can be a pain. The **Ultimate Turkey Rack** ($29.95), a metal stand that holds a handled spit, presents a viable alternative: Just slip the bird onto the spit, roast, and turn—no heavy lifting necessary. Its manufacturer claims it can handle any size bird, from 3-pound chickens to 30-pound turkeys. We used it to roast a 3½-pound chicken plus 14- and 24-pound turkeys. All of the birds fit and were easy to flip. However, once the turkeys were breast side up and ready to go back in the oven, we hit a snag: The birds protruded higher above the roasting pan and no longer fit in our smaller ovens. Luckily, we had larger ovens so the turkeys could finish roasting. In sum: The rack made flipping a snap. But before you buy, measure your oven: You need at least 15 inches between the ceiling (or top heating element) and the rack when set in the lowest position (where the roasting pan will sit). See AmericasTestKitchen.com for updates on this testing.

oven 45 minutes later. After 2½ hours, the whole turkey was done.

And the result? Well, the legs and thighs were fantastic. Seasoned from the inside out, they were tender and juicy. Our colleagues were also suitably impressed when we sliced the deboned thighs crosswise. The stuffing, however, was a little too wet and there certainly wasn't enough of it—though it did have that irresistible savory taste of stuffing that's been cooked in the bird, something we've missed in the years since we all stopped stuffing turkeys out of concern for food safety.

But while the stuffing had potential, the breast was another story: Dry, tough, and underseasoned, it needed some serious attention. We got to work.

To address the chalky, bland breast meat, we decided to employ our go-to saltwater brining strategy. The meat would absorb some of the brine, and that would subtly alter the structure of the protein, enabling it to retain more moisture during cooking: turkey breast, salt, water, fridge, 6 hours—done.

But when we roasted this first brined breast, it released its saltwater juices onto the stuffing, rendering it wet and inedibly salty. To address this problem, we started by adding 50 percent more bread in order to absorb the liquid. Before adding the bread cubes to the mix and assembling the stuffing, however, we dried them out in the oven. We've used this technique many times in the test kitchen for stuffing recipes, and even Julia dries out the bread for her stuffing—just not enough. The key to a moist-but-not-too-moist stuffing cooked under a brined breast, we learned, was to start with thoroughly dried bread cubes. The second tweak was to omit the sausage: Since all of the turkey fat dripped into the stuffing, sausage was making the mixture overly rich and heavy, not to mention saltier. Third, we tossed some dried cranberries in along with the sautéed onions and celery we'd retained from Julia's recipe, thinking that a sweet/tart note would be welcome. Finally, though stuffing recipes usually call for some added liquid, with all of the turkey juices present, we added only eggs for a custardy richness.

When everything came out of the oven, this stuffing tasted great: It was perfectly moist and beautifully seasoned. The breast, though better, was still a bit too dry and the skin somewhat pale. We'd have to be more creative.

At this point, the breast was taking about 2½ hours to cook—a pretty long time at a moderate oven temperature. Perhaps the solution was to speed up the cooking? This would eliminate some of the time in which all that moisture could evaporate. Some recipes jump-start the turkey at a higher temp and then lower it to finish—but we knew that would incinerate our stuffing. But who said the stuffing had to be part of the equation from the beginning?

For our next turkey, we used the skillet in which we had softened the onions and celery for the stuffing to begin cooking the breast. We arranged the breast skin side down to protect the delicate white meat and blasted it at 425 degrees for 30 minutes while we set up our roasting pan with the stuffing and leg quarters. Then we transferred the breast, now skin side up, on top of the stuffing in the roasting pan and placed the whole assembly on the oven's upper-middle rack for better browning. After 30 minutes more, we turned the oven temperature down to 350 degrees. Forty minutes later, our turkey was all cooked through. We transferred the breast and legs

to a cutting board to rest for 30 minutes and stirred the stuffing to redistribute the juices before returning it to the now-off but still-warm oven. We snuck a taste before summoning our colleagues to give it a try and sighed with relief—this was the juiciest of them all.

At serving time, we reassembled our deconstructed turkey by mounding the stuffing in the center of a platter, placing the breast on top, and resting a leg quarter on each side. A simple step with important results. This reassembled bird was a showstopper indeed. And with that our turkey problems were solved, Julia style.

Julia Child's Stuffed Turkey, Updated

SERVES 10 TO 12

This recipe calls for a natural, unenhanced turkey and requires brining the turkey breast in the refrigerator for 6 to 12 hours before cooking. If using a self-basting turkey (such as a frozen Butterball) or a kosher turkey, do not brine in step 3 and omit the salt in step 2. Trim any excess fat from the bird before cooking to ensure the stuffing doesn't become greasy. The bottom of your roasting pan should be 7 to 8 inches from the top of the oven. In this recipe, we leave the stuffing in a warm oven while the turkey rests. If you need your oven during this time, you may opt to leave the stirred stuffing in the uncovered roasting pan at room temperature while the turkey rests and then reheat it in a 400-degree oven for 10 minutes before reassembling your turkey.

1 **(12- to 15-pound) turkey, neck and**
  giblets removed and reserved for gravy
1 **teaspoon plus 2 tablespoons minced**
  fresh sage
  Salt and pepper
  Wooden skewers
1½ **pounds hearty white sandwich bread,**
  cut into ½-inch cubes
1 **tablespoon vegetable oil**
3 **tablespoons unsalted butter**
3 **onions, chopped fine**
6 **celery ribs, minced**
1 **cup dried cranberries**
4 **large eggs, beaten**

1. With turkey breast side up, using boning or paring knife, cut through skin around leg quarter where it attaches to breast. Bend leg back to pop leg bone out of socket. Cut through joint to separate leg quarter. Repeat to remove second leg quarter. Working with 1 leg quarter at a time and with skin side down, use tip of knife to cut along sides of thighbone to expose bone, then slide knife under bone to free meat. Cut joint between thigh and leg and remove thighbone. Reserve thighbones for gravy.

2. Rub interior of each thigh with ½ teaspoon sage, ½ teaspoon salt, and ¼ teaspoon pepper. Truss each thigh closed using wooden skewers and kitchen twine. Place leg quarters on large plate, cover, and refrigerate for 6 to 12 hours.

3. Using kitchen shears, cut through ribs following vertical line of fat where breast meets back, from tapered end of breast to wing joint. Using your hands, bend back away from breast to pop shoulder joint out of socket. Cut through joint between bones to separate back from breast. Reserve back for gravy. Trim excess fat from breast. Dissolve ¾ cup salt in 6 quarts cold water in large container. Submerge breast in brine, cover, and refrigerate for 6 to 12 hours.

4. Adjust oven racks to upper-middle and lower-middle positions and heat oven to 300 degrees. Spread bread cubes in even layer on 2 rimmed baking sheets and bake until mostly dry and very lightly browned, 25 to 30 minutes, stirring occasionally during baking. Transfer dried bread to large bowl. Increase oven temperature to 425 degrees.

5. While bread dries, remove breast from brine and pat dry with paper towels (leave leg quarters in refrigerator). Tuck wings behind back. Brush surface with 2 teaspoons oil. Melt butter in 12-inch nonstick ovensafe skillet over medium heat. Add onions and cook, stirring occasionally, until softened, 10 to 12 minutes. Add celery, remaining 2 tablespoons sage, and 1½ teaspoons pepper; continue to cook until celery is slightly softened, 3 to 5 minutes longer. Transfer vegetables to bowl with bread and wipe out skillet with paper towels. Place turkey breast skin side down in skillet, and roast in oven for 30 minutes.

6. While breast roasts, add cranberries and eggs to bread mixture and toss to combine (mixture will be dry). Transfer stuffing to 16 by 13-inch roasting pan and, using rubber spatula, pat stuffing into level 12 by 10-inch rectangle.

7. Remove breast from oven, and using 2 wads of paper towels, flip breast and place over two-thirds of stuffing. Arrange leg quarters over remaining stuffing and brush with remaining 1 teaspoon oil. Lightly season breast and leg quarters with salt. Tuck any large sections of exposed stuffing under bird so most of stuffing is covered by turkey. Transfer pan to oven and cook for 30 minutes.

8. Reduce oven temperature to 350 degrees. Continue to roast until thickest part of breast registers 160 to 165 degrees and thickest part of thigh registers 175 to

180 degrees, 40 minutes to 1 hour 20 minutes longer. Transfer breast and leg quarters to cutting board and let rest for 30 minutes. While turkey rests, using metal spatula, stir stuffing well, scraping up any browned bits. Redistribute stuffing over bottom of roasting pan, return to oven, and turn off oven.

9. Before serving, season stuffing with salt and pepper to taste. Mound stuffing in center of platter. Place breast on top of stuffing with point of breast resting on highest part of mound. Remove skewers and twine from leg quarters and place on each side of breast. Carve and serve.

Turkey Gravy for Julia Child's Stuffed Turkey, Updated

MAKES ABOUT 4 CUPS

If you do not have ¼ cup reserved turkey fat in step 4, supplement with unsalted butter.

> Reserved turkey giblets, neck, backbone, and thighbones, hacked into 2-inch pieces
> 2 onions, chopped coarse
> 1 carrot, peeled and cut into 1-inch pieces
> 1 celery rib, cut into 1-inch pieces
> 6 garlic cloves, unpeeled
> 1 tablespoon vegetable oil
> 3½ cups chicken broth
> 3 cups water
> 2 cups dry white wine
> 6 sprigs fresh thyme
> ¼ cup all-purpose flour
> Salt and pepper

1. Adjust oven rack to middle position and heat oven to 450 degrees. Place turkey parts, onions, carrot, celery, and garlic in large roasting pan. Drizzle with oil and toss to combine. Roast, stirring occasionally, until well browned, 40 to 50 minutes.

2. Remove pan from oven and place over high heat. Add broth and bring to boil, scraping up any browned

DECONSTRUCTED TURKEY

Removing the leg quarters from a turkey and deboning the thighs may sound intimidating, but it really is a snap. Julia used a meat cleaver and rubber mallet to remove the backbone. But we found it easier to use only kitchen shears and a boning or paring knife, concentrating on severing the easy-to-cut ligaments, tendons, and cartilage between the bones instead of trying to hack through the bones themselves. Added bonus? Removing bones now makes it easier to carve later.

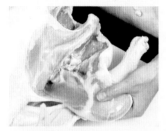

1. Using boning or paring knife, cut through skin around leg where it attaches to breast. Bend leg back to pop leg bone out of socket. Cut through joint to separate leg quarter.

4. Cut through ribs, following line of fat where breast meets back, from tapered end of breast up to wing joint.

2. With tip of knife, cut along sides of thighbone to expose bone, then slide knife under bone to free meat. Without severing skin, cut joint between thigh and leg and remove thighbone.

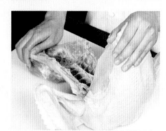

5. Using your hands, bend back away from breast to pop shoulder joint out of socket.

3. Rub interior of each thigh with sage, salt, and pepper. Truss thighs closed with wooden skewers and kitchen twine.

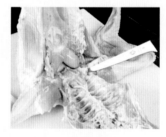

6. Cut through joint between bones to separate back from breast.

---

bits. Transfer contents of pan to Dutch oven. Add water, wine, and thyme; bring to boil over high heat. Reduce heat to low and simmer until reduced by half, about 1½ hours.

3. Strain contents of pot through fine-mesh strainer set in large bowl. Press solids with back of spatula to extract as much liquid as possible. Discard solids. Transfer liquid to fat separator and let settle 5 minutes.

4. Transfer ¼ cup fat to medium saucepan and heat over medium-high heat until bubbling. Whisk in flour and cook, whisking constantly, until combined and honey-colored, about 2 minutes. Gradually whisk in hot liquid and bring to boil. Reduce heat to medium-low and simmer, stirring occasionally, until thickened, about 5 minutes. Season to taste with salt and pepper and serve with turkey. (Gravy can be refrigerated up to 2 days.)

ROASTED ROOT VEGETABLES

ROASTED ROOT VEGETABLES

✔ WHY THIS RECIPE WORKS: Roasted root vegetables develop complex flavors with just a quick toss in oil, salt, and pepper and a stint in a hot oven—until you try to roast different vegetables at once. We wanted a medley of vegetables that would cook through evenly. The trick was to carefully prep each vegetable according to how long it took to cook through. With each vegetable cut into the right size and shape, we could roast them together in one batch for uniformly tender results. To speed up the roasting, we briefly microwaved the vegetables, then placed them on a preheated baking sheet to jump-start the browning. A fruity salsa garnish, a rich bacon topping, and an easy spice blend gave us some flavorful seasoning options.

WANT TO TRANSFORM HUMBLE ROOT VEGETABLES into a side dish that's the star of the dinner? Stick them in the oven.

Well, OK, it's not quite that easy. But it's pretty close. Few techniques are more effective at transforming a root vegetable into something richly flavored and complex than roasting, and it takes almost no effort. The key to success is cutting whatever root you are cooking into equal-size pieces so they all cook evenly. After that, you just toss them with some oil and pop them into a hot oven to cook until they become tender inside and their exteriors brown and caramelize.

Of course, that's if you're cooking just one vegetable. We wanted to roast an assortment, a dish that's become very popular during the past couple of years for its rich variety of textures and flavors. Easy enough, it seemed. Since the technique for roasting one type of vegetable worked so well, we didn't question the advice of recipes that directed us to do the same when we diversified. We put together a complementary combination—sweet carrots, parsnips, and shallots; earthy celery root; and peppery turnips—and then cut everything except the shallots into uniform chunks.

It took only one test to convince us that this was not a good idea. After roasting the lot in a 400-degree oven for 1½ hours, we found ourselves with a medley of every possible bad result, from raw and crunchy to charred and desiccated. Only the shallots, which we'd simply peeled and left whole, came out tender with crisp, caramelized exteriors.

Roasting each vegetable separately would surely get us better results, but that much effort was out of the question for this side dish. We wanted to find an approach that would reliably produce an assortment of perfectly roasted root vegetables, all on the same sheet pan. And if we could somehow shorten the usual lengthy cooking time, all the better.

Instead of trying to cut the veggies into equal pieces, we decided to let the density and texture of each vegetable determine its particular shape. We started with the carrots. Since cutting them into chunks had left them undercooked, this time we cut them into sticks about 2½ inches long, halving or quartering pieces so the diameter of each was no more than an inch. Our thought was that the greater surface area of this shape would allow the interior to cook faster. We were pleased to find that after the same 90 minutes in a 400-degree oven, these roots were now tender and nicely browned.

Parsnips were up next. Since both are cylindrical, we cut them into the same shape as the carrots. But parsnips are more fibrous than carrots, and they came out a little stringy and chewy. It occurred to us that a trick we use to make tough cuts of meat seem more tender—cutting them across the grain to shorten their fibers—might help here. We sliced the parsnips on the bias into 1-inch-wide oblong disks, and roasted them at 400 degrees with the carrot sticks. After 90 minutes, the cross-cut parsnips were nearly as soft and tender as the roasted carrots.

Clearly we'd found the secret to this dish. We peeled and cut the celery root, which we now knew to be the slowest-cooking veggie in the bunch, into ¾-inch-thick slices, which we then cut into planks, creating the optimal amount of direct contact with the baking sheet. Sure enough, when added to the next test with the carrots and parsnips, the celery root was as tender and well browned as its two compatriots.

Finally, we considered the turnips. Since they had charred while the other roots remained too hard in our initial tests, it made sense to take the opposite approach with them and minimize surface area. After trying several different methods of cutting the turnips into eighths, we found that the most effective was to cut them horizontally and then slice each half into four wedges. With their relatively small surface area, these pieces cooked through at just the right slow tempo.

With each vegetable cut to the right shape, all were cooking at the same rate, but we wanted to see if we could bring them in at less than 90 minutes. We had noticed that during the first hour of cooking, the veggies were merely warming up and not actually browning or even softening. We tried covering them with foil when they first went into the oven to see if that would speed up cooking. With the foil trapping moisture and creating steam, the veggies were piping hot after just 20 minutes, but they still took nearly an hour more to brown once we took off the foil. Not good enough.

But we also noticed that after we removed the foil, the vegetables sat in a pool of juices that took at least 15 minutes to evaporate. So for our next test, instead of covering the raw vegetables with foil, we put all except the quick-cooking turnips in the microwave. A 10-minute zap in a bowl softened them enough so they released liquid, which we then drained off. After incorporating the uncooked turnips and giving them all a quick toss in oil, we spread them over a baking sheet that we'd preheated while the roots were in the microwave, for even faster cooking and better browning. Just 25 minutes later, the bottoms of the vegetables were golden brown. We stirred them so the unbrowned sides faced down and rotated the pan for even cooking. After 15 minutes more, we removed the pan from the oven. To our delight, all the veggies were moist on the inside and sported crisp, golden-brown crusts—and we'd done it in less than an hour. A simple garnish of chopped parsley was all that these richly flavored vegetables really needed, but we couldn't resist the urge to dress them up further. For deep savory flavor, we created a topping made from crispy bacon, minced shallot, sherry vinegar, and chives. A bright salsa made of orange, parsley, almonds, and cumin highlighted their sweet caramelized notes. Finally, a Turkish spice blend brought thyme, sesame seeds, and orange and lemon zests to the mix.

Roasted Root Vegetables

SERVES 6

Use turnips that are roughly 2 to 3 inches in diameter. Instead of sprinkling the roasted vegetables with chopped herbs, try garnishing them with one of the toppings that follow.

1 celery root (14 ounces), peeled

4 carrots, peeled and cut into 2½-inch lengths, halved or quartered lengthwise if necessary to create pieces ½ to 1 inch in diameter

12 ounces parsnips, peeled and sliced 1 inch thick on bias

5 ounces small shallots, peeled
Kosher salt and pepper

12 ounces turnips, peeled, halved horizontally, and each half quartered

3 tablespoons vegetable oil

2 tablespoons chopped fresh parsley, tarragon, or chives

1. Adjust oven rack to middle position, place rimmed baking sheet on rack, and heat oven to 425 degrees. Cut celery root into ¾-inch-thick rounds. Cut each round into ¾-inch-thick planks about 2½ inches in length.

2. Toss celery root, carrots, parsnips, and shallots with 1 teaspoon salt and pepper to taste in large microwave-safe bowl. Cover bowl and microwave until small pieces of carrot are just pliable enough to bend, 8 to 10 minutes, stirring once halfway through microwaving. Drain vegetables well. Return vegetables to bowl, add turnips and oil, and toss to coat.

3. Working quickly, remove baking sheet from oven and carefully transfer vegetables to baking sheet; spread into even layer. Roast for 25 minutes.

4. Using thin metal spatula, stir vegetables and spread into even layer. Rotate pan and continue to roast until vegetables are golden brown and celery root is tender when pierced with tip of paring knife, 15 to 25 minutes longer. Transfer to platter, sprinkle with parsley, and serve.

NOTES FROM THE TEST KITCHEN

SHAPING ROOTS FOR ROASTING

The trouble with roasting a medley of vegetables is that each type cooks at a different rate. For uniformly tender, caramelized results, cut each one into a specific shape and size.

CELERY ROOT PLANKS
Cut dense celery root into wide, flat shapes to accelerate cooking and browning.

CARROT STICKS
Long, slender sticks have large surface area that browns quickly.

PARSNIP DISKS
Cut on bias across fibrous cores to create oblong disks that will become more tender.

TURNIP CHUNKS
Cut quick-cooking turnips into eighths to minimize surface area.

Bacon-Shallot Topping

MAKES ABOUT ⅓ CUP

    4 slices bacon, cut into ¼-inch pieces
    ¼ cup water
    2 tablespoons minced shallot
    1 tablespoon sherry vinegar
    2 tablespoons minced fresh chives

Bring bacon and water to boil in 8-inch skillet over high heat. Reduce heat to medium and cook until water has evaporated and bacon is crisp, about 10 minutes. Transfer bacon to paper towel–lined plate and pour off all but ½ teaspoon fat from skillet. Add shallot and cook, stirring frequently, until softened, 2 to 4 minutes. Remove pan from heat and add vinegar. Transfer shallot mixture to bowl and stir in bacon and chives. Sprinkle over vegetables before serving.

Orange-Parsley Salsa

MAKES ABOUT ½ CUP

    ¼ cup slivered almonds
    ¼ teaspoon ground cumin
    ¼ teaspoon ground coriander
    1 orange
    ½ cup fresh parsley leaves, minced
    2 garlic cloves, minced
    2 teaspoons extra-virgin olive oil
    1 teaspoon cider vinegar
    ¼ teaspoon kosher salt

1. Toast almonds in 10-inch skillet over medium-high heat until fragrant and golden brown, 5 to 6 minutes. Add cumin and coriander; continue to toast, stirring constantly, until fragrant, about 45 seconds. Immediately transfer to bowl.

2. Cut away peel and pith from orange. Use paring knife to slice between membranes to release segments. Cut segments into ¼-inch pieces. Stir orange pieces, parsley, garlic, oil, vinegar, and salt into almond mixture. Let stand for 30 minutes. Spoon over vegetables before serving.

Turkish Spice Blend

MAKES ABOUT ¼ CUP

    2 tablespoons sesame seeds, toasted
    4 teaspoons minced fresh thyme
    ¼ teaspoon kosher salt
    ¼ teaspoon finely grated orange zest
    ¼ teaspoon finely grated lemon zest

Combine all ingredients in bowl. Sprinkle over vegetables before serving.

RATING INNOVATIVE NONSTICK SKILLETS

The biggest problem with nonstick skillets is that sooner or later they all quit being nonstick. Next on the list of gripes would be health concerns about the use of polytetrafluoroethylene (PTFE), a chemical that can release harmful fumes if heated to above 650 degrees. Luckily, new models promise superior nonstick performance—without PTFE. To see if any of them work as promised, we gathered three and compared them against our favorite nonstick skillet, the T-Fal Professional Non-Stick Fry Pan. Two of the pans we tested use ceramic finishes, while the third is a five-layer stainless-steel and aluminum pan that promises to be nonstick without a coating. We tested them by making a series of single fried eggs without fat, not stopping until an egg stuck (our established winner, the T-Fal, made it to 76 eggs in this test). Next we made crêpes to test for even browning and then moved on to beef stir-fry; frittata; and, lastly, scrambled eggs (which we also made without fat). The ceramic pans released more eggs before sticking—both were into the 70s, comparable to the T-Fal—and were easier to maneuver than the stainless-steel and aluminum pan, which felt heavy and awkward. While this testing gave us hope that a ceramic nonstick pan to rival our traditional favorite might come along someday, the current models proved that we're not quite there yet. Brands are listed in order of preference. See AmericasTestKitchen.com for updates and further information on this testing.

TEST KITCHEN FAVORITE (NONSTICK SKILLET)

T-FAL Professional Non-Stick Fry Pan (12.5 Inches)
MODEL: E9380864   **PRICE:** $34.99   **COOKING SURFACE:** 9.75 in
OVENSAFE TEMPERATURE: 410°
COOKING: ★★★   **DESIGN:** ★★½   **COATING DURABILITY:** ★★★
COMMENTS: This inexpensive pan has a slick, durable nonstick coating that released food perfectly throughout testing. It is lightweight and well proportioned, with a comfy handle and a generous cooking surface.

RECOMMENDED WITH RESERVATIONS

MONETA Padella Whitech Frypan, 28 Cm (11 inches)
MODEL: 3820128   **PRICE:** $110   **COOKING SURFACE:** 9 in
OVENSAFE TEMPERATURE: 350°
INNOVATION: Aluminum pan with ceramic interior, enamel exterior
DOES INNOVATION WORK? Partly
COOKING: ★★★   **DESIGN:** ★   **COATING DURABILITY:** ★★½
COMMENTS: This lightweight pan fried 77 eggs without fat before the coating began to wear off—almost as many as our favorite nonstick skillet. We liked its smooth interior and low flared sides; it nicely browned beef for stir-fry and wiped out easily throughout testing. But the handle loosened and was impossible to fix. The pan is also ovensafe to only 350 degrees (our winner is ovensafe to 450 degrees). A heat indicator spot on the handle stopped working. With these flaws, it's a hard sell.

NOT RECOMMENDED

BERNDES SignoCast Pearl Ceramic Coated Cast Aluminum 11½-Inch Open Fry Pan
MODEL: 697628   **PRICE:** $119.98   **COOKING SURFACE:** 9.75 in
OVENSAFE TEMPERATURE: 350°
INNOVATION: Cast aluminum pan with ceramic coating
DOES INNOVATION WORK? Partly
COOKING: ★★   **DESIGN:** ★★   **COATING DURABILITY:** ★★
COMMENTS: This gorgeous pan started out strong but eventually lost slickness: The 73rd fried egg stuck firmly. It seared meat for beef stir-fry well but was hard to clean after we made scrambled eggs without fat, revealing the loss of some nonstick capability. It developed stains on its surface. Its handle loosened, though we retightened it. Far more expensive than our favorite nonstick pan, with none of its durability, this pan is a no go.

GUNTER WILHELM 12-Inch Fry Pan with Standing Lid
MODEL: 305   **PRICE:** $179   **COOKING SURFACE:** 10 in
OVENSAFE TEMPERATURE: 450°
INNOVATION: Five-ply stainless-steel and aluminum pan described as "nonstick" without special coating
DOES INNOVATION WORK? No
COOKING: ★   **DESIGN:** ★   **COATING DURABILITY:** N/A
COMMENTS: This pricey pan was supposed to be nonstick. But the first egg we fried in it stuck completely. A handsome traditional pan, it was also a heavy, unwieldy beast that was slow to heat up but then accumulated too much heat, scorching the meat for our stir-fry and the eggs in our frittata. Its surface was not very durable, becoming scratched when we sliced frittata.

Meat & Potatoes with Panache

We came up with a way to braise small red potatoes in a skillet, delivering super-creamy potatoes and crispy skins.

BOEUF BOURGUIGNON IS THE ULTIMATE BEEF STEW: THIS CLASSIC French dish offers tender chunks of meat, a luxurious, velvety sauce, and a rich-tasting mushroom and pearl onion garnish. But achieving the intensity and depth of flavor promised by traditional boeuf bourguignon recipes takes hours of cooking, a laborious, multistep procedure, and enough prep work that one might consider hiring an extra pair of hands for the day. We were in search of an easier path to beef Burgundy heaven, and hoped to find ways to impart our stew with complexity and depth that didn't involve standing at the stovetop for most of the day.

Roasted potatoes deliver a golden-brown, super-crisp exterior, but often they dry out too much on the inside and become crumbly and flavorless. Steamed potatoes offer tender, creamy bites, but the skins tend to become mealy. We wanted to know if there was a way to combine the two methods for a recipe that yielded crispy yet creamy spuds. And if we could do it all on the stovetop, all the better—that way, this simple side dish could be prepared while we had an entrée cooking away in the oven.

MODERN BEEF BURGUNDY

MODERN BEEF BURGUNDY

✔️ **WHY THIS RECIPE WORKS:** We wanted to update the French classic *boeuf bourguignon* to get tender braised beef napped with a silky sauce with bold red wine flavor—without all the work that traditional recipes require. To eliminate the time-consuming step of searing the beef, we cooked the stew uncovered in a roasting pan in the oven so that the exposed meat browned as it braised. This method worked so well that we also used the oven, rather than the stovetop, to render the salt pork and to caramelize the traditional mushroom and pearl onion garnish. Salting the beef before cooking and adding some anchovy paste and porcini mushrooms enhanced the meaty savoriness of the dish without making our recipe too fussy.

JULIA CHILD ONCE WROTE THAT BOEUF BOURGUIGNON "is the best beef stew known to man," and we're inclined to agree. This hearty braise, arguably one of the most defining dishes in French cuisine, is the ultimate example of how rich, savory, and satisfying a beef stew can be: By gently simmering large chunks of well-marbled meat in beef stock and a good amount of red wine, you end up with fork-tender beef and a braising liquid that's transformed into a silky, full-bodied sauce. The result is equally suitable for a Sunday-night supper or an elegant dinner party.

Problem is, boeuf bourguignon is a pain to make. Most recipes, Child's included, require a serious time commitment: roughly 40 minutes of browning bacon lardons and batch-searing beef, in addition to the lengthy braising time. Then there's the "garnish"—in this case not a quick embellishment but an integral serving of pearl onions and button mushrooms that get cooked in separate pans and added to the stew toward the end of cooking. The combination of all three is enough to deter most of us busy home cooks from attempting the dish even on weekends, which is a shame. But what if there was a way to revise the old-school technique, eliminating some of the fuss while staying true to this stew's bold, sumptuous profile? We couldn't resist trying.

The classic bourguignon formula goes something like this: Crisp strips of salt pork in a Dutch oven, sear the beef in batches, sprinkle it with flour, and toss it over the heat to create a sauce-thickening roux. Then add a few cups of beef stock, a bottle of wine, and some tomato paste and aromatics (onions, garlic, herbs, and peppercorns); bring the pot to a boil; cover it; and set it in a low (325-degree) oven to simmer until the meat is tender and the sauce is full-bodied and lush. That takes a good 3 hours, during which time you make the garnish by browning and braising the onions in one pan and lightly sautéing the mushrooms in another. When the meat is done, the sauce gets strained and reduced, and vegetables join the pot just before serving.

We decided to start with the original and see where we could pare down. On our first attempts, we also incorporated a couple of tweaks from other test kitchen beef stew recipes: salting the meat (well-marbled chuck-eye roast is our go-to for stews) for 30 minutes, which seasons it and helps it retain moisture during cooking, and beefing up the lackluster commercial broth we were using with *umami* enhancers like anchovy paste and porcini mushrooms. (However, the latter wouldn't replace the mushrooms in the garnish.) To build body, we added a couple of packets of powdered gelatin; when stirred into the braising liquid, it mimics the rich, glossy consistency of stock made from gelatin-rich beef bones.

We'd be lying if we said the stew didn't taste beefy and sumptuous, with wine flavor that was full if a bit flat-tasting after cooking. But, as predicted, we'd hovered at the stove for well over 30 minutes, and all that searing had produced a greasy mess. Our knee-jerk reaction was to try something drastic, so we started another batch, this time ditching the browning step altogether. Unsurprisingly, it was a flop; sure, it radically cut back on the active work time, but without all those new complex flavors that develop in meat during browning (known as the Maillard reaction), the sauce was downright dull.

Fortunately, we had a better approach to try thanks to a braised meat discovery that we made a few years back: Given enough time, and provided the pieces are not fully submerged in liquid, braising meat can develop color because its exposed surface will eventually reach 300 degrees—the temperature at which meat begins to

on lots of color, and that rich browning flavor seeped into the sauce. (Defatting and reducing the sauce on the stove were still necessary, but with the searing step gone it didn't seem too much to ask.)

We were so pleased with our roasting pan technique that we wondered if we could streamline our recipe even further and brown the salt pork in the roasting pan before we added the beef. This, too, turned out to be easy. By initially cranking the oven to 500 degrees, we mimicked the stove's searing heat and got the pork pieces good and crispy. We also realized that the salt pork could serve as a platform for the beef chunks to sit on as they cooked, raising them even higher out of the liquid and encouraging more browning. And since we were going for the meatiest flavor we could get, we tossed in the trimmed beef scraps and browned them with the salt pork.

Now that the oven was doing most of the flavor-development work for us, we wanted to pare down the time-consuming garnish steps, too. Cooking the mushrooms and pearl onions separate from the stew was already asking a lot, to say nothing of the good hour that we spent browning and braising just the onions. We tried simply tossing the vegetables into the stew, but the spongy, bland result was a nonstarter. Instead, we spread the onions and mushrooms on a baking sheet with a pat of butter and slid the sheet onto the lower of the two oven racks while the salt pork and beef scraps cooked above in the roasting pan. Stirred once or twice, the vegetables were nicely glazed by the time the pork and beef scraps were rendered. Tossing the vegetables with a touch of sugar before roasting deepened their caramelized color and flavor.

The only matter left unattended? Punching up the wine flavor. Adding part of another bottle to the braising liquid seemed extravagant, and the flavor wasn't much better. A more successful—and economical—solution was to hold back part of the wine until the final reduction of the sauce, which left the flavor noticeably brighter.

We had no doubt that our mostly hands-off method was considerably less fussy than classic recipes, but we were curious to see just how much time we'd trimmed. We went back to our notes about how long it had taken

brown. Figuring that the same logic would apply here, we proceeded with another test, placing the raw meat chunks on top of the aromatics so that they broke the liquid line. Indeed, after 3 hours in the oven, the bare surfaces looked almost seared, and our tasters attested to the meat's savoriness. But they wanted even more flavorful browning. The only problem was that the liquid covered too much of the meat to generate sufficient browning. If only we had a wider vessel to use in the oven.

But it occurred to us that we did have one: a roasting pan. It would be plenty deep to contain the stew, and its generous surface area would ensure that the braising liquid pooled less deep, exposing more of the beef chunks for better browning. When we tried it, the result was better than we'd expected: The tops of the meat chunks took

us to make Julia Child's boeuf bourguignon recipe. Turns out that we'd saved a very respectable 45 minutes. What's more, the flavors of the stews were remarkably similar.

An almost entirely hands-off boeuf bourguignon that tasted just as rich and complex as the classic version? The thought was almost as satisfying as the stew itself.

Modern Beef Burgundy

SERVES 6 TO 8

If the pearl onions have a papery outer coating, remove it by rinsing them in warm water and gently squeezing individual onions between your fingertips. Two minced anchovy fillets can be used in place of the anchovy paste. To save time, salt the meat and let it stand while you prep the remaining ingredients. Serve with mashed potatoes or buttered noodles.

1	**(4-pound) boneless beef chuck-eye roast, trimmed and cut into 1½- to 2-inch pieces, scraps reserved**
	Salt and pepper
6	**ounces salt pork, cut into ¼-inch pieces**
3	**tablespoons unsalted butter**
1	**pound cremini mushrooms, trimmed, halved if medium or quartered if large**
1½	**cups frozen pearl onions, thawed**
1	**tablespoon sugar**
⅓	**cup all-purpose flour**
4	**cups beef broth**
1	**(750-ml) bottle red Burgundy or Pinot Noir**
5	**teaspoons unflavored gelatin**
1	**tablespoon tomato paste**
1	**teaspoon anchovy paste**
2	**onions, chopped coarse**
2	**carrots, peeled and cut into 2-inch lengths**
1	**garlic head, cloves separated, unpeeled, and crushed**
2	**bay leaves**
½	**teaspoon black peppercorns**
½	**ounce dried porcini mushrooms, rinsed**
10	**sprigs fresh parsley, plus 3 tablespoons minced**
6	**sprigs fresh thyme**

1. Toss beef and 1½ teaspoons salt together in bowl and let stand at room temperature for 30 minutes.

2. Adjust oven racks to lower-middle and lowest positions and heat oven to 500 degrees. Place salt pork, beef scraps, and 2 tablespoons butter in large roasting pan. Roast on lower-middle rack until well browned and fat has rendered, 15 to 20 minutes.

3. While salt pork and beef scraps roast, toss cremini mushrooms, pearl onions, remaining 1 tablespoon butter, and sugar together on rimmed baking sheet. Roast on lowest rack, stirring occasionally, until moisture released by mushrooms evaporates and vegetables are lightly glazed, 15 to 20 minutes. Transfer vegetables to large bowl, cover, and refrigerate.

4. Remove roasting pan from oven and reduce temperature to 325 degrees. Sprinkle flour over rendered fat and whisk until no dry flour remains. Whisk in broth, 2 cups wine, gelatin, tomato paste, and anchovy paste until combined. Add onions, carrots, garlic, bay leaves, peppercorns, porcini mushrooms, parsley sprigs, and thyme to pan. Arrange beef in single layer on top of vegetables. Add water as needed to come three-quarters up side of beef (beef should not be submerged). Return roasting pan to oven and cook until meat is tender, 3 to 3½ hours, stirring after 90 minutes and adding water to keep meat at least half-submerged.

5. Using slotted spoon, transfer beef to bowl with cremini mushrooms and pearl onions; cover and set aside. Strain braising liquid through fine-mesh strainer set over large bowl, pressing on solids to extract as much liquid as possible; discard solids. Stir in remaining wine and let cooking liquid settle, 10 minutes. Using wide shallow spoon, skim fat off surface and discard.

6. Transfer liquid to Dutch oven and bring mixture to boil over medium-high heat. Simmer briskly, stirring occasionally, until sauce is thickened to consistency of heavy cream, 15 to 20 minutes. Reduce heat to medium-low, stir in beef and mushroom-onion garnish, cover, and cook until just heated through, 5 to 8 minutes. Season with salt and pepper to taste. Stir in minced parsley and serve. (Stew can be made up to 3 days in advance.)

RATING POTATO RICERS

For smooth and fluffy mashed potatoes, a potato ricer is the best tool. Potato ricers look and work just like giant garlic presses: You put the cooked potatoes in a hopper and squeeze the handles to force the spuds through a perforated disk. The best ricers produce a uniform texture that is not lumpy, overworked, or gummy. To find the best one, we tested six brands, ranging in price from $10 to $30. Every ricer got the job done; the difference was in how easy or difficult it was for the cook. Some ricers required a considerable amount of brute force, but others pressed the potatoes effortlessly. After taking a closer look, we found a few key design differences that explained why. The number of perforations was one of the biggest factors. While all ricers had holes similar in size, having more holes on the bottom of the hopper made the job much easier. Perforations on the sides as well as the bottom of the hopper didn't help; instead, they usually squirted spuds out of the bowl, making a mess. The plunger's angle of approach was also important: Most plungers hit the potatoes lopsided—making some spuds spurt up and out of the hopper. Only two models sported different designs that resulted in more efficient ricing. Both kept potatoes neatly under the plunger during the entire process, for more efficient ricing and easier squeezing. Finally, some models were much easier and more intuitive to dismantle, clean, and reassemble than others. A few took real force to pull apart and required the instruction manual to put them back together. Brands are listed in order of preference. See AmericasTestKitchen.com for updates and further information on this testing.

HIGHLY RECOMMENDED

RSVP INTERNATIONAL Potato Ricer
MODEL: SPUD   **PRICE:** $13.95
NUMBER OF PERFORATIONS (FINE DISK): 347
EASE OF USE: ★★★   **PERFORMANCE:** ★★★
CLEANING: ★★★
COMMENTS: This rectangular, highly efficient plastic model with comfortable handles was the easiest ricer to squeeze. Its interchangeable disks neatly produce a range of fine to coarse textures, and its sturdy hook rests securely on a pot rim.

RECOMMENDED

OXO 3-in-1 Adjustable Potato Ricer
MODEL: 1129780   **PRICE:** $29.99
NUMBER OF PERFORATIONS (FINE DISK): 201
EASE OF USE: ★★   **PERFORMANCE:** ★★★   **CLEANING:** ★★★
COMMENTS: This new model from OXO features an innovative adjustable dial to set the size of the perforations with a twist. The ricer dismantles easily for cleaning, and we liked its sturdy pot hook and cushioned grip. However, as we squeezed the handles, potatoes came up and around the plunger. Finally, fewer perforations than our winner meant more effort to process the potatoes.

KUHN RIKON Potato Ricer
MODEL: 2665   **PRICE:** $24
NUMBER OF PERFORATIONS (FINE DISK): 271
EASE OF USE: ★½   **PERFORMANCE:** ★★★   **CLEANING:** ★½
COMMENTS: Overall this was a solid performer, with an angled hopper that matched the angle of the plunger for neat, efficient ricing. Unfortunately, there were enough small flaws that lost it points: Complicated parts and the lack of instructions made dismantling this tool a chore. Numerous nooks and crannies collect water and make it a pain to dry.

NOT RECOMMENDED

NORPRO Potato Ricer
MODEL: 162   **PRICE:** $10.41
NUMBER OF PERFORATIONS: 569 (209 on bottom, 360 on sides)
EASE OF USE: ★   **PERFORMANCE:** ★   **CLEANING:** ★★★
COMMENTS: This was one of two ricers with perforations running along the walls as well as the bottom of the hopper, causing potatoes to squirt out the sides. This no-frills gadget doesn't have a pot hook and its plunger did not fit snugly in the hopper. What's more, it left a ¼-inch layer of unprocessed potatoes in the hopper.

WESTON Potato Ricer
MODEL: 83-3040-W   **PRICE:** $11.69
NUMBER OF PERFORATIONS: 529 (169 on bottom, 360 on sides)
EASE OF USE: ★   **PERFORMANCE:** ★★   **CLEANING:** ★★
COMMENTS: Almost identical to the Norpro ricer in design, this product shared its problems and added a few of its own. Aside from having no pot hook, shooting potatoes out the sides, and leaving a ¼-inch layer of unprocessed potatoes in the hopper, the tool was flimsy and warped with use. The ricer required considerable force to push the potatoes through.

TRUDEAU Stainless Steel Ricer
MODEL: 0990067   **PRICE:** $17.50
NUMBER OF PERFORATIONS (FINE DISK): 170
EASE OF USE: ★   **PERFORMANCE:** ★★   **CLEANING:** ★
COMMENTS: The round plunger required lots of adjusting to actually squeeze into the hopper (the smallest in the lineup) and left a sizable gap between the plunger and the hopper. Also, it has no pot hook. But the worst thing about this ricer was trying to clean it: While the disk pops out easily when clean, when clogged with potatoes it takes force to remove the sharp-edged disk. Our testers ripped fingernails and cut a thumb attempting to dismantle it.

BRAISED RED POTATOES

✔ **WHY THIS RECIPE WORKS:** What if you could get red potatoes with the creamy interiors created by steaming and the crispy browned exteriors produced by roasting—without doing either? That's the result promised by recipes for braised red potatoes, but they rarely deliver. To make good on the promise, we combined halved small red potatoes, butter, and salted water (plus thyme for flavoring) in a 12-inch skillet and simmered the spuds until their interiors were perfectly creamy and the water was fully evaporated. Then we let the potatoes continue to cook in the now-dry skillet until their cut sides browned in the butter, developing the rich flavor and crisp edges of roasted potatoes. These crispy, creamy potatoes were so good they needed only a minimum of seasoning: We simply tossed them with some minced garlic (softened in the simmering water along with the potatoes), lemon juice, chives, and pepper.

WE LOVE THE VERSATILITY OF WAXY POTATOES LIKE Red Bliss. Steamed whole, they turn tender and creamy—perfect canvases for tossing with butter and fresh herbs. They also take well to halving and roasting, which browns their cut surfaces. So when we came across recipes for braised new potatoes, we wondered if this approach, which pairs dry heat for browning with moist heat for simmering, would yield the best of both worlds. In fact, we thought there might be a third benefit to braising: Since many recipes call for simmering the spuds in chicken broth, we reasoned that the potatoes would soak up all that flavorful liquid like little savory sponges. All in all, it sounded like a promising—and super-simple—alternative method for cooking waxy potatoes.

Except it wasn't that simple. To our surprise, the recipes we made were failures. Any flavor that the potatoes might have picked up from the chicken broth was barely discernible—even after we'd halved or thin-sliced the spuds to expose their flesh to the cooking liquid. Worse,

the typical brown-and-then-simmer approach to braising had been a bust, as all the flavorful brown color that the potatoes developed during searing washed off by the time they had cooked through in the liquid.

But by this point, we were fixated on braised potatoes and convinced that if we could revise the technique, the results would surely be ideal. Enter our first change: ditching the chicken broth, since there was no point in using broth if it wasn't considerably improving the potatoes' flavor. Instead, we would use heavily salted water. (While most of the aromatic flavor molecules in chicken are fat-soluble and won't penetrate water-filled potatoes, salt is water-soluble and will seep into the spuds' flesh.) We halved 1½ pounds of small red potatoes—enough to feed at least four—placed them cut side down in an oiled 12-inch skillet, and turned the dial to medium-high. Once they'd browned, we reexamined the steaming step by adding 2 cups of seasoned water (to evenly cover the surface of the pan), covering the pan, and leaving the potatoes to braise until tender. Removing the lid revealed potatoes with smooth and creamy interiors. But as expected, their cut sides were wan in appearance—and flavor.

That's when we realized we should reverse the order of operations and brown the potatoes after simmering them to guarantee good browning. We moved ahead with this plan and, once the potatoes were tender, carefully drained off the water, added some oil to the dry pan, and let the pieces brown over high heat. This time, our colleagues assured us that we were getting somewhere, as the salt had thoroughly seasoned the spuds and searing after simmering had produced the rich, deeply flavorful browning that we'd had in mind.

The downside was that straining off simmering water from a large skillet was cumbersome, and rearranging each of the hot potato halves cut side down to ensure that they browned properly was fussy—too fussy for a simple side dish. When a colleague suggested that we simply simmer the potatoes uncovered so that the water would evaporate, we were skeptical: The time it would take to simmer off a full 2 cups of liquid would certainly mean overcooking the spuds. But at that

BRAISED RED POTATOES

point, we didn't have any better ideas, so we decided to give it a shot.

It did, in fact, take about 35 minutes for the water to cook off, at which point we expected to find a mushy, overcooked mess. Imagine our surprise, then, when we stuck a fork into a few of the potatoes and found that they were holding together just fine. More than that, these potatoes were remarkably silky and smooth—by far the best texture we'd produced to date. Pleased by the results, we researched an explanation and learned that if low-starch potatoes like Red Bliss are cooked long enough, they exude a fluid gel that keeps the potato "glued" together and also gives the impression of extreme creaminess.

Still, our newfound cooking method for waxy potatoes wasn't entirely without fault: In our excitement over these ultracreamy spuds, we'd ignored that their undersides, now in contact with a dry, hot skillet, were stuck fast to the pan and scorched.

The more we thought about it the more we realized that our recipe shared the basic framework of a classic Chinese dish: potstickers. After browning these flat-sided dumplings in an oil-coated skillet, you add water and simmer them until the water evaporates and the dumplings once again make contact with the skillet and crisp in the oil. The main difference was that with potstickers, the oil goes in at the beginning. We wondered if adding the fat earlier in the potato-cooking process might gloss the potatoes and prevent them from sticking after the water evaporated.

So we combined everything—water, salt, potatoes, and a few tablespoons of oil—in the skillet and brought it to a simmer. After a few minutes of covered cooking (which ensured that any sections of unsubmerged potato would steam), we removed the lid and cranked the burner to medium-high. Our hope was that, just as with potstickers, the water would evaporate and leave the oil and potatoes alone in the pan to brown. About 15 minutes later, we got our wish: As the last few wisps of steam escaped, the oil sizzled and the potatoes developed rich color—but we knew that we could do even better if we switched

from oil to butter. Indeed, the protein in the butter's milk solids magnified the effects of browning (known as the Maillard reaction) and left the potatoes significantly richer and more complex-tasting.

Even better, as we poked a fork into the velvety pieces, every bit of their deeply browned surface pulled away cleanly from the pan's surface. We were thrilled with this unlikely approach to potato cookery. All we had left to do was jazz up the potatoes' earthy flavor.

Tossing a few sprigs of thyme into the pan during the covered simmering step was an easy way to add some herbal depth (thyme is soluble in both water and fat),

THE BENEFITS OF OVERCOOKING WAXY POTATOES

The rules for cooking potatoes seem pretty straightforward: Undercook them and they'll stay intact; overcook them and they'll break down into crumbly bits. But while developing our recipe for braised red potatoes, we allowed a batch of halved red potatoes to simmer for an extra-long 35 minutes and noticed that they not only stayed intact but actually cooked up incredibly creamy and smooth. Had we been wrong about the effects of overcooking potatoes in general, or was there something different about the low-starch red kind?

To find out, we prepared two batches of our working recipe, one with low-starch red potatoes and another with high-starch russets (quartering these larger spuds) and simmering each for 35 minutes. Just as they had before, the red potatoes held their shape and boasted remarkably silky interiors. The russets, however, broke down and turned crumbly and mushy.

A little-known but key difference between waxy potatoes (such as red or new potatoes) and starchy potatoes (such as russets) is that they contain different ratios of two different starches: amylopectin and amylose. Waxy potatoes contain very little amylose; as they cook, the starch granules in waxy potatoes burst, releasing very sticky amylopectin, which in essence glues the potato structure together, giving the impression of creaminess. In a russet or other starchy potato, there is a higher amount of the second starch—amylose—which is made up of smaller molecules that are less sticky. Despite the fact that, overall, russets contain more starch than do waxy potatoes (hence they are often described as being "high starch"), russets simply fall apart once overcooked because most of their starch is the less sticky amylose.

CRUMBLY
Overcooked starchy russets break apart.

CREAMY
Overcooked waxy new potatoes hold together.

but garlic was trickier. Though a natural partner with potatoes, garlic burned when added while the spuds browned, and stirring in raw minced garlic at the end led to a flavor that was unpalatably sharp. Instead, we simmered whole cloves with the potatoes to mellow their bite before mincing them into a paste, which we stirred into the finished potatoes. Tasters loved the now-mellow garlic's flavor, not to mention the body that it lent to the sauce. After a few grinds of black pepper, a squeeze of fresh lemon juice, and a sprinkling of minced chives, these spuds had it all: creamy, well-seasoned interiors; flavorful browned exteriors; and a heady sauce. (We also worked up a variation with Dijon mustard and tarragon and a super-savory version with miso and scallions.) Best of all, we'd done little hands-on cooking and dirtied just one pan.

Braised Red Potatoes with Lemon and Chives
SERVES 4 TO 6

Use small red potatoes measuring about 1½ inches in diameter.

- 1½ **pounds small red potatoes, unpeeled, halved**
- 2 **cups water**
- 3 **tablespoons unsalted butter**
- 3 **garlic cloves, peeled**
- 3 **sprigs fresh thyme**
- ¾ **teaspoon salt**
- 1 **teaspoon lemon juice**
- ¼ **teaspoon pepper**
- 2 **tablespoons minced fresh chives**

1. Arrange potatoes in single layer, cut side down, in 12-inch nonstick skillet. Add water, butter, garlic, thyme, and salt and bring to simmer over medium-high heat. Reduce heat to medium, cover, and simmer until potatoes are just tender, about 15 minutes.

2. Remove lid and use slotted spoon to transfer garlic to cutting board; discard thyme. Increase heat to

medium-high and vigorously simmer, swirling pan occasionally, until water evaporates and butter starts to sizzle, 15 to 20 minutes. When cool enough to handle, mince garlic to paste. Transfer paste to bowl and stir in lemon juice and pepper.

3. Continue to cook potatoes, swirling pan frequently, until butter browns and cut sides of potatoes turn spotty brown, 4 to 6 minutes longer. Off heat, add garlic mixture and chives and toss to thoroughly coat. Serve immediately.

VARIATIONS

Braised Red Potatoes with Dijon and Tarragon
Substitute 2 teaspoons Dijon mustard for lemon juice and 1 tablespoon minced fresh tarragon for chives.

Braised Red Potatoes with Miso and Scallions
Reduce salt to ½ teaspoon. Substitute 1 tablespoon red miso paste for lemon juice and 3 thinly sliced scallions for chives.

Special-Occasion Roasts

*Our crunchy peppercorn crust
stays intact, even when Julia
slices it, because we coat the
roast first with a mixture of
kosher salt, sugar, and baking
soda.*

A POT ROAST IS FINE FOR A CASUAL FAMILY DINNER, BUT WHEN YOU really want to add flair to a holiday meal or other celebratory dinner, only a fancy roast will do. Yet preparing a large roast for a dinner party can be intimidating—not to mention costly. One misstep, and a pricey cut of meat is ruined.

Take beef tenderloin. The challenge lies in not only cooking the roast properly so the interior is perfectly rosy-pink, but also infusing the mild-tasting meat with big flavor. One way to do this is to coat the exterior with peppercorns. However, as with pepper-crusted steaks, getting the peppercorns to adhere and balancing their spicy heat pose challenges.

Leg of lamb is another guaranteed-to-impress dish, but this daunting cut requires expert timing for evenly cooked meat and a carving class to turn out attractive slices worthy of your fancy china. We wondered if starting at square one—revisiting the cut of meat—might give us a leg up (no pun intended) on perfecting this elegant main course.

PEPPER-CRUSTED BEEF TENDERLOIN ROAST

✔ **WHY THIS RECIPE WORKS:** For a tender, rosy roast with a spicy, yet not harsh-tasting, peppercorn crust that didn't fall off, we relied on a few tricks. Rubbing the raw tenderloin with an abrasive mixture of kosher salt, sugar, and baking soda transformed its surface into a magnet for the pepper crust. To tame the heat of the pepper crust, we simmered cracked peppercorns in oil, then strained them from the oil. To replace some of the subtle flavors we had simmered away, we added some orange zest and nutmeg. With the crust in place, we gently roasted the tenderloin in the oven until it was perfectly rosy, then served it with a tangy, fruity sauce to complement the rich beef.

WHEN IT COMES TO SPECIAL-OCCASION ENTRÉES, IT'S hard to beat beef tenderloin. It's easy to make—just oven-roast it until it's done—and, as the absolute tenderest cut of beef, it's luxurious to eat.

But that tenderness comes at a cost—and we're not just talking about the very high price it fetches at the butcher's counter. In addition to buttery texture, these roasts are renowned for the meekness of their beef flavor. To counter this, they are often dressed up with flavor-packed flourishes. One such enhancement is a pepper crust. Though we've always put this particular embellishment on individual filets mignons, pepper is such a great complement to beef that we were eager to give it a try on a whole roast.

We knew that the idea had merit as soon as we started digging for recipes: There were dozens. But when we prepared the most promising of the bunch, a number of problems revealed themselves that hadn't when we'd put peppercorns on steaks. First, we had to tie the roast with kitchen twine to ensure that it cooked evenly from end to end, but when we removed the string, the surrounding peppercorns came with it. More cracked pepper rained down on the carving board as we sliced the roast—even when we used our sharpest carving knife and the gentlest strokes. Worst of all, the peppercorns' crunch was wimpy, while their heat was pungent and lingering. The only good part: the meat itself, which had been gently cooked and, as a result, was juicy and uniformly rosy.

Our goal was clear: Create a crunchy crust that stayed put but was not punishingly spicy.

Initially, we drew on prior test kitchen solutions for crusting meat, coating the surface with various sticky substances before packing on the peppercorns. Our edible "glues" included a mixture of mayonnaise and gelatin, another of finely grated Parmesan cheese and olive oil, and one that's named for a painter's trick: We "primed" the roast with a dusting of cornstarch before brushing it with foamed egg white.

We immediately dismissed the mayo-gelatin and cornstarch–egg white combinations due to the unattractive white residue they left on the meat. The Parmesan-oil paste fixed the crust beautifully and lent a rich, flavorful punch, but the cheesiness obscured the pepper and beef flavors that we wanted to highlight.

We turned to the beef itself, wondering if we might be able to transform its surface into a pepper magnet through mechanical or chemical means. A colleague suggested that we try roughing up its surface with a sandpaper-like mixture of gritty kosher salt enhanced with some baking soda. The latter would raise the beef's pH, in turn triggering enzymes in the meat to dissolve some of the surface proteins, which we hoped would create a tacky exterior. Not wanting to turn the roast's exterior to mush, we kept the amount of baking soda small—only ¼ teaspoon—and skipped any resting time. Sure enough, the surface became sticky after a brief rubdown. We pressed on ½ cup of cracked peppercorns that we mixed with a few tablespoons of oil. We then sprayed the twine we would use to tie the roast with vegetable oil—that way, it wouldn't stick to the meat when we removed it—and transferred the roast to a 300-degree oven.

This time, the peppercorns held tight to the tenderloin even after slicing, and our tasters applauded the gorgeously crusted roast we served for lunch that day. Until they dug in. Then they winced and reached for water, complaining that the heat was too aggressive now that every bite was loaded with peppercorns.

It was time to bring down the heat level to the point at which it was enhancing rather than overpowering

PEPPER-CRUSTED BEEF TENDERLOIN ROAST WITH RED WINE–ORANGE SAUCE

the meat's flavor. To do so, we took a cue from a study funded by the National Institutes of Health that demonstrated that both sucrose (table sugar) and citric acid can effectively temper the spiciness of black pepper. We tried mixing a little sugar into the salt rub, and we found that it not only lessened tasters' perception of heat but also enhanced the pepper's more subtle flavors, thus lending more complexity. We tabled the addition of citric acid until later, imagining tart fruit juices as a good base for an accompanying sauce.

The sugar hadn't tamed the heat enough, though, so we abandoned all further attempts to dampen the pepper's heat with other ingredients and turned to an approach that the test kitchen has used in other such situations: simmering the cracked pepper in oil. We've found this an effective way to mellow piperine, the flavor compound responsible for peppercorns' pungency. But as we did some further reading, we learned that piperine is also soluble in alcohol and acid, which inspired our next test. We simmered a batch of peppercorns in each of the three liquids (using neutral-flavored vodka for the alcohol test and white vinegar for the acid test), drained away the spicy liquids, and then mixed the tamed pepper with fresh oil (to help the crust stick).

Tasters' universal verdict: All three methods were highly successful at mellowing the heat, but vodka and vinegar were nonstarters because the former gave the meat a boozy taste while the latter turned it gray. The oil-simmered peppercorns, on the other hand, lent a pleasant spiciness without generating any off-flavors or negatively affecting appearance.

That said, less heat came at a cost. Simmering the peppercorns in oil had drawn out not only their spiciness but also the nuanced piney and floral flavors that contributed much to making this dish so good. Essentially, we'd been pitching the best part of the peppercorns into the trash.

Looking for a way to restore these flavors, we did more digging and discovered some interesting information. It turns out that three of the main flavor compounds in peppercorns—sabinene, pinene, and limonene—are also found in high concentrations in the oil in orange zest (95 percent limonene) and nutmeg (58 percent pinene and sabinene). Intrigued, we tried adding both to the rub. Sure enough, mixing 1 tablespoon of zest and ½ teaspoon of ground nutmeg with the simmered and drained peppercorns hit the mark, restoring a balance of flavors that made the crust taste more like, well, pepper.

We were ready for the final flourish: those tangy fruit juice–based sauces. We'd already stripped the orange's zest, so we figured we'd squeeze out the juice and combine it with some red wine, beef broth, and other pantry staples for a complex-tasting finish. Liking those results, we also mixed up a version with pomegranate juice and port. Both sauces were hits, their fruity tang slightly tempering the peppercorns' aromatic, toasty heat, not to mention gussying up this luxe cut to qualify as holiday dinner-party fare.

NOTES FROM THE TEST KITCHEN

PREPARING—AND PACKING ON—A PEPPERCORN CRUST
Most peppercorn crusts either bring big crunch or grip the meat—but rarely both. Here's how we got it right.

1. For a crunchy crust that also sticks, coarsely crack—don't pulverize—peppercorns.

2. To remove dusty bits of ground pepper, sift cracked peppercorns in strainer.

3. Rub meat with salt, sugar, and baking soda to make surface tacky.

Pepper-Crusted Beef Tenderloin Roast

SERVES 10 TO 12

Not all pepper mills produce a coarse enough grind for this recipe. Coarsely cracked peppercorns are each about the size of a halved whole one.

4½ teaspoons kosher salt

1½ teaspoons sugar

¼ teaspoon baking soda

9 tablespoons olive oil

½ cup coarsely cracked black peppercorns

1 tablespoon finely grated orange zest

½ teaspoon ground nutmeg

1 (6-pound) whole beef tenderloin, trimmed

1. Adjust oven rack to middle position and heat oven to 300 degrees. Combine salt, sugar, and baking soda in bowl; set aside. Heat 6 tablespoons oil and peppercorns in small saucepan over low heat until faint bubbles appear. Continue to cook at bare simmer, swirling pan occasionally, until pepper is fragrant, 7 to 10 minutes. Using fine-mesh strainer, drain cooking oil from peppercorns. Discard cooking oil and mix peppercorns with remaining 3 tablespoons oil, orange zest, and nutmeg.

2. Set tenderloin on sheet of plastic wrap. Sprinkle salt mixture evenly over surface of tenderloin and rub into tenderloin until surface is tacky. Tuck tail end of tenderloin under about 6 inches to create more even shape. Rub top and side of tenderloin with peppercorn mixture, pressing to make sure peppercorns adhere. Spray three 12-inch lengths kitchen twine with vegetable oil spray; tie head of tenderloin to maintain even shape, spacing twine at 2-inch intervals.

3. Transfer prepared tenderloin to wire rack set in rimmed baking sheet, keeping tail end tucked under. Roast until thickest part of meat registers about 120 degrees for rare and about 125 degrees for medium-rare (thinner parts of tenderloin will be slightly more done), 60 to 70 minutes. Transfer to carving board and let rest for 30 minutes.

4. Remove twine and slice meat into ½-inch-thick slices. Serve.

Red Wine–Orange Sauce

MAKES 1 CUP

2 tablespoons unsalted butter, plus 4 tablespoons cut into 4 pieces and chilled

2 shallots, minced

1 tablespoon tomato paste

2 teaspoons sugar

3 garlic cloves, minced

2 cups beef broth

1 cup red wine

¼ cup orange juice

2 tablespoons balsamic vinegar

1 tablespoon Worcestershire sauce

1 sprig fresh thyme

Salt and pepper

1. Melt 2 tablespoons butter in medium saucepan over medium-high heat. Add shallots, tomato paste, and sugar; cook, stirring frequently, until deep brown, about 5 minutes. Add garlic and cook until fragrant, about 1 minute. Add broth, wine, orange juice, vinegar, Worcestershire, and thyme, scraping up any browned bits. Bring to simmer and cook until reduced to 1 cup, 35 to 40 minutes.

2. Strain sauce through fine-mesh strainer and return to saucepan. Return saucepan to medium heat and whisk in remaining 4 tablespoons butter, 1 piece at a time. Season with salt and pepper to taste.

RATING PEPPER GRINDERS

For our money, a pepper mill has one purpose: to swiftly crank out the desired size and amount of fresh ground pepper, without any guesswork in grind selection or extra strain on our wrists. Simple criteria, and yet many models fail to measure up. To find one that would, we rounded up nine contenders, both manual and battery-powered, priced from $27 to nearly $100, and got grinding. We tested each mill by timing how long it took to produce the equivalent of 2 tablespoons of finely ground pepper. We also looked at how easily each mill allowed us to control the grind size and whether the mills could produce a range of sizes from fine to coarsely ground. Brands are listed in order of preference. See AmericasTestKitchen.com for updates and complete testing results.

HIGHLY RECOMMENDED

COLE & MASON Derwent Gourmet Precision Pepper Mill
MODEL: H59401G PM **PRICE:** $40
GRIND MECHANISM: Carbon steel **CAPACITY:** Scant ½ cup
GRIND QUALITY: ★★★ **EASE OF USE:** ★★★
FINE-GRIND SPEED: ★★ (3 min)
COMMENTS: When it comes to grind quality, this mill is tops. It made grind selection a snap, with clear markings corresponding to grind size, and every one of its six fixed settings performed well. Its transparent acrylic body proved easy to load and grasp.

RECOMMENDED

PEUGEOT Daman u'Select Shaftless Pepper Mill
MODEL: PM25441 **PRICE:** $75
GRIND MECHANISM: Carbon steel **CAPACITY:** ½ cup
GRIND QUALITY: ★★½ **EASE OF USE:** ★★
FINE-GRIND SPEED: ★★★ (2 min 15 sec)
COMMENTS: This high-performing mill was fast and consistent, but if its peppercorn supply fell below 1 inch, output slowed. However, with no center shaft and a clever magnetized lid, this mill is a snap to refill. We would prefer that the grind-size adjuster click firmly into place: It can slip if you grab it during grinding.

TRUDEAU Easy Grind 6½-Inch Pepper Mill
MODEL: 0716027 **PRICE:** $33.99
GRIND MECHANISM: Carbon steel **CAPACITY:** ⅔ cup
GRIND QUALITY: ★★ **EASE OF USE:** ★★
FINE-GRIND SPEED: ★★★ (1 min 40 sec)
COMMENTS: This inexpensive crank-style mill lived up to its name with an easy-to-grip handle that had us cranking out pepper at a rapid clip. A downside: The grind adjustment dial has no fixed grind sizes, making it hard to get just the right pepper size.

UNICORN Magnum Plus Pepper Mill
MODEL: 61695 **PRICE:** $45
GRIND MECHANISM: Stainless steel **CAPACITY:** 1⅛ cups
GRIND QUALITY: ★★ **EASE OF USE:** ★★
FINE-GRIND SPEED: ★★★ (1 min 55 sec)
COMMENTS: Our old favorite remains fast and efficient, with a generous capacity and a smooth operation, but its "fine" grind looked more like medium. There are no fixed grind settings, requiring trial and error to get the right grind size, and the loading ring twisted open during grinding, spilling out peppercorns.

RECOMMENDED WITH RESERVATIONS

VIC FIRTH 8-Inch Federal Pepper Mill
MODEL: FED08PM21 **PRICE:** $45.95
GRIND MECHANISM: Stainless steel **CAPACITY:** ¼ cup
GRIND QUALITY: ★★★ **EASE OF USE:** ★★
FINE-GRIND SPEED: ★½ (4 min 5 sec)
COMMENTS: Comfortable to hold and twist, this wood mill produced uniform grinds in each setting. Its major flaws were a very small capacity to hold peppercorns, which were difficult to load, and poor output: It finely ground pepper at a very slow pace, even when we loosened the setting a few notches.

UNICORN KeyTop Professional Pepper Mill
MODEL: 91597 **PRICE:** $27
GRIND MECHANISM: Stainless steel **CAPACITY:** Scant ½ cup
GRIND QUALITY: ★★½ **EASE OF USE:** ★★
FINE-GRIND SPEED: ★★ (3 min)
COMMENTS: The grind mechanism on this mill from Unicorn is smaller than that of its predecessor, and its key top was hard to grasp, slowing our efforts. It made a better fine grind than did the Magnum Plus but didn't produce uniformly coarse pepper.

NOT RECOMMENDED

WILLIAM BOUNDS Robo Steel Pepper Mill
MODEL: 30121 **PRICE:** $60
GRIND MECHANISM: Ceramic **CAPACITY:** ¼ cup
GRIND QUALITY: ★★★ **EASE OF USE:** ★★
FINE-GRIND SPEED: ★ (14 min)
COMMENTS: Although it ground pepper to a uniform size, the coarse setting was troublesome, and this battery-powered mill took a lifetime to produce either one. Plus, the dial at the base, which controls the grind setting, got stuck, requiring pliers to loosen.

PEUGEOT Saint Malo 5.7 Inch Pepper Mill
MODEL: PM27483 **PRICE:** $49.95
GRIND MECHANISM: Carbon steel **CAPACITY:** Scant ¼ cup
GRIND QUALITY: ★½ **EASE OF USE:** ★
FINE-GRIND SPEED: ★★★ (1 min 55 sec)
COMMENTS: This small crank-style mill ground pepper in a flash, but it was uncomfortable to hold and crank and fussy to load. Its fine grind produced too many large pieces—most likely because its crank handle loosened the finial that controls the grind setting.

ROAST LEG OF LAMB

✔ **WHY THIS RECIPE WORKS:** Roast leg of lamb is both delicious and daunting. The usual bone-in or boned, rolled, and tied leg options cook unevenly and are tricky to carve. Choosing a butterflied leg of lamb did away with these problems; we simply pounded it to an even thickness and salted it for an hour to encourage juicy, evenly cooked meat. To cook the lamb, we first roasted it gently in the oven until it was just medium-rare, then we passed it under the broiler to give it a crisp, browned crust. We tried a standard spice rub, but it scorched under the broiler, so we ditched it in favor of a spice-infused oil. The oil seasoned the lamb during cooking then became a quick sauce for serving alongside the juicy, boldly spiced lamb.

WHO COOKS LAMB? NOT MANY PEOPLE. NOT OFTEN. Not in America, anyway. We know. Not even we cook it, and it's not because we don't enjoy eating it. Lamb has a richness of flavor unmatched by beef or pork, with a meaty texture that can be as supple as that of tenderloin. It pairs well with a wide range of robust spices, and our favorite cut, the leg, can single-handedly elevate a holiday meal from ordinary to refined. The real reason we avoid leg of lamb is that our past experiences cooking it were undermined by the many challenges it can pose.

Roasting a bone-in leg of lamb invariably delivers meat of different degrees of doneness; the super-thin sections of muscle near the shank go beyond well-done while you wait for the meat closest to the bone to come up to temperature. And even when we've successfully roasted this cut, carving it off the bone into presentable pieces proved humbling. Opting for a boneless, tied leg of lamb partly alleviates these issues—the meat cooks more evenly and carving is simplified. But this approach presents problems of its own, the biggest being the poor ratio of well-browned crust to tender meat and the unavoidable pockets of sinew and fat that hide between the mosaic of muscles.

Maybe it would be easiest to just pick up a user-friendly rack of lamb next time we're in the ovine mood, but that smacks of defeat, and we love a challenge. We wanted a roast leg of lamb with a good ratio of crispy crust to evenly cooked meat, one that was dead simple to carve and serve and that provided us with a ready-made sauce. We guess you could say we were after a lazy man's roast leg of lamb.

We immediately decided to forgo bone-in and tied boneless roasts in favor of a different preparation: a butterflied leg of lamb. Essentially a boneless leg in which the thicker portions have been sliced and opened up to yield a relatively even slab of meat, this cut is most often chopped up for kebabs or tossed onto a hot grill. But its uniformity and large expanse of exterior made us think it might do well as a roast, too. Our first move was to ensure an even thickness by pounding any thicker areas to roughly 1 inch. Examining this large slab of lamb on our cutting board, we realized an unexpected benefit of this preparation: access to big pockets of intermuscular fat and connective tissue. These chewy bits, which aren't accessible even in boneless roasts, don't render or soften enough during cooking. Now we were able to carve out and remove them easily. Another benefit was the ability to season this roast far more efficiently than either a bone-in or a boneless leg.

Though many people brine lamb, we noticed that the profile of this butterflied leg resembled that of a very large, thick-cut steak. We decided to treat it like one: We seasoned both sides with kosher salt and let it sit for an hour. Treating the lamb this way provided many of the benefits of a brine: It was better seasoned, juicier, and more tender than untreated samples. Unlike brining, however, salting left our lamb with a relatively dry surface—one that could brown and crisp far better during roasting. To ensure that the salt would cover more of the meat, we crosshatched the fat cap on the top surface of the leg by scoring just down to the meat in ½-inch intervals. Roasted to 130 degrees on a baking sheet in a moderate oven, the lamb was well seasoned and featured a decent crust, but still the exterior portions

ROAST BUTTERFLIED LEG OF LAMB

were overcooked by the time the center came up to temperature. We knew we could do better.

Years of roasting meat have helped us figure out how to do it well. One thing we know is that roasting low and slow ensures good moisture retention and even cooking. The exterior and interior temperatures will be much closer in a roast cooked at 300 degrees than in one blasted at 500 degrees. With this in mind, we tried roasting our salted lamb at a range of relatively low oven temperatures, from 225 degrees up to 325 degrees. Sure enough, going lower resulted in juicier, more evenly cooked meat. We struck a balance between time and temperature at 250 degrees. So far so good: We were turning out tender, juicy leg of lamb in only 40 minutes of roasting.

But now we ran up against a second tenet of good roasting: High heat develops the rich, meaty flavors associated with the Maillard reaction. It's a paradox we commonly address by cooking at two different heat levels—sear in a skillet over high heat and then gently roast. But our roast was too large for stovetop searing. It was clear that we'd need to sear it in the oven, where our options for high heat were 500 degrees or the broiler. We tested both options and found that beginning in a 500-degree oven was too slow for our thin roast. By the time we rendered and crisped the exterior, we'd overcooked the meat below the surface. Broiling was markedly better. We achieved the best results by slow-roasting the lamb first and then finishing it under the broiler, which allowed us to further dry the meat's surface and promote faster browning. Just 5 minutes under the broiler produced a burnished, crisped crust but left the meat below the surface largely unaffected. Now it was time to address the spices.

Lamb's bold flavor is complemented, rather than overpowered, by a liberal use of spices. We wanted to find the ideal way to incorporate a blend of them, and our first thought was to include them from the outset. We toasted equal parts cumin, coriander, and mustard seeds and rubbed the mixture over both sides of the lamb along with the salt. Things looked (and smelled) quite good while the lamb gently cooked at 250 degrees, but they took a turn for the worse once we transitioned to broiling.

The broiler's intense heat turned the top layer of spices into a blackened, bitter landscape in a matter of minutes.

Luckily it wasn't all bad news—the spices under the lamb had started to bloom and soften during their stay in the oven, adding texture and bursts of flavor where they clung to the meat. What if we ditched the top layer of spices and focused on getting the most out of what was underneath? After salting our next lamb, we placed whole coriander, cumin, and mustard seeds, as well as smashed garlic and sliced ginger, on a baking sheet along with a glug of vegetable oil and popped it in the oven. This would take full advantage of the concept of blooming—a process in which, through the application of heat, fat-soluble flavor compounds in a spice (or other aromatic ingredient) are released from a solid state into a solution, where they mix together and physically interact with one another, thereby gaining even more complexity. When the lamb was ready to be cooked, we simply removed the baking sheet from the oven, placed the lamb (fat side up) on top of the spice-oil mixture, and returned it to the oven to roast.

We had hit the roast-lamb jackpot. Without a layer of spices to absorb the heat, the top of the roast once again turned a handsome golden brown under the broiler, while the aromatics and infused oil clung to the bottom and provided rich flavor. Tasters were pleased but wanted more complexity, so we added shallots, strips of lemon zest, and bay leaves (which we removed before adding the lamb) to the pan oil. This lamb was close to our ideal: a browned crust encasing medium-rare meat, perfumed with pockets of spice and caramelized alliums. The last step was to put all of that infused oil to good use.

While the lamb rested, we strained the infused oil and pan juices into a bowl and whisked in some lemon juice, shallot, cilantro, and mint. This vinaigrette was meaty, aromatic, and fresh-tasting. The time had come to carve (a term we now used quite loosely), and it proved as simple as slicing up a steak. We transferred the meat to a platter, dressed it with some of the sauce, and—in less than 2 hours—were ready to eat. Lazy man's leg of lamb, indeed.

Roast Butterflied Leg of Lamb with Coriander, Cumin, and Mustard Seeds
SERVES 8 TO 10

We prefer the subtler flavor and larger size of lamb labeled "domestic" or "American" for this recipe. The amount of salt (2 tablespoons) in step 1 is for a 6-pound leg. If using a larger leg (7 to 8 pounds), add an additional teaspoon of salt for every pound.

LAMB

- 1 (6- to 8-pound) butterflied leg of lamb
  Kosher salt
- ⅓ cup vegetable oil
- 3 shallots, sliced thin
- 4 garlic cloves, peeled and smashed
- 1 (1-inch) piece ginger, sliced into ½-inch-thick rounds and smashed
- 1 tablespoon coriander seeds
- 1 tablespoon cumin seeds
- 1 tablespoon mustard seeds
- 3 bay leaves
- 2 (2-inch) strips lemon zest

SAUCE

- ⅓ cup chopped fresh mint
- ⅓ cup chopped fresh cilantro
- 1 shallot, minced
- 2 tablespoons lemon juice
  Salt and pepper

1. FOR THE LAMB: Place lamb on cutting board with fat cap facing down. Using sharp knife, trim any pockets of fat and connective tissue from underside of lamb. Flip lamb over, trim fat cap so it's between ⅛ and ¼ inch thick, and pound roast to even 1-inch thickness. Cut slits, spaced ½ inch apart, in fat cap in crosshatch pattern, being careful to cut down to but not into meat. Rub 2 tablespoons salt over entire roast and into slits. Let stand, uncovered, at room temperature for 1 hour.

2. Meanwhile, adjust oven racks 4 to 5 inches from broiler element and to lower-middle position and heat oven to 250 degrees. Stir together oil, shallots, garlic, ginger, coriander seeds, cumin seeds, mustard seeds, bay leaves, and lemon zest on rimmed baking sheet and bake on lower-middle rack until spices are softened and fragrant and shallots and garlic turn golden, about 1 hour. Remove sheet from oven and discard bay leaves.

3. Thoroughly pat lamb dry with paper towels and transfer, fat side up, to sheet (directly on top of spices). Roast on lower-middle rack until lamb registers 120 degrees, 30 to 40 minutes. Remove sheet from oven and heat broiler. Broil lamb on upper rack until surface

NOTES FROM THE TEST KITCHEN

CONFIGURED FOR EASY CARVING

First position meat so that long side is facing you. Then slice lamb with the grain into three equal pieces. Turn each piece so that you can now cut across grain, and cut into ¼-inch-thick slices.

is well browned and charred in spots and lamb registers 125 degrees, 3 to 8 minutes for medium-rare.

4. Remove sheet from oven and, using 2 pairs of tongs, transfer lamb to carving board (some spices will cling to bottom of roast); tent loosely with aluminum foil and let rest for 20 minutes.

5. FOR THE SAUCE: Carefully pour pan juices through fine-mesh strainer into medium bowl, pressing on solids to extract as much liquid as possible; discard solids. Stir in mint, cilantro, shallot, and lemon juice. Add any accumulated lamb juices from carving board to sauce and season with salt and pepper to taste.

6. With long side facing you, slice lamb with grain into 3 equal pieces. Turn each piece and slice across grain into ¼-inch-thick slices. Serve with sauce. (Briefly warm sauce in microwave if it has cooled and thickened.)

VARIATIONS

Roast Butterflied Leg of Lamb with Coriander, Rosemary, and Red Pepper

Omit cumin and mustard seeds. Toss 6 sprigs fresh rosemary and ½ teaspoon red pepper flakes with oil mixture in step 2. Substitute parsley for cilantro in sauce.

Roast Butterflied Leg of Lamb with Coriander, Fennel, and Black Pepper

Substitute 1 tablespoon fennel seeds for cumin seeds and 1 tablespoon black peppercorns for mustard seeds in step 2. Substitute parsley for mint in sauce.

Grilling Goes International

Halving the tomatoes before grilling eliminates excess moisture, which would otherwise turn our Tunisian-inspired vegetable dish soggy.

DURING GRILLING SEASON, DO YOU EVER TIRE OF BASIC BURGERS and steaks? We do. To liven up our grilling repertoire, we looked across the globe to the Middle East and North Africa for inspiration.

Kofte, a dish popular in Armenia and other parts of the Middle East, puts a spin on the traditional kebab by starting with ground lamb, which is seasoned with spices and herbs, shaped into sausagelike links, and skewered. These lamb patties are then tossed on the flame until the exterior becomes crisp and the inside is tender and juicy before being wrapped in pita and drizzled with a tangy yogurt sauce. Kofte is immensely appealing and satisfying, but the reality is that nailing the texture can be tricky—getting a good amount of char on the crust while keeping the interior from overcooking is tough. We hoped to develop our own recipe for this exotic dish that would deliver great flavor and the ideal texture—inside and out.

In Tunisia, a vegetable dish known as *mechouia* derives its depth of flavor from the embers of a hot fire. Once charred, the skins of the vegetables (most commonly onions, bell peppers, and chiles) are discarded and the tender flesh is pureed and infused with warmth and complexity from a variety of spices. We wanted to transform this recipe into an effortless side dish of boldly spiced vegetables cut into fork-friendly pieces, rather than a puree, that would pair well with any number of grilled entrées.

LAMB KOFTE

✔ WHY THIS RECIPE WORKS: In the Middle East, kebabs called *kofte* feature ground meat, not chunks, mixed with lots of spices and fresh herbs. For ours, we started with preground lamb for convenience. Kneading the meat ensured the kofte had a sausagelike spring. To help keep the meat firm, we added a small amount of gelatin and then refrigerated it. Ground pine nuts ensured a perfect texture and prevented toughness, plus they gave the kofte a noticeably richer flavor. Hot smoked paprika, cumin, and cloves contributed warm spice notes, while parsley and mint offered bright, grassy flavors. Adding a little tahini to the tangy garlic and yogurt serving sauce gave it more complexity.

WHEN A COLLEAGUE OF OURS AT THE TEST KITCHEN was growing up, his Armenian family had two basic meat-grilling modes for warm-weather events: skewered leg of lamb—shish kebab—or spiced ground lamb patties. Armenians call these *losh* kebabs, but they are known nearly everywhere else in the Middle East as kofte.

His family's version of kofte falls in line with some of the more common versions served in the Middle East, so when we set out to develop our own recipe, we used his father's recipe as a baseline. It uses a mixture of hand-ground lamb, bread crumbs, grated onion, cumin, chiles, and whatever fresh herbs are available, kneading the ingredients together to disperse the fat and flavor and form an almost sausagelike springiness. The boldly spiced patties are quickly grilled over high heat on long metal skewers, making them tender and juicy on the inside and encased in a smoky, crunchy coating of char. To serve, the kofte are stuffed in pita and drizzled with a tangy yogurt-garlic sauce.

When we began our testing we quickly learned that the problem with kofte is that it's finicky. Because the patties are small, the meat easily overcooks and becomes dry. And since kofte is kneaded by hand in order to get the meat proteins to cross-link and take on a resilient texture, we found that it's easy to make it too springy—or not springy enough. We rounded up a handful of existing kofte recipes using a range of binders, spices, and kneading times, but we found that most produced results that were dry and crumbly or simply tough. We wanted our kofte to be warm and flavorful, with a cooling sauce; tender yet intact; and easy to boot. And we wanted to achieve this without needing years of practice.

Kofte is traditionally made by mincing meat—usually lamb—by hand with a cleaver. Unlike machine grinding, which roughs up the meat fibers to the point that they can't easily hold on to moisture upon cooking, hand mincing is far gentler and leads to kofte that is juicy and tender. But hand mincing is a lot of work—and therefore, for us, a nonstarter. Even using the food processor to grind our own meat seemed like too much. We would stick with preground meat from the grocery store. And though we decided to go with lamb—its rich flavor pairs so well with earthy spices and smoky grill char—we wanted to develop a recipe that worked with ground beef, too.

After cobbling together a working recipe of ground lamb and grated onion, along with a little cumin, chile, and fresh parsley (knowing that we would return to deal with the spices later), we began trying to solve the moisture issue. In the test kitchen we usually turn to panades made from soaked bread or bread crumbs to keep ground meat patties moist when cooked through, since their starches help hold on to moisture released by the meat as it cooks. Many kofte recipes also use some form of binder, but when we tried bread crumbs, standard sandwich bread, torn-up pita bread, and all-purpose flour, these add-ins introduced some other problems. While our tasters found that all helped retain a bit of moisture and kept the kofte together, when enough was used to prevent drying out on the grill, the starchy panades gave the kofte an unwelcome pastiness, and they muted the flavor of the lamb. But what other options did we have?

GRILLED LAMB KOFTE

We thought about meatballs. In prior test kitchen development for a recipe for Italian meatballs, we used a panade along with powdered gelatin. Gelatin holds up to 10 times its weight in water, and the gel that forms when it hydrates is highly viscous (which is why sauces made from gelatin-rich reduced meat stocks are so silky smooth). And unlike starches, you need very tiny amounts of gelatin to see benefits, so it doesn't usually have negative effects on texture or flavor. Could gelatin work solo in our kofte? We tried adding a mere teaspoon per pound of lamb and then refrigerated the kofte to help the meat firm up and hold fast to the skewer, and we were pleased by the results: We now had nice, juicy kofte.

But we were still left with a problem. With the pre-ground meat plus a solid 2 minutes of kneading, which was not only traditional but also necessary to help keep the kofte together on the grill, many of our finished products were so springy that they could practically bounce. We remembered a recipe we'd seen that had included bulgur. This coarse cracked wheat most likely wouldn't melt into the meat like bread crumbs but would instead keep the ground meat a bit separated and therefore less springy and more tender when cooked. We had high hopes. But when we tried bulgur, adding a couple of tablespoons to the mix, we found that it only made the kofte gritty. We tried it again in smaller quantities, but the unpleasant texture remained.

The bulgur gave us an idea, though: What about incorporating something of a similar size but of a softer consistency? We'd seen a few kofte recipes containing ground pine nuts or pistachios, and we'd assumed that the nuts were used for flavor rather than texture. Coarsely ground nuts might be just the thing. So for our next test, we added a few tablespoons of ground pine nuts to the mixture. The results were even better than we'd hoped. The nuts helped prevent toughness in the kofte without adding their own texture. And best of all, thanks to the oil they contained, they gave the kofte a subtle but noticeable boost in richness.

Now all that remained was to sort out the flavorings and a sauce. Many kofte recipes contain *baharat*, a Middle Eastern spice blend that is a common seasoning for meat dishes. Recipes vary widely, but the common denominators are usually black pepper, cumin, coriander, and chile pepper. We came up with our own combination of these, with cumin as the dominant player and hot smoked paprika as the chile. To these we also added smaller amounts of ground cinnamon, nutmeg, and cloves. As for herbs, equal amounts of fresh parsley and mint did the trick. For the sauce, we borrowed an idea from a recipe we'd found in *Jerusalem*, the latest cookbook from British chefs Yotam Ottolenghi and Sami Tamimi: We added a small amount of tahini to the traditional mixture of crushed garlic, lemon juice, and yogurt usually served with kofte since this gave the sauce a depth to match that of the kofte itself.

With that, there was one last test to perform: Serve the kofte to our colleague's family. The result? Our kofte was a big hit. Even his dad asked for the recipe.

Grilled Lamb Kofte

SERVES 4 TO 6

Serve with rice pilaf or make sandwiches with warm pita bread, sliced red onion, and chopped fresh mint.

YOGURT-GARLIC SAUCE

- 1 cup plain whole-milk yogurt
- 2 tablespoons lemon juice
- 2 tablespoons tahini
- 1 garlic clove, minced
- ½ teaspoon salt

KOFTE

- ½ cup pine nuts
- 4 garlic cloves, peeled
- 1½ teaspoons hot smoked paprika
- 1 teaspoon salt
- 1 teaspoon ground cumin

½ teaspoon pepper

¼ teaspoon ground coriander

¼ teaspoon ground cloves

⅛ teaspoon ground nutmeg

⅛ teaspoon ground cinnamon

1½ pounds ground lamb

½ cup grated onion, drained

⅓ cup minced fresh parsley

⅓ cup minced fresh mint

1½ teaspoons unflavored gelatin

1 large disposable aluminum roasting
  pan (if using charcoal)

1. FOR THE YOGURT-GARLIC SAUCE: Whisk all ingredients together in bowl. Set aside.

2. FOR THE KOFTE: Process pine nuts, garlic, paprika, salt, cumin, pepper, coriander, cloves, nutmeg, and cinnamon in food processor until coarse paste forms, 30 to 45 seconds. Transfer mixture to large bowl. Add lamb, onion, parsley, mint, and gelatin; knead with your hands until thoroughly combined and mixture feels slightly sticky, about 2 minutes. Divide mixture into 8 equal portions. Shape each portion into 5-inch-long cylinder about 1 inch in diameter. Using 8 (12-inch) metal skewers, thread 1 cylinder onto each skewer, pressing gently to adhere. Transfer skewers to lightly greased baking sheet, cover with plastic wrap, and refrigerate for at least 1 hour or up to 24 hours.

3A. FOR A CHARCOAL GRILL: Using skewer, poke 12 holes in bottom of disposable pan. Open bottom vent completely and place pan in center of grill. Light large chimney starter filled two-thirds with charcoal briquettes (4 quarts). When top coals are partially covered with ash, pour into pan. Set cooking grate in place, cover, and open lid vent completely. Heat grill until hot, about 5 minutes.

3B. FOR A GAS GRILL: Turn all burners to high, cover, and heat grill until hot, about 15 minutes. Leave all burners on high.

4. Clean and oil cooking grate. Place skewers on grill (directly over coals if using charcoal) at 45-degree angle to grate. Cook (covered if using gas) until browned and

meat easily releases from grill, 4 to 7 minutes. Flip skewers and continue to cook until browned on second side and meat registers 160 degrees, about 6 minutes longer. Transfer skewers to platter and serve, passing yogurt–garlic sauce separately.

VARIATION

Grilled Beef Kofte

Substitute 80 percent lean ground beef for lamb. Increase garlic to 5 cloves, paprika to 2 teaspoons, and cumin to 2 teaspoons.

RATING SKEWERS

We've been burned by skewers before. Bamboo and wood scorches; super-thin double prongs are flimsy; smooth, rounded prongs let food spin in place when you're trying to flip it. Still, manufacturer innovations promise improvement, so we gathered six sets ($6.85 to $29.95), including our previous no-frills favorite, and threaded them with chicken-vegetable kebabs; scallops; and kofte, a kebab of ground meat and herbs. Metal was best, but solid tab handles on one set retained heat, so serving was a burn risk; loop handles on our two favorite models dispersed heat quickly. One model's "heat-resistant" plastic slider melted. Double-pronged skewers splayed out awkwardly, so threading them through food was a struggle; their thickness also tore tender scallops. Curved rods occupied too much grill real estate, tangled easily, and only let us turn food 180 degrees. In the end, our former champ again came in on top: Not only does it have the smartest design, but it's also the cheapest. Brands are listed in order of preference. See AmericasTestKitchen.com for updates and complete testing results.

RECOMMENDED

NORPRO 12-Inch Stainless Steel Skewers
PRICE: $6.85 for six
COMMENTS: The only set to ace every task, these top-ranked stainless-steel spears supported kebabs, and their looped handles cooled quickly.

NOT RECOMMENDED

CHARCOAL COMPANION CIRCLE Kabobs
PRICE: $8.99 for four
COMMENTS: These curved prongs sank toward the bottom of the pack as they hogged space, tangled easily, and limited turning options.

SLIDERS by Quirky
PRICE: $24.99 for four
COMMENTS: These bottom-ranking double prongs were flimsy, and the plastic sliding guide melted and fused to the handles during grilling.

TUNISIAN-STYLE GRILLED VEGETABLES

✓ **WHY THIS RECIPE WORKS:** For our take on this robustly flavored Tunisian dish of grilled vegetables, we started by scoring the vegetables (a mix of bell peppers, eggplant, zucchini, and plum tomatoes) before putting them over the coals so they would release their moisture. We used a Tunisian spice blend called *tabil* to infuse our vegetables with exotic flavor. The heat of the grill worked to bloom the flavor of the spices so they didn't taste raw or harsh, and more tabil, plus garlic, lemon, and a trio of herbs, provided a bright, fresh-tasting vinaigrette.

GRILLING BRINGS OUT THE BEST IN SUMMER VEGetables, calling forth their sweetness and adding an accent of smoke. But by midsummer, we're ready for something different from the same old tender-firm produce simply dressed with oil and vinegar. We knew that the Mediterranean region—particularly North Africa—has a rich tradition of grilling vegetables. Maybe we could learn from it. The particular recipe that caught our eye was *mechouia*, a Tunisian dish in which whole bell peppers or chiles, tomatoes, and sometimes onions or shallots are either buried in live embers or grilled until their skins blacken. After the carbonized exterior is peeled away, the soft, smoky flesh (the vegetables are cooked beyond a tender-firm state) is chopped or pounded into a coarse puree and mixed with a blend of warm spices called tabil, plus garlic, lemon juice, and olive oil. The dish can be served as a salad with pita bread, as a side dish to grilled meat, or even as a light lunch accompanied by canned tuna and hard-cooked eggs.

Lured by the promise of new flavors and textures, we oiled two bell peppers, eight plum tomatoes, and two shallots and grilled them over a medium-hot fire until they were entirely soft. When the vegetables were cool, we peeled them and mashed them with a fork and then drizzled on a garlic-lemon vinaigrette laced with tabil. (Recipes vary: Our version included coriander, caraway, and cumin seeds; paprika; and cayenne.) The vegetables were wonderfully supple, with a smokier taste than that of most grilled vegetables, thanks to spending a longer time over the coals. The downsides were a somewhat soupy consistency and flavors that were a little too raw and pungent.

We'd deal with flavor issues later. To address consistency, for our next batch we chopped the vegetables into ½-inch pieces instead of mashing them, an approach preferred by some recipes we'd found. But the resulting salad was still watery. Thinking that our juicy, height-of-summer tomatoes were the culprit, we replaced half of them with sturdier eggplant and zucchini. (Since we weren't intending to remove the zucchini's skin, we grilled it only until browned.)

Surprisingly, the mixture was still waterlogged. That's when we realized that grilling the vegetables whole trapped all of their moisture, which then flooded the salad. We would have to cut the vegetables before putting them over the coals, so they would release moisture during cooking and not after. We halved the zucchini and

tabil-spiced oil. The spices bloomed on the grill and lost any trace of raw, dusty flavor. And to tame the harsh taste of the garlic, we sizzled it in some of the spiced oil before combining it with lemon juice to make the vinaigrette. The only thing missing was freshness. Lemon zest plus a trio of fresh herbs brought a tangy, lively taste. We now had grilled vegetables that enticed us as both cooks and diners.

Tunisian-Style Grilled Vegetables (Mechouia)
SERVES 4 TO 6

Serve as a side dish to grilled meats and fish; with grilled pita as a salad course; or with hard-cooked eggs, olives, and premium canned tuna as a light lunch. Equal amounts of ground coriander and cumin can be substituted for the whole spices.

VINAIGRETTE

- 2 teaspoons coriander seeds
- 1½ teaspoons caraway seeds
- 1 teaspoon cumin seeds
- 5 tablespoons olive oil
- ½ teaspoon sweet paprika
- ⅛ teaspoon cayenne pepper
- 3 garlic cloves, minced
- ¼ cup chopped fresh parsley
- ¼ cup chopped fresh cilantro
- 2 tablespoons chopped fresh mint
- 1 teaspoon grated lemon zest plus
  2 tablespoons juice
  Salt

VEGETABLES

- 2 bell peppers (1 red and 1 green)
- 1 small eggplant, halved lengthwise
- 1 zucchini (8 to 10 ounces), halved lengthwise
- 4 plum tomatoes, cored and halved lengthwise
  Salt and pepper
- 2 medium shallots, unpeeled

eggplant and cut deep crosshatch marks in their flesh. We also halved the tomatoes and opened the peppers into long planks. It was a winning move: Our salad was no longer soupy, and the whole operation took only about 15 minutes.

There was yet another benefit: We could now season the vegetable flesh before grilling. In addition to sprinkling the vegetables with salt, we also brushed on

TUNISIAN-STYLE GRILLED VEGETABLES (MECHOUIA)

1. FOR THE VINAIGRETTE: Grind coriander seeds, caraway seeds, and cumin seeds in spice grinder until finely ground. Whisk ground spices, oil, paprika, and cayenne together in bowl. Reserve 3 tablespoons oil mixture. Heat remaining oil mixture and garlic in small skillet over low heat, stirring occasionally, until fragrant and small bubbles appear, 8 to 10 minutes. Transfer to large bowl and let cool, about 10 minutes. Whisk parsley, cilantro, mint, and lemon zest and juice into oil mixture; season with salt to taste.

2. FOR THE VEGETABLES: Slice ¼ inch off tops and bottoms of bell peppers and remove cores. Make slit down 1 side of each bell pepper and then press flat into 1 long strip, removing ribs and remaining seeds with knife as needed. Using sharp knife, cut slits in flesh of eggplant and zucchini, spaced ½ inch apart, in crosshatch pattern, being careful to cut down to but not through skin. Brush cut sides of bell peppers, eggplant, zucchini, and tomatoes with reserved oil mixture and season with salt to taste.

3. Grill vegetables, starting with cut sides down, over medium-hot fire, until tender and well browned and skins of bell peppers, eggplant, tomatoes, and shallots are charred, 8 to 16 minutes, turning and moving vegetables as necessary. Transfer vegetables to baking sheet as they are done. Place bell peppers in bowl, cover with plastic wrap, and let steam to loosen skins.

4. When cool enough to handle, peel bell peppers, eggplant, tomatoes, and shallots. Chop all vegetables into ½-inch pieces and transfer to bowl with vinaigrette; toss to coat. Season with salt and pepper to taste, and serve warm or at room temperature.

RATING HUMMUS

With just five ingredients—chickpeas, tahini, garlic, olive oil, and lemon juice—plus a smattering of spices, hummus should be nearly impossible to get wrong. The ideal spread is appealingly smooth and creamy, with the fresh, clean flavor of buttery chickpeas in balance with the earthy toasted-sesame taste of tahini, set off by a lemon-garlic bite. But some store-bought hummus doesn't even come close, with funky off-flavors and a stodgy, grainy consistency. We tasted eight nationally available samples of plain hummus, including a shelf-stable hummus that uses no oil, a soy-chickpea-blend hummus, and a box mix that has you stir in hot water and olive oil. Many weren't worth buying, but a few hit the mark with a nutty, earthy flavor and a wonderfully thick, creamy texture. Our favorite brands were those that had higher fat and protein levels—from more tahini—and those that used ripe, mature chickpeas. Brands are listed in order of preference. See AmericasTestKitchen.com for updates and further information on this tasting.

RECOMMENDED

SABRA Classic Hummus
PRICE: $4.49 for 10 oz ($0.45 per oz)
FAT: 18.8% SODIUM: 420 mg in 100 g
PROTEIN: 7.4% WATER/MOISTURE: 55.4%
COMMENTS: This "hearty but not dense" hummus had a "very clean flavor of tahini" that was also "earthy," and had tasters praising it as "tahini heaven." Its richness made it taste "like good homemade: real, buttery, almost sweet." One taster confessed, "I'd eat this with a spoon."

CEDAR'S All Natural Hommus, Classic Original
PRICE: $3.49 for 8 oz ($0.44 per oz)
FAT: 12.1% SODIUM: 370 mg in 100 g
PROTEIN: 6.8% WATER/MOISTURE: 67.2%
COMMENTS: This less tahini-forward, "lemony" hummus had a "super-soft and silky," "smooth" texture. With its high degree of moisture, it struck some tasters as "watered down" and "lacking substance." But most found it "good all around." "Now this is a hummus I can get with," one taster raved.

TRIBE Classic Hummus
PRICE: $3.49 for 8 oz ($0.44 per oz)
FAT: 15.4% SODIUM: 430 mg in 100 g
PROTEIN: 7% WATER/MOISTURE: 59.9%
COMMENTS: "Creamy," with a "thick and smooth," "very likable texture," this "clean-tasting" hummus had "deep savory notes." A few tasters acknowledged its "strong tahini flavor," which was "almost like peanut butter." For some, it was overload: "Not to be Goldi-hummus, but this has too much tahini."

NOT RECOMMENDED

ATHENOS Original Hummus
PRICE: $3.75 for 7 oz ($0.54 per oz)
FAT: 8.9% SODIUM: 580 mg in 100 g
PROTEIN: 6.3% WATER/MOISTURE: 65.2%
COMMENTS: "Tastes like taco night," and not in a good way, with "too much cumin." Tasters also complained that it was "too tangy." Its "creamy" texture was undermined by "random grains of chunky chickpeas." For others it was "a touch bitter."

NOT RECOMMENDED *(cont.)*

WILD GARDEN Traditional Hummus Dip
PRICE: $1.90 for 1.76-oz Tetra Pack ($1.08 per oz)
FAT: 7.4% SODIUM: 580 mg in 100 g
PROTEIN: 5.4% WATER/MOISTURE: 71.3%
COMMENTS: With the highest amount of water and the lowest amount of protein and fat among the products in our lineup, this shelf-stable hummus was "like mustard," with a "runny" texture "reminiscent of baby food." Some tasters found its "citrusy," "garlicky" flavors "almost abrasive."

FANTASTIC WORLD FOODS Original Hummus
PRICE: $3.65 for 12 oz prepared from 6-oz box ($0.30 per oz)
FAT: 10.4% SODIUM: 410 mg in 100 g
PROTEIN: 6.6% WATER/MOISTURE: 64.1%
COMMENTS: Reconstituted from chickpea flour and dried tahini and seasonings, this box mix hummus failed mainly on the basis of its "dry" and "sandy" texture. It was also "bland" and "stale," with "lots of raw spice in there," and most of us "could barely taste any tahini."

ATHENOS Greek-Style Hummus
PRICE: $3.75 for 7 oz ($0.54 per oz)
FAT: 10.2% SODIUM: 490 mg in 100 g
PROTEIN: 5.7% WATER/MOISTURE: 67.1%
COMMENTS: If this was hummus, some tasters didn't believe it. With "very little chickpea except in the finish," it "tastes like sandwich spread" or "like an Italian seasoning packet." Several tasters found it "sour," and a few faulted it for being "quite salty."

NASOYA Classic Original Super Hummus
PRICE: $2.99 for 10 oz ($0.30 per oz)
FAT: 10.1% SODIUM: 350 mg in 100 g
PROTEIN: 12.9% WATER/MOISTURE: 65.7%
COMMENTS: With a "very creamy," "mousse-like" texture, this soybean-chickpea hummus had "maple-like undertones." No wonder: It was the only product in our lineup that lists sugar in its ingredients. Though it was high in protein, the soybeans made this hybrid hummus taste strange; some tasters speculated that it was "fermented."

Quick & Easy Rib Dinner

Simmering the ribs indoors then grilling them outdoors produces tender-chewy, flavorful ribs that are ready in about an hour.

BARBECUE DIE-HARDS KNOW THAT FOR REALLY GOOD RIBS, ONLY A lengthy stint on the grill or in the smoker will do, because the low, slow temperature works to break down the meat's collagen and render it incredibly tender. But a long spell on the grill isn't something we can tackle just anytime—we have to reserve a full Saturday or Sunday for the job. We wanted to know if there was a way to make deeply flavored, tender ribs in just an hour, for a casual weeknight dinner. Our plan was to jump-start their cooking indoors, so we could then finish them on the grill with a simple glaze—and a minimal amount of time spent standing on the patio holding a pair of tongs.

Fire up the grill for a summer supper, and most likely you'll be adding a few ears of corn to the grate for a super-easy side that goes well with everything from ribs to chicken breasts to fish. To gussy them up, most recipes simply swipe them with an herb-laced butter. But after it melts and drips off, all that's left behind are a few specks of green and a charred ear of corn. We set out to find the best way to cook corn on the grill so that it was not only tender and sweet, but also infused with rich, bright flavor.

GRILLED GLAZED BABY BACK RIBS

✔ **WHY THIS RECIPE WORKS:** Instead of spending hours tending a grill for flavorful, tender ribs, we started ours on the stovetop, then moved them outside. Boiling is an established rib-cooking shortcut, but we found this led to unevenly cooked ribs, so we turned down the heat and simmered them; the gentler heat kept the thinner ends from overcooking and becoming dry. Salting the water prevented them from losing too much of their pork flavor to the cooking liquid. Once they reached 195 degrees, we removed our ribs from the pot, applied a flavorful glaze, and tossed them on the grill, for tender-chewy ribs that were ready in a fraction of the time.

IT'S A WIDELY KNOWN TRUTH AMONG RIB AFICIONADOS that boiling a rack in water before grilling it is the most effective rib-cooking shortcut you can take. Precooked this way, the meat's tough collagen breaks down exponentially faster than it does when ribs are cooked according to the traditional barbecue method: from start to finish over a low, steady fire for several hours. That's because unlike air, water conducts heat extremely efficiently—about 25 times faster than air, according to research. It's also well-known that, unfortunately, this shortcut comes at a considerable cost, as boiling ribs is guaranteed to wash out rich pork flavor.

Such was the predicament we faced as we set out to develop a method for "weeknight" ribs—a recipe that we were pursuing because, as much as we love the smoky, super-tender results produced by hours of barbecuing, we simply don't have that kind of time (or patience) most nights of the week. All the same, we weren't willing to completely forgo flavor for the sake of speed. But we were willing to compromise some on tenderness—and even on barbecue smokiness—if it meant that we could have ribs any night of the week. Besides, who says that ribs have to be fall-off-the-bone tender? We like the meat to have

a little resistance. We set our sights on grilled ribs that were reasonably tender but still boasted some satisfying chew. Our ideal cooking time: about an hour.

Even though we weren't aiming for barbecue-tender results, we still needed to come up with a cooking method that tenderized the tough meat, so we started with a review of why barbecuing works so effectively. Like other tough cuts, ribs are full of collagen, the protein that holds meat fibers together and also holds muscle tissue to bone. As collagen heats up during cooking, it not only unravels, making the meat more tender, but it also slowly turns into gelatin. Since gelatin holds up to 10 times its weight in water, it helps keep some of the moisture in meat that would otherwise be lost during cooking. Slow, steady barbecuing maximizes the conversion of collagen into gelatin, since the meat lingers between 160 and 190 degrees—the so-called sweet spot for collagen breakdown. The longer the meat hovers in this zone (particularly around the 190-degree mark) the more of its collagen converts into gelatin.

We kept those tenets in mind as we surveyed our rib options and looked for the quickest-cooking cut we could get. Though meaty, spareribs, which are cut from near the pig's belly, are also gristly and tough and really best left for slow cooking. That also eliminated St. Louis–style ribs, which are just spareribs that have been trimmed of some meat and excess cartilage. Instead, we stocked up on baby back ribs—a slab that cooks faster because the ribs are smaller and come from the more tender loin area of the pig.

Shopping questions addressed, we looked into alternative moist-heat methods that would speed along the rib-cooking process but wouldn't wash away the pork's flavor. We thought that we might have some luck with the oven, as most of the "quick" rib recipes we came across called for wrapping the racks in aluminum foil and baking them before transferring them to the grill. The idea is that the ribs "steam" in their own exuded moisture—a method that should save time while saving flavor, too. It sounded promising, so we wrapped a pair of 2-pound racks (enough to feed at least four

GRILLED GLAZED BABY BACK RIBS

rib enthusiasts) in aluminum foil and baked them in a 325-degree oven until they reached 165 degrees, at which point it seemed reasonable to move them out to the grill to finish cooking. There, we unwrapped them, basted them with bottled barbecue sauce (we'd develop our own sauces later), and grilled them over a moderately hot fire until they hit the target doneness temperature—195 degrees at the thickest part—and had developed a nice lacquered crust.

Baking the foil-wrapped racks did hasten the cooking process as promised, and the results were pretty good: firm but not leathery, with decent charring. But the method hadn't been nearly the timesaver we were hoping for. Forty-five minutes of oven steaming had passed by the time the ribs reached 165 degrees, and they needed another solid hour of grilling time before they hit 195 degrees—not a feasible plan for a weeknight. Pressed for time (and out of other ideas), we reluctantly moved our operation to the stove. After all, we hadn't actually tried boiling a rack of ribs. Maybe we'd discover a way to make cooking them in water work.

This time, we cut the two rib racks in half, which allowed them to fit snugly in a large Dutch oven. Then we poured in just enough water to cover them (2½ quarts), cranked the dial to high, and set the lid in place. The cooking time difference was even more dramatic than we'd expected: Barely 10 minutes had ticked by before the thick end of the rack reached 165 degrees. Trouble was, the thin end was also cooking at a much faster rate and now registered 20 degrees more than the meaty section, and a discrepancy remained when we moved the racks out to the grill to finish cooking. By the time the thick portion reached 195 degrees, the slimmer end had blown by that target and hit 210 degrees, and its meat tasted predictably dry and stringy. And of course boiling the ribs had dulled their flavor.

Putting aside the flavor issue for a moment, we wondered if simmering the ribs would help prevent the thin sections of meat from overcooking since simmering occurs at around 200 degrees—much closer to the meat's target doneness temperature than boiling, which happens at 212 degrees. We brought another pot of water and ribs to a simmer, turned the dial to low, and let the pot bubble gently until the meaty portions reached 165 degrees, about 15 minutes. These ribs were considerably more tender from end to end than the boiled batch, and we quickly realized how significant that 12-degree temperature drop had been: Now the temperature difference between the two ends was about 10 degrees, and lowering the temperature cost us only another 5 minutes. Even better, starting the ribs in cold water and then simmering them made for more tender ribs: As the ribs heated gradually with the water, the meat had more time to break down the tough collagen, and because the meat simmered (rather than boiled), it spent longer in that ideal collagen-breakdown temperature range.

Now that the ribs were cooking quickly indoors, we moved out to the grill to see if we could speed up that leg of the process, too. The challenge was that the 165-degree ribs lost a good 20 degrees in their travels from the Dutch oven to the grill—and then cooled further every time we brushed on a coat of sauce during cooking. It occurred to us that the best approach would be to take full advantage of simmering and bring the racks to 195 degrees in the water, and then use the grill just to char them. Since we weren't going for barbecue, we didn't need lots of grilling time to infuse the meat with smoke, and briefly grilling the ribs probably wouldn't overcook the meat. Our expectations panned out: About 20 minutes of simmering plus roughly 20 minutes of searing produced ribs that were reasonably tender but pleasantly chewy and beautifully lacquered. We even managed to squeeze in a 10-minute rest after the ribs came off the grill and still keep the overall cooking time to about an hour.

Of course, cooking the ribs quickly wasn't much of a success if their flavor was subpar. We tried to use the cooking water to our advantage, "infusing" it with every addition we could think of: garlic, paprika, chiles,

REMOVING THE RIB MEMBRANE

1. At 1 end of rack, loosen edge of membrane with tip of paring knife or your fingernail.

2. Grab membrane with paper towel and pull slowly—it should come off in 1 piece. The membrane itself is very thin, so removing it should not expose rib bones.

soy sauce, chicken broth, onion powder, bacon, kombu (a seaweed known for its high glutamate content), and lots of salt. While none of those flavors penetrated beyond the ribs' exterior, the salt was surprisingly effective at offsetting the small loss of porky taste. We settled on 2 tablespoons for the 2½ quarts of cooking water, essentially cooking the ribs in a "brine."

That left just the sauce. The bottled stuff was out. In fact, since these ribs weren't barbecued, we saw no reason to limit ourselves to the usual tomato-based condiment. Instead, we paired no-cook ingredients that would color quickly over the fire: hoisin sauce and coconut milk, lime juice and ketchup, and orange marmalade and cider vinegar. We brushed these glazes over the racks before, during, and after grilling and made sure to rotate and flip the ribs as needed to ensure that they colored evenly.

As our tasters tore into these final batches of ribs, we couldn't decide which was more satisfying: the racks' meaty chew and nicely glazed char or the fact that we could easily pull off this recipe any night of the week.

Grilled Glazed Baby Back Ribs

SERVES 4 TO 6

Try one of the glaze recipes that follow, or use 1 cup of your favorite glaze or barbecue sauce.

- 2 tablespoons salt
- 2 (2-pound) racks baby back or loin back ribs, trimmed, membrane removed, and each rack cut in half
- 1 recipe glaze (recipes follow)

1. Dissolve salt in 2½ quarts water in Dutch oven; place ribs in pot so they are fully submerged. Bring to simmer over high heat. Reduce heat to low, cover, and cook at bare simmer until thickest part of ribs registers 195 degrees, 15 to 25 minutes. While ribs are simmering, set up grill. (If ribs come to temperature before grill is ready, leave in pot, covered, until ready to use.)

2A. FOR A CHARCOAL GRILL: Open bottom vent halfway. Light large chimney starter filled with charcoal briquettes (6 quarts). When top coals are partially covered with ash, pour evenly over grill. Set cooking grate in place, cover, and open lid vent halfway. Heat grill until hot, about 5 minutes.

2B. FOR A GAS GRILL: Turn all burners to high, cover, and heat grill until hot, about 15 minutes. Turn all burners to medium-high.

3. Clean and oil cooking grate. Remove ribs from pot and pat dry with paper towels. Brush both sides of ribs with ⅓ cup glaze. Grill ribs, uncovered, flipping and rotating as needed, until glaze is caramelized and charred in spots, 15 to 20 minutes, brushing with another ⅓ cup glaze halfway through cooking. Transfer ribs to cutting board, brush both sides with remaining glaze, tent loosely with aluminum foil, and let rest for 10 minutes. Cut ribs between bones to separate, and serve.

Hoisin-Coconut Glaze

MAKES ABOUT 1 CUP

- ⅔ cup hoisin sauce
- ⅓ cup canned coconut milk
- 3 tablespoons rice vinegar
- ¾ teaspoon pepper

Whisk all ingredients together in bowl.

Lime Glaze

MAKES ABOUT 1 CUP

- ⅔ cup lime juice (6 limes)
- ⅓ cup ketchup
- ¼ cup packed brown sugar
- 1 teaspoon salt

Whisk all ingredients together in bowl.

Spicy Marmalade Glaze

MAKES ABOUT 1 CUP

- ⅔ cup orange marmalade
- ⅓ cup cider vinegar
- 2 tablespoons hot sauce
- ¾ teaspoon salt

Whisk all ingredients together in bowl.

GRILLED CORN

✓ **WHY THIS RECIPE WORKS:** To infuse grilled corn with the flavor of herbed and spiced butters, we first charred the corn over a hot fire, then transferred it to a roasting pan full of flavored butter. Covering the pan with aluminum foil trapped the heat so the corn would continue to cook, while it also picked up the rich flavors of the butter. Shaking the pan a few times ensured that each ear was evenly coated.

A WHOLE YEAR GOES BY WHILE WE WAIT FOR THAT perfect matchup: fresh summer corn and the lick of the grill flame. Fire does something magical to the kernels, toasting them and deepening their natural sweetness. When it's corn season, we toss ears on the grill a couple of times a week, so we wanted to find a way to incorporate herbs, spices, and other seasonings with the usual smear of butter.

Whipping up a flavored butter is easy, but getting it to penetrate the corn is a different story: Simply slathering grilled corn with a compound butter fails to infuse flavor into the kernels. We'd have to apply the butter before or during cooking. We considered two methods of preparing the ears: entirely shucked or partially shucked (peeling away all but the inner layers of husk). We tried the latter first, mixing softened butter with fresh chopped basil, parsley, and grated lemon zest, and then smearing it onto the ears and reassembling the husks.

The result was one hot mess—literally. Once on the blazing fire, the butter leaked out of the husks and dripped—and dripped and dripped—into the grill until an inferno singed the entire setup.

As for the naked-ear method, we knew that to avoid flare-ups, we'd have to use a less aggressive fire. We smeared more basil butter onto a batch and set it on a moderate grill. No flare-ups—good. But the butter still trickled off before it could season the kernels, which picked up no char at all.

We took stock: To char the corn as quickly as possible, we would have to at least start it over a hot fire. We also had to find a way to keep the butter on the corn. For our next try, we brushed the kernels with vegetable oil—to prevent them from drying out—and placed the corn on the hot grill. After it charred, we scooped basil butter onto several pieces of foil and topped each dollop with a hot ear of corn. Using our faux flameproof "husks," we were able to wrap up each ear tightly—that butter was going nowhere. We returned the shrouded corn to the grill until we could hear the butter sizzling. Once we unwrapped the corn, we got an instant whiff of aromatic basil and lemon and toasty corn. But opening the hobo packs was about as enjoyable as holding a hot potato—with a bonus of molten butter running down our arm.

We switched gears, ditching the foil packets for a disposable pan. After searing the corn, we placed it in the pan along with the herb butter. We sealed the pan with foil, put it on the grill, and after a few minutes heard that sweet sizzling sound. To make sure that the corn was well coated, we shook the pan a few times—consider it our homage to Jiffy Pop.

For variations on the basil mixture, we stuck to "summery" flavors. One combo blended sweet honey and spicy red pepper flakes; one with smoky chipotles,

GRILLED CORN WITH BASIL AND LEMON BUTTER

cilantro, and tangy orange zest gave a nod to Latin flavors; a "barbecue" butter boasted bold Cajun flavors; and a final spicy butter was flavored with Old Bay seasoning and lemon. As it turns out, you can improve on hot, buttered grilled corn.

Grilled Corn with Flavored Butter

SERVES 4 TO 6

Use a disposable aluminum roasting pan that is at least 2¾ inches deep.

- 1 recipe flavored butter (recipes follow)
- 1 (13 by 9-inch) disposable aluminum roasting pan
- 8 ears corn, husks and silk removed
- 2 tablespoons vegetable oil
  Salt and pepper

1. Place flavored butter in disposable pan. Brush corn evenly with vegetable oil and season with salt and pepper to taste.

2. Grill corn over hot fire, turning occasionally, until lightly charred on all sides, 5 to 9 minutes. Transfer corn to pan and cover tightly with aluminum foil.

3. Place pan on grill and cook, shaking pan frequently, until butter is sizzling, about 3 minutes. Remove pan from grill and carefully remove foil, allowing steam to escape away from you. Serve corn, spooning any butter in pan over individual ears.

Basil and Lemon Butter

Serve with lemon wedges if desired.

- 6 tablespoons unsalted butter, softened
- 2 tablespoons minced fresh basil
- 1 tablespoon minced fresh parsley
- 1 teaspoon finely grated lemon zest
- ½ teaspoon salt
- ¼ teaspoon pepper

Combine all ingredients in small bowl.

NOTES FROM THE TEST KITCHEN

EASIEST-EVER WAY TO SHUCK CORN
Removing the husk and silk from an ear of corn is a chore (see Julia and Chris at work, above). And a "corn de-silker" gadget that we tested proved to be a bust. But now we've found a better way: A short stint in the microwave and a quick shake are all it takes to cleanly slide off the corn husk and silk. The cob will heat up a bit, but the kernels won't be cooked.

With a sharp chef's knife, cut off the stalk end of the cob just above the first row of kernels. Place 3 or 4 ears at a time on a plate and microwave for 30 to 60 seconds.

Hold each ear by the uncut end in 1 hand. Shake the ear up and down until the cob slips free, leaving behind the husk and silk.

Honey Butter

- **6 tablespoons unsalted butter, softened**
- **2 tablespoons honey**
- **½ teaspoon salt**
- **¼ teaspoon red pepper flakes**

Combine all ingredients in small bowl.

Latin-Spiced Butter

Serve with orange wedges if desired.

- **6 tablespoons unsalted butter, softened**
- **2 tablespoons minced fresh cilantro**
- **1 tablespoon minced fresh parsley**
- **1 teaspoon minced canned chipotle chile in adobo sauce**
- **½ teaspoon finely grated orange zest**
- **½ teaspoon salt**

Combine all ingredients in small bowl.

New Orleans "Barbecue" Butter

- **6 tablespoons unsalted butter, softened**
- **1 garlic clove, minced**
- **1 tablespoon Worcestershire sauce**
- **1 teaspoon tomato paste**
- **½ teaspoon minced fresh rosemary**
- **½ teaspoon minced fresh thyme**
- **½ teaspoon cayenne pepper**

Combine all ingredients in small bowl.

Spicy Old Bay Butter

Serve with lemon wedges if desired

- **6 tablespoons unsalted butter, softened**
- **1 tablespoon hot sauce**
- **1 tablespoon minced fresh parsley**
- **1½ teaspoons Old Bay seasoning**
- **1 teaspoon finely grated lemon zest**

Combine all ingredients in small bowl.

RATING CHARCOAL GRILLS

In search of a well-engineered, user-friendly charcoal grill that's up to any outdoor cooking task, we lined up seven models. Our battery of tests included burgers, sticky glazed beef satay, thick salmon fillets, and barbecued ribs. To check their height, we shut each grill's lid over a whole turkey; we monitored temperature retention; and we kept track of how easy the grills were to set up and to clean up. In the end, we found one grill that delivered on all fronts, but it comes with a high price tag. Fortunately, we also found a Best Buy that performed almost as well, although without all the bells and whistles. Brands are listed in order of preference. See AmericasTestKitchen.com for updates and complete testing results.

HIGHLY RECOMMENDED

WEBER Performer Platinum 22.5-Inch Charcoal Grill with Touch-n-Go Gas Ignition

MODEL: 1481001   PRICE: $349
GRATE: Steel, 363 sq in
GRILLING: ★★★
BBQ/HEAT RETENTION: ★★★
DESIGN: ★★★   ASSEMBLY: ★★★
CLEANUP: ★★★   CAPACITY: ★★★
CONSTRUCTION QUALITY: ★★★

FAVORITE FEATURES: Push-button gas ignition, rolling cart, charcoal storage bin, Tuck-Away lid holder, ash catcher, thermometer
COMMENTS: The convenience of gas plus the flavor of charcoal makes this grill a worthwhile (albeit pricey) upgrade from the basic model. Built around our favorite 22.5-inch Weber kettle is a roomy, easy-to-roll cart (much sturdier than the kettle's legs) with a pullout charcoal storage bin; a lid holder; and, most significant, a gas ignition system that lights coals with the push of a button—no chimney starter needed.

WEBER One-Touch Gold 22.5-Inch Charcoal Grill   [BEST BUY]

MODEL: 1351001   PRICE: $149
GRATE: Steel, 363 sq in
GRILLING: ★★★   BBQ/HEAT RETENTION: ★★★
DESIGN: ★★½   ASSEMBLY: ★★★   CLEANUP: ★★★
CAPACITY: ★★★   CONSTRUCTION QUALITY: ★★½
FAVORITE FEATURES: Ash catcher, thermometer (on newest model), hinged grate
COMMENTS: Weber's versatile, well-designed classic kettle is an expert griller and maintains heat well, and its well-positioned vents allow for excellent air control. The sturdy ash catcher makes cleanup a breeze, and it was the fastest and easiest model to assemble and move. We wish its tripod legs were sturdier and that the hinged portions of its grate were slightly larger.

RECOMMENDED

RÖSLE 24-Inch Charcoal Grill

MODEL: 25004   PRICE: $400
GRATE: Steel, 416 sq in
GRILLING: ★★★   BBQ/HEAT RETENTION: ★★
DESIGN: ★★½   ASSEMBLY: ★★★   CLEANUP: ★★★
CAPACITY: ★★★   CONSTRUCTION QUALITY: ★★★
FAVORITE FEATURES: Ash catcher, lever that marks vent position, hinged lid, thermometer
COMMENTS: This pricey kettle is sturdier than the Weber One-Touch and offers more cooking space, plus a few perks: a lever that marks vent positions and a hinged lid. But while it grilled well, its roomy interior lost heat relatively quickly. Its top vent sits in the center of the lid—a disadvantage for indirect cooking.

RECOMMENDED (cont.)

STOK Tower Charcoal Grill

MODEL: SCC0140   PRICE: $122
GRATE: Cast iron, 363 sq in
GRILLING: ★★★   BBQ/HEAT RETENTION: ★★½
DESIGN: ★★   ASSEMBLY: ★★   CLEANUP: ★★
CAPACITY: ★★   CONSTRUCTION QUALITY: ★★
FAVORITE FEATURES: Cast-iron grate, built-in chimney starter, thermometer

COMMENTS: Its cast-iron grate is just as big as the Weber's (and seared beautifully), but everything else about this inexpensive kettle is small—from its footprint to the space above and below the grates. Consequently, it holds heat well but struggles with indirect cooking since there is little room for a cooler zone. We appreciated its built-in chimney starter.

RECOMMENDED WITH RESERVATIONS

BRINKMANN Trailmaster Limited Edition Grill and Smoker

MODEL: 855-6305-S   PRICE: $299
GRATE: Steel, 938 sq in
GRILLING: ★★
BBQ/HEAT RETENTION: ★★
DESIGN: ★½   ASSEMBLY: ★
CLEANUP: ★   CAPACITY: ★★
CONSTRUCTION QUALITY: ★★★
FAVORITE FEATURE: Small firebox for smoking, thermometer
COMMENTS: This grill-smoker combo boasts plenty of cooking surface (including a separate firebox for smoking), but since opening the lid uncovered only part of that space, visibility was limited and smoke blew into our eyes. Without an ash catcher, shoveling is the only option. Also, it's a big, heavy beast: Moving it was a chore, and storing it was a challenge.

NOT RECOMMENDED

CHAR-BROIL 30-Inch Charcoal Grill

MODEL: 12301672   PRICE: $199
GRATE: Cast iron, 504 sq in
GRILLING: ★★½
BBQ/HEAT RETENTION: ½
DESIGN: ★★   ASSEMBLY: ½   CLEANUP: ★★
CAPACITY: ★★★   CONSTRUCTION QUALITY: ★
FAVORITE FEATURES: Crank for adjusting coal height, rolling cart, cast-iron grate, flip-up side tables, thermometer, warming shelf
COMMENTS: This grill was a heartbreaker. Though outfitted with great features its cheap construction defeated it. Paper-thin walls and an ill-fitting lid leaked heat (ribs were not finished after 4 hours). Assembly took hours. When it rolled, it rattled horribly.

Grilled & Glazed

To speed browning and help the glaze adhere, we first sprinkle the chicken breasts with a surprisingly simple ingredient.

LIKE A LOT OF COOKS, AT HOME WE TURN TO LEAN, QUICK-COOKING cuts of meat like pork tenderloin and boneless chicken breasts again and again. Grilling these mild-flavored cuts is quick and convenient and can boost the flavor, but the grill can also render the meat dry. We were in search of the right way to grill pork tenderloin and chicken breasts so they came off the grill tender and juicy. In addition, we wanted to come up with a few glazes to add even more flavor.

Starting with pork tenderloin, we'd address the shape of this roast—with a thin end and a thicker end, getting the meat to cook evenly can be a challenge. And the same goes for boneless, skinless chicken breasts. Their uneven shape, coupled with the absence of skin to protect the meat from the hot fire, can pose a host of problems for the outdoor cook. As for the glazes, we've most often seen fruit-based glazes, but we wanted a change of pace here—and we wanted them to be easy, so we decided to try savory glazes, spiked with pantry powerhouse ingredients like miso, coconut milk, and hoisin sauce. Join us as we grill and glaze our way to some new weeknight options.

GRILLED GLAZED PORK TENDERLOIN ROAST

GRILLED GLAZED PORK TENDERLOIN ROAST

✓ **WHY THIS RECIPE WORKS:** To solve the problem of the end of the tenderloin cooking faster than the thicker head and also to create a more presentation-worthy cut, we tied two tenderloins together, making a larger roast. Brining and then cooking partially over indirect heat ensured maximum retained juices, and scraping the insides of the tenderloins with a fork helped them stick together after cooking. Finally, we put together a few potent protein-rich glazes that undergo flavorful Maillard browning on the grill.

PORK TENDERLOIN IS WONDERFULLY TENDER AND versatile, it doesn't require much prep, and it's relatively inexpensive. But alas, this cut also comes with a certain set of challenges. Because tenderloin is so incredibly lean, it's highly susceptible to drying out during cooking. Then there's its ungainly tapered shape: By the time the large end hits a perfect medium (140 degrees), the skinnier tail is guaranteed to be overdone. And while our favorite way to prepare mild meats like tenderloin is grilling (to develop a rich, meaty crust), extreme heat and natural fluctuations in temperature make this hard to do well. We wanted to find a way to make grilled pork tenderloin a bit more foolproof and at the same time elevate this cut above its "casual supper" status to something more special and elegant. Into the kitchen—and out to the grill—we went.

Keeping meat of any kind juicy on the grill is a perennial challenge. In the test kitchen, we have a couple of tricks for addressing the problem, namely salting and brining. Both techniques introduce salt into the flesh, where it tenderizes the meat and increases water retention. Using our preferred type of pork, unenhanced (or natural)—meaning that it has not been injected with a solution of water, salt, and sodium phosphate—we ran a side-by-side test in which we salted or brined a few tenderloins, slicked them with oil, and grilled them. Tasters reported that while both options proved juicier

and more evenly seasoned than an untreated control, the brined samples were the most succulent. Settling on brining, we moved on to another variable that affects juiciness: grill setup.

Many pork tenderloin recipes call for grilling the meat directly over a hot fire the entire time. The result? A well-browned exterior with a thick band of dry, overcooked meat below its surface—no thanks. A better approach, we've found, is to employ a combination high-low method: High heat provides great browning—which means great flavor—and low heat cooks meat evenly. And recently, we've favored cooking first over low heat followed by searing over high heat. During its initial stay on the cooler side of the grill, the meat's surface warms and dries, making for fast, efficient browning (and therefore precluding overcooking) when it hits the hotter part of the grate. Sure enough, when we gave this approach a try, we produced meat with rosy interiors surrounded by thin, flavorful crusts—at least at the thick ends. Unsurprisingly, the thin, tapered ends of the tenderloins (we were cooking two in order to serve six guests) were terribly overdone.

There was nothing we could do to the grill setup to make the unevenly shaped meat cook evenly, so what about altering the tenderloins themselves? Assuming the role of mad butcher, we pounded and portioned untold samples in search of a more uniform shape. Flattening the thicker end of the roast certainly made for more even cooking, but it also turned the cut into what looked like a gigantic, malformed pork chop. Slicing the tenderloin into medallions produced an awkward group of scallop-size pieces that were fussy to grill.

After a long, unsuccessful afternoon, a light bulb went on when we stood before the last two raw tenderloins on the cutting board: Why not tie them together? If we stacked the tenderloins the way that shoes come packed in a box—with the thick end of one nestled against the thin end of the other—we'd produce a single, evenly shaped roast. We gave it a shot, fastening together our brined double-wide roast with lengths of kitchen twine and brushing it with oil before heading out to the hot grill. About 35 minutes later, we had a piece of meat that was perfectly cooked from one end to the other. This

FUSION COOKING: TURNING TWO TENDERLOINS INTO ONE

To get around the usual problems with grilling pork tenderloin, we "fused" two together and cooked them as a single roast.

ROUGH UP
Scrape the flat sides of each tenderloin with a fork until the surface is covered with shallow grooves. This releases sticky proteins that will act as "glue."

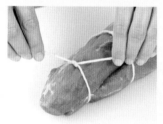

TIE TOGETHER
Arrange the tenderloins with the scraped sides touching and the thick end of one nestled against the thin end of the other. Tie the tenderloins together.

larger roast took longer to come up to temperature, but the added grill time was a boon to taste: More time over the fire meant more smoky grill flavor.

These successes aside, there was still an obstacle in the way. When we carved our impressive-looking roast, each slice inevitably flopped apart into two pieces. While this wasn't a deal breaker, we were eager to see if we could establish a more permanent bond between the tenderloins.

Trying to get meat to stick together might sound unorthodox, but it's something that happens naturally all the time, at least with ground meat. In sausages, burgers, meatballs, and meatloaf, tiny individual pieces of protein fuse together to form a cohesive whole. We weren't working with ground meat, but maybe we could use it as inspiration.

It turns out that any time meat is damaged (such as during grinding, slicing, or even pounding), sticky proteins are released. The proteins' gluey texture is what makes it possible to form a cohesive burger from nothing but ground beef. If salt is added—as it is to make

sausage—the proteins become even tackier. When heated, the protein sets into a solid structure, effectively binding the meat together. To see if we could use this information for our tenderloins, we tried roughing up their surfaces in a variety of ways: lightly whacking them with a meat mallet, scraping them with a fork, and rubbing them vigorously with coarse salt. We tested these methods before brining, after brining, and both before and after brining.

The key to getting two tenderloins to bind together? A few simple scrapes of a fork along the length of each one before brining, followed by a very thorough drying after brining. The scrapes, acting much like grinding, released plenty of sticky proteins, which the salty brine made even stickier. Finally, thorough drying ensured that moisture wouldn't interfere with this bond during cooking (the sticky mixture continued to exude from the meat even after we blotted off moisture). The technique is simple and, while not perfect (some slices had better cling than others), it provided a platter of attractive, mostly intact slices. Hurdle cleared, we turned our attention to flavoring the roast.

We wanted to dress up our beautifully browned pork tenderloin roast, and a bold, burnished glaze seemed like the ideal choice. Most glazes contain sugar, which caramelizes when exposed to heat, deepening flavor. But we wanted to add still more complexity—even meatiness. And we knew how to do it: by including glutamate-rich ingredients that enhance savory flavor. With this in mind, we combined glutamate-rich miso with sugar, mustard, mirin, and ginger. For our next version, we created a sweet and spicy glaze that benefited from the glutamates found in sweet and tangy hoisin sauce. And a satay-inspired version containing brown sugar, coconut milk, curry paste, and lime juice got its glutamate infusion from fish sauce. When we tried out these new glazes on the pork, we were surprised by how much more flavor—and yes, meatiness—they contributed. It turns out that pork has a high concentration of nucleotides. When glutamates and nucleotides are combined, these compounds have a synergistic effect that magnifies meaty, savory flavor significantly more than glutamates alone do.

The only thing left was to refine how we applied the glaze. After slowly grilling the roast on the cooler side of the grill, we slid it to the hotter side to brown. We then glazed one side at a time, allowing the glaze to char before repeating the process with the other three sides. We also reserved some glaze to add an extra blast of flavor at the table. Time to get the party started.

Grilled Glazed Pork Tenderloin Roast

SERVES 6

Since brining is a key step in having the two tenderloins stick together, we don't recommend using enhanced pork in this recipe.

- 2 (1-pound) pork tenderloins, trimmed
  Salt and pepper
  Vegetable oil
- 1 recipe glaze (recipes follow)

1. Lay tenderloins on cutting board, flat side (side opposite where silverskin was) up. Holding thick end of 1 tenderloin with paper towels and using dinner fork, scrape flat side lengthwise from end to end 5 times, until surface is completely covered with shallow grooves. Repeat with second tenderloin. Dissolve 3 tablespoons salt in 1½ quarts cold water in large container. Submerge tenderloins in brine and let stand at room temperature for 1 hour.

2. Remove tenderloins from brine and pat completely dry with paper towels. Lay 1 tenderloin, scraped side up, on cutting board and lay second tenderloin, scraped side down, on top so that thick end of 1 tenderloin matches up with thin end of other. Spray five 14-inch lengths of kitchen twine thoroughly with vegetable oil spray; evenly space twine underneath tenderloins and tie. Brush roast with vegetable oil and season with pepper. Transfer ⅓ cup glaze to bowl for grilling; reserve remaining glaze for serving.

3A. FOR A CHARCOAL GRILL: Open bottom vent completely. Light large chimney starter filled with charcoal briquettes (6 quarts). When top coals are partially covered with ash, pour into steeply banked pile against side of grill. Set cooking grate in place, cover, and open lid vent completely. Heat grill until hot, about 5 minutes.

3B. FOR A GAS GRILL: Turn all burners to high, cover, and heat grill until hot, about 15 minutes. Leave primary burner on high and turn off other burner(s).

4. Clean and oil cooking grate. Place roast on cooler side of grill, cover, and cook until meat registers 115 degrees, 22 to 28 minutes, flipping and rotating halfway through cooking.

5. Slide roast to hotter side of grill and cook until lightly browned on all sides, 4 to 6 minutes. Brush top of roast with about 1 tablespoon glaze and grill, glaze side down, until glaze begins to char, 2 to 3 minutes; repeat

glazing and grilling with remaining 3 sides of roast, until meat registers 140 degrees.

6. Transfer roast to carving board, tent loosely with aluminum foil, and let rest for 10 minutes. Carefully remove twine and slice roast into ½-inch-thick slices. Serve with remaining glaze.

Miso Glaze

MAKES ABOUT ¾ CUP

3	tablespoons sake
3	tablespoons mirin
⅓	cup white miso paste
¼	cup sugar
2	teaspoons Dijon mustard
1	teaspoon rice vinegar
¼	teaspoon grated fresh ginger
¼	teaspoon toasted sesame oil

Bring sake and mirin to boil in small saucepan over medium heat. Whisk in miso and sugar until smooth, about 30 seconds. Remove pan from heat and continue to whisk until sugar is dissolved, about 1 minute. Whisk in mustard, vinegar, ginger, and sesame oil until smooth.

Sweet and Spicy Hoisin Glaze

MAKES ABOUT ¾ CUP

1	teaspoon vegetable oil
3	garlic cloves, minced
1	teaspoon grated fresh ginger
½	teaspoon red pepper flakes
½	cup hoisin sauce
2	tablespoons soy sauce
1	tablespoon rice vinegar

Heat oil in small saucepan over medium heat until shimmering. Add garlic, ginger, and pepper flakes; cook until fragrant, about 30 seconds. Whisk in hoisin and soy sauce until smooth. Remove pan from heat and stir in vinegar.

Satay Glaze

MAKES ABOUT ¾ CUP

1	teaspoon vegetable oil
1	tablespoon red curry paste
2	garlic cloves, minced
½	teaspoon grated fresh ginger
½	cup canned coconut milk
¼	cup packed dark brown sugar
2	tablespoons peanut butter
1	tablespoon lime juice
2½	teaspoons fish sauce

Heat oil in small saucepan over medium heat until shimmering. Add curry paste, garlic, and ginger; cook, stirring constantly, until fragrant, about 1 minute. Whisk in coconut milk and sugar and bring to simmer. Whisk in peanut butter until smooth. Remove pan from heat and whisk in lime juice and fish sauce.

GRILLED GLAZED CHICKEN BREASTS

✔ **WHY THIS RECIPE WORKS:** To produce great grilled flavor and glaze the meat in a relatively short period of time, we brined the meat while the grill heats to season it and keep it moist during cooking. We dusted the chicken with milk powder to hasten the Maillard reaction and provide a surface for the glaze to adhere to. For a savory glaze with balanced flavor, we used a small amount of corn syrup, which is less sweet than other sweeteners, to provide viscosity but not a lot of sweetness.

THROWING A FEW BONELESS, SKINLESS CHICKEN breasts on the grill and painting them with barbecue sauce always sounds like a good idea. This lean cut is available everywhere, it cooks fast, and it makes a light, simple meal. The trouble is that the results are usually flawed. Because these disrobed specimens cook in a flash over coals, it's hard to get chicken that not only tastes grilled but also has a good glaze without overcooking it. Here's the dilemma: If you wait to apply the glaze until the meat is browned with grill marks, it's usually dry and leathery by the time you've lacquered on a few layers. (And you need a few layers to build anything more than a superficial skim of sauce.) But if you apply the glaze too soon, you don't give the chicken a chance to brown, a flavor boost that this bland cut badly needs. Plus the sugary glaze is liable to burn before the chicken cooks through.

But the ease of throwing boneless, skinless breasts on the grill is too enticing to pass up. We decided to fiddle with the approach until we got it right: tender, juicy chicken with the smoky taste of the grill, glistening with a thick coating of glaze. While we were at it, we wanted to create glazes specifically designed to accentuate, not overwhelm, this lean cut's delicate flavors.

Our first step was to brine the meat. We knew that a 30-minute saltwater soak would help keep the chicken juicy and well-seasoned and could be accomplished while the grill was heating. We also opted for a two-level fire, which means that we piled two-thirds of the coals on one side of the kettle and just one-third on the other side. This would allow us to sear the breasts over the coals and then move them to the cooler side to avoid burning when we applied the glaze.

Our real challenge was to figure out how to speed up browning, also known as the Maillard reaction, and the consequent formation of all those new flavor compounds that help meat taste rich and complex. If the chicken browned faster, it would leave us more time to build a thick glaze that would add even more flavor. Our first thought was to enlist the aid of starch in absorbing some of the moisture on the exterior of the meat that normally would need to burn off before much browning could occur. First we tried dredging the breasts in flour, but this made them bready. Next we tried cornstarch, but this approach turned the breasts gummy. A technique we have employed in pan-searing chicken breasts—creating an artificial "skin" using a paste of cornstarch, flour, and melted butter—had better results. The starches, which break down into sugars, and butter proteins helped achieve a browned surface more quickly, and the porous surface readily held a glaze. Unfortunately, though, the chicken still tasted more breaded than grilled.

Switching gears, we tried rubbing the surface of the chicken with baking soda. Baking soda increases the pH of the chicken, making it more alkaline, which in turn speeds up the Maillard reaction. Alas, while this did speed up browning, even small amounts left behind a mild soapy aftertaste.

We were unsure of what to do next. But then we remembered a really unlikely sounding test that a colleague tried when attempting to expedite the browning of pork chops—dredging the meat in nonfat dry milk powder. While this strange coating did brown the meat more quickly, it made the chops taste too sweet. But might it work for browning chicken? It was worth a try. After lightly dusting the breasts with milk powder (½ teaspoon per breast) and lightly spraying them with

GRILLED GLAZED BONELESS, SKINLESS CHICKEN BREASTS

vegetable oil spray to help ensure that the powder stuck, we threw them on the grill. We were thrilled when the chicken was lightly browned and had nice grill marks in less than 2 minutes, or about half the time of our most successful previous tests. Why was milk powder so effective? It turns out that dry milk contains about 25 percent protein. But it also contains about 50 percent lactose, a so-called reducing sugar. And the Maillard reaction takes place only after large proteins break down into amino acids and react with certain types of sugars—reducing sugars like glucose, fructose, and lactose. In sum, milk powder contained just the two components that we needed to speed things up.

But that wasn't the only reason milk powder was so successful in quickly triggering browning. Like starch, it's a dry substance that absorbs the excess moisture on the meat. This is helpful because moisture keeps the temperature too low for significant browning to take place until the wetness evaporates. There was yet one more benefit to using the milk powder: It created a thin, tacky surface that was perfect for holding on to the glaze. And now, with expedited browning in place, we had time to thoroughly lacquer our chicken with glaze by applying four solid coats before the chicken finished cooking.

Next it was time to focus on perfecting the glaze itself. We started with flavor. Since we knew that we wanted to limit the amount of sweetness so as not to overpower the mild flavor of the chicken, we began by testing a host of ingredients that would be thick enough to serve as a clingy base but weren't sugary. We settled on a diverse group that included hoisin sauce, mustard, and coconut milk. Then, to add balance and complexity, we introduced acidity in the form of citrus juice or vinegar, as well as a healthy dose of spices and aromatics, like red curry paste, fresh ginger, and spicy Sriracha sauce.

Our next step was to add a sweet (but not too sweet) element, which would provide further balance, promote browning, and give even more of a sticky cling to the glaze. Sweeteners like maple syrup, honey, brown sugar,

and fruit jams made the glazes saccharine. Corn syrup, which is about half as sweet as the other sweeteners, worked far better, giving the glaze a goodly amount of stickiness while keeping the sweetness level under control. Two to 3 tablespoons, depending on the other ingredients, was just the right amount.

But all was not perfect: The glazes still had a tendency to become too loose when applied to the hot chicken after it browned. Whisking in a teaspoon of cornstarch helped.

At this point we were feeling pretty good. But many tasters wanted an even thicker glaze. This time we looked to adjust our cooking technique. The fix? We switched up the point at which we applied the glaze. Instead of brushing it on right before flipping the chicken, we began to apply the glaze immediately after it was flipped. This meant that less glaze stuck to the grill—and the glaze applied to the top of the chicken had time to dry out and cling. The result? Chicken breasts robed in a thick, lacquered glaze. Dinner was ready.

Grilled Glazed Boneless, Skinless Chicken Breasts

SERVES 4

¼ cup salt

¼ cup sugar

4 (6- to 8-ounce) boneless, skinless chicken breasts, trimmed

2 teaspoons nonfat dry milk powder

¼ teaspoon pepper

Vegetable oil spray

1 recipe glaze (recipes follow)

1. Dissolve salt and sugar in 1½ quarts cold water. Submerge chicken in brine, cover, and refrigerate for at least 30 minutes or up to 1 hour. Remove chicken from brine and pat dry with paper towels. Combine milk powder and pepper in bowl.

2A. FOR A CHARCOAL GRILL: Open bottom vent completely. Light large chimney starter mounded with charcoal briquettes (7 quarts). When top coals are partially covered with ash, pour two-thirds evenly over half of grill, then pour remaining coals over other half of grill. Set cooking grate in place, cover, and open lid vent completely. Heat grill until hot, about 5 minutes.

2B. FOR A GAS GRILL: Turn all burners to high, cover, and heat grill until hot, about 15 minutes. Leave primary burner on high and turn other burner(s) to medium-high.

3. Clean and oil cooking grate. Sprinkle half of milk powder mixture over 1 side of chicken. Lightly spray coated side of chicken with oil spray until milk powder is moistened. Flip chicken and sprinkle remaining milk powder mixture over second side. Lightly spray with oil spray.

4. Place chicken, skinned side down, on hotter side of grill and cook until browned on first side, 2 to 2½ minutes. Flip chicken, brush with 2 tablespoons glaze, and cook until browned on second side, 2 to 2½ minutes. Flip chicken, move to cooler side of grill, brush with 2 tablespoons glaze, and cook for 2 minutes. Repeat flipping and brushing 2 more times, cooking for 2 minutes on each side. Flip chicken, brush with remaining glaze, and cook until chicken registers 160 degrees, 1 to 3 minutes. Transfer chicken to plate and let rest for 5 minutes before serving.

Spicy Hoisin Glaze

MAKES ABOUT ⅔ CUP

For a spicier glaze use the larger amount of Sriracha.

- 2 tablespoons rice vinegar
- 1 teaspoon cornstarch
- ⅓ cup hoisin sauce
- 2 tablespoons light corn syrup
- 1–2 tablespoons Sriracha sauce
- 1 teaspoon grated fresh ginger
- ¼ teaspoon five-spice powder

Whisk vinegar and cornstarch together in small saucepan until cornstarch has dissolved. Whisk in hoisin, corn syrup, Sriracha, ginger, and five-spice powder. Bring mixture to boil over high heat. Cook, stirring constantly, until thickened, about 1 minute. Transfer glaze to bowl.

Honey Mustard Glaze

MAKES ABOUT ⅔ CUP

- 2 tablespoons cider vinegar
- 1 teaspoon cornstarch
- 3 tablespoons Dijon mustard
- 3 tablespoons honey
- 2 tablespoons corn syrup
- 1 garlic clove, minced
- ¼ teaspoon ground fennel seeds

Whisk vinegar and cornstarch together in small saucepan until cornstarch has dissolved. Whisk in mustard, honey, corn syrup, garlic, and fennel seeds. Bring mixture to boil over high heat. Cook, stirring constantly, until thickened, about 1 minute. Transfer glaze to bowl.

NOTES FROM THE TEST KITCHEN

WHERE GRILLING AND GLAZING GO WRONG

Here's what usually happens when you try for a deep sear and a thick glaze.

NICE GLAZE, DRY MEAT

If you wait to apply the sauce, you'll get good grill marks and a thick glaze but dry, overcooked chicken.

BURNT GLAZE, BLAND MEAT

Layer on glaze from the get-go and it tends to burn. The chicken may be moist, but it lacks flavorful browning.

THE POWER OF MILK POWDER

To make sure our chicken breasts could be both browned and glazed in the time it took the meat to cook, we had to accelerate browning. A surprising ingredient—milk powder—was the solution. Milk powder contains both protein and so-called reducing sugar (in this case, lactose), the keys to the Maillard reaction, or the chemical reaction that causes browning. Faster browning gave us more time to layer on the glaze.

Coconut-Curry Glaze

MAKES ABOUT ⅔ CUP

2	tablespoons lime juice
1½	teaspoons cornstarch
⅓	cup canned coconut milk
3	tablespoons corn syrup
1	tablespoon fish sauce
1	tablespoon red curry paste
1	teaspoon grated fresh ginger
¼	teaspoon ground coriander

Whisk lime juice and cornstarch together in small saucepan until cornstarch has dissolved. Whisk in coconut milk, corn syrup, fish sauce, curry paste, ginger, and coriander seeds. Bring mixture to boil over high heat. Cook, stirring constantly, until thickened, about 1 minute. Transfer glaze to bowl.

Miso-Sesame Glaze

MAKES ABOUT ⅔ CUP

3	tablespoons rice vinegar
1	teaspoon cornstarch
3	tablespoons white miso paste
2	tablespoons corn syrup
1	tablespoon sesame oil
2	teaspoons grated fresh ginger
¼	teaspoon ground coriander

Whisk vinegar and cornstarch together in small saucepan until cornstarch has dissolved. Whisk in miso, corn syrup, sesame oil, ginger, and coriander. Bring mixture to boil over high heat. Cook, stirring constantly, until thickened, about 1 minute. Transfer glaze to bowl.

Molasses-Coffee Glaze

MAKES ABOUT ⅔ CUP

3	tablespoons balsamic vinegar
1½	teaspoons cornstarch
¼	cup molasses
2	tablespoons corn syrup
2	tablespoons brewed coffee
1	garlic clove, minced
¼	teaspoon ground allspice

Whisk vinegar and cornstarch together in small saucepan until cornstarch has dissolved. Whisk in molasses, corn syrup, coffee, garlic, and allspice. Bring mixture to boil over high heat. Cook, stirring constantly, until thickened, about 1 minute. Transfer glaze to bowl.

RATING INEXPENSIVE CHEF'S KNIVES

One chef's knife has been a champ in our kitchen for nearly two decades. During the past 20 years, we've conducted five chef's knife evaluations to find out what makes a great cheap knife. Those tests have covered dozens of blades in many styles. And at the end of every test, we've told the same story: One bargain knife, the $27 Victorinox Fibrox, has typically trounced the competition—including knives costing 10 times its price tag. Every so often we revisit the category and this time we sought out 8-inch chef's knives (the most all-purpose size) and capped our budget at $50. Ten models met our criteria—including a new Victorinox knife called the Swiss Classic that the company considers to be the "consumer" version of the Fibrox, a model that will eventually be available only commercially. We enlisted six testers, male and female and with varying hand sizes and kitchen abilities, and got each of them to spend weeks hacking, dicing, and chopping their way through whole chickens, butternut squashes, onions, and bunches of parsley. We are always looking for a sharp yet agile blade that feels comfortable and secure in our hands. By the time we wrapped up testing, we'd found one standout favorite and a couple of other knives that passed muster. Once again, it was the Victorinox Fibrox that effortlessly ascended to the top spot for its exceptional cutting ability and a grip that all testers found particularly comfortable. Brands are listed in order of preference. See AmericasTestKitchen.com for updates and complete testing results.

HIGHLY RECOMMENDED

VICTORINOX Swiss Army Fibrox 8-Inch Chef's Knife
MODEL: 47520 **PRICE:** $27.21
BLADE ANGLE: 15 degrees **STEEL TYPE:** x50CrMoV15
BLADE DESIGN ★★★ **HANDLE** ★★★
KITCHEN TASKS ★★★ **EDGE RETENTION** ★★★
COMMENTS: Still the best—and a bargain—after 20 years, this knife's "super-sharp" blade was "silent" and "smooth," even as it cut through tough squash, and it retained its edge after weeks of testing. Its textured grip felt secure for a wide range of hand sizes, and thanks to its gently rounded edges and the soft, hand-polished top spine, we could comfortably choke up on the knife for "precise," "effortless" cuts.

RECOMMENDED

VICTORINOX Swiss Army Swiss Classic 8-Inch Chef's Knife
MODEL: 6.8063.20US1 **PRICE:** $37.62
BLADE ANGLE: 15 degrees **STEEL TYPE:** x50CrMoV15
BLADE DESIGN ★★★ **HANDLE** ★★
KITCHEN TASKS ★★★ **EDGE RETENTION** ★★★
COMMENTS: Marketed as the consumer version of the Fibrox with an identical blade (and a higher price tag), this sibling made equally sharp, agile cuts. The downside was the handle, which exchanges the textured grip for a "hard," "slippery" one with a "bigger belly" curve and an indented ridge. Testers complained that their hands were "pulled open wider" and that they were forced to grip "too far back," resulting in less comfort and control.

MERCER Renaissance Forged Riveted 8-Inch Chef's Knife
MODEL: M23510 **PRICE:** $31.99
BLADE ANGLE: 15 degrees **STEEL TYPE:** x50CrMoV15
BLADE DESIGN ★★½ **HANDLE** ★★
KITCHEN TASKS ★★½ **EDGE RETENTION** ★★
COMMENTS: This knife's blade was "sturdy" and "plenty sharp"—splitting bone is "no problem," one tester said—and its curve "rocked well." However, we deducted minor points for a semisharp spine that dug into a few testers' hands. Some testers liked that the "heavier handle" felt "solid" and "nicely balanced"; others did not prefer the "heft."

RECOMMENDED WITH RESERVATIONS

MESSERMEISTER Four Seasons 8-Inch Chef's Knife
MODEL: 5025-8 **PRICE:** $42
BLADE ANGLE: 20 degrees **STEEL TYPE:** x55CrMoV14
BLADE DESIGN ★½ **HANDLE** ★★
KITCHEN TASKS ★★ **EDGE RETENTION** ★★
COMMENTS: "Chunky" and "fat" is how testers described this blade—the thickest and broadest that we tested. As a result, it "wedged" through squash instead of slicing it, but it made for a "solid butchering knife." Its "sharp" spine drew some complaints from testers using the pinch grip to choke up, but the handle was "comfortable."

NOT RECOMMENDED

SCHMIDT BROTHERS Cutlery Bonded Teak Series 8-Inch Chef Knife
MODEL: SBOCH08 **PRICE:** $49.95
BLADE ANGLE: 19 degrees **STEEL TYPE:** x50CrMoV15
BLADE DESIGN ★½ **HANDLE** ★½
KITCHEN TASKS ★½ **EDGE RETENTION** ★★
COMMENTS: The "maneuverable" blade made "quick work" of a whole chicken, but its "dull" edge sprayed onion juice and got stuck, marooned halfway down a butternut squash. Testers wanted to choke up on the knife, but its sharp spine forced them to hold it farther back on the "rough wood" handle, decreasing leverage. Larger-handed testers struck their knuckles on the cutting board due to the lack of clearance underneath the handle.

HENCKELS INTERNATIONAL Classic 8-Inch Chef's Knife
MODEL: 31161-201 **PRICE:** $49.95
BLADE ANGLE: 17.5 degrees **STEEL TYPE:** x55CrMoV15
BLADE DESIGN ★½ **HANDLE** ★
KITCHEN TASKS ★½ **EDGE RETENTION** ★★½
COMMENTS: This knife's squared-off, "uncomfortable" handle dug into testers' palms, the blade's spine into their fingers. Though the blade was "reasonably sharp," the last bit of edge near the handle was left unsharpened (the bolster blocks sharpening); as a result, we lost a centimeter of cutting real estate.

Easy Summer Supper

Executive chef Keith Dresser finds that the easiest path to tender, flavorful beets is halving and braising them in a small amount of water.

FOR AN EASY SUMMER SUPPER, WE OFTEN TURN TO THE GRILL. Beyond quick and convenient burgers and chicken breasts, we'd had our eye on developing a recipe for grilled whole chicken—one with rich, bone-in flavor—but we wanted to keep it easy and relatively quick-cooking. But cooking a whole chicken on the grill can be challenging. The bulky shape can make even cooking elusive, and the fatty skin, while delicious when crisped and charred, can cause flare-ups. In addition to finding the best way to grill our chicken, we also wanted to add flavor to the meat. We've seen dozens of recipes for rosemary lemon chicken, but few deliver flavor that's more than skin deep. We wanted bright citrus flavor and woodsy rosemary notes straight down to the bone.

Alongside our chicken, we wanted a side dish that wasn't the same old green beans or potatoes. Beets came to mind and we needed to find the best way to cook this vegetable that wouldn't be time-consuming—the usual method, roasting, can take upward of 90 minutes. We also wanted to incorporate complementary flavors into this sweet, earthy vegetable. Together these recipes make a summer supper easy enough for the weeknight table and elegant enough for entertaining.

GRILLED LEMON CHICKEN

✔ **WHY THIS RECIPE WORKS:** Grilling a whole chicken can be a recipe for disaster thanks to flare-ups caused by the fatty skin. Usually recipes address this problem with a two-stage grilling process: low heat to gently render the fat and then high heat to char the meat and crisp the skin. We found a much faster way to solve the problem: We skipped the rendering step by removing the skin before grilling. To ensure that our chicken got plenty of color and char without overcooking, we butterflied it so it was an even thickness, then we brined it in a sugar and salt solution for juicy meat. For flavor that penetrated all the way to the bone, we cut deep channels in the meat and rubbed it with lemon and herb seasoning. Basting the chicken with a flavorful butter sauce and tenting it with aluminum foil partway through cooking kept the surface moist and tender as it cooked. We quickly charred lemon wedges to squeeze over each portion before serving for even more moisture and flavor.

THE EMBARRASSING TRUTH IS THAT GRILLING A WHOLE chicken brings out our insecurities. The problem is that you can't treat a chicken like a steak and simply throw it over a blazing fire. The fat in the skin will melt and rain onto the coals, sending up flames that carbonize the exterior before the interior is cooked. For this reason, most grilled chicken recipes call for variable heat: low and slow first—to gently render fat and initiate cooking—and then high heat to finish cooking, crisp the skin, and get that enticing char.

Determined to vanquish our combustible nemesis once and for all, we headed for the grill. We would start with a half fire, made by pouring all the lit coals over one side of the grill for intense heat and leaving the other side empty for indirect cooking—in other words, a prime whole-chicken-cooking environment. We would keep grilling until we could consistently produce moist, well-flavored, pleasantly charred birds—and without the intervention of the local fire department.

We started simply: one whole chicken and a grill. We knew that cooking a 3½-pounder would take a while, but this was tedious even by our tolerant standards: We placed the chicken breast side down over low heat to cook off some of the fat and then flipped it. By the time we got to the hotter side, the coals no longer had enough oomph to brown the skin. Yes, it was simple, and there were no flare-ups; but with no high-temperature char, the meat looked and tasted more roasted than grilled, and the white meat was as dry as one might expect after 90 minutes on the grill.

Brining the next chicken in a saltwater solution helped keep it more moist, but it still required a solid chunk of time on the grill. In an attempt to shorten the cooking time of the next bird, we employed a technique we've used when roasting chickens: butterflying. That is, we removed the backbone with a pair of kitchen shears and pressed on the breastbone to flatten the bird to a more-or-less uniform thickness. Butterflying the bird would speed up cooking by increasing the meat's exposure to heat. We rubbed some lemon zest, mustard, rosemary, and seasoning on the skin of the chicken for added flavor.

We placed the wide, flat chicken breast side down over the cooler side of the grill, and then we flipped it to finish the rendering job before moving it over to the hotter side (after 30 minutes it was still plenty hot) to get grill marks on each side. This chicken had promise—evenly cooked meat, a bit of char, and no scary fire—but it still took almost an hour, and tasters observed that the meat was a bit dry. The good news was that they liked the lemon-herb rub; the bad news was that its flavor was only skin-deep.

Thinking about dishes that combine poultry and high heat, we remembered tandoori chicken, which is traditionally cooked in a 900-degree clay oven without bursting into flames. Why does it work? Because the skin has been removed before cooking.

GRILLED LEMON CHICKEN WITH ROSEMARY

The three separate problems we were trying to fix—flare-ups, long cooking time, and lack of flavor penetration—were all caused by the same thing: the skin. Yes, the skin protects the meat during cooking—but remove it and you remove most of the fat, so you can put the chicken directly over high heat without fear of flare-ups, not to mention that the chicken cooks so quickly that it has less time to dry out.

A whole chicken with no skin seemed odd at first—we like chicken skin. But we also know that not everyone does; we've witnessed many a guest discreetly set it aside before eating. Maybe a naked chicken was worth a try.

Turns out that taking the skin off a butterflied chicken is pretty easy; using our hands, a paper towel to improve our grip, and the kitchen shears, we got the job done in just a couple of minutes, and we were even able to remove the small pockets of fat that lay on the surface of the meat. However, we had underestimated the structural service provided by the skin, and the legs

dangled precariously. We strategically threaded a couple of skewers through the thighs and breast to fix that. After drying off the bird, we applied the rub directly to the meat and then placed the chicken breast side down over the hotter side of the grill (7 quarts of coals strong) and closed the lid to modify the flow of oxygen and discourage flare-ups.

There was smoke, the smell of charring, and a lot of sizzling noises, too. When we peeked, we did see some flames, but they were weak. After a mere 10 minutes, we flipped the chicken, and after another 10 minutes, we moved it over to the cooler side of the grill to finish cooking. When it reached the target temperature (160 degrees in the breast, 175 in the thigh) in just 8 more minutes, we knew we were onto something. This chicken was the juiciest yet, and who can find fault with a whole chicken that cooks in just 28 minutes?

We can, of course. It was good, but it wasn't perfect. The brief time over intense heat (necessary to prevent overcooking) meant that the surface of the meat was a bit pale and, while not exactly dry, it had a tight, cauterized feel to it. And the flavor of the rub was still a bit superficial.

To address the paleness problem, we spiked the brine with sugar, which we hoped would be absorbed into the bird and aid browning. To solve the flavor penetration issue, we turned once again to tandoori chicken for inspiration. Tandoori cooks cut deep slits in meat before it goes into the oven, so we did the same before brining the bird. When it came out of the brine, we massaged the rub deep into the knife cuts. We reserved a bit of the flavoring agents from the rub—lemon juice, rosemary, mustard, and pepper—and mixed them into a small amount of melted butter to use as a basting sauce. Thinking ahead, we cut an additional lemon into quarters and brought it out to the grill with our chicken and sauce.

Once again, we laid the chicken skinned side down over the hotter side, and this time we also placed the lemon quarters on the grate to char. The sugar in the brine caused this bird to achieve a beautiful brown color after just 8 minutes. When we flipped it, we brushed the cooked surface with the flavored butter to prevent it from tightening up, and we tented it with foil as extra insurance. The lemons went into a bowl to cool. After another 8 minutes, we moved the chicken to the cooler side and basted it again, and in 8 more minutes it was done. We took it off the grill and basted it with the last of the butter.

The moist brown exterior of this chicken was accented with hints of tasty black char, and carving it revealed a juiciness that went all the way to the bone and took the flavorful rub along for the ride. A spritz of charred lemon over the top completed the dish. We had met the enemy and emerged victorious. No fire department necessary.

NOTES FROM THE TEST KITCHEN

Here's how to prep a whole chicken for even, rapid cooking on the grill.

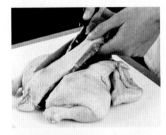

1. REMOVE BACKBONE: Cut through the bones on either side of the backbone; discard.

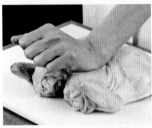

2. FLATTEN: Flip the chicken and crack and flatten its breastbone for fast, even grilling.

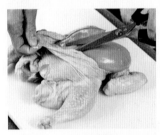

3. PEEL OFF SKIN: Fat rendering from the skin can cause flare-ups. We take it off.

4. SLASH: Deep cuts in the meat allow seasonings to penetrate to the bone.

5. SKEWER: Skewers inserted through the thighs and legs provide stability.

NOTES FROM THE TEST KITCHEN

NO SKIN—REALLY?

Trust us: This "naked" chicken is good. Really good. While skin can provide protection against the high heat of grilling, we make up for its absence with two measures: After the bird is flipped and the risk of flare-ups is receding, we brush a melted butter mixture on the exposed flesh to prevent the meat from becoming leathery, and we also tent the chicken with foil. The result? Juicy, tender chicken.

COVER UP

We use melted butter and foil to protect the bird.

Grilled Lemon Chicken with Rosemary

SERVES 4

For a better grip, use a paper towel to grasp the skin when removing it from the chicken.

1	(3½- to 4-pound) whole chicken, giblets discarded
¾	cup sugar
	Salt and pepper
2	lemons
1	tablespoon vegetable oil
2	teaspoons minced fresh rosemary
1½	teaspoons Dijon mustard
2	tablespoons unsalted butter

1. With chicken breast side down, use kitchen shears to cut through bones on either side of backbone; discard backbone. Flip chicken over and press on breastbone to flatten. Using fingers and shears, peel skin off chicken, leaving skin on wings.

2. Tuck wings behind back. Turn legs so drumsticks face inward toward breasts. Using chef's knife, cut ½-inch-deep slits, spaced ½ inch apart, in breasts and legs. Insert skewer through thigh of 1 leg, into bottom of breast, and through thigh of second leg. Insert second skewer, about 1 inch lower, through thigh and drumstick of 1 leg and then through thigh and drumstick of second leg.

3. Dissolve sugar and ¾ cup salt in 3 quarts cold water in large, wide container. Submerge chicken in brine, cover, and refrigerate for at least 30 minutes or up to 1 hour.

4. Zest lemons (you should have 2 tablespoons grated zest). Juice 1 lemon (you should have 3 tablespoons juice) and quarter remaining lemon lengthwise. Combine zest, oil, 1½ teaspoons rosemary, 1 teaspoon mustard, and ½ teaspoon pepper in small bowl; set aside. Heat butter, remaining ½ teaspoon rosemary, remaining ½ teaspoon mustard, and ½ teaspoon pepper in small saucepan over low heat, stirring occasionally, until butter is melted and ingredients are combined. Remove pan from heat and stir in lemon juice; leave mixture in saucepan.

5. Remove chicken from brine and pat dry with paper towels. With chicken skinned side down, rub ½ teaspoon zest mixture over surface of legs. Flip chicken over and rub remaining zest mixture evenly over entire surface, making sure to work mixture into slits.

6A. FOR A CHARCOAL GRILL: Open bottom vent completely. Light large chimney starter mounded with charcoal briquettes (7 quarts). When top coals are partially covered with ash, pour evenly over half of grill. Set cooking grate in place, cover, and open lid vent completely. Heat grill until hot, about 5 minutes.

6B. FOR A GAS GRILL: Turn all burners to high, cover, and heat grill until hot, about 15 minutes. Leave primary burner on high and turn off other burner(s).

7. Clean and oil cooking grate. Place chicken, skinned side down, and lemon quarters over hotter side of grill. Cover and cook until chicken and lemon quarters are well browned, 8 to 10 minutes. Transfer lemon quarters to bowl and set aside. Flip chicken over and brush with one-third of butter mixture (place saucepan over cooler side of grill if mixture has solidified). Cover chicken loosely with aluminum foil. Continue to cook, covered, until chicken is well browned on second side, 8 to 10 minutes.

8. Remove foil and slide chicken to cooler side of grill. Brush with half of remaining butter mixture, and re-cover with foil. Continue to cook, covered, until breasts register 160 degrees and thighs/drumsticks register 175 degrees, 8 to 10 minutes longer.

9. Transfer chicken to carving board, brush with remaining butter mixture, tent loosely with foil, and let rest for 5 to 10 minutes. Carve into pieces and serve with reserved lemon quarters.

STREAMLINED BEETS

✔ **WHY THIS RECIPE WORKS:** We sought a streamlined recipe for beets that maximized their sweet, earthy flavor. To achieve this goal in less than an hour, we braised the halved beets on the stovetop in minimal water, reduced the residual cooking liquid, and added light brown sugar and vinegar. This flavor-packed glaze was just thick enough to coat the wedges of peeled beets. For flavor and texture contrast, we added toasted nuts (or pepitas), fresh herbs (or scallions), and aromatic citrus zest (or pungent freshly grated ginger) just before serving.

BEETS ARE PACKED WITH COMPLEX EARTHY SWEETNESS, but preparing them is no small feat. Roasting them concentrates their flavor but can take more than 90 minutes—way too long for a weeknight side dish. Boiling might shave off time, but one taste of the earthy, sweet crimson cooking liquid proves that this convenience exacts its own toll. Not wanting to pour flavor down the drain or wait longer than an hour, we went in search of a more streamlined approach to bringing out the best in beets.

Most quick-cooking beet recipes begin by cutting the beets down to bite size. While this reduces the roasting time to less than a half-hour, peeling and cutting the rock-hard raw beets is a tedious and messy task. Part of the satisfaction of cooking beets whole (either roasting or boiling) is slipping their skins off post-cooking with the simple rub of a paper towel and easily slicing their softened flesh with a knife. We wanted the same easy technique—but faster.

We decided to turn to the epitome of speed and convenience: the microwave. But as it turns out, this is the wrong appliance for beets. When we pulled a tender batch from the microwave after 12 minutes, we found that their skins were impossible to remove without some

BEETS WITH LEMON AND ALMONDS

arm strength and a vegetable peeler. This is because the microwave heats the outermost inch of food so fast that moisture in the beet flesh doesn't have time to evaporate and cause the flesh to shrink and separate slightly from the skin—the key to easy removal. And easy removal of the skins was a must.

We knew we would have to use a more traditional method, and boiling had the most potential for speed. We tried halving the raw beets before placing them in a large saucepan with about a quart of water to cover (turning a blind eye to any consequential flavor loss for now). This small investment in prep work cost less than a minute but shaved 10 to 15 minutes off the hour of cooking time typically required for whole beets. As an added benefit, the cooked beet halves cooled to handling temperature more quickly than whole beets and shed their peels just as easily under the pressure of our thumbs and the gentle friction of a paper towel. Done.

Our next step? We had to face the flavor lost to all that cooking water. Instead of sheepishly pouring the vibrant "beet broth" down the drain after cooking up our next batch, we decided that we would reduce it to about a tablespoon and use it to build a dressing for the beets—nothing wasted and no flavor lost. Unfortunately, reducing a quart of water took upwards of 25 minutes.

Not wanting to devote this much time to reduction, we tried cooking the beets in less water to begin with. A mere 1¼ cups was enough to submerge a small portion of each beet and provide ample steam. By reducing the amount of liquid, we effectively switched from boiling to braising, relying on a small amount of water to gently simmer and steam the beets in a tightly covered pot. For even braising, we needed to make certain that the beets were in a single layer, so we switched from a large saucepan to a broader covered straight-sided skillet. (A Dutch oven worked, too.) The beets finished cooking in the same time period and were just as tender, but now the leftover braising liquid reduced in only 5 minutes flat.

To play up the earthy sweetness of the beets and introduce a complementary acidity, we added a tablespoon of light brown sugar and 3 tablespoons of vinegar

to the beet reduction. Just 1 more minute of cooking gave the resultant sweet-and-sour sauce enough body to coat the peeled wedges. Thin slices of shallot underscored the savory depth, while toasted nuts, aromatic citrus zest, and fresh herbs added just enough contrast without overshadowing the robust beet flavor we had worked so hard to preserve. As the self-proclaimed roasted beet lovers went back for seconds, we considered our work done. Armed with a simple method that took less than an hour, we were ready to add beets to our midweek vegetable roster.

Beets with Lemon and Almonds

SERVES 4 TO 6

To ensure even cooking, we recommend using beets that are of similar size—roughly 2 to 3 inches in diameter. The beets can be served warm or at room temperature. If serving at room temperature, wait until right before serving to sprinkle on the almonds and herbs.

1½ **pounds beets, trimmed and halved horizontally**
1¼ **cups water**
    Salt and pepper
  3 **tablespoons white vinegar**
  1 **tablespoon packed light brown sugar**
  1 **shallot, sliced thin**
  1 **teaspoon grated lemon zest**
 ½ **cup whole almonds, toasted and chopped**
  2 **tablespoons chopped fresh mint**
  1 **teaspoon chopped fresh thyme**

1. Place beets, cut side down, in single layer in 11-inch straight-sided sauté pan or Dutch oven. Add water and ¼ teaspoon salt; bring to simmer over high heat. Reduce heat to low, cover, and simmer until beets are tender and tip of paring knife inserted into beets meets no resistance, 45 to 50 minutes.

2. Transfer beets to cutting board. Increase heat to medium-high and reduce cooking liquid, stirring occasionally, until pan is almost dry, 5 to 6 minutes. Add vinegar and sugar, return to boil, and cook, stirring constantly with heat-resistant spatula, until spatula leaves wide trail when dragged through glaze, 1 to 2 minutes. Remove pan from heat.

3. When beets are cool enough to handle, rub off skins with paper towel or clean dish towel and cut into ½-inch wedges. Add beets, shallot, lemon zest, ½ teaspoon salt, and ¼ teaspoon pepper to glaze and toss to coat. Transfer beets to serving dish; sprinkle with almonds, mint, and thyme; and serve.

VARIATIONS

Beets with Lime and Pepitas

Omit thyme. Substitute lime zest for lemon zest, toasted pepitas for almonds, and cilantro for mint.

Beets with Orange and Walnuts

Substitute orange zest for lemon zest; walnuts, toasted and chopped, for almonds; and parsley for mint.

Beets with Ginger and Cashews

Omit thyme. Substitute 4 scallions, white parts sliced thin, for shallot and green parts sliced thin on bias for mint; 1 teaspoon grated fresh ginger for lemon zest; and ½ cup roasted cashews, toasted and chopped, for almonds.

RATING INNOVATIVE SAUCEPANS

We wondered whether newfangled designs could improve on—or even stand up to—the tried-and-true saucepan we've used for years. Our favorite All-Clad saucepan is a kitchen workhorse; its hefty frame, deep bowl, long arm, and tight-fitting lid make it our go-to vessel for rice, soups, sauces, and even pastry cream. What could possibly be improved? Mainly space management, we discovered when we began to peruse cutting-edge options. Two saucepans have removable handles, which allow the cook to fit more pans on a small stovetop, in the dishwasher, or in a cupboard. One pan also boasts a lid that doubles as a trivet. And we were hopeful that another pan, with an integrated strainer and a keep-warm bowl, would work. We tested these three new models by making pastry cream, sautéed onions, and rice pilaf. The results? Disappointing. While they did save space, the two pans with removable handles either were out of balance or did not feel secure. One pan's wooden lid/trivet performed its heat-shield function well but prevented us from using the clamp-style handle, since the lid won't fit when the handle is attached. Bulky solids tended to block the opening of the innovative lid with strainer. The only innovation that held up was that same pan's nesting bowl: Placing the pan in the bowl let us take it to the table and kept the contents warm. None of the innovators came close to performing as well as our favorite. Brands are listed in order of preference. See AmericasTestKitchen.com for updates and further information on this testing.

TEST KITCHEN FAVORITE (LARGE SAUCEPAN)

ALL-CLAD Stainless 4-Quart Saucepan with Lid and Loop
MODEL: 4204
PRICE: $224.95
CAPACITY: 4 qt **COOKING SURFACE:** 8 in
WEIGHT: 3.3 lb
COOKING: ★★★ **DESIGN:** ★★½
COMMENTS: Our longtime champ features a hefty frame, deep bowl, long arm with comfortable handle, and tight-fitting lid. It also has rounded corners that a whisk can reach into. It heats slowly and evenly enough to prevent onions from scorching and pastry cream and rice from overcooking.

RECOMMENDED WITH RESERVATIONS

ABCT Low Casserole with Universal Handle and Mahogany Lid
MODEL: AB10324; handle AB200; lid AB10024
PRICE: $158 (pan $72; handle $40; lid $46)
CAPACITY: 2 qt **COOKING SURFACE:** 9 in
WEIGHT: 1.45 lb
INNOVATION: Removable handle, lid doubles as trivet
DOES INNOVATION WORK? No
COOKING: ★★ **DESIGN:** ★
COMMENTS: With its white ceramic coating and wooden lid that doubles as a trivet, this pan is designed to go elegantly from stovetop to table. But the removable tonglike handle, the clamp of which is wrapped in rubber to affix to the pan's walls, required near-constant squeezing to stay secure, which hurt our hands. The pan made great rice pilaf, but the very thin aluminum scorched onions and broke our pastry cream. With vigilance on the part of the cook, this pan does perform, but that makes extra work.

RECOMMENDED WITH RESERVATIONS *(cont.)*

CRISTEL MultiPly Stainless 4.5 Quart Sauce Pan with Glass Lid
MODEL: F22QMPKP; handle PLSX
PRICE: $319.90 (pan $289.95; handle $29.95)
CAPACITY: 4.5 qt **COOKING SURFACE:** 8.25 in
WEIGHT: 5.15 lb (with handle)
INNOVATION: Removable handle
DOES INNOVATION WORK? No
COOKING: ★★ **DESIGN:** ★
COMMENTS: With five layers of metal—it's tri-ply throughout, with two additional layers on the bottom—this pan was heavy and out of balance when lifted by its stumpy, removable handle. The handle also got too hot to hold close to the pan, making it awkward to stir pastry cream. Though it produced decent rice pilaf, it repeatedly scorched onions since its thick disk bottom heated slowly and then raced. For its price, this pan should have been perfect.

NOT RECOMMENDED

TWIZTT BY JOAN LUNDEN 2-Quart Cook, Strain and Serve 3-Piece Set
MODEL: CW0004775
PRICE: $49.99
CAPACITY: 2 qt **COOKING SURFACE:** 5.75 in
WEIGHT: 3.25 lb
INNOVATION: Strainer lid, keep-warm serving bowl
DOES INNOVATION WORK? Partly
COOKING: ★½ **DESIGN:** ★
COMMENTS: This thin, flimsy steel pan bulges out from its aluminum- and steel-clad disk-bottom base, which scorched onions and browned rice too much along the pan's sides. Its lid locks to allow safe straining, but solids pushed against the narrow opening when we poured, holding back the liquid. The pan fits into a keep-warm melamine bowl that let us bring it to the table, where it successfully kept the contents hot.

Best Barbecued Chicken & Cornbread

Indirect cooking is key to grilling juicy and evenly cooked chicken parts. Here Julia "temps" a barbecued chicken breast to be sure it's time to take it off the fire.

WHO DOESN'T LIKE SAUCY, STICKY BARBECUED CHICKEN AND BIG squares of fresh cornbread? We admit that over the years our tastes in both of these barbecue treats have become more demanding. As kids, we were perfectly happy with bottled barbecue sauce—and if the chicken was dry, well, we'd just add more sauce and grab some napkins. Today, we don't want to settle for anything less than smoky, well-seasoned, juicy chicken. But even when cooked on the bone, chicken has a tendency to dry out over a fiery grill or, because of its shape, cook unevenly. We'd need to find a way around these issues. As for the sauce, we wanted it to complement, not camouflage, the meat, so only a thoughtfully developed homemade sauce would do.

Like barbecued chicken, cornbread is no stranger to mediocrity—and frankly, even the squares served at our favorite barbecue joints are tasty when slathered with butter, but in truth, it could be so much better. Why? Most cornbread recipes, whether Northern- or Southern-style, lack real corn flavor. This isn't suprising given that recipes typically call for cornmeal alone. We'd need to find a way to infuse our cornbread with fresh, summery corn flavor for a bread truly worth eating.

SWEET AND TANGY BARBECUED CHICKEN

BARBECUED CHICKEN

✔ WHY THIS RECIPE WORKS: To produce juicy, evenly cooked chicken parts on the grill, indirect cooking is key, as it provides a hotter side for briefly searing the parts and a cooler side for them to cook through gently. We lined up the fattier leg quarters closer to the coals and the leaner white meat farther from the heat, as well as adding a water pan underneath the cooler side, to help the dark and white pieces cook slowly and evenly. Applying a simple spice rub deeply seasoned the meat, and the salt in it helped retain moisture, while brushing on a homemade sauce in stages allowed it to cling nicely to the skin and also develop layers of tangy-sweet flavor.

WE HAVE FOND MEMORIES OF EATING BARBECUED chicken when we were growing up, but not because the chicken was any good. This summertime staple involved dousing chicken parts with bottled sauce and dumping the pieces over a ripping hot fire. The grill minder would then spend the next 45 minutes flipping and shuffling them around on the grate in a vain effort to get the pieces to cook evenly. Some of the pieces always cooked up dry, while others were raw at the bone. Worse, flare-ups caused by fat dripping onto the coals carbonized the skin well before its underbelly had a chance to fully render. But it was summer, it was fun to eat outside, and if we poured enough of the (inevitably) ultrasweet sauce on the chicken, we could mask its shortcomings.

Throughout the years we've eaten enough subpar barbecued chicken to realize that a lot of cooks don't know how to produce juicy, deeply seasoned, evenly cooked chicken parts on the grill. With decades of test kitchen barbecuing experience on our side, we set out to foolproof this American classic.

There were a few basic barbecue tenets we put in place from the get-go. First, we ditched the single-level fire (recommended by a surprising number of recipes) and built an indirect one: We corralled all the coals on one side of the kettle, enabling us to sear the chicken over the hotter side and then pull it over to the cooler side, where the meat would cook gently and the skin could render slowly. Cooking the chicken opposite from (rather than on top of) the coals for most of the time would also cut back on flare-ups. Second, we salted the meat and let it sit for several hours before grilling it, since we assumed that this pretreatment would change the meat's protein structure so that it would hold on to more moisture as it cooked—added insurance against overcooking. Finally, we would wait to apply barbecue sauce (which usually contains sugary ingredients) until after searing; this would prevent the sauce from burning and give the skin a chance to develop color first.

We proceeded to sear 6 pounds of breasts and leg quarters on the hotter part of the grill. Once both sides of the meat were brown, we dragged the pieces to the cooler part of the kettle, painted on some placeholder bottled sauce, and considered our core challenge: how to ensure that both the white and dark pieces cooked at an even pace.

Since food that sits closest to the fire cooks faster, we lined up the fattier, more heat-resistant leg quarters closest to the coals and the leaner, more delicate breasts farther away and covered the grill. About an hour later, the breast meat was just about done, the skin was nicely rendered and thin, and the sauce was concentrated and set. The problem was that several leg quarters were chewy and dry. Salting clearly wasn't enough to protect them from the heat, even when positioned next to the coals instead of on top of them.

We thought that swapping the dark and white pieces midway through cooking to even out their exposure to the heat would help, but this just made things worse: Now both the white and dark pieces overcooked. Building a smaller fire wasn't an option either: When we used 25 percent less charcoal, the heat dwindled before the meat finished cooking.

Reducing the coals didn't work, but that didn't mean that we couldn't adjust the heat another way—by setting a disposable aluminum pan opposite the coals and partially filling it with water, a trick that we've used in other

recipes that require low, even heat. Both the pan and the water absorb heat, lowering the overall temperature inside the kettle and eliminating hot spots.

We cooked another batch using the water pan and finally made some headway. The ambient temperature inside the grill had dropped by about 50 degrees—a good sign. We checked the pieces midway through grilling and were pleased to see that the dark meat was cooking at a slower, steadier pace. By the end of the hour, both the white and dark pieces were hitting their target temperatures (160 and 175 degrees, respectively).

Our cooking method had come a long way, but we could hardly call our results "barbecued." For one thing, we needed a homemade alternative for the characterless bottled sauce. Our tasters also reminded us that, although the chicken was nicely seasoned after salting, the flavor of the meat itself was unremarkable once you got past the skin.

But salting the chicken reminded us that we could easily apply bolder flavor in the same way—with a rub.

We kept the blend basic: In addition to kosher salt, we mixed together equal amounts of onion and garlic powders and paprika; a touch of cayenne for subtle heat; and a generous 2 tablespoons of brown sugar, which would caramelize during cooking.

For the sauce, we fell back on the test kitchen's go-to recipe, which smartens the typical ketchup-based concoction. Molasses adds depth, while cider vinegar, Worcestershire sauce, and Dijon mustard keep sweetness in check. Grated onion, minced garlic, chili powder, cayenne, and pepper round out the flavors.

But there was a downside to applying the sauce just after searing: After cooking for an hour, it lost a measure of its bright tanginess. Instead, we applied the sauce in stages, brushing on the first coat just after searing and then applying a second midway through grilling. That minor adjustment made a surprisingly big difference. We also reserved some of the sauce for passing at the table.

This was perfectly cooked, seriously good chicken worthy of taking center stage at the next family barbecue.

Sweet and Tangy Barbecued Chicken

SERVES 6 TO 8

When browning the chicken over the hotter side of the grill, move it away from any flare-ups. Try to select similar-size chicken parts for even cooking.

CHICKEN

- 2 tablespoons packed dark brown sugar
- 4½ teaspoons kosher salt
- 1½ teaspoons onion powder
- 1½ teaspoons garlic powder
- 1½ teaspoons paprika
- ¼ teaspoon cayenne pepper
- 6 pounds bone-in chicken pieces (split breasts and/or leg quarters), trimmed

SAUCE

- 1 cup ketchup
- 5 tablespoons molasses
- 3 tablespoons cider vinegar
- 2 tablespoons Worcestershire sauce
- 2 tablespoons Dijon mustard
- ¼ teaspoon pepper
- 2 tablespoons vegetable oil
- ⅓ cup grated onion
- 1 garlic clove, minced
- 1 teaspoon chili powder
- ¼ teaspoon cayenne pepper

- 1 large disposable aluminum roasting pan (if using charcoal) or 2 disposable aluminum pie plates (if using gas)

1. FOR THE CHICKEN: Combine sugar, salt, onion powder, garlic powder, paprika, and cayenne in bowl. Arrange chicken on rimmed baking sheet and sprinkle both sides evenly with spice rub. Cover with plastic wrap and refrigerate for at least 6 hours or up to 24 hours.

2. FOR THE SAUCE: Whisk ketchup, molasses, vinegar, Worcestershire, mustard, and pepper together in bowl. Heat oil in medium saucepan over medium heat until shimmering. Add onion and garlic; cook until onion is softened, 2 to 4 minutes. Add chili powder and cayenne and cook until fragrant, about 30 seconds. Whisk in ketchup mixture and bring to boil. Reduce heat to medium-low and simmer gently for 5 minutes. Set aside ⅔ cup sauce to baste chicken and reserve remaining sauce for serving. (Sauce can be refrigerated for up to 1 week.)

3A. FOR A CHARCOAL GRILL: Open bottom vent halfway and place disposable pan filled with 3 cups water on 1 side of grill. Light large chimney starter filled with charcoal briquettes (6 quarts). When top coals are partially covered with ash, pour evenly over other half of grill (opposite disposable pan). Set cooking grate in place, cover, and open lid vent halfway. Heat grill until hot, about 5 minutes.

3B. FOR A GAS GRILL: Place 2 disposable pie plates, each filled with 1½ cups water, directly on 1 burner of gas grill (opposite primary burner). Turn all burners to high, cover, and heat grill until hot, about 15 minutes. Turn primary burner to medium-high and turn off other burner(s). (Adjust primary burner as needed to maintain grill temperature of 325 to 350 degrees.)

4. Clean and oil cooking grate. Place chicken, skin side down, over hotter part of grill and cook until browned and blistered in spots, 2 to 5 minutes. Flip chicken and

---

NOTES FROM THE TEST KITCHEN

TRIM YOUR LEG QUARTERS
Some leg quarters come with the backbone still attached. Here's an easy way to remove it.

Holding the leg quarter skin side down, grasp the backbone and bend it back to pop the thigh bone out of its socket. Place the leg on a cutting board and cut through the joint and any attached skin.

Small-batch barbecue sauces promise pit-master magic—but are they worth their higher price tags? To find out, we tested four mail-order products that had some buzz, were award winners, or were marketed by barbecue pros. We sampled the sauces plain and on grilled chicken, focusing on sweetness, complexity, texture, and overall appeal. Our two least favorite sauces were too sweet, containing twice the amount of sugar per serving as the others. A third sauce was watery and mild. But the fourth, our winner, delivered. With generous additions of vinegar, salt, and chili paste along with liquid smoke, it was tart, spicy, and more savory than sweet. It also had enough body to cling to the chicken. To see how our high-end winner compared with our supermarket winner, Bull's-Eye Original BBQ Sauce ($2.39 for 18 ounces)—a sweet, tomato-based classic—we held a taste test on grilled chicken. Votes were evenly split on these very different sauces. For traditionalists, our supermarket winner is best, but for a savory, tangy sauce with a kick, we recommend splurging on our high-end winner. Brands are listed in order of preference. See AmericasTestKitchen.com for updates and further information on this tasting.

RECOMMENDED

PORK BARREL ORIGINAL BBQ Sauce
PRICE: $5.49 for 12 oz ($0.46 cents per oz)
COMMENTS: This "big, bold" winner boasted a "robust," "vinegary" kick.

RECOMMENDED WITH RESERVATIONS

BONE SUCKIN' SAUCE
PRICE: $6.79 for 16 oz ($0.42 cents per oz)
COMMENTS: Some tasters noted "interesting honey and fruit" flavors. For others, the sauce was "thin" and "boring."

STEVEN RAICHLEN BEST OF BARBECUE
Chipotle Molasses Barbecue Sauce
PRICE: $9.99 for 18 oz ($0.56 cents per oz)
COMMENTS: The "licorice," "molasses," and "hoisin" flavors of this sauce were too much of a good thing.

NOT RECOMMENDED

AMERICAN STOCKYARD
Harvest Apple BBQ Sauce
PRICE: $6.95 for 22 oz ($0.32 cents per oz)
COMMENTS: This last-place sauce was "too runny," with a "cloying sweetness."

cook until second side is browned, 4 to 6 minutes. Move chicken to cooler side of grill and brush both sides of chicken with ⅓ cup sauce. Arrange chicken, skin side up, with leg quarters closest to fire and breasts farthest away. Cover (positioning lid vent over chicken if using charcoal) and cook for 25 minutes.

5. Brush both sides of chicken with remaining ⅓ cup sauce and continue to cook, covered, until breasts register 160 degrees and leg quarters register 175 degrees, 25 to 35 minutes longer.

6. Transfer chicken to serving platter, tent loosely with aluminum foil, and let rest for 10 minutes.

FRESH CORN CORNBREAD

✔ **WHY THIS RECIPE WORKS:** For cornbread packed with fresh, concentrated corn flavor, we pureed fresh corn kernels and cooked them down into a "corn butter" that we incorporated into the batter. Buttermilk added tang, while egg yolks and a little bit of extra butter ensured that the bread would be moist.

CORNBREAD FALLS INTO TWO MAIN STYLES: THE SWEET, cakey Northern type and the crusty, savory kind more often found in Southern kitchens. Each has its die-hard fans, but—let's face the facts—neither tastes much like corn. This is because most cornbreads are made with cornmeal alone, and no fresh corn at all. Furthermore, the so-called "field" or "dent" corn used to make cornmeal is far starchier (read: less flavorful) than the sweet corn grown to eat off the cob.

So what would it take to get real corn flavor in cornbread? It wouldn't be as simple as just tossing some fresh-cut kernels into the batter. When we tried, we found that we needed to add at least 2 whole cups of kernels for the corn flavor to really shine, and that created a slew of problems. Since fresh kernels are full of moisture, the crumb of the cornbread was now riddled with unpleasant gummy pockets. What's more, the kernels turned chewy and tough as the bread baked. But there had to be a way to get true sweet corn flavor in our cornbread, and we were determined to figure it out.

We decided to work on the cornbread base first. In our earlier tests, tasters found that the little bit of sweetener added to the Northern-style versions helped fresh corn flavor break through, so we settled on that cornbread archetype. For our working recipe, we used slightly more cornmeal than flour and decided to abandon fine-ground cornmeal in favor of the stone-ground type, which contains both the hull and the oil-rich germ of the corn kernel. The upshot: a more rustic texture and fuller flavor. For sweetness, honey, maple syrup, and brown sugar all masked the fresh corn taste, but 2 tablespoons of regular granulated sugar fell neatly in

line. For the liquid component, we would stick with traditional tangy buttermilk. Three tablespoons of melted butter and two eggs provided richness, and baking the cornbread in a cast-iron skillet allowed it to develop a brown, crisp crust.

With the batter figured out, we turned back to the problems of the fresh corn. We wondered if we could get rid of the unpleasantly steamed, chewy texture of the kernels by soaking them in a solution of water and baking soda before adding them to the batter—a technique we recently used to tenderize kernels for a fresh corn salsa. The alkaline environment provided by the baking soda helps soften the hulls of the kernels. Sure enough, the kernels were tender…that is, until they were baked in the bread and the heat of the oven toughened them right back up. And we still had the issue of all those wet, gummy pockets.

With no new ideas to try, we were idly flipping through cookbooks when we came across a recipe for "corn butter" made by pureeing fresh kernels and then reducing the mixture on the stove until thick. We tried it using three large ears of corn and found that the puree thickened and turned deep yellow in minutes, transforming into a "butter" packed with concentrated corn flavor. While the recipes we found used the corn butter as a spread, we had another idea: We added the reduced puree to a batch of batter, baked it—and rejoiced. For the first time, our cornbread tasted like real corn—and without any distracting chewiness.

This method offered another benefit: Since cooking the corn puree drove off moisture, our bread no longer had gummy pockets surrounding the kernels. In fact, the bread was almost too dry and even a little crumbly—a result of the large amount of natural cornstarch (released by pureeing the kernels) that was now absorbing surrounding moisture in the batter. Happily, this problem was easy to solve by simply increasing the amount of fat in the batter: an extra egg yolk and 2 more tablespoons of butter did the trick. We had one more tweak: We melted a pat of butter in the skillet before adding the batter, which gave the bread a more crispy and buttery-tasting bottom crust.

Moist, tender, and bursting with corn flavor, our cornbread tasted like a bite of corn on the cob.

FRESH CORN CORNBREAD

Fresh Corn Cornbread

SERVES 6 TO 8

We prefer to use a well-seasoned cast-iron skillet in this recipe, but an ovensafe 10-inch skillet can be used in its place. Alternatively, in step 4 you can add 1 tablespoon of butter to a 9-inch cake pan and place it in the oven until the butter melts, about 3 minutes.

1⅓ cups (6⅔ ounces) stone-ground cornmeal
1 cup (5 ounces) all-purpose flour
2 tablespoons sugar
1½ teaspoons baking powder
¼ teaspoon baking soda
1¼ teaspoons salt
3 ears corn, kernels cut from cobs (2¼ cups)
6 tablespoons unsalted butter, cut into 6 pieces
1 cup buttermilk
2 large eggs plus 1 large yolk

1. Adjust oven rack to middle position and heat oven to 400 degrees. Whisk cornmeal, flour, sugar, baking powder, baking soda, and salt together in large bowl.

2. Process corn kernels in blender until very smooth, about 2 minutes. Transfer puree to medium saucepan (you should have about 1½ cups). Cook puree over medium heat, stirring constantly, until very thick and deep yellow and it measures ¾ cup, 5 to 8 minutes.

3. Remove pan from heat. Add 5 tablespoons butter and whisk until melted and incorporated. Add buttermilk and whisk until incorporated. Add eggs and yolk and whisk until incorporated. Transfer corn mixture to bowl with cornmeal mixture and, using rubber spatula, fold together until just combined.

4. Melt remaining 1 tablespoon butter in 10-inch cast-iron skillet over medium heat. Scrape batter into skillet and spread into even layer. Bake until top is golden brown and toothpick inserted in center comes out clean, 23 to 28 minutes. Let cool on wire rack for 5 minutes. Remove cornbread from skillet and let cool for 20 minutes before cutting into wedges and serving.

Three Ways with Eggs

Eggs are placed in a half-inch of boiling water before the pan is covered for foolproof soft-cooked eggs.

WE ARE HEARTENED BY THE FACT THAT EGGS SEEM SO SIMPLE to prepare and that there are almost always eggs in our refrigerator. But we know that simple doesn't necessarily mean easy. We were after the very best versions of three egg favorites: soft-cooked eggs, fried eggs, and ultimate omelets.

Soft-cooked eggs are often served with fingers of toast at breakfast but they also make a deliciously decadent addition to boldly dressed salad greens for dinner, where their rich, runny yolks can cut the richness of the vinaigrette. But unless you make soft-cooked eggs often or are a short-order cook, your technique may be rusty. And think about it—because the egg is encased in the shell during cooking, you really don't know if you've achieved a soft, tender white and fluid yolk until you're at the table—and at that point, all bets are off. We wanted to come up with a foolproof method for this anytime egg treat.

Omelets can be refined or hearty but we wanted to make an omelet that was both—and we wanted it to be as at home on the dinner table as it was at breakfast. After perfecting our omelet technique and folding the soufflé-like eggs over a savory filling, we had just that.

Everyone knows how to fry an egg, right? Well, it depends on what your goals are. We wanted to make a classic diner-syle fried egg that had a tender white with crisp, lacy, brown edges and a fluid but lightly thickened yolk—at home.

FOOLPROOF
SOFT-COOKED EGGS

✔ **WHY THIS RECIPE WORKS:** Traditional methods for making soft-cooked eggs are hit or miss. We wanted one that delivered a set white and a fluid yolk every time. Calling for fridge-cold eggs and boiling water has two advantages: It reduces temperature variables, which makes the recipe more foolproof, and it provides the steepest temperature gradient, which ensures that the yolk at the center stays fluid while the white cooks through. Using only ½ inch of boiling water instead of several cups to cook the eggs means that the recipe takes less time and energy from start to finish. Because of the curved shape of the eggs, they actually have very little contact with the water so they do not lower the water temperature when they go into the saucepan. This means that you can use the same timing for anywhere from one to four eggs without altering the consistency of the finished product.

IN RETROSPECT, WE CAN SEE WHY SOME STAGES OF OUR quest for the perfect soft-cooked egg caused our coworkers to think we had gone off the deep end. We can understand why they were surprised and even alarmed to see one of us furtively slipping into a darkened restroom armed with a high-powered flashlight, an empty toilet paper roll, a permanent marker, and two cartons of U.S. grade A eggs, size large. (For the record, we were trying to determine the precise location of the yolk within each egg, because we were convinced that it influenced the way the egg cooked.) And we concede that it was a mistake to spend five weeks vigorously shaking raw eggs in their shells in an effort to encourage even cooking; the fact that 25 percent of the shaken eggs exploded in the saucepan probably should have tipped us off.

But we figured that achieving our goal would be worth a little embarrassment along the way. A soft-cooked egg—its smoothly gelled white encasing a sphere of warm liquid yolk—is every bit as satisfying to eat as a poached egg, but it looks tidier, and preparing it requires less equipment. It's a one-ingredient recipe; how hard could it be to get it right?

Turns out that soft-cooked eggs are a bit of a crapshoot because you can't rely on any visual cues to monitor the eggs' progress. You don't know if you've succeeded or failed until you're already seated at the breakfast table.

Granted, many people successfully make soft-cooked eggs every day, but here's the thing: Those folks have precisely tailored their individual methods to suit their kitchens. They use the same saucepan, the same amount of water, the same burner, and the same number of eggs every time. If any one of these variables changes, all bets are off.

That wasn't good enough for us. We wanted a method that would produce consistent results for any cook, in any kitchen, using any equipment, whether he or she was cooking one egg, four eggs, or even a half-dozen.

The problem with eggs is that they aren't just one ingredient. Tucked within that porous shell are really two very distinct ingredients: the white and the yolk. Each is composed of different types and ratios of proteins, fats, and water, which means that they react differently to heat. Most important: The white and the yolk begin to coagulate, or solidify, at very different temperatures. The egg white begins to coagulate at 142 degrees and is fully solid at around 180 degrees, while the yolk solidifies at about 158 degrees.

What does this mean? When cooking an egg that we want to be ultimately both solid (the white) and liquid (the yolk) at once, we have to bring the whites up to a much higher temperature—and do so carefully.

To begin, we figured that we had two choices for cooking: aggressively high heat or low-and-slow heat. The test kitchen's go-to method for making hard-cooked eggs is the epitome of a low-heat cooking method: Place the cold eggs in a saucepan, cover them with cold water, bring them to a boil, and then turn off the heat. Cover the saucepan and let the eggs finish cooking in the cooling water for 10 minutes. A quick chill in ice water, and *voilà*! Eggs with fully set whites and firm yolks. Could the key to soft-cooked eggs be as simple as halting the process a little earlier, before the heat penetrates to the center and sets the yolk?

SOFT-COOKED EGGS

No such luck. We followed our hard-cooked egg method, but to monitor the progress of the eggs, we cracked one open as soon as the water came to a boil and then another at each 1-minute interval after that. Sure, that first egg boasted a beautifully fluid yolk, but it was accompanied by a lot of slippery, transparent white. After 1 minute, part of the yolk of the next egg had started to solidify, but there was still a lot of undercooked white. By the time the white was fully set at the 3-minute mark, about half of the yolk had already coagulated and was beginning to turn chalky.

High heat it was. So we would simply take cold eggs from the fridge, drop them into boiling water, and then remove them as soon as the whites were cooked but before the heat penetrated all the way to the yolks.

Admittedly, this is your basic soft-cooked egg recipe, and folks have been doing it this way for millennia. It took a bit of testing to find the timings and quantities that worked for us in the test kitchen, but after some trial and error, we landed on the following method: We placed two large, cold eggs in 4 cups of boiling water in a small, heavy saucepan and fished them out after 6½ minutes. After running cold water over them for 30 seconds, we peeled them and sliced them open to reveal set whites and warm, liquid yolks.

However, this was not a flexible method. When we added extra eggs, there were still some watery whites in evidence after 6½ minutes. That's because adding the cold eggs to the saucepan temporarily lowers the temperature of the water. With more eggs, the water's temperature dipped lower and took longer to return to 212 degrees; with fewer eggs, the water recovered more quickly. So changing the number of eggs changed the amount of time that it took for the eggs to cook perfectly.

If only we could somehow use boiling water to cook the eggs without actually submerging them in it, we thought. That seemed like an absurd idea—until it occurred to us to try a steamer basket. We brought 1 inch of water to a boil in a large saucepan while we loaded the steamer basket with two large, fridge-cold eggs. We lowered the steamer into the saucepan, covered it, and let the eggs steam for 6½ minutes, after which we transferred the steamer to the sink and ran cold water over the eggs before breaking them open. They were perfect. Eggs cooked in steam took exactly the same amount of time as eggs that were submerged in an ample amount of boiling water.

When we tested batches of one to six eggs with exactly the same cook time and got exactly the same results, we were sure we had cracked the case: The key to a perfect yet still flexible recipe for soft-cooked eggs was not to boil them but to steam them. But could we simplify it even more?

We wondered about steamerless steaming. If an egg cooked in steam takes the same amount of time to cook as an egg that is submerged in boiling water, doesn't it follow that if you cook the same egg partially in water and partially in steam, it will still cook evenly?

This time we brought a mere ½ inch of water to a boil in our saucepan, and then we placed two cold eggs directly on the bottom of the pot, covered it, and steamed/boiled them. Because of the curved exterior of the eggs, we reasoned, they wouldn't make enough contact with the water to lower the temperature significantly, so the cook time would remain the same as it did with the steamer. At the end of 6½ minutes, we cooled the eggs by transferring the whole pot to the sink and running cold water into it for 30 seconds. We peeled the eggs and cut each one in half, revealing two beautifully tender yet fully set whites cradling warm, fluid yolks.

Subsequent tests with different-size batches (from one to six eggs) worked equally well using exactly the same timing. And with only ½ inch of water to heat, this recipe was not only the surest and most flexible but also the quickest. Just in time, our reputation as serious and sane test cooks was restored. Never again would we stress about producing perfect soft-cooked eggs for breakfast anytime, anywhere, under any conditions.

Soft-Cooked Eggs

MAKES 4

Be sure to use large eggs that have no cracks and are cold from the refrigerator. Because precise timing is vital to the success of this recipe, we strongly recommend using a digital timer. You can use this method for one to six large, extra-large, or jumbo eggs without altering the timing. If you have one, a steamer basket does make lowering the eggs into the boiling water easier. We recommend serving these eggs in eggcups and with buttered toast for dipping, or you may simply use the dull side of a butter knife to crack the egg along the equator, break the egg in half, and scoop out the insides with a teaspoon.

4 **large eggs**

Salt and pepper

1. Bring ½ inch water to boil in medium saucepan over medium-high heat. Using tongs, gently place eggs

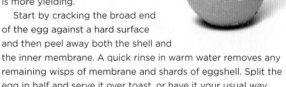

YES, YOU CAN PEEL A SOFT-COOKED EGG

Though it seemed unlikely to us, soft-cooked eggs are actually easier to peel than are hard-cooked eggs. This is because the soft-cooked white is more yielding.

Start by cracking the broad end of the egg against a hard surface and then peel away both the shell and the inner membrane. A quick rinse in warm water removes any remaining wisps of membrane and shards of eggshell. Split the egg in half and serve it over toast, or have it your usual way.

WHAT DOES PERFECTLY COOKED MEAN?

The proteins in egg whites and egg yolks solidify at different temperatures, making the perfect soft-cooked egg an exercise in precision. Whites that are firm yet tender must reach 180 degrees, while the yolk must stay below 158 degrees to remain runny. To achieve this temperature differential, it's essential to start cooking your eggs in hot water (versus the cold-water start that we've proven conclusively works best for hard-cooked eggs) so that the whites will be blasted with enough heat to solidify before the heat has time to penetrate to the yolks.

WHITE: 180°
YOLK: LESS THAN 158°

in boiling water (eggs will not be submerged). Cover saucepan and cook eggs for 6½ minutes.

2. Remove cover, transfer saucepan to sink, and place under cold running water for 30 seconds. Remove eggs from pan and serve, seasoning with salt and pepper to taste.

Soft-Cooked Eggs with Salad

SERVES 2

Combine 3 tablespoons olive oil, 1 tablespoon balsamic vinegar, 1 teaspoon Dijon mustard, and 1 teaspoon minced shallot in jar, seal lid, and shake vigorously until emulsified, 20 to 30 seconds. Toss with 5 cups assertively flavored salad greens (arugula, radicchio, watercress, or frisée). Season with salt and pepper to taste, and divide between 2 plates. Top each serving with 2 peeled soft-cooked eggs, split crosswise to release yolks, and season with salt and pepper to taste.

Soft-Cooked Eggs with Sautéed Mushrooms

SERVES 2

Heat 2 tablespoons olive oil in large skillet over medium-high heat until shimmering. Add 12 ounces sliced white or cremini mushrooms and pinch salt and cook, stirring occasionally, until liquid has evaporated and mushrooms are lightly browned, 5 to 6 minutes. Stir in 2 teaspoons chopped fresh herbs (chives, tarragon, parsley, or combination). Season with salt and pepper to taste, and divide between 2 plates. Top each serving with 2 peeled soft-cooked eggs, split crosswise to release yolks, and season with salt and pepper to taste.

Soft-Cooked Eggs with Steamed Asparagus

SERVES 2

Steam 12 ounces asparagus (spears about ½ inch in diameter, trimmed) over medium heat until crisp-tender, 4 to 5 minutes. Divide between 2 plates. Drizzle each serving with 1 tablespoon extra-virgin olive oil and sprinkle each serving with 1 tablespoon grated Parmesan. Season with salt and pepper to taste. Top each serving with 2 peeled soft-cooked eggs, split crosswise to release yolks, and season with salt and pepper to taste.

RATING EGG TOPPERS

Egg toppers neatly slice off the tops of eggs, whether you are serving them soft-cooked or using a raw eggshell as a vessel. These devices claim to be faster, neater, and more precise than the standard method of breaking the shell with the back of a butter knife. The designs fall into two categories: scissor-style and spring-loaded. Not surprisingly, scissor-style toppers look like a pair of scissors that end in a loop instead of straight blades. The loop goes over the tapered end of an egg; when you squeeze the handle, metal teeth emerge to latch into the shell and remove the top half-inch of the egg. Spring-loaded toppers look like little metal plungers: The bowl fits over the end of the egg like a dunce cap. Two pulls on the spring-loaded lever in the handle punctures a circle around the top of the egg that can be gently pried off. Scissor-style models were faster and did the job, but their shell-puncturing teeth left a jagged edge flecked with shell shards. One model's flimsy handles bent after only a few uses. Spring-loaded versions fared better. We sliced a dozen eggs with each of these models; while neither perfectly topped every egg, the Rösle Egg Topper produced many more shells with precise, clean edges. Brands are listed in order of preference. See AmericasTestKitchen.com for updates and complete testing results.

HIGHLY RECOMMENDED

RÖSLE Egg Topper
PRICE: $22
COMMENTS: This sturdy, plunger-shaped model was the most precise, quickly topping eggs with neat, even breaks.

RECOMMENDED

PADERNO WORLD CUISINE
Stainless-Steel Egg Top Cutter
PRICE: $26.18
COMMENTS: This spring-loaded model occasionally created perfectly topped eggs but too often cracked the bottom shell.

FOX RUN Egg Topper
PRICE: $6.02
COMMENTS: This scissor-style egg topper worked, but its handles were flimsy and it left behind jagged shards.

FLUFFY OMELETS

✔ **WHY THIS RECIPE WORKS:** A different breed than French-style rolled omelets or diner-style omelets folded into half-moons, fluffy omelets are made by baking whipped eggs in a skillet until they rise above the lip of the pan. We love their impressive height and delicate texture. But most recipes result in oozing soufflés or dry, bouncy rounds—or eggs that barely puff up at all. To give our omelet lofty height without making it tough, we folded butter-enriched yolks into stiffly whipped whites stabilized with cream of tartar. The whipped whites gave the omelet great lift while the yolks and butter kept it tender and rich-tasting. We chose light but flavorful fillings that satisfied without weighing down the omelet.

WE'VE MADE OUR FAIR SHARE OF OMELETS. MOST OF those have been either the refined French roll with its pure yellow surface and creamy, sparingly filled center or the hearty diner version that's browned spottily, generously stuffed with cheese and other fillings, and folded into a half-moon. But there's a third, less familiar style that's nothing like these other two. Often referred to as a fluffy omelet, this version dwarfs the diner type by at least a couple of inches. Some specimens are so puffed up that they look like folded-over soufflés—which, in a sense, they are. Most call for whipping air into the eggs and baking the omelet in the oven, where it rises above the lip of the skillet. Beyond the appeal of this omelet's lofty height and its promise of a delicate, airy texture, we've always been attracted to the idea of cooking an omelet in the oven, since this would eliminate the usual fiddling with the burner flame to prevent overcooking. Using the oven's ambient heat also seemed like a more forgiving approach.

With high expectations, we tried several recipes, figuring we'd pull pan after pan of tall, gently set omelets from the oven. We did not. With few exceptions, we got a motley crew of oozing soufflés and dry, bouncy Styrofoam rounds, as well as some omelets that barely puffed up at all. Where had these recipes taken a wrong turn?

Texturewise, the most promising recipe we tried began with whipping four whole eggs in a stand mixer until the mixture was foamy (aerating the eggs helps them rise), then pouring the whipped eggs into a buttered nonstick skillet and baking them in a 375-degree oven for 7 minutes. The omelet's inside had set nicely, but its sides and bottom had toughened up. Adjusting the cooking times and oven temperature didn't improve the results. We even introduced a lid to the pan, hoping that trapping steam would prevent the omelet from drying out, but this kept only the top tender and moist; the bottom still formed a tough, scaly crust. Flavorwise, it was also pretty lean.

Leaving the oven alone, we moved on to examine the other core variable: the eggs. The omelets were cooking up tough, so our job was to tenderize them, which meant figuring out a way to weaken the structure of the egg foam—the cluster of air bubbles made by whipping them. Adding dairy seemed logical, since it contains the dual tenderizers water and fat (we add it to scrambled eggs for these very reasons). When the proteins in eggs are heated, they bond to form a latticed gel in a process known as coagulation. Fat from the dairy coats the proteins and prevents the bonds from becoming so strong that the eggs toughen, while the dairy's water dilutes the proteins and makes it more difficult for them to come into contact with each other in the first place.

We tried 1 tablespoon each of milk, heavy cream, and—mindful of our omelet's lean taste—melted butter. But each one weakened the egg foam so dramatically that it couldn't hold enough air to increase in volume. The melted butter added a particularly nice richness, so we decided to stick with it. For a second attempt, we whipped the eggs before adding the butter, thinking that building structure before introducing a tenderizer might help. But that method flopped, too. The egg foam wasn't strong enough to support the extra fat and collapsed before cooking—hardly the more tender structure we had in mind.

We were several dozen tests in at this point, but these experiments had clarified a valuable point: While we needed to tenderize the eggs, we also needed to start with the strongest possible egg foam. That wasn't going to happen by whipping whole eggs, since the fat in the yolks was already tenderizing the mixture a little. Instead,

FLUFFY OMELET WITH MUSHROOM FILLING

we separated the eggs, whipping just the whites to form stiff peaks (think meringues) and whisking 1 tablespoon of melted butter with the yolks before folding them into the whites. This test was the turning point. Now that the whites were stiff and stable, they were able to support the additional fat of the yolks and butter.

Well, at least they held on for a couple of minutes. Then the mixture separated and finally deflated again. We felt defeated, until we thought more about that meringue analogy. Whipping the egg whites to stiff peaks is part of what ensures stable meringues; the other part is adding a stabilizer such as cream of tartar. The acidic ingredient preserves that stability by slowing the formation of sulfur bonds in egg whites; if too many bonds form, the white's protein structure becomes too rigid, and the network that holds the whipped air and water in place begins to collapse. We saw no reason why it wouldn't have the same effect in our omelet. Before beating the whites, we sprinkled ¼ teaspoon of cream of tartar evenly over their surface. This batch of whites didn't look any different as they whipped, but the results were convincing after we folded in the yolk mixture and waited. Seven minutes later, they were still standing tall.

We proceeded with our method, melting a pat of butter in the skillet, pouring in the airy eggs, smoothing the top with a spatula, and sliding the pan into a preheated oven. About 4 minutes later, we pulled a gorgeously puffed omelet out of the oven. It not only looked beautiful and held its shape but was also perfectly tender, with the requisite richness.

Our only remaining task was to come up with fillings. The delicate nature of this omelet meant that we couldn't throw just anything in there—and certainly not in large quantities. Instead, we would need to use small amounts of bold ingredients. A light sprinkle of Parmesan made for a nice minimalist option, but we also worked up a few more substantial variations: one with asparagus and smoked salmon, one with mushrooms, and another with artichokes and bacon.

The trick was figuring out when, exactly, to add the fillings. Sprinkling them on after the omelet had baked meant that the filling rested on—but did not mesh with—the puffy bed of eggs. Filling the omelets before they went into the oven was a better solution. To make

sure that the eggs set but didn't brown too thoroughly, we poured them into the hot buttered skillet and then immediately removed the skillet from the heat to sprinkle on the fillings. Then into the oven it went. When we pulled the baked omelet from the oven, the eggs were beautifully puffed up and, what's more, gently surrounded the fillings, ensuring that each bite contained a flavor and texture contrast: rich but delicate eggs, a hit of salty Parmesan, and savory vegetables or meat.

It was safe to say that our puffy omelet was the most impressive-looking omelet we'd ever made—and now it was the most forgiving to pull off, too.

Fluffy Omelet

SERVES 2

A teaspoon of white vinegar or lemon juice can be used in place of the cream of tartar, and a hand-held mixer or a whisk can be used in place of a stand mixer. We recommend using the fillings that accompany this recipe; they are designed not to interfere with the cooking of the omelet.

4	large eggs, separated
1	tablespoon unsalted butter, melted, plus 1 tablespoon unsalted butter
¼	teaspoon salt
¼	teaspoon cream of tartar
1	recipe filling (recipes follow)
1	ounce Parmesan cheese, grated (½ cup)

1. Adjust oven rack to middle position and heat oven to 375 degrees. Whisk egg yolks, melted butter, and salt together in bowl. Place egg whites in bowl of stand mixer and sprinkle cream of tartar over surface. Fit stand mixer with whisk and whip egg whites on medium-low speed until foamy, 2 to 2½ minutes. Increase speed to medium-high and whip until stiff peaks just start to form, 2 to 3 minutes. Fold egg yolk mixture into egg whites until no white streaks remain.

2. Heat remaining 1 tablespoon butter in 12-inch ovensafe nonstick skillet over medium-high heat, swirling to coat bottom of pan. When butter foams, quickly add egg mixture, spreading into even layer with spatula. Remove pan from heat and gently sprinkle filling and

Parmesan evenly over top of omelet. Transfer to oven and cook until center of omelet springs back when lightly pressed, 4½ minutes for slightly wet omelet and 5 minutes for dry omelet.

3. Run spatula around edges of omelet to loosen, shaking gently to release. Slide omelet onto cutting board and let stand for 30 seconds. Using spatula, fold omelet in half. Cut omelet in half crosswise and serve immediately.

Asparagus and Smoked Salmon Filling
MAKES ¾ CUP

- 1 teaspoon olive oil
- 1 shallot, sliced thin
- 5 ounces asparagus, trimmed and cut on bias into ¼-inch lengths
  Salt and pepper
- 1 ounce smoked salmon, chopped
- ½ teaspoon lemon juice

Heat oil in 12-inch nonstick skillet over medium-high heat until shimmering. Add shallot and cook until softened and starting to brown, about 2 minutes. Add asparagus, pinch salt, and pepper to taste, and cook, stirring frequently, until crisp-tender, 5 to 7 minutes. Transfer asparagus mixture to bowl and stir in salmon and lemon juice.

Mushroom Filling
MAKES ¾ CUP

- 1 teaspoon olive oil
- 1 shallot, sliced thin
- 4 ounces white or cremini mushrooms, trimmed and chopped
  Salt and pepper
- 1 teaspoon balsamic vinegar

Heat oil in 12-inch nonstick skillet over medium-high heat until shimmering. Add shallot and cook until softened and starting to brown, about 2 minutes. Add mushrooms, ⅛ teaspoon salt, and pepper to taste. Cook until liquid has evaporated and mushrooms begin to brown, 6 to 8 minutes. Transfer mixture to bowl and stir in vinegar.

Artichoke and Bacon Filling
MAKES ¾ CUP

- 2 slices bacon, cut into ¼-inch pieces
- 1 shallot, sliced thin
- 5 ounces frozen artichoke hearts, thawed, patted dry, and chopped
  Salt and pepper
- ½ teaspoon lemon juice

Cook bacon in 12-inch nonstick skillet over medium-high heat until crisp, 3 to 6 minutes. Using slotted spoon, transfer bacon to paper towel–lined plate. Pour off all but 1 teaspoon fat from skillet. Add shallot and cook until softened and starting to brown, about 2 minutes. Add artichokes, ⅛ teaspoon salt, and pepper to taste. Cook, stirring frequently, until artichokes begin to brown, 6 to 8 minutes. Transfer artichoke mixture to bowl and stir in bacon and lemon juice.

PERFECT FRIED EGGS

✔️ **WHY THIS RECIPE WORKS:** There are two common problems when it comes to fried eggs: undercooked whites and an overcooked yolk. A hot nonstick skillet, a touch of butter, and a lid combine to produce perfectly cooked fried eggs—with crisp edges, tender whites, and runny yolks—in just a few minutes.

TO US, A FRIED EGG SHOULD BE FRIED. WE'RE TALKING about the sort you find at the best diners: sunny-side up and crisp on its underside and edges, with a tender and opaque white and a perfectly runny yolk.

Ideally, we'd whip up this diner-style breakfast in our own kitchen, but the fried egg recipes we'd tried (and we'd run through our fair share) had failed to produce the results we wanted. Perhaps seasoned short-order cooks can consistently turn out great fried eggs because of their years of sheer practice. Or maybe a hot, slick commercial griddle is the key. All we knew for sure was that our home-cooked sunny-side-up eggs always had one of two possible defects. The first was undercooked whites—specifically, a slippery, transparent ring of white surrounding the yolk. The second was an overcooked yolk—often it was fluid on top but cooked solid on the underside.

These faults are due to a predicament that plagues most types of egg cookery: Yolks and whites set at different temperatures. This means that yolks, which start to solidify at around 158 degrees, are inevitably overcooked by the time the whites, which set up at 180 degrees, are opaque. Our objective, then, was to get the whites to cook through before the yolks did. We also wanted whites with beautifully bronzed, crispy edges. We had our work cut out for us.

There are two basic approaches for tackling an egg's disparate doneness temperatures: Cook low and slow or hot and fast. The former calls for breaking the egg into a warm, greased nonstick skillet and letting it gradually come to temperature over low heat, which can take 5 or more minutes. If the flame is low enough, the heat will firm up the white before the yolk sets. The downside: This technique doesn't add browning or crispiness. Raising the heat toward the end of cooking only overcooks the entire egg.

The opposite method blasts the egg with fierce heat from the start in an attempt to cook the white so quickly that it is out of the pan before the yolk even considers setting up. The best example that we've tried comes from Spanish chef José Andrés, who calls for shallow-frying an egg in a tilted skillet containing an inch or so of very hot olive oil. Within seconds, the bottom of the white bubbles and browns, and as you continuously baste the egg with hot oil, the top of the white cooks through as well. The whole process happens so quickly (just 30 seconds or so) that the yolk can't possibly overcook, and the result—a filigree of browned, crispy egg surrounding a tender white and a runny yolk—is just what we wanted.

And yet, there were drawbacks. The flavor of the egg wasn't quite what we had in mind. Olive oil gave it a great savory taste, but it lacked the buttery richness of a diner-style egg. What's more, the sputtering oil made a mess of our stovetop and threatened to burn our forearms. The method also required cooking only one egg at a time. Sure, they cooked quickly, but we wanted to produce two or four eggs at one time. Could we use high heat and far less oil and be able to feed two people breakfast in one go?

We reviewed what we had learned: First, it was difficult to get the eggs to cook evenly when we broke them one by one into the pan. Breaking the eggs into small bowls ahead of time so that all we had to do was slide them into the pan saved time—and went a long way in a recipe in which mere seconds make a difference. Plus, it worked equally well with two or four eggs. Second, it was important to let the pan fully preheat low and slow. A quick blast of high heat can cause hot spots to form and, thus, the eggs to cook at different rates. We got the best results by adding a teaspoon of vegetable oil to the skillet and setting it over low heat for a full 5 minutes. You also need a pan roomy enough for the eggs to spread out but not so much that large areas of the pan remain empty, which could cause the fat to burn. A 12- or 14-inch pan works best for four eggs,

PERFECT FRIED EGGS

an 8- or 9-inch pan for two. Finally, adding a couple of pats of butter to the pan right before slipping in the eggs resulted in great flavor and browning due to the butter's milk proteins.

Going forward, we fried a few rounds of eggs on medium-high heat after preheating the skillet on low. The butter and oil sizzled nicely and the eggs started to brown almost immediately. But (perhaps predictably) things deteriorated from there, with the whites undercooking or the yolks overcooking, depending on when we reached for our spatula. Lowering the heat once the whites were browned at the edges did let them solidify before the yolks set up, but that process took so long that the whites, in effect, oversolidified, turning tough and rubbery.

For a moment we were stumped—until we thought back to the key to Andrés's shallow-fried eggs: basting. Basting the eggs with hot fat helped quickly cook the top and bottom of the white before the yolk could set up. We weren't up for basting due to its accompanying splatter, but how else could we rapidly generate heat from above? We pictured ourself in a diner, watching a line cook perch an overturned aluminum bowl on top of griddle-fried eggs to speed cooking. How about a lid? The reflected heat and steam trapped by a lid might just work.

For our next test, we covered the pan as soon as the eggs were in place. Ninety seconds later, we lifted the lid for a peek, fingers crossed, before using a spatula to quickly remove our specimens. The good news was that the vexing ring of jiggly, uncooked white around the yolk was gone, and the white was perfectly tender, with a nicely browned underside and edges. The bad news was that the lid had trapped too much heat: The yolk was now a bit overcooked.

Instead, we slid the covered skillet off the burner entirely, hoping the gentle residual heat of the pan would firm up the white but not the yolk. It took a few dozen more eggs to get the timing just right but—stopwatch in hand—we finally nailed down the proper intervals: One minute over medium-high heat followed by an additional 15 to 45 seconds off heat produced beautifully bronzed edges; just-set, opaque whites; and fluid yolks every time.

Mission accomplished: perfect diner-style fried eggs—no diner necessary.

Perfect Fried Eggs

SERVES 2

When checking the eggs for doneness, lift the lid just a crack to prevent loss of steam should they need further cooking. When cooked, the thin layer of white surrounding the yolk will turn opaque, but the yolk should remain runny. To cook two eggs, use an 8- or 9-inch nonstick skillet and halve the amounts of oil and butter. You can use this method with extra-large or jumbo eggs without altering the timing.

2 teaspoons vegetable oil
4 large eggs
   Salt and pepper
2 teaspoons unsalted butter, cut into 4 pieces and chilled

1. Heat oil in 12- or 14-inch nonstick skillet over low heat for 5 minutes. Meanwhile, crack 2 eggs into small bowl and season with salt and pepper. Repeat with remaining 2 eggs and second small bowl.

2. Increase heat to medium-high and heat until oil is shimmering. Add butter to skillet and quickly swirl to coat pan. Working quickly, pour 1 bowl of eggs in 1 side of pan and second bowl of eggs in other side. Cover and cook for 1 minute. Remove skillet from burner and let stand, covered, 15 to 45 seconds for runny yolks (white around edge of yolk will be barely opaque), 45 to 60 seconds for soft but set yolks, and about 2 minutes for medium-set yolks. Slide eggs onto plates and serve.

Elegant Brunch Favorites

Chef Ashley Moore prepares to gently whisk in whipped egg whites for light and tender lemon ricotta pancakes.

SOMETIMES WE LIKE TO STEP IT UP AT BRUNCH AND SERVE DISHES outside our usual repertoire. Take brioche. Whether served as a thick slice from a distinctively shaped large loaf or a small bun, the bread is pillow soft and of course richly flavored from the hefty amount of butter this bread requires. In reviewing recipes we were surprised to see that the butter is often added piece by piece to the dough—a tedious process. And striking the right ratio can be tricky—we wanted a buttery, but not greasy, bread. Our goal was twofold: Find a simpler way to make brioche at home and be sure that our method resulted in a loaf (or buns) just as good as those crafted by artisan bakers at our favorite bakery.

Sure, you can get away with serving traditional pancakes at brunch, but if you really want to serve something special, try ricotta pancakes. Often brightened with lemon, these light and fluffy flapjacks are sure to impress—if you can get them right. Some ricotta cakes are heavy and wet from an overload of cheese. We'd need to strike the right balance. And skip the maple syrup; you'll want to serve these cakes with a warm, complementary fruit compote—and we have just the right recipes for you.

BRIOCHE

✓ **WHY THIS RECIPE WORKS:** The average brioche recipe is 50 percent butter, and the high fat content can make the brioche incredibly tender—or it can cause the dough to separate into a greasy mess. For rich, tender brioche without the hassle of painstakingly adding softened butter to the dough little by little as it is kneaded, we melted the butter and added it directly to the eggs. Then we dispensed with the stand mixer and opted for an equally effective no-knead approach that lets time do most of the work: An overnight rest in the fridge developed both structure and flavor. We used two simple loaf pans and then, to build structure and ensure an even, fine crumb, we shaped the dough into four tight balls before placing two in each pan. The dough can also be divided to make brioche buns or traditionally shaped loaves using fluted brioche molds.

WELL-MADE BRIOCHE IS SOMETHING OF A MIRACLE: Despite being laden with butter and eggs, it manages to avoid the density of a pound cake and turn out incredibly light and airy. Yet this gossamer-wing texture still provides brioche with enough structure to serve as a base for a sandwich or toast slathered with jam, or even as the foundation for bread pudding. But achieving these results is a balancing act—and a tricky one at that.

Most butter-enriched doughs, like those for sandwich bread or dinner rolls, contain between 10 and 20 percent butter. The average brioche recipe brings the ratio up to 50 percent (or 5 parts butter to 10 parts flour). Because fat lubricates the wheat proteins in the flour, any amount at all will inhibit their ability to form gluten, the network of cross-linked proteins that gives bread its structure. The more fat the greater the interference. This can make brioche incredibly tender—or it can cause the dough to separate into a greasy mess.

The typical brioche method goes as follows: After a sponge of flour, yeast, and water sits overnight in order to ferment and build flavor, additional flour, yeast, and water, as well as salt, sugar, and several eggs, are added, and the mixture is kneaded in a stand mixer until a strong gluten network has begun to form. The next step is to add butter, softened to just the right temperature, a few tablespoons at a time. Only after one portion is fully incorporated into the dough is the next added. This painstaking process, which can take more than 20 minutes, is necessary to ensure that the butter is completely and evenly combined without causing the dough to separate. Next, the dough is left to rise at room temperature for a few hours and then chilled in the refrigerator for anywhere from an hour to overnight to firm up the butter—an essential step when shaping a sticky, wet dough. Once cold, the dough is shaped into loaves, left to rise yet again, and—at long last—baked. Phew.

Our goal: to make tender, plush brioche with butter-rich flavor but no butter-induced headache.

Though it was tempting, we knew that dumping everything (butter included) together at the start and letting the stand mixer knead it all into submission wouldn't work. All that softened butter would coat the wheat proteins (which normally come together to form gluten as soon as water is added to the mix) so thoroughly that no amount of kneading would develop sufficient structure.

But what about using cold butter? Cut into the flour before adding other ingredients, the solid little chunks surely wouldn't coat the proteins as readily as softened fat, making it possible to develop at least some gluten—or so we hoped.

Using a respectable 45 percent fat-to-flour ratio and simplifying things by leaving out the sponge, we began by cutting cold butter into flour in a food processor. After transferring the mixture to the bowl of a stand mixer, we threw in the yeast, sugar, and salt. With the dough hook turning, we gradually added some water and a few beaten eggs. The dough was quite wet but still had a surprising amount of structure. After putting the dough through the usual steps—proof, chill, proof—we baked it, fingers crossed.

NO-KNEAD BRIOCHE

The results? Not great, but not half bad either. The interior crumb was far too open, with large, irregular holes, and the bread had a cottony, crumbly texture, both of which suggested that it needed more gluten development. But its having any structure at all meant that we were onto something.

A familiar approach popped to mind: the "no-knead" bread technique first popularized by Mark Bittman and Jim Lahey in the *New York Times*. Basically, you combine all your ingredients and let the mixture sit for hours. During this long rest, enzymes naturally present in wheat help untangle the wheat proteins that eventually come together to form an organized gluten network. This allows the dough to stitch itself together into a loaf containing plenty of structure with only a bit of stirring and a couple of folds—no actual kneading required. The key to this technique is a very wet dough (the more water

the more efficient the enzymes). And happily, brioche dough is highly hydrated.

We gave the no-knead approach a whirl, cutting the butter into the flour in the food processor like before but then simply mixing the liquid ingredients into the dry ones and stirring with a wooden spoon. This produced a dough that was soupy—exactly what we wanted. We covered it and let it sit at room temperature while it proofed, giving it a series of folds at 30-minute intervals to encourage the gluten to form. As we'd hoped, after several hours, the dough had just as much strength as the previous machine-kneaded one. Even better: After being chilled, shaped, and proofed a second time, it baked up just as nicely. Feeling emboldened, we wondered if we could eliminate the food processor step as well. So this time, we simply melted the butter, let it cool, and then whisked it into the egg and milk mixture before adding the liquid to the dry ingredients. To our gratification, this simplification produced a loaf that was indistinguishable from the one in which we'd cut the butter into the flour first.

Still, our loaves remained cottony and open-crumbed—a sure sign that they needed more gluten than our hand-mixed method could provide on its own. But we had a few tricks up our sleeve.

First, the flour: Since its protein content is directly related to its ability to form gluten (the more protein it has, the more structure it can provide to the dough), it was no shock that brioche made with flour containing the highest amount of protein—bread flour—was the clear winner.

Next, we'd let the dough sit even longer, a process that would not only increase gluten development but also add more flavor, since it would give the starches in the dough more time to ferment (a role normally played by a sponge). Gluten development and fermentation are slowed but not halted by cold temperatures, so we'd also extend the dough's second rest in the fridge (where it wouldn't run the risk of overproofing and collapsing), giving it even more strength. Sure enough, brioche made from dough that was allowed to rest overnight in the fridge was much improved: It had a more fine-textured and resilient crumb than any previous versions, as well as a more complex flavor.

Lastly, we gave some consideration to our shaping method. Until now, we'd been forming the dough into a single long loaf. We realized that we could add even more strength and structure to the dough by dividing it in two and shaping each half into a tight, round ball instead. Placed side by side in the pan, the two balls merged during rising and baking to form a single loaf. Even this little bit of extra manipulation made the crumb a bit finer and more uniform. And if shaping them once was good, we figured that twice might be even better. After letting the dough rounds rest, we patted them flat once more and then reshaped them into tight balls. As expected, the interior crumb was fine-textured, uniform, and resilient but still delicate.

Finally, we had a reliable and relatively hands-off brioche recipe that could hold its own against those from the best bakeries in town.

No-Knead Brioche
MAKES 2 LOAVES

High-protein King Arthur Bread Flour works best with this recipe, though other bread flours will suffice. The test kitchen's preferred loaf pan measures 8½ by 4½ inches; if you use a 9 by 5-inch pan, start checking for doneness 5 minutes earlier. If you don't have a baking stone, bake the bread on a preheated rimmed baking sheet.

3¼ cups (17¾ ounces) bread flour
2¼ teaspoons instant or rapid-rise yeast
1½ teaspoons salt
7   large eggs (1 lightly beaten with pinch salt)
½   cup water, room temperature
⅓   cup (2⅓ ounces) sugar
16   tablespoons unsalted butter, melted and cooled slightly

1. Whisk flour, yeast, and salt together in large bowl. Whisk 6 eggs, water, and sugar together in medium bowl until sugar has dissolved. Whisk in butter until smooth. Add egg mixture to flour mixture and stir with wooden spoon until uniform mass forms and no dry flour remains, about 1 minute. Cover bowl with plastic wrap and let stand for 10 minutes.

2. Holding edge of dough with your fingertips, fold dough over itself by gently lifting and folding edge of dough toward middle. Turn bowl 45 degrees; fold again. Turn bowl and fold dough 6 more times (total of 8 folds). Cover with plastic and let rise for 30 minutes. Repeat folding and rising every 30 minutes, 3 more times. After fourth set of folds, cover bowl tightly with plastic and refrigerate for at least 16 hours or up to 48 hours.

3. Transfer dough to well-floured counter and divide into 4 equal pieces. Working with 1 piece of dough at a time, pat dough into 4-inch disk. Working around circumference of dough, fold edges of dough toward center

NOTES FROM THE TEST KITCHEN

LOOK, MA: NO KNEADING

Folding the dough as it proofs is an important step—and the only active work you'll have to do. Gently lift an edge of the dough and fold it over itself, turning the bowl 45 degrees and repeating until you've made a full circle (total of eight folds).

MELTED BUTTER EASES THE WAY

Traditionally, making a rich dough like brioche means kneading all of the ingredients to develop gluten—except butter. Butter (softened to 68 degrees) is added tablespoon by tablespoon only after the mixture begins to develop into dough. This is a long and painstaking process. It's an important one, too: If the butter isn't added slowly, the dough can break into a greasy mess. When we decided to ditch tradition and use a "no-knead" technique, we realized that this would also solve our tricky butter problem. In a no-knead approach, the dough (which must be very wet) sits for a long time, stitching itself together to form gluten—all without any help from a mixer. With kneading out of the equation, we were able to melt the butter and add it all at once—a faster and far less demanding approach.

BRIOCHE FOR BRUNCH

DAY BEFORE:
- Make dough; let rest for 10 minutes
- Fold every 30 minutes for 2 hours
- Refrigerate overnight

MORNING OF, 7:00 A.M.:
- Shape; let rise for 1½ to 2 hours
- Bake for 35 to 45 minutes
- Let cool for 2 hours

until ball forms. Flip dough over and, without applying pressure, move your hands in small circular motions to form dough into smooth, taut round. (If dough sticks to your hands, lightly dust top of dough with flour.) Repeat with remaining dough. Cover dough rounds loosely with plastic and let rest for 5 minutes.

4. Grease two 8½ by 4½-inch loaf pans. After 5 minutes, flip each dough ball so seam side is facing up, pat into 4-inch disk, and repeat rounding step. Place 2 rounds, seam side down, side by side into prepared pans and press gently into corners. Cover loaves loosely with plastic and let rise at room temperature until almost doubled in size (dough should rise to about ½ inch below top edge of pan), 1½ to 2 hours. Thirty minutes before baking, adjust oven rack to middle position, place baking stone on rack, and heat oven to 350 degrees.

5. Remove plastic and brush loaves gently with remaining 1 egg beaten with salt. Set loaf pans on stone and bake until golden brown and internal temperature registers 190 degrees, 35 to 45 minutes, rotating pans halfway through baking. Transfer pans to wire rack and let cool for 5 minutes. Remove loaves from pans, return to wire rack, and let cool completely before slicing and serving, about 2 hours.

VARIATIONS
No-Knead Brioche Buns
MAKES 10 BUNS

1. Line 2 rimmed baking sheets with parchment paper. Transfer dough to well-floured counter and divide into 10 equal pieces. Working with 1 piece of dough at a time, pat dough into disk. Working around circumference of dough, fold edges of dough toward center until ball forms. Flip dough over and, without applying pressure, move your hands in small circular motions to form dough into smooth, taut round. (Tackiness of dough against counter and circular motion should work dough into smooth, even ball, but if dough sticks to your hands, lightly dust top of dough with flour.) Repeat with remaining dough.

2. Arrange buns on prepared sheets, five per sheet. Cover loosely with plastic and let rise at room temperature until almost doubled in size, 1 to 1½ hours. Thirty minutes before baking, adjust oven racks to upper-middle and lower-middle positions and heat oven to 350 degrees.

3. Remove plastic and brush rolls gently with remaining 1 egg beaten with salt. Bake until golden brown and internal temperature registers 190 degrees, 15 to 20 minutes, rotating and switching sheets halfway through baking. Transfer sheets to wire rack and let cool for 5 minutes. Transfer buns to wire rack. Serve warm or at room temperature.

No-Knead Brioche à Tête
MAKES 2 LOAVES

Traditional loaves of *brioche à tête* achieve their fluted sides and conical shape from brioche pans.

1. Transfer dough to well-floured counter and divide into 2 equal pieces. Remove golf ball–size piece of dough from each. Pat 2 large pieces of dough into 4-inch disks and 2 small pieces of dough into ½-inch disks. Working with 1 piece of dough at a time, work around circumference of dough; fold edges of dough toward center until ball forms. Flip dough over and, without applying pressure, move your hands in small circular motions to form dough into smooth, taut round. (Tackiness of dough against counter and circular motion should work dough into smooth, even ball, but if dough sticks to your hands, lightly dust top of dough with flour.) Repeat with remaining dough. Cover dough rounds loosely with plastic and let rest for 5 minutes.

2. Grease two 8- to 8½-inch fluted brioche pans. After 5 minutes, flip each dough ball so seam side is facing up, pat into 4-inch and ½-inch disks, and repeat rounding step. Place larger rounds, seam side down, into prepared pans and press gently into corners. Place smaller rounds, seam side down, in center of larger rounds, pushing down gently so only top halves of smaller rounds are showing. Cover loaves loosely with plastic and let rise at room

temperature until almost doubled in size (dough should rise to about ½ inch below top edge of pan), 1½ to 2 hours. Thirty minutes before baking, adjust oven rack to middle position, place baking stone on rack, and heat oven to 350 degrees.

3. Remove plastic and brush loaves gently with remaining 1 egg beaten with salt. Set pans on stone and bake until golden brown and internal temperature registers 190 degrees, 35 to 45 minutes, rotating pans halfway through baking. Transfer pans to wire rack and let cool for 5 minutes. Remove loaves from pans, return to wire rack, and let cool completely before slicing and serving, about 2 hours.

EQUIPMENT CORNER

RATING BRIOCHE PANS

Traditional loaves of *brioche à tête* achieve their fluted sides and conical shape from brioche pans. We tested four large brioche pans, 8 to 8½ inches in diameter, rating them on handling and release, browning, crumb structure, and the shape of the finished loaves. We found that each 8-inch brioche pan held the equivalent of one loaf pan. All released the breads easily (after being coated with vegetable oil spray) and were simple to clean.

Only our favorite pan, the **Gobel 8-Inch Tinned Steel Brioche Mold, 6-Cup** ($10), a French import with a traditional shiny finish, produced loaves that were perfect, with a golden crust, airy crumb, and a flawless shape. See AmericasTestKitchen.com for updates and complete testing results.

GOBEL'S 8-INCH TINNED STEEL BRIOCHE MOLD GIVES OUR BREAD A CLASSIC SHAPE

LEMON RICOTTA PANCAKES

✓ **WHY THIS RECIPE WORKS:** Light, fluffy ricotta pancakes are more sophisticated than traditional pancakes, making them perfect for special occasions, but you have to get the balance of cheese and structure just right or your pancakes will fall flat. We compensate for the extra weight of the ricotta by doubling the amount of egg whites and whipping them for added lightness. To ensure maximum lift, we add plenty of lemon juice and baking soda, which combine to produce carbon dioxide that super-inflates the egg foam. Warm fruit compotes provide the perfect finishing touch.

WE'VE ALWAYS LIKED PANCAKES, BUT UNTIL RECENTLY we'd never actually been wowed by them. That all changed when we were served ricotta pancakes at a brunch. We'd been seeing this style of pancake on upscale restaurant menus around town, but with a signature ingredient like ricotta, we'd always imagined them to be somewhat heavy and damp. These cakes were anything but. They had a remarkably light, tender, pillowy texture and a sweet, milky flavor that made them more intriguing than the usual griddle cakes. While we wouldn't consider making plain old pancakes and syrup for brunch guests, we could easily imagine dressing up the ricotta kind with confectioners' sugar or fresh fruit toppings and serving them to company.

We gathered a handful of recipes, which by and large looked like variations on a typical pancake formula: flour, salt, a leavener, eggs, milk, sugar and vanilla extract for flavor, melted butter, and of course ricotta. Mostly it was the cheese content that varied; some batters were enriched with just a few spoonfuls of ricotta while others were loaded with it (more than a 2:1 ratio of cheese to flour). Presumably, the recipes that called for a conservative amount of cheese were trying to ensure that its moisture wouldn't weigh down the cakes, but with so little cheese in the mix, the results hardly earned their ricotta name. Meanwhile, the cheese-laden recipes confirmed that ricotta cakes could indeed be wet and heavy.

LEMON RICOTTA PANCAKES WITH PEAR-BLACKBERRY TOPPING

our working recipe and then beating the whites with the sugar and whisking just the yolks with the ricotta and milk before adding them to the dry ingredients. But it turns out that there's only so much heavy lifting two whipped whites and a little baking powder can do. The pancakes weren't exactly dense, but they'd maintained that somewhat starchy, conventional pancake texture.

We realized that if we wanted pancakes that were more soufflé-like, we'd have to cut back on the "bready" element: the flour. We took it down to ⅔ cup, and for a few minutes it seemed that our work was done. The cakes rose beautifully and only collapsed a bit when flipped, but they completely deflated when they hit the plate. Then it occurred to us that we might get better results if we added a second leavener, so ½ teaspoon of baking soda went into the mix. Of course, baking soda requires an acid to react, so we squeezed a few teaspoons of lemon juice into the batter as well and hoped that the lemon's brightness would complement the cheese. As it turned out, the lemon-ricotta flavor match was great—so we bolstered it with some lemon zest—and the hotcakes rose high on the griddle. Two leaveners seemed to be the answer—until the pancakes again fell flat on the plate.

At this point we either had to cut back on the cheese or call in reinforcements. Hedging our bets, we did a bit of both. We trimmed the cheese back to 1 cup and, invoking the "many hands make light work" principle, whipped two more whites. This, finally, was the combination we were looking for: The lift from the leavener combined with the four whipped egg whites made for the lightest pancakes ever. And yet, our scientific side made us wonder if all three leavening sources—baking soda, baking powder, and a large amount of egg foam— were really necessary, so we made one more batch and ditched the baking powder (ditching the baking soda was out of the question since the lemon juice was a keeper). Happily, nobody missed it.

There was another bonus to switching to baking soda: The cakes were browning a little more deeply and evenly. While we were pleased by this effect, which boosted flavor, we were also a little surprised. Alkaline baking soda

The obvious solution was to go down the middle, so we started with a moderate 1¼ cups of ricotta, which we stirred together with two eggs, a couple of tablespoons of melted butter, ⅓ cup of milk, and a little sugar and vanilla. Separately, we whisked ¾ cup of flour with ½ teaspoon each of baking powder and salt and then combined the wet and dry ingredients and ladled the batter onto a hot griddle, where the pancakes cooked until golden on each side. It was a decent start, we thought, noticing the ricotta's rich, creamy presence when we took a bite. But texturewise, we had a ways to go: The pancakes had none of the billowy lightness of the ones we'd tasted at brunch.

Several recipes we'd found called for incorporating whipped egg whites into the batter like for a soufflé. We gave the technique a go, separating the two eggs in

can enhance browning by raising the pH of a food, but we'd assumed that with a pure acid like lemon juice in the mix, its effect would be neutralized. But our science editor explained that there were two other acid neutralizers in the batter: egg whites, which contribute alkalinity, and cheese, which contains casein proteins that buffer the action of the acid. As a result, the batter's pH was more than high enough to allow for rapid browning.

These exquisitely light, tender, and golden-brown pancakes were so good that we found ourselves eating them straight from the pan without even a dusting of powdered sugar. But to dress them up for company, we threw together a few quick fruit toppings, one made with apples, cranberries, and nutmeg; one with pears, blackberries, and cardamom; and another with plums, apricots, and cinnamon. Conveniently, we were able to soften the fruits (with a little sugar) in the microwave while the pancakes cooked.

With pancakes this easy and this good, we might never go back to ordinary flapjacks.

Lemon Ricotta Pancakes

MAKES 12 (4-INCH) PANCAKES; SERVES 3 TO 4

An electric griddle set at 325 degrees can also be used to cook the pancakes. We prefer the flavor of whole-milk ricotta, but part-skim will work, too; avoid nonfat ricotta. Serve with confectioners' sugar or one of our fruit toppings.

- ⅔ cup (3⅓ ounces) all-purpose flour
- ½ teaspoon baking soda
- ½ teaspoon salt
- 8 ounces (1 cup) whole-milk ricotta cheese
- 2 large eggs, separated, plus 2 large whites
- ⅓ cup whole milk
- 1 teaspoon grated lemon zest plus 4 teaspoons juice
- ½ teaspoon vanilla extract
- 2 tablespoons unsalted butter, melted
- ¼ cup (1¾ ounces) sugar
- 1-2 teaspoons vegetable oil

1. Adjust oven rack to middle position and heat oven to 200 degrees. Spray wire rack set inside rimmed baking sheet with vegetable oil spray; place in oven. Whisk flour, baking soda, and salt together in medium bowl and make well in center. Add ricotta, egg yolks, milk, lemon zest and juice, and vanilla and whisk until just combined. Gently stir in butter.

2. Using stand mixer fitted with whisk, whip egg whites on medium-low speed until foamy, about 1 minute. Increase speed to medium-high and whip whites to soft, billowy mounds, about 1 minute. Gradually add sugar and whip until glossy, soft peaks form, 1 to 2 minutes. Transfer one-third of whipped egg whites to batter and whisk gently until mixture is lightened. Using rubber spatula, gently fold remaining egg whites into batter.

3. Heat 1 teaspoon oil in 12-inch nonstick skillet over medium heat until shimmering. Using paper towels, wipe out oil, leaving thin film on bottom and sides of pan. Using ¼-cup measure or 2-ounce ladle, portion batter into pan in 3 places, leaving 2 inches between portions. Gently spread each portion into a 4-inch round. Cook until edges are set and first side is deep

NOTES FROM THE TEST KITCHEN

WHAT MAKES THESE CAKES SO LIGHT?
Here's how we keep the wet, milky ricotta from weighing down the pancakes.

LOTS OF WHIPPED WHITES
Just as when making soufflé, we whip the egg whites—in this case, four of them—which creates an egg foam that lightens the batter.

NOT TOO MUCH FLOUR
A moderate ⅔ cup of flour adds enough starch to shore up the egg foam's structure but not so much that the pancakes become bready.

AN ACID PLUS A BASE
Lemon juice not only contributes tangy flavor but also reacts with the alkaline baking soda to produce carbon dioxide that inflates the egg foam.

golden brown, 2 to 3 minutes. Using thin, wide spatula, flip pancakes and continue to cook until second side is golden brown, 2 to 3 minutes longer. Serve pancakes immediately or transfer to wire rack in preheated oven. Repeat with remaining batter, using remaining oil as needed.

Apple-Cranberry Pancake Topping
MAKES 2½ CUPS

- 3 Golden Delicious apples, peeled, cored, halved, and cut into ¼-inch pieces
- ¼ cup dried cranberries
- 1 tablespoon sugar
- 1 teaspoon cornstarch
  Pinch salt
  Pinch ground nutmeg

Combine all ingredients in bowl and microwave until apples are softened but not mushy and juices are slightly thickened, 4 to 6 minutes, stirring once halfway through microwaving. Stir and serve.

Pear-Blackberry Pancake Topping
MAKES 3 CUPS

- 3 ripe pears, peeled, halved, cored, and cut into ¼-inch pieces
- 1 tablespoon sugar
- 1 teaspoon cornstarch
  Pinch salt
  Pinch ground cardamom
- 5 ounces (1 cup) blackberries, berries more than 1 inch long cut in half crosswise

Combine pears, sugar, cornstarch, salt, and cardamom in bowl and microwave until pears are softened but not mushy and juices are slightly thickened, 4 to 6 minutes, stirring once halfway through microwaving. Stir in blackberries and serve.

Plum-Apricot Pancake Topping
MAKES 2½ CUPS

- 1½ pounds plums, halved, pitted, and cut into ¼-inch pieces
- ¼ cup dried apricots, chopped coarse
- 1 tablespoon sugar
- 1 teaspoon cornstarch
  Pinch salt
  Pinch ground cinnamon

Combine all ingredients in bowl and microwave until plums are softened but not mushy and juices are slightly thickened, 4 to 6 minutes, stirring once halfway through microwaving. Stir and serve.

RATING SUPERMARKET BACON

These days, buying bacon means choosing from a slew of options that range from center-cut to pepper-crusted, maple-flavored, specialty-wood-smoked, low-salt, or even reduced-fat. The latest style vying for market share is thick-cut strips. Since we last compared major brands in 2004, a bevy of heftier bacons have shown up alongside the traditional thin, shingled slices. But does a thicker cut offer anything more than just a bigger bite of bacon? To find out, we rounded up six thick strips (based partly on actual thickness rather than labels, since some fatter slices weren't identified as such) and four traditional slices from nationally available supermarket brands (choosing both styles from the same brand when possible) and invited colleagues to a tasting. Brands are listed in order of preference. See AmericasTestKitchen.com for updates and complete tasting results.

HIGHLY RECOMMENDED

FARMLAND Thick Sliced Bacon
PRICE: \$7.99 for $1\frac{1}{2}$ lb (\$0.33 per oz) **THICKNESS:** $\frac{1}{6}$ in
SALT: 2.17 g **PROTEIN:** 11.36 g **FAT:** 36.88 g
COMMENTS: This thick strip was also one of the meatiest, with saltiness offset by sweetness, all combining to deliver bacon balance. Tasters described it as "a good meaty slice" that was "sweet," "smoky, porky, and salty."

PLUMROSE Premium Thick Sliced Bacon
PRICE: \$5.99 for 1 lb (\$0.37 per oz) **THICKNESS:** $\frac{1}{8}$ in
SALT: 1.95 g **PROTEIN:**13.96 g **FAT:** 30.48 g
COMMENTS: With one of the highest amounts of protein, this "substantially meaty" bacon was "pleasantly smoky," "with very little fat." Plumrose is the only brand cured with brown sugar, which contributed to its "deeply browned, Maillard flavor."

RECOMMENDED

WRIGHT Naturally Hickory Smoked Bacon
PRICE: \$7.48 for $1\frac{1}{2}$ lb (\$0.31 per oz) **THICKNESS:** $\frac{1}{5}$ in
SALT: 1.28 g **PROTEIN:** 11.42 g **FAT:** 35.37 g
COMMENTS: This thick-cut bacon was "good all around," delivering "great smoky flavor with enough salt and sweet." Other tasters rated it the smokiest in the lineup and also praised its "meaty" taste and "substantial" texture.

WELLSHIRE FARMS Black Forest Dry Rubbed Salt Cured Bacon
PRICE: \$8.99 for $1\frac{1}{2}$ lb (\$0.50 per oz) **THICKNESS:** $\frac{1}{5}$ in
SALT: 1.2 g **PROTEIN:** 11.45 g **FAT:** 41.92 g
COMMENTS: This "substantial" thick-cut slice, the only bacon we tasted that was dry cured, was "smoky, sweet, salty, meaty—the four basic bacon food groups!" Others compared its sweetness with "barbecued brisket" or "burnt ends," with its "porky, sweet-but-not-too-sweet" taste.

RECOMMENDED *(cont.)*

OSCAR MAYER Naturally Hardwood Smoked Thick Cut Bacon
PRICE: \$7.49 for 1 lb (\$0.47 per oz) **THICKNESS:** $\frac{1}{6}$ in
SALT: 1.67 g **PROTEIN:** 12.86 g **FAT:** 38.28 g
COMMENTS: The thick version of classic Oscar Mayer bacon ranked in the middle of the pack for smokiness, just ahead of its thinner companion product. It was "deeply porky" and "meaty"—"a very nice, satisfying slice."

OSCAR MAYER Naturally Hardwood Smoked Bacon
PRICE: \$7.49 for 1 lb (\$0.47 per oz) **THICKNESS:** $\frac{1}{10}$ in
SALT: 1.60 g **PROTEIN:** 13.24 g **FAT:** 37.86 g
COMMENTS: With "a nice ratio of fat to lean meat," this regular-sliced strip cooked up "smoky" and "sweet," and tasted "not bad for thin bacon," as one taster deemed it. "Perfect in terms of crispness," summed up another.

HORMEL Black Label Bacon
PRICE: \$6.99 for 1 lb (\$0.44 per oz) **THICKNESS:** $\frac{1}{11}$ in
SALT: 1.58 g **PROTEIN:** 10.85 g **FAT:** 43.39 g
COMMENTS: Some found this bacon—one of two in our lineup that was sprayed with vaporized liquid smoke rather than dry smoked—"leathery" and "not very smoky." Others deemed it "good" and "decently meaty."

FARMLAND Hickory Smoked Bacon
PRICE: \$5.99 for 1 lb (\$0.37 per oz) **THICKNESS:** $\frac{1}{11}$ in
SALT: 1.58 g **PROTEIN:** 10.37 g **FAT:** 48.65
COMMENTS: While many tasters enjoyed our former favorite supermarket bacon's "woodsy smoke" and good "bacony flavor," perhaps due to unavoidable variation in agricultural products, it was far fattier than its thick-cut cousin. One taster described biting into it this way: "like eating a slab of fat."

Oatmeal Muffins & Granola

Dan explains to Chris that it is indeed necessary to process the toasted oats for muffins that are flavorful and tender, not tough.

THE HEARTY, NUTTY FLAVOR OF ROLLED OATS HOLDS LOTS OF APPEAL. Even in a bowl of simple oatmeal they're satisfying. We were looking to go further afield with oats and aimed to develop two portable oatmeal treats—a muffin and a great version of homemade granola—for those times when we didn't want the same old bowl of porridge.

We've made oatmeal cookies and even oatmeal cake but had never tackled an oatmeal muffin. We imagined a moist muffin with a light but hearty crumb and lightly spiced, great oatmeal flavor. Initial attempts resulted in heavy muffins with chewy bits of oats throughout, but the flavor of the oats wasn't coming through. We wanted to find a way to pack these muffins with great oat flavor but still ensure a moist and tender texture. We thought warm spices might provide a nice accent to the oat flavor; determining just what spice or spices would be another challenge.

Over the years, granola, once synonymous with hippie diets (i.e., more good for you than great-tasting), has gone gourmet. You can spend quite a lot for a small package that will be gone in a few bowlfuls or you can buy the mass-produced stuff that's dusty and overly sweetened. We wanted to develop our own recipe for really great granola. We pictured a mix of crunchy, lightly sweetened clusters of oats, nuts, and dried fruit. To achieve our ideal, we'd have to find the right balance of these ingredients as well as the right sweetener. And because fat adds flavor and crunch to granola, we'd need to determine whether to use butter or oil and how much we would need to deliver taste and texture, without greasiness. We wanted a recipe easy enough to make it a once-a-week or every-other-week ritual.

OATMEAL MUFFINS

☑ **WHY THIS RECIPE WORKS:** For an oatmeal muffin that is packed with oat flavor but also has a fine, tender texture, we processed old-fashioned rolled oats into a flour in the food processor. To boost the oat flavor further, we first toasted the oats in a couple of tablespoons of butter and eliminated extraneous spices from the batter. To ensure a lump-free batter, we used a whisk to fold the wet and dry ingredients together and allowed the batter to sit and hydrate for 20 minutes before baking. Finally, we made an apple crisp–inspired topping of crunchy oats, nuts, and brown sugar.

WE'VE ALWAYS BEEN INTERESTED IN THE IDEA OF A breakfast that boasts the best qualities of a great bowl of oatmeal—lightly sweet, oaty flavor and satisfying heartiness—in the portable form of a muffin. But we've yet to find a decent example of the confection. Oats are dry and tough, making them difficult to incorporate into a tender crumb. And what chance does their mild, nutty flavor have of shining through when it is clouded by loads of spices and sugar? We were determined to bake our way to a richly flavored, moist, and tender oatmeal muffin.

The real problem with most of the initial recipes we tested was the oats themselves. The most common approach was to toss a few handfuls of the old-fashioned rolled type (our usual choice for baking) into a quick bread–style muffin batter. This calls for separately combining the wet ingredients (melted butter, milk, light brown sugar, and eggs) and dry ingredients (all-purpose flour, baking powder, baking soda, and salt) and then blending the two mixtures together. The result of this dead-simple style? Muffins speckled with dry, chewy oats featuring raw white centers.

It was clear that simply stirring raw oats into the batter wasn't enough to sufficiently hydrate and cook them. A few recipes sought to avoid the problem by calling for quick oats, which are precooked and rolled into thin flakes before packaging, but these muffins presented their own issues. Gone were the dry, uncooked bits flecking the crumb, but with them went any trace of oat taste.

Sticking with the more robust old-fashioned rolled oats, we set about trying to find the best way to ensure that they would cook through. When a soak in cold milk failed to soften the sturdy flakes, we tried heating the milk first. We poured 2 cups of boiling milk over an equal amount of oats and after allowing the mixture to cool to room temperature, we incorporated the oatmeal mush into our batter. Still no luck: The muffins were now riddled with gummy pockets. We produced similar results when we simmered the oats and milk as we would for a bowl of oatmeal. What had gone wrong?

Well, it turns out that when oats are hydrated and heated, they release gobs of starch. This is good news if you're trying to make a creamy bowl of porridge, but it spells disaster when it comes to baking muffins. The oat starch ends up trapping some of the moisture in the batter, thus preventing the flour from evenly hydrating. The result: those ruinous thick, gummy patches.

Frustrated, we scratched soaking the oats from our list and took a step back to reflect. When we used quick oats, the texture of the muffins had been perfect. Because they are broken down and precooked, quick oats absorb liquid more readily than do thicker rolled oats and thus fully soften during baking. What if we processed the rolled oats so that they would drink up liquid more easily?

We broke out the food processor and whizzed 2 cups of chunky rolled oats into a pile of fine oat flour—just 30 seconds did the trick. Exactly as we'd hoped, the finely ground meal readily absorbed milk (heating it was now unnecessary) and fully softened once incorporated into the batter and baked. There was just one caveat: Our home-ground oat flour absorbed liquid much more slowly than wheat flour did, producing a batter that was too thin. This was an easy problem to fix: After mixing the batter, we gave it a 20-minute rest to fully hydrate, thereby ensuring that the batter would be thick enough to scoop.

Making progress on the texture, we switched our attention to flavor. Our muffins boasted a prominent oat flavor. Still, we wanted their nutty taste to be even more noticeable, so we turned to a technique that we've used to intensify oat flavor when making granola: toasting. We evaluated two options: tossing the whole oats in a dry skillet over medium heat versus sautéing them in a couple tablespoons of butter. It was no contest: The muffins

OATMEAL MUFFINS

made with butter-toasted oats won hands down for their richer, more complex taste and aroma. While we were focused on flavor, we experimented with adding spices and seasonings. Time and again tasters singled out the muffins without any extras.

There was one issue that we had yet to address: When mixed with the wet ingredients, the oat flour occasionally developed a few large clumps that refused to hydrate and dissolve during baking, leaving dry, floury pockets in the finished muffins. We tried vigorously folding with a spatula, whisking energetically, and even processing the mixture in a blender. But manhandling the batter to smooth it out only resulted in a crumb with a tough texture—a repercussion of overworking the oat starch and gluten.

Seeing our predicament, a colleague suggested we try a technique called whisk folding: A whisk is gently drawn down and then up through the batter before being tapped lightly against the side of the bowl to knock any clumps back into the mixture. The wires of the whisk exert very little drag and thus develop minimal gluten, while the tapping action helps rupture pockets of dry ingredients. Whisk folding made all the difference, ridding the batter of large clumps and preserving a tender, moist texture.

Happy with our tender, jam-packed-with-oats muffins, it was time to come up with a topping. Just as one might garnish a bowl of oatmeal with crunchy nuts or chewy, sweet raisins, we wanted a contrasting adornment on our muffins that featured crunch and a bit of sweetness. We played around with toasted nuts, a cinnamon sugar mixture, and even an unconventional broiled icing, but nothing tasted quite right. While pondering our next

move, we watched a colleague pull a bubbling hot apple crisp from the oven and we thought a crisplike topping would be just right.

We excitedly stirred together more oats, finely chopped pecans, brown sugar, flour, melted butter, salt, and a hint of cinnamon, and crumbled our crisp-inspired topping evenly over the muffin batter before baking. Our muffins emerged with a proud crown of crunchy, chewy, sweet, and salty oats and nuts—the perfect accent to the rich crumb. Finally, we'd succeeded in turning the best traits of a humble bowl of oatmeal into a satisfying breakfast on the go.

Oatmeal Muffins

MAKES 12 MUFFINS

Do not use quick or instant oats in this recipe. Walnuts may be substituted for the pecans. The easiest way to grease and flour the muffin tin is with a baking spray with flour.

TOPPING

- ½ cup (1½ ounces) old-fashioned rolled oats
- ⅓ cup (1⅔ ounces) all-purpose flour
- ⅓ cup pecans, chopped fine
- ⅓ cup packed (2⅓ ounces) light brown sugar
- 1¼ teaspoons ground cinnamon
- ⅛ teaspoon salt
- 4 tablespoons unsalted butter, melted

MUFFINS

- 2 tablespoons unsalted butter, plus
  6 tablespoons melted
- 2 cups (6 ounces) old-fashioned rolled oats
- 1¾ cups (8¾ ounces) all-purpose flour
- 1½ teaspoons salt
- ¾ teaspoon baking powder
- ¼ teaspoon baking soda
- 1⅓ cups packed (9⅓ ounces) light brown sugar
- 1¾ cups milk
- 2 large eggs, beaten

1. FOR THE TOPPING: Combine oats, flour, pecans, sugar, cinnamon, and salt in medium bowl. Drizzle melted butter over mixture and stir to thoroughly combine; set aside.

2. FOR THE MUFFINS: Grease and flour 12-cup muffin tin. Melt 2 tablespoons butter in 10-inch skillet over medium heat. Add oats and cook, stirring frequently, until oats turn golden brown and smell of cooking popcorn, 6 to 8 minutes. Transfer oats to food processor and process into fine meal, about 30 seconds. Add flour, salt, baking powder, and baking soda to oats and pulse until combined, about 3 pulses.

3. Stir 6 tablespoons melted butter and sugar together in large bowl until smooth. Add milk and eggs and whisk until smooth. Using whisk, gently fold half of oat mixture into wet ingredients, tapping whisk against side of bowl to release clumps. Add remaining oat mixture and continue to fold with whisk until no streaks of flour remain. Set aside batter for 20 minutes to thicken. Meanwhile, adjust oven rack to middle position and heat oven to 375 degrees.

4. Using ice cream scoop or large spoon, divide batter equally among prepared muffin cups (about ½ cup batter per cup; cups will be filled to rim). Evenly sprinkle topping over muffins (about 2 tablespoons per muffin). Bake until toothpick inserted in center comes out clean, 18 to 25 minutes, rotating muffin tin halfway through baking.

5. Let muffins cool in muffin tin on wire rack for 10 minutes. Remove muffins from muffin tin and serve or let cool completely before serving.

NOTES FROM THE TEST KITCHEN

GETTING ROLLED OATS TO BAKE INTO MOIST, FLAVORFUL MUFFINS
Old-fashioned rolled oats have a subtle taste and don't easily absorb the liquid in a batter. Here are the steps we took to transform their flavor and texture.

TOAST IN BUTTER
Browning the oats in butter develops rich, complex flavor and aroma.

GRIND INTO FLOUR
Processing the oats into a fine meal ensures that they will absorb liquid.

MIX INTO BATTER; LET SIT
A 20-minute rest gives the oat flour time to hydrate in the batter.

SUPER-CHUNKY GRANOLA

✔ **WHY THIS RECIPE WORKS:** Store-bought granola suffers from many shortcomings. It's often loose and gravelly and/or shockingly expensive. We wanted to make our own granola at home, with big, satisfying clusters and crisp texture. The secret was to firmly pack the granola mixture into a rimmed baking sheet before baking. Once it was baked, we had a granola "bark" that we could break into crunchy lumps of any size.

WHETHER PAIRED WITH MILK, FRESH FRUIT, OR yogurt—or eaten by the fistful as a snack—granola is a must-have. Too bad the commercially prepared kind is such a letdown. Whether dry and dusty, overly sweet, infuriatingly expensive ($10 for a 12-ounce bag?), or all of the above, it is universally disappointing.

Of course, that meant that if we wanted to enjoy granola, we had to make our own. Sure, do-it-yourself granola afforded us the opportunity to choose exactly which nuts and dried fruit we wanted to include, as well as how much. But there was a downside: The slow baking and frequent stirring that most recipes recommend results in a loose, granular texture. We wanted substantial clumps of toasty oats and nuts. Our ideal clusters would be markedly crisp yet tender enough to shatter easily when bitten—we definitely didn't want the density or tooth-chipping crunch of a hard granola bar.

Starting from square one, we laid out our plan of attack: We would nail down the oats and nuts first and then set our sights on achieving substantial chunks.

We baked test batches using instant, quick, steel-cut, and old-fashioned whole rolled oat varieties. It was no surprise that instant and quick oats baked up unsubstantial and powdery. Steel-cut oats suffered the opposite problem: Chewing them was like munching gravel. Whole rolled oats were essential for a hearty, crisp texture.

Nuts, on the other hand, offered much more flexibility. Almost any type did just fine, contributing rich, toasty flavor that developed as the cereal roasted in the oven, along with plenty of crunch. While many recipes

ALMOND GRANOLA WITH DRIED FRUIT

advocate adding them whole, we preferred chopping them first for more even distribution.

As for other potential dry add-ins, more unusual grains (such as quinoa or amaranth) and seeds (sunflower, flax, pumpkin, and so on) are terrific choices, but since we planned on making granola often, we wanted granola that could be made anytime, using ingredients most home cooks routinely stock in their pantries.

With two of the primary players settled, we mixed up a batch using 5 cups of rolled oats and 2 cups of chopped almonds coated with our placeholder liquids: honey and vegetable oil (plus a touch of salt). We used a rubber spatula to spread the sticky concoction onto a baking sheet that we'd first lined with parchment for easier cleanup. We settled on a relatively moderate 375-degree oven to ward off scorching and allow the ingredients to brown slowly and evenly. We stirred the mixture every 10 minutes or so until it was evenly golden, which took about 30 minutes. The granola boasted a fantastic toasty scent, but there were no hearty chunks.

Setting texture aside, we considered sweeteners. Honey and maple syrup are the most common choices, but the honey struck many tasters as too distinct. Maple syrup was preferred for its milder character, especially when balanced with the subtle molasses notes offered by light brown sugar. One-third cup of each for 7 cups of nuts and oats gave just the right degree of sweetness.

The other major component in most granola recipes is fat. But because fat-free commercial versions are so popular and we didn't want to leave any stone unturned, we whipped up a batch in which we left the oil out of the recipe completely. No dice: The fat-free cereal was so dry and powdery that no amount of milk or yogurt could rescue it. We eventually determined that ½ cup was the right amount of oil for a super crisp—but not greasy—texture. Our science editor explained that fat is essential for a substantial crisp texture: Fat and liquid sweeteners form a fluid emulsion that thoroughly coats ingredients, creating crunch as the granola bakes. Without any fat, the texture is bound to be dry and fragile. We did two final fat experiments, swapping butter for the oil in the first, only to find that it was prone to burning. Extra-virgin olive oil gave the cereal a savory slant, so we stuck with our original choice: neutral-tasting vegetable oil.

Our granola now possessed well-balanced flavor and perfectly crisp oats and nuts, but we still had to deal with the issue of how to create big clumps. As we paged through cookbooks looking for a magic bullet, we uncovered a lot of interesting suggestions, including adding dry milk powder, egg whites, and sweet, sticky liquids like apple juice or cider to the mix. Sadly, none produced the clusters of our dreams.

If an additional ingredient couldn't help create the substantial chunks we sought, how about adjusting our technique? We'd been reaching into the oven to repeatedly stir the granola as it baked, so we decided to try skipping this step. To make sure that the cereal wouldn't burn in the absence of stirring, we dropped the oven temperature to 325 degrees and extended the cooking time to 45 minutes. Sure enough, some olive-size pieces did form in a no-stir sample—but we wanted more (and larger) chunks. For our next try, we used a spatula to press the hot granola firmly into the pan as soon as it emerged from the oven so that the cooling syrup would bind the solids together as it hardened. This worked, but only to a point. Could we take this idea to the next level?

Since the raw granola mixture was so sticky with syrup and oil, we wondered if muscling it into a tight, compact layer before baking would yield larger nuggets. We happily found that it remained in a single sheet as it cooled. Now we had more of a granola "bark," which was ideal, since we could break it into clumps of any size. Not only had we finally achieved hefty yet breakable chunks, but this granola was now hands-off, except for having to rotate the pan halfway through baking.

All that our chunky granola needed now was sweet bits of dried fruit. We tested a variety of choices—raisins, apple, mango, pineapple, cranberries, and pear—finding that they all either burned or turned leathery when baked with the other ingredients. To rectify this, we tried plumping the fruit in water or coating it with oil to help prevent moisture loss. And yet time and time again, it emerged from the oven overcooked. It eventually became clear that the best way to incorporate the fruit was to keep it away from heat altogether, only stirring it in once the granola was cool.

Our simple recipe was nearly complete, but we wanted to create a tiny bit more depth. After some tinkering, we found that a healthy dose of vanilla extract (we used a whopping 4 teaspoons) was just the ticket, accenting the maple, nut, and fruit flavors without overwhelming them.

Finally, we developed a few twists on our basic formula by switching up the fruit-and-nut pairings and accenting them with flavor boosters like coconut, citrus zest, and warm spices.

Forget the store-bought stuff. Home is where you'll find the holy grail of granola: big, satisfying clusters and moist, chewy fruit.

Almond Granola with Dried Fruit

MAKES ABOUT 9 CUPS

Chopping the almonds by hand is the first choice for superior texture and crunch. If you prefer not to hand-chop, substitute an equal quantity of slivered or sliced almonds. (A food processor does a lousy job of chopping whole nuts evenly.) Use a single type of your favorite dried fruit or a combination. Do not use quick oats.

- ⅓ **cup maple syrup**
- ⅓ **cup packed (2⅓ ounces) light brown sugar**
- 4 **teaspoons vanilla extract**
- ½ **teaspoon salt**
- ½ **cup vegetable oil**
- 5 **cups (15 ounces) old-fashioned rolled oats**
- 2 **cups (10 ounces) raw almonds, chopped coarse**
- 2 **cups raisins or other dried fruit, chopped**

1. Adjust oven rack to upper-middle position and heat oven to 325 degrees. Line rimmed baking sheet with parchment paper.

2. Whisk maple syrup, brown sugar, vanilla, and salt in large bowl. Whisk in oil. Fold in oats and almonds until thoroughly coated.

3. Transfer oat mixture to prepared baking sheet and spread across sheet into thin, even layer (about ⅜ inch thick). Using stiff metal spatula, compress oat mixture until very compact. Bake until lightly browned, 40 to 45 minutes, rotating pan once halfway through baking. Remove granola from oven and cool on wire rack to room temperature, about 1 hour. Break cooled granola into pieces of desired size. Stir in dried fruit. (Granola can be stored in airtight container for up to 2 weeks.)

VARIATIONS

Pecan-Orange Granola with Dried Cranberries
Add 2 tablespoons finely grated orange zest and 2½ teaspoons ground cinnamon to maple syrup mixture in step 2. Substitute coarsely chopped pecans for almonds. After granola is broken into pieces, stir in 2 cups dried cranberries.

Spiced Walnut Granola with Dried Apple
Add 2 teaspoons ground cinnamon, 1½ teaspoons ground ginger, ¾ teaspoon ground allspice, ½ teaspoon freshly grated nutmeg, and ½ teaspoon pepper to maple syrup mixture in step 2. Substitute coarsely chopped walnuts for almonds. After granola is broken into pieces, stir in 2 cups chopped dried apples.

Tropical Granola with Dried Mango
Reduce vanilla extract to 2 teaspoons and add 1½ teaspoons ground ginger and ¾ teaspoon freshly grated nutmeg to maple syrup mixture in step 2. Substitute coarsely chopped macadamias for almonds and 1½ cups unsweetened shredded coconut for 1 cup oats. After granola is broken into pieces, stir in 2 cups chopped dried mango or pineapple.

Hazelnut Granola with Dried Pear
Substitute coarsely chopped, skinned hazelnuts for almonds. After granola is broken into pieces, stir in 2 cups chopped dried pears.

RATING AUTOMATIC DRIP COFFEE MAKERS

The success of our favorite—but very pricey—Dutch automatic drip coffee maker spurred the launch of new rivals over the last five years. We wondered if any of them would produce coffee as reliably good, and with as little fuss, as the Technivorm. To find out, we tested seven automatic drip coffee makers with thermal carafes including an updated Technivorm (now a staggering $299). All claimed to reach the optimal time and temperature standards for great coffee flavor; a few have even won certification from the Specialty Coffee Association of America (SCAA). We used the same batch of freshly roasted, freshly ground beans; brewed the beans with spring water; and followed manufacturer directions for a full pot. We held a blind taste test, assessing flavor, acidity, body, and overall appeal. We assessed the coffee maker's and the carafe's construction and user-friendliness. Carafes that kept the most heat got more stars. We listed the water capacity of each machine in ounces because the definition of a "cup" is not standardized throughout the coffee industry. After brewing gallons of coffee, we still think the Technivorm Moccamaster is the best auto drip machine on the market. It's utterly consistent and intuitive to use. That said, we also identified an excellent alternative for half the money. Brands are listed in order of preference. See AmericasTestKitchen.com for updates and complete testing results.

HIGHLY RECOMMENDED

TECHNIVORM MOCCAMASTER 10-Cup Coffee Maker with Thermal Carafe
MODEL: KBGT 741 **PRICE:** $299
AVERAGE BREW TIME: 6 min, 11 sec
BREW TEMPERATURE IN IDEAL RANGE: 87%
WATER CAPACITY: 40 oz
BREW FLAVOR: ★★★ **DESIGN:** ★★★ **CARAFE:** ★
COMMENTS: Certified by the SCAA, the updated version of our old favorite (the KBT 741, now also $299) meets time and temperature guidelines with utter consistency. As a result, it produces a "smooth," "velvety" brew. It's also intuitive to use. The carafe lost some heat after 2 hours but still kept the coffee above 150 degrees.

BONAVITA 8-Cup Coffee Maker with Thermal Carafe
MODEL: BV 1800 TH **PRICE:** $149 `BEST BUY`
AVERAGE BREW TIME: 6 min, 43 sec
BREW TEMPERATURE IN IDEAL RANGE: 78%
WATER CAPACITY: 40 oz
BREW FLAVOR: ★★★ **DESIGN:** ★★½ **CARAFE:** ★
COMMENTS: Simple to use and SCAA-certified, this brewer spends most of the cycle in the ideal temperature range. Its coffee had "bright," "full" flavor that was a bit more "acidic" than the Technivorm's. The widemouthed carafe is easy to clean, but there's no brew-through lid; you must remove the brew basket and screw on a separate lid to keep coffee hot.

RECOMMENDED

BUNN HT Phase Brew 8-Cup Thermal Carafe Coffee Maker
MODEL: HT **PRICE:** $139.99
AVERAGE BREW TIME: 4 min, 49 sec
BREW TEMPERATURE IN IDEAL RANGE: 87%
WATER CAPACITY: 40 oz
BREW FLAVOR: ★★½ **DESIGN:** ★★★ **CARAFE:** ★★
COMMENTS: This SCAA-certified pot heats the water completely before releasing it over the grounds. That explained its temperature accuracy, though the coffee was somewhat "acidic." (Note: Early versions of this model shorted out when home voltage fluctuated; Bunn has solved this problem, and our machine worked fine.)

NOT RECOMMENDED

CAPRESSO MT600 PLUS 10-Cup Programmable Coffee Maker with Thermal Carafe
MODEL: 485 **PRICE:** $129.99
AVERAGE BREW TIME: 10 min, 26 sec
BREW TEMPERATURE IN IDEAL RANGE: 35%
WATER CAPACITY: 40 oz
BREW FLAVOR: ★½ **DESIGN:** ★½ **CARAFE:** ★★
COMMENTS: This model's water temperature climbed above the ideal zone for most of the cycle—prompting "burnt" complaints. Its cycle also ran too long. The design wasn't great: Controls were confusing, loading the reservoir was awkward (you must peer around the side to see the water level), and the carafe dribbles.

BODUM BISTRO b. over Coffee Machine
MODEL: 11001-565US **PRICE:** $250
AVERAGE BREW TIME: 5 min, 54 sec
BREW TEMPERATURE IN IDEAL RANGE: 35%
WATER CAPACITY: 40 oz
BREW FLAVOR: ★½ **DESIGN:** ★ **CARAFE:** ★★★
COMMENTS: This machine's brew cycle was erratic (running first cool and then hot); its design was flimsy; and, most damning, its small brew basket overflowed, pouring coffee and grounds onto its power button, which stuck "on." The carafe was the best heat retainer of the lineup and was easy to pour from.

BREVILLE YouBrew Drip Coffee Maker with Built-In Grinder
MODEL: BDC600XL **PRICE:** $279.95
AVERAGE BREW TIME: 10 min, 57 sec
BREW TEMPERATURE IN IDEAL RANGE: 16%
WATER CAPACITY: 60 oz
BREW FLAVOR: ★½ **DESIGN:** ★ **CARAFE:** ★★
COMMENTS: This is a pricey grind-and-brew machine that does the thinking for you—after you fuss with the endless customizable options. It spent a measly 16 percent of its long brew cycle in the ideal temperature zone—no wonder the coffee tasted "weak" and "bitter." Most important, the brew basket is too small to hold the SCAA-recommended amount of coffee when brewing a full pot.

From an Italian Bakery

A small amount of butter and finely ground nuts keep our biscotti crunchy but not too hard.

ITALIAN COOKIES, LIKE BISCOTTI AND FLORENTINES, WERE ONCE found only in neighborhood Italian bakeries, but they've since entered the mainstream through the multitudes of chain coffeehouses looking to pair their espressos, cappuccinos, and lattes with a baked treat. We wanted to develop foolproof versions of each one—but we wanted them to be better than what we get at the local coffee shop.

Biscotti are cooked twice. First the dough is formed into logs, usually two, and baked through. The logs are then sliced into individual cookies and baked a second time so they turn out dry and crisp. Many biscotti get the dry part right, so much so that they're jawbreakers. Others are so soft they're simply biscotti-shaped sugar cookies. We wanted something in between. Since texture is key, that's where we'd start. Flavor is important in biscotti too. Yes, they're often dunked in coffee or wine, but we wanted to find the best way to impart the toasty flavor and crunch of nuts to our cookies.

Florentines are at the fancier end of Italian cookie offerings. Delicate and lacy rounds of ground almonds in a buttery caramel, they are incredibly elegant with their thin drizzle of chocolate; sometimes Florentines are made into sandwich cookies with the chocolate in the middle. Getting the thin, crisp texture right can be tricky—they can sometimes bake up too thick or spread into uneven blobs. And Florentines are often accented with orange, but getting that bright citrusy flavor to come through the caramel can be difficult. With some test kitchen ingenuity and a lot of trial and error, we were determined to come up with our own foolproof Florentines.

RETHINKING BISCOTTI

✓ WHY THIS RECIPE WORKS: We wanted biscotti that were hard and crunchy (but not hard to eat) and bold in flavor. To keep the crumb crisp, we used just a small amount of butter (4 tablespoons), and to keep the biscotti from being too hard, we ground some of the nuts to a fine meal, which helped minimize gluten development in the crumb. To ensure bold flavor in a biscuit that gets baked twice, we increased the quantities of almond extract and of the aromatic herbs and spices such as anise, rosemary, cardamom, and cloves.

BISCOTTI LITERALLY MEANS "TWICE-BAKED." THESE classic Italian cookies are baked once as a single, oblong loaf. The loaf is then sliced into thin planks, which are returned to the oven to fully dry. The result: crunchy, nutty, finger-shaped cookies that are perfect alongside a cup of coffee—or, as in Italy, a glass of sweet *vin santo*.

What separates one style from another mostly is texture—specifically, just how crunchy or soft the cookies are. The most traditional biscotti, known as *cantuccini*, or *biscotti di Prato*, are extremely hard; they are meant to be dunked into a liquid to soften them (that's where the vin santo comes in). American biscotti—the big, buttery, much softer kind sold in coffeehouse chains—are more like sugar cookies masquerading as biscotti. For our own recipe, we wanted a hybrid: a cookie with big flavor and even bigger crunch—a cookie that could be dipped into coffee but didn't need to be.

A quick scan of several recipes—and a biscotti bake-off—confirmed that the cookies' crunch corresponded with the amount of butter in the dough. Batches made with little (or even no) fat were rock-hard, while doughs enriched with a full stick of butter baked up much softer, thanks to the fat's tenderizing effect. We began experimenting with a basic creaming formula—beat the butter and sugar; alternately fold in the dry ingredients with the wet—and varying the amount of butter in each batch.

Half a stick turned out to be the ideal compromise; the dough was neither too hard nor too lean. The only problem was that a mere 4 tablespoons of butter (plus 1 cup of sugar) didn't give the stand mixer enough to work with. Instead of beating air into the butter to lighten it, all the mixer could do was soften the fat, and the resulting biscotti were dense and squat. Our other idea to give the dough some lift was to up the baking powder, but this was only effective to a point; any more than 2 teaspoons and the biscotti baked up crumbly. (The carbon dioxide produced is more effective at expanding existing air bubbles than it is at creating its own.)

It was time to brainstorm: What other elements of the dough could be aerated in the mixer? We landed on an obvious ingredient: eggs. Reversing the order of operations, we whipped two eggs until they were light in color and then added the sugar and continued to beat the mixture. Finally, we folded in the melted butter, followed by the dry ingredients. We deliberately portioned the dough into two short, wide logs; that way, the cut cookies would span 4 inches—perfect for repeat dunking. To give the finished cookies a nice sheen, we brushed the logs with a beaten egg white. We then baked the logs for about a half-hour, sliced them on the bias into ½-inch-thick cookies, and returned those to the oven for round two.

Our unorthodox dough-mixing technique was a major breakthrough: The whipped eggs gave the dough the lightness and lift it had been lacking. But despite their lighter, more open crumb, the biscotti were still making our teeth work too hard for a bite. Also, we'd added a judicious amount of almond extract to bring out the nuts' flavor, but its distinct taste was surprisingly faint.

Too little fat had been partially responsible for our overly hard cookies, but apparently it wasn't the only factor. Our experience baking bread made us wonder if the dough had developed too much gluten (the network of proteins that gives baked goods their structure). In moist bread dough, lots of gluten produces chewiness, as the gluten strands resist being pulled apart; in a dry cookie, the result is hardness, as the gluten resists breaking.

Our first thought was to try using lower-protein cake flour in place of the all-purpose, since its reduced gluten content would result in weaker gluten structure. The swap did make the biscotti easier to eat but not in a good way: To the extent that the cake flour made the biscotti less hard, it also made them more fragile. Even mixing all-purpose and cake flours was a bust.

ALMOND BISCOTTI

We were starting to realize that less gluten was not the answer. What we really needed was a way to modify the texture of the biscotti so that the gluten it contained had less impact on the overall hardness of the cookie, while still providing the crumb itself with plenty of structure.

That's when we remembered that one of the early recipes we tried called for finely ground (rather than chopped) almonds. The nuts had gotten lost in the biscotti, but they'd also made the cookies much more crumbly—and a little more crumbliness might be just what these cookies needed. Moving ahead with this idea, we swapped out ½ cup of flour for an equal amount of almonds ground to a fine powder in the food processor. We knew we were onto something. These biscotti were still plenty hard, but the almond meal made them far easier to bite into. In fact, they were breaking apart too easily, so we tried again, using ¼ cup almond meal. This time the cookies' texture was perfect: crunchy but easy to bite.

What was it about the nut meal that produced a more breakable cookie? According to our science editor, the ground nuts broke up the gluten structure so that there were smaller pockets of gluten rather than one large one. As a result, the cookies gave way more easily when bitten, but the crumb itself didn't lose its hard crunch (see "Why Nuts Take Some Bite Out of Biscotti"). And to appease those who missed the bursts of nuttiness from whole pieces, we added back 1 cup of coarsely chopped almonds when it came time to fold in the dry ingredients.

All that remained was to beef up the still-weak almond flavor. The almond extract aroma was strong during the first baking but had all but vanished by the time the cookies had baked twice. A little research explained: As it turns out, benzaldehyde, the main compound responsible for the flavor and aroma of almonds, is highly volatile and had evaporated during the twice-baked cookies' long exposure to heat. To compensate, we figured we needed to start with a higher-than-average dose and experimented until we found that 1½ teaspoons—triple the amount that we had started with—did the trick. Similarly, we found that we had to load up on other ingredients with volatile compounds like aromatic herbs, spices, and zest when we developed our anise, hazelnut-orange, and pistachio-spice variations. (Since vanilla extract was only providing background notes to the biscotti flavor, we found that we could keep its amount at just ½ to 1 teaspoon.)

At last, we had a set of biscotti recipes we could be proud of: Boldly flavored and crunchy, these biscotti were hard, yes, but far from hard to eat.

Almond Biscotti
MAKES 30 COOKIES

The almonds will continue to toast while the biscotti bake, so toast the nuts only until they are just fragrant.

- 1¼ cups whole almonds, lightly toasted
- 1¾ cups (8¾ ounces) all-purpose flour
- 2 teaspoons baking powder
- ¼ teaspoon salt
- 2 large eggs, plus 1 large white beaten with pinch salt
- 1 cup (7 ounces) sugar
- 4 tablespoons unsalted butter, melted and cooled
- 1½ teaspoons almond extract
- ½ teaspoon vanilla extract
- Vegetable oil spray

1. Adjust oven rack to middle position and heat oven to 325 degrees. Using ruler and pencil, draw two 8 by 3-inch rectangles, spaced 4 inches apart, on piece of parchment paper. Grease baking sheet and place parchment on it, marked side down.

2. Pulse 1 cup almonds in food processor until coarsely chopped, 8 to 10 pulses; transfer to bowl and set aside.

Process remaining ¼ cup almonds in food processor until finely ground, about 45 seconds. Add flour, baking powder, and salt; process to combine, about 15 seconds. Transfer flour mixture to second bowl. Process 2 eggs in now-empty food processor until lightened in color and almost doubled in volume, about 3 minutes. With processor running, slowly add sugar until thoroughly combined, about 15 seconds. Add melted butter, almond extract, and vanilla and process until combined, about 10 seconds. Transfer egg mixture to medium bowl. Sprinkle half of flour mixture over egg mixture and, using spatula, gently fold until just combined. Add remaining flour mixture and chopped almonds and gently fold until just combined.

3. Divide batter in half. Using floured hands, form each half into 8 by 3-inch rectangle, using lines on parchment as guide. Spray each loaf lightly with oil spray. Using rubber spatula lightly coated with oil spray, smooth tops and sides of rectangles. Gently brush tops of loaves with egg white wash. Bake until loaves are golden and just beginning to crack on top, 25 to 30 minutes, rotating pan halfway through baking.

4. Let loaves cool on baking sheet for 30 minutes. Transfer loaves to cutting board. Using serrated knife, slice each loaf on slight bias into ½-inch-thick slices. Lay slices, cut side down, about ¼ inch apart on wire rack set in rimmed baking sheet. Bake until crisp and golden brown on both sides, about 35 minutes, flipping slices halfway through baking. Let cool completely before serving. Biscotti can be stored in airtight container for up to 1 month.

VARIATIONS

Anise Biscotti
Add 1½ teaspoons anise seeds to flour mixture in step 2. Substitute anise-flavored liqueur for almond extract.

Hazelnut-Orange Biscotti
Substitute lightly toasted and skinned hazelnuts for almonds. Add 2 tablespoons minced fresh rosemary to flour mixture in step 2. Substitute orange-flavored liqueur for almond extract and add 1 tablespoon grated orange zest to egg mixture with butter.

SCIENCE DESK

WHY NUTS TAKE SOME BITE OUT OF BISCOTTI
We wanted our biscotti to pack just as much crunch as the traditional Italian kind but also to break apart easily when you take a bite. Adding extra butter to the dough helped, but our ultimate solution was cutting the flour with finely ground nuts. While butter merely made the cookie more tender, ground nuts actually weakened its structure.

Both ingredients influence the texture because of their effect on gluten, the web of flour proteins that gives baked goods structure. The fat in butter "shortens" the gluten strands by surrounding individual strands and preventing them from linking up into larger networks. Ground nuts interfere with gluten formation in a slightly different way, getting in between pockets of gluten to create microscopic "fault lines" in the biscotti, which allow the hard cookie to break apart easily under the tooth.

Pistachio-Spice Biscotti
Substitute shelled pistachios for almonds. Add 1 teaspoon ground cardamom, ½ teaspoon ground cloves, ½ teaspoon pepper, ¼ teaspoon ground cinnamon, and ¼ teaspoon ground ginger to flour mixture in step 2. Substitute 1 teaspoon water for almond extract and increase vanilla extract to 1 teaspoon.

FLORENTINE LACE COOKIES

✔ **WHY THIS RECIPE WORKS:** These wafer-thin almond cookies have a reputation for being fussy and unpredictable, but we ensured success with just a few tweaks. Instead of temping the hot sugar mixture that forms the base of the dough, we removed it from the heat when it thickened and began to brown. We substituted orange marmalade for the usual candied orange peel and corn syrup combo, producing a more complex citrus flavor. These cookies are baked much darker than most cookies, which enhances their delicate crispiness, and a flourish of carefully melted chocolate completes the professional pastry shop effect.

"YOU CAN NEVER BE TOO RICH OR TOO THIN." THAT familiar adage is debatable when applied to people, but it's spot-on if you're talking about Florentine cookies. Slim, lacy disks of ground or chopped almonds bound with buttery caramel and gilded with bittersweet chocolate, Florentines are a familiar presence in upscale pastry shops (although they're often called by other names), and their crunchy appeal ensures that they are the first to disappear from a cookie plate. But make them at home? Most people never even try.

That's because Florentines have a solid reputation for being fussier and more unpredictable than the average cookie. They start out like candy: Butter, sugar, cream, and either honey or corn syrup are cooked in a saucepan until the mixture reaches 238 degrees, the temperature at which most of the water has evaporated. Then they veer into cookie territory, as flour, almonds, candied citrus, and sometimes dried fruit are stirred in to form a loose, slippery dough. Spoonfuls of dough are then deposited on baking sheets and baked until each forms a crispy, thin, perfectly browned disk—or, if things don't go well, a mottled, chewy, amoeba-like blob. Factor in the uncertainty of whether the chocolate is going to set up firm and shiny or remain sticky and dull, and it's no wonder most people leave this cookie to the pros.

But here's the thing about Florentines: they're actually less work to make than many more conventional cookies because the dough requires just a brief stir in a saucepan. Plus, these cookies are stylish and keep well for several days, making them ideal for holiday baking.

First, we concentrated on the cookie itself. We melted butter with cream, sugar, and neutral-flavored corn syrup and cooked the mixture for 6 to 8 minutes, until it reached 238 degrees. We weren't keen on breaking out our thermometer for cookie making, so as the caramel mixture cooked, we watched for visual indicators. The mixture turned a distinctive creamy beige color and started to catch on the bottom of the pan just as the temperature approached 238 degrees—exactly the kind of cue we'd been hoping for. Off the heat, we stirred in chopped almonds, flour, a bit of vanilla, and a good amount of candied orange peel to give the cookies a citrusy brightness to offset their richness. We scooped 1-tablespoon portions of dough onto baking sheets and baked them for 12 minutes.

This early batch was disappointing. The cookies hadn't spread enough, so they were chunky and sported tight fissures instead of the fine, lacy holes that are characteristic of Florentines. Their texture was also tough and a bit chewy. Finally, the candied peel didn't taste like anything.

It occurred to us that finely grinding the almonds might give the cookies a flatter profile, and upping the cream might encourage them to spread more. Those changes did indeed move us toward a thinner Florentine, but didn't produce the crispiness and delicate filigreed appearance of bakery-quality cookies. Three extra minutes in the oven allowed the cookies to crisp and turn deeply golden brown, and a touch less flour helped them spread even thinner. Since more spreading also encouraged amorphous shapes, we took a minute to pat each mound of dough into a flat circle. Bingo: These thin, round, crispy wafers looked like prime pastry shop offerings. If only there was a way to boost that backbone of orange flavor.

Swapping the candied orange peel for grated orange zest helped, but wasn't enough. If we added more zest the little bits became too noticeable. But there was one bakery cookie that we'd tasted that had exactly the orange profile we were after. It came from the Lakota Bakery in

FLORENTINE LACE COOKIES

Arlington, Massachusetts, and proprietor Barbara Weniger generously divulged her secret: orange marmalade.

When we added ¼ cup of marmalade to our working recipe (swapping it for the corn syrup), the difference was incredible. The marmalade's concentrated flavor had the perfect bright, citrusy, and faintly bitter taste we wanted, and the jam provided a contrast to the richness and sweetness of the caramel base. Satisfied with our thin, crispy, orangey cookie, we moved on to the chocolate.

The classic Florentine has a thin, smooth coat of bittersweet chocolate on its underside, an elegant effect achieved by dipping the entire bottom surface of each cookie into a large container of melted chocolate. This approach presents two problems for the home cook: First, you wind up with loads of leftover chocolate. Second, to ensure that the chocolate retains an attractive sheen, you have to either temper it (a painstaking process of melting and cooling the chocolate to ensure that it stays within the optimal temperature range) or get your hands on special coating chocolate, which contains a small amount of a highly saturated vegetable fat that extends the temperature range at which the chocolate can safely melt. We needed to come up with an easier, more practical alternative.

After some trial and error, we devised a great faux-tempering method that involved melting part of the chocolate in the microwave and then stirring in the remainder—a very gentle approach that kept the chocolate glossy when it resolidified (for more information, see "Don't Lose Your Temper"). We tried spreading a small amount of chocolate onto the undersides of the cookies,

but that looked messy. The chocolate seeped through those lacy holes, and it was difficult to get a skim coat, meaning the chocolate flavor overwhelmed the delicate cookies. In the end, we took a different approach: piping decorative zigzags over the top of each cookie. (In lieu of a pastry bag, we poured the melted chocolate into a plastic bag and snipped off the corner.)

With Florentines as crispy, flavorful, and elegant as these, we know exactly what we'll be giving for holiday gifts this year.

Florentine Lace Cookies
MAKES 24 COOKIES

It's important to cook the cream mixture in the saucepan until it is thick and starting to brown at the edges; undercooking will result in a dough that is too runny to portion. Do not be concerned if some butter separates from the dough while you're portioning the cookies. For the most uniform cookies, use the flattest baking sheets you have and make sure that your parchment paper lies flat. When melting the chocolate, pause the microwave and stir the chocolate often to ensure that it doesn't get much warmer than body temperature.

- 2 cups slivered almonds
- ¾ cup heavy cream
- 4 tablespoons unsalted butter, cut into 4 pieces
- ½ cup (3½ ounces) sugar
- ¼ cup orange marmalade
- 3 tablespoons all-purpose flour
- 1 teaspoon vanilla extract
- ¼ teaspoon grated orange zest
- ¼ teaspoon salt
- 4 ounces bittersweet chocolate, chopped fine

1. Adjust oven racks to upper-middle and lower-middle positions and heat oven to 350 degrees. Line 2 baking sheets with parchment paper. Process almonds in food processor until they resemble coarse sand, about 30 seconds.

2. Bring cream, butter, and sugar to boil in medium saucepan over medium-high heat. Cook, stirring frequently, until mixture begins to thicken, 5 to 6 minutes.

NOTES FROM THE TEST KITCHEN

DON'T LOSE YOUR TEMPER
Tempering is a complex process that involves carefully heating and cooling chocolate to prevent its fat crystals from dissolving and reforming into less stable crystals. If this happens (a common occurrence when chocolate gets too warm), the chocolate's surface will turn soft, grainy, and dull—fine for incorporating into cake batter and cookie dough but not suitable for decorating. For an equally gentle but less fussy way to keep chocolate in temper, we microwave most of it at 50 percent power until about two-thirds melted and then stir in the remainder of the chocolate until all of it is fully melted.

Continue to cook, stirring constantly, until mixture begins to brown at edges and is thick enough to leave trail that doesn't immediately fill in when spatula is scraped along pan bottom, 1 to 2 minutes longer (it's OK if some darker speckles appear in mixture). Remove pan from heat and stir in almonds, marmalade, flour, vanilla, orange zest, and salt until combined.

3. Drop 6 level tablespoons dough at least 3½ inches apart on prepared sheets. When cool enough to handle, use damp fingers to press each portion into 2½-inch circle.

4. Bake until deep brown from edge to edge, 15 to 17 minutes, switching and rotating sheets halfway through baking. Transfer cookies, still on parchment, to wire racks and let cool. Let baking sheets cool for 10 minutes, line with fresh parchment, and repeat portioning and baking remaining dough.

5. Microwave 3 ounces chocolate in bowl at 50 percent power, stirring frequently, until about two-thirds melted, 1 to 2 minutes. Remove bowl from microwave, add remaining 1 ounce chocolate, and stir until melted, returning to microwave for no more than 5 seconds at a time to complete melting if necessary. Transfer chocolate to small zipper-lock bag and snip off corner, making hole no larger than ¹⁄₁₆ inch.

6. Transfer cooled cookies directly to wire racks. Pipe zigzag of chocolate over each cookie, distributing chocolate evenly among all cookies. Refrigerate until chocolate is set, about 30 minutes, before serving. (Cookies can be stored at cool room temperature for up to 4 days.)

RATING MEDIUM-ROAST COFFEE

Well into the 1990s, most of the coffee consumed in this country was a medium roast. The classic American cup was lighter and more acidic than today's espresso-dark brew. It took West Coast coffeehouse roasters to show us another side of coffee flavor when they began roasting coffee dark. But fans of medium-roast coffee resisted, insisting that ultradark roasts tasted charred. These holdouts helped ensure that lighter coffee continued to do a brisk business in stores. Since some of the big-name dark-roast pioneers have come out with lighter options we decided it was time to give medium roasts a closer look. We selected a lighter whole-bean roast from Peet's and one from Starbucks, along with the medium roasts of five other top-selling supermarket brands. We sampled the coffees without milk or sweeteners. An independent laboratory analyzed each coffee to obtain its Agtron rating (a measure of roast darkness), the number of defective green "quaker" beans, pH level, and moisture content. Brands are listed in order of preference. See AmericasTestKitchen.com for updates and complete tasting results.

RECOMMENDED

PEET'S COFFEE CAFÉ DOMINGO
PRICE: $13.95 for 1-pound bag ($0.87 per oz)
AGTRON: 39 **QUAKERS:** 1
pH: 5.33 **MOISTURE:** 1.28 percent
COMMENTS: The darkest roast in the lineup, this sample came across as "extremely smooth" and "bold-tasting," with a "stronger finish" than other samples. It tied for smallest number of defective beans and had low acidity and optimal moisture. Its "rich," "chocolate," and "toast" flavors make it the perfect brew for those who want a break—but not too much of one—from ultra-dark French roasts.

MILLSTONE BREAKFAST BLEND
PRICE: $9.17 for 12-ounce bag ($0.76 per oz)
AGTRON: 47 **QUAKERS:** 2
pH: 5.22 **MOISTURE:** 1.6 percent
COMMENTS: This "satiny" coffee was "lemony" and "very enjoyable," with a "slightly nutty aftertaste." It hit the middle for "acidity, earthiness, and complexity." As with our winner, lab results showed low acidity, few defective beans, and ideal moisture. A good choice for those who enjoy brighter, livelier medium-roast flavors.

RECOMMENDED WITH RESERVATIONS

CARIBOU COFFEE DAYBREAK
PRICE: $12.54 for 12-ounce bag ($1.05 per oz)
AGTRON: 46 **QUAKERS:** 1
pH: 5.19 **MOISTURE:** 0.06 percent
COMMENTS: Some tasters were able to detect a "slight berry taste" with "black tea-like" undertones. For others, it was "flat," "bland," and "not very distinctive." "Smells nutty but no taste," is how one taster put it. Lab results indicated extremely low moisture in the beans, which almost certainly weakened the brew.

Summertime Desserts

Chris admires the summer berry trifle that Julia is assembling with our simplified from-scratch components: light cake, silky pastry cream, flavored whipped cream, and luscious berries.

DURING THE SUMMER, WHEN FRESH BERRIES AND PEACHES ARE AT their peak, we tend to eat them out of hand and dress them up in desserts that really make them shine. While we are happy to eat them plain or piled onto shortcakes, we like to think about how to show off these fruits in a more company-worthy way.

Classic English trifle is a beautiful construction of cake or ladyfingers, custard, jam, flavored whipped cream, and fresh fruit all layered together in a tall clear glass bowl. But modern renditions of trifle tend to look better than they taste. Given the time and effort needed for all of the components, shortcuts are frequently taken. It's no surprise that putting together store-bought cake, pudding from a box, and faux whipped topping results in a dessert tasting less than impressive. We wanted a luscious trifle made completely from scratch that was manageable to pull off. We imagined a simple, buttery cake, fresh berries, rich pastry cream, and lots of fluffy, whipped cream layered together. In short, we wanted a trifle that was a beauty, inside and out.

Peach pie is a quintessential summer dessert, theoretically one made all the better with fresh summer peaches. But their sugary juice causes all kinds of problems, including peach filling that is soupy or overly sweet. We wanted a filling that was juicy but sliceable and full of peach flavor. We also wanted a buttery, flaky crust that was crisp—top and bottom. Since lattice tops help moisture to evaporate, we thought that might be the best approach to our juicy pie. Weaving a lattice, however, can be tricky. Our dream peach pie would be a challenge, but one we were ready to face.

SUMMER BERRY TRIFLE

SUMMER BERRY TRIFLE

✔ **WHY THIS RECIPE WORKS:** Trifles usually look a lot better than they taste because busy cooks simplify the complicated preparation by subbing in premade or instant components. We wanted to streamline the components so that the entire trifle could be made from scratch in just a few hours. We added a little extra flour to a classic chiffon cake so we could bake it in an 18 by 13-inch sheet, which bakes and cools much more quickly than the traditional tall chiffon cake, and we prevented our pastry cream from turning runny during assembly by adding 25 percent more cornstarch than other recipes. Rather than leaving all our berries whole, we mashed one-third of them so their juices would help the trifle components meld. A bit of cream sherry, mixed into the whipped cream and drizzled on each layer of cake, adds a sophisticated layer of flavor and pulls the dessert together.

THE ELEGANT TRIFLE HAD HUMBLE BEGINNINGS. It originated in 16th-century England as a soupy combination of sweetened cream, rose water, and spices, and by the 17th century the mixture was being called into service to soak stale bread and cake. Things got a bit more upscale with the introduction of wine and custard, but it wasn't until the Victorian era that trifle blossomed into its most awe-inspiring form, one involving ladyfingers, almond macaroons, jam, custard, whipped cream, brandy, sherry, candied fruits, and edible flowers.

Few people have the time or energy for that kind of trifle labor these days, but that hasn't diminished the celebratory appeal of this showstopper dessert. We wanted to make a luscious trifle completely from scratch—without going crazy in the process.

Our goal was to combine four basic components—light cake, silky pastry cream, whipped cream, and lush summer berries—to make a simple but elegant trifle full of flavor from top to bottom. But as soon as we began testing recipes, we realized that there would be a few hurdles. First, many light cakes were also weak cakes, falling apart into a mushy mess as soon as they began to

absorb moisture in the trifle. The pastry cream, which should be dense and silky, tended to break down as soon as we spread it in layers in the bowl. We also wanted the flavors of the sherry and fruit to permeate each bite.

We first focused on the cake. A tender butter cake was a disaster in trifle. The sherry and creamy elements turned it to mush. Instead we tried taking the historical route by using ladyfingers. Crisp and dry, they required so much booze to soften that the alcohol burn swamped the delicate cream and fruit. But they did hold their shape. This is because ladyfingers are simply small, dry angel food cakes based on a protein-rich whipped egg white foam. Because protein doesn't readily absorb water, ladyfingers hold up nicely against moisture.

An angel food cake wouldn't be dry like ladyfingers but it would require a tube pan—the center tube is essential in helping it rise. Plus, an angel food cake must thoroughly cool before being removed from the pan or it will collapse. We needed a cake that would bake and cool quickly in a regular cake pan but with an angel food cake's ability to stand up to moisture.

A chiffon cake is similar to an angel food cake but contains more flour for structure. We wondered if adding more flour to a chiffon cake would enable us to bake the batter in a rimmed baking sheet, allowing it to bake and cool very rapidly. To our delight, by doubling the amount of flour we were able to bake a slim, fluffy modified chiffon cake in an 18 by 13-inch baking sheet in 15 minutes. It cooled in just 30 minutes.

Pastry cream is typically made with a mixture of heavy cream and milk, egg yolks, sugar, cornstarch, and a bit of butter and vanilla. Since our trifle was already going to be rich with whipped cream, we decided to make an all-milk pastry cream. But spreading the cream between layers of cake caused it to turn runny. The lower fat content was partially to blame, and cornstarch-thickened pastry cream loses structure if you disturb the gel too much. Starting with a firmer gel by upping the cornstarch gave us a bit more leeway to stir and spread.

Next: berries. Arranging whole berries in decorative layers misses the point: A trifle's components are supposed to coalesce. Whole berries don't release any juice, so they don't meld. Crushing all of our gorgeous berries seemed criminal so we settled on mashing one-third of the fruit and heating the mash with just a bit of cornstarch to thicken it, and adding a bit of sugar to balance the flavor.

Then the fun part: construction. We spread a small amount of pastry cream to anchor the first layer of cake. Then we sprinkled sherry on top of the cake and piled on the juicy berries. Next came the silky pastry cream, topped by a thin layer of whipped cream. We repeated

the layers before refrigerating the trifle to set. Before serving, we garnished the top with a handful of berries.

Every component of our edible centerpiece had been made from scratch and fit together into a cohesive whole—without any headache.

NOTES FROM THE TEST KITCHEN

REFINING THE ELEMENTS

Here's how we tweaked three main components of our trifle so they all worked in tandem. The trifle is also prepared 6 to 36 hours in advance to give flavors and textures time to meld.

MAKE A STURDIER CAKE
An egg foam–based chiffon cake stands up better to a trifle's moisture than butter cake. By adding extra flour to it, we can bake it quickly in a rimmed baking sheet.

DEVELOP BERRY FLAVOR
We mash some of our berries. This allows the fruit juice—and therefore the flavor—to reach every bite of trifle.

STABILIZE THE CUSTARD
Adding extra cornstarch to the pastry cream keeps it from turning runny when spread between layers of cake.

LAYERING CAKE JUST RIGHT

Cutting and shingling the cake is the key to making it fit—and using every bit. First, slice the cake into 24 equal pieces and then shingle them (12 per layer), like fallen dominos, in the bowl.

Summer Berry Trifle

SERVES 12 TO 16

For the best texture, this trifle should be assembled at least 6 hours before serving. Use a glass bowl with at least a 3½-quart capacity; straight sides are preferable.

PASTRY CREAM
3½ cups whole milk
1 cup (7 ounces) sugar
6 tablespoons cornstarch
 Pinch salt
5 large egg yolks (reserve whites for cake)
4 tablespoons unsalted butter, cut into ½-inch pieces and chilled
4 teaspoons vanilla extract

CAKE
1⅓ cups (5⅓ ounces) cake flour
¾ cup (5¼ ounces) sugar
1½ teaspoons baking powder
¼ teaspoon salt
⅓ cup vegetable oil
¼ cup water
1 large egg
2 teaspoons vanilla extract
5 large egg whites (reserved from pastry cream)
¼ teaspoon cream of tartar

FRUIT FILLING
1½ pounds strawberries, hulled and cut into ½-inch pieces (4 cups), reserving 3 halved for garnish
12 ounces (2⅓ cups) blackberries, large berries halved crosswise, reserving 3 whole for garnish
12 ounces (2⅓ cups) raspberries, reserving 3 for garnish
¼ cup (1¾ ounces) sugar
½ teaspoon cornstarch
 Pinch salt

WHIPPED CREAM

- **1 cup heavy cream**
- **1 tablespoon sugar**
- **1 tablespoon plus ½ cup cream sherry**

1. FOR THE PASTRY CREAM: Heat 3 cups milk in medium saucepan over medium heat until just simmering. Meanwhile, whisk sugar, cornstarch, and salt together in medium bowl. Whisk remaining ½ cup milk and egg yolks into sugar mixture until smooth. Remove milk from heat and, whisking constantly, slowly add 1 cup to sugar mixture to temper. Whisking constantly, return tempered sugar mixture to milk in saucepan.

2. Return saucepan to medium heat and cook, whisking constantly, until mixture is very thick and bubbles burst on surface, 4 to 7 minutes. Remove saucepan from heat; whisk in butter and vanilla until butter is melted and incorporated. Strain pastry cream through fine-mesh strainer set over medium bowl. Press lightly greased parchment paper directly on surface and refrigerate until set, at least 2 hours or up to 24 hours.

3. FOR THE CAKE: Adjust oven rack to middle position and heat oven to 350 degrees. Lightly grease 18 by 13-inch rimmed baking sheet, line with parchment, and lightly grease parchment. Whisk flour, sugar, baking powder, and salt together in medium bowl. Whisk oil, water, egg, and vanilla into flour mixture until smooth batter forms.

4. Using stand mixer fitted with whisk, whip reserved egg whites and cream of tartar on medium-low speed until foamy, about 1 minute. Increase speed to medium-high and whip until soft peaks form, 2 to 3 minutes. Transfer one-third of whipped egg whites to batter; whisk gently until mixture is lightened. Using rubber spatula, gently fold remaining egg whites into batter.

5. Pour batter into prepared sheet; spread evenly. Bake until top is golden brown and cake springs back when pressed lightly in center, 13 to 16 minutes.

6. Transfer cake to wire rack; let cool for 5 minutes. Run knife around edge of sheet, then invert cake onto wire rack. Carefully remove parchment, then re-invert cake onto second wire rack. Let cool completely, at least 30 minutes.

7. FOR THE FRUIT FILLING: Place 1½ cups strawberries, 1 cup blackberries, 1 cup raspberries, sugar, cornstarch, and salt in medium saucepan. Place remaining berries in large bowl; set aside. Using potato masher, thoroughly mash berries in saucepan. Cook over medium heat until sugar is dissolved and mixture is thick and bubbling, 4 to 7 minutes. Pour over berries in bowl and stir to combine. Set aside.

8. FOR THE WHIPPED CREAM: Using stand mixer fitted with whisk, whip cream, sugar, and 1 tablespoon sherry on medium-low speed until foamy, about 1 minute. Increase speed to high and whip until soft peaks form, 1 to 2 minutes.

9. Trim ¼ inch off each side of cake; discard trimmings. Using serrated knife, cut cake into 24 equal pieces (each piece about 2½ inches square).

10. Briefly whisk pastry cream until smooth. Spoon ¾ cup pastry cream into trifle bowl; spread over bottom. Shingle 12 cake pieces, fallen domino–style, around bottom of trifle, placing 10 pieces against dish wall and 2 remaining pieces in center. Drizzle ¼ cup sherry evenly over cake. Spoon half of berry mixture evenly over cake, making sure to use half of liquid. Using back of spoon, spread half of remaining pastry cream over berries, then spread half of whipped cream over pastry cream (whipped cream layer will be thin). Repeat layering with remaining 12 cake pieces, sherry, berries, pastry cream, and whipped cream. Cover bowl with plastic wrap and refrigerate for at least 6 hours or up to 36 hours. Garnish top of trifle with reserved berries and serve.

FRESH PEACH PIE

✔️ **WHY THIS RECIPE WORKS:** Juicy summer peaches usually produce soupy peach pies. We corralled the moisture that peaches give off during cooking in a number of ways. First, we macerated the peaches to draw out some of their juices and added a measured portion back to the filling. Second, we used both cornstarch and pectin to bind up what remained. Using two thickeners left the pie with a clear, silky texture without any of the gumminess or gelatinous texture that larger amounts of either one alone produced. Finally, we used a reliable, delicious lattice crust, the open nature of which let moisture cook off as the pie baked.

WHILE THE ALMOST-IMPOSSIBLE JUICINESS OF A RIPE peach is the source of the fruit's magnificence, it's also the reason that fresh peaches can be tricky to use in pies. Ripe peaches exude so much juice that they require an excess of flavor-dampening binders to create a filling that isn't soup. Fresh peaches can also differ dramatically in water content, so figuring out how much thickener to add can be a guessing game. Finally, ripe peaches are delicate, easily disintegrating into mush when baked. In our book, a perfect slice of peach pie is a clean slice of pie, with fruit that's tender yet intact.

In the past, we've had some success in perfecting a filling by using potato starch, but this ingredient isn't always readily available, and it still leaves the filling a little looser than we'd like. We wanted to make a peach pie with a filling that holds the slices in place without preventing any of the fresh peach flavor from shining through.

But before we could nail down the filling, we'd need a reliable crust. Experimenting taught us one thing: The fillings in pies with lattice-tops had far better consistencies, since the crosshatch allows moisture to evaporate during cooking. Moreover, lattices served as windows into the pies' interiors, making it easy to know when the filling was bubbly at the center, a sure sign that it was fully cooked.

When making a lattice, it's actually helpful to have a dough with a little more structure. Our dough calls for a little more water and a little less fat, both of which help create a sturdy dough that can withstand the extra handling involved in making a lattice. And this dough still manages to bake up tender and taste rich and buttery.

We moved on to thinking about building the lattice itself. Whether you cut out strips and then weave them directly over the filling or do this handiwork on the side and then transfer the finished lattice to the pie, it takes practice to create neat, professional-looking results. We wanted a lattice that a novice baker could do perfectly. The best approach we found skips the weaving in favor of simply laying one strip over the previous one in a pattern that allows some of the strips to appear woven (see "Building a 'No-Weave' Lattice Top"). Even with less handling, we still found it helpful to freeze the strips for 30 minutes before creating the lattice. Done.

Now it was time to get down to the fruit. Most recipes we'd tested called for tossing thinly sliced peaches with sugar and spices before throwing them into the pie crust. But we'd noted that the peaches handled this way shed a lot of moisture, thanks to the sugar's osmotic action on the slices. Sugar is hygroscopic—meaning it easily attracts water to itself—making it superbly capable of pulling juice out of the peaches' cells. If we were going to gain control over the consistency of the filling, that's where we'd need to start. Since osmosis occurs on the surface, we made the peach slices relatively large to minimize total surface area. We cut the peaches into quarters and then cut each of these into thick 1-inch chunks.

We let the sugared peaches macerate for a bit and then drained off the juice, adding back only enough juice to moisten the filling. This would allow us to control how much liquid the peaches contributed from batch to batch. We tossed 3 pounds of peaches with ½ cup of sugar, 1 tablespoon of lemon juice, and a pinch of salt. When we drained the peaches 30 minutes later, they yielded more than ½ cup of juice. We settled on using exactly ½ cup as the right amount to moisten the filling. We added just enough cinnamon and nutmeg to accent the flavor of the peaches.

Now it was time to experiment with thickeners that would tighten up the fruit and juice while maintaining the illusion that nothing was in the pie but fresh peaches. Flour left the filling grainy and cloudy, while tapioca pearls never completely dispersed, leaving visible beads of

FRESH PEACH PIE

gel behind. (Grinding the rock-hard tapioca pearls into finer grains helped but was a pain.) Potato starch and cornstarch each worked admirably up to a point, but after that they did not eliminate further runniness so much as turn the filling murky and gluey. More important, all these starches dulled the flavor of the peaches.

Maybe adding starch was not the best approach. We thought about apple pie, which barely needs any thickener to create a filling that slices cleanly. Apples are less juicy than peaches, but they also contain lots of pectin, which helps them hold on to their moisture and remain intact during baking. Peaches, on the other hand, contain much less pectin. For our next test we stirred some pectin (we used the low-sugar kind since we wanted to keep sweeteners to a minimum) into our reserved peach juice, heated the mixture briefly on the stove, and then folded it into the peach chunks. This filling turned out smooth and clear and tasted brightly of peaches. But it was still runnier than we wanted. Adding more pectin wasn't the

solution; a hair too much and the filling turned bouncy. Then we thought back to a recipe that used a combination of pectin and cornstarch. When we had added cornstarch alone, it left the pie gluey but still fluid. But could we find the sweet spot using both thickeners? Yes: Two tablespoons of pectin and 1 tablespoon of cornstarch left us with a filling that was smooth, clear, and moist from edge to center without being soupy.

One problem remained: a tendency for the peach chunks to fall out of the pie slices—because of the chunks' irregular shapes, they never fit together perfectly. Mashing a small amount of the macerated peaches to a coarse pulp with a fork and using it as a form of mortar to eliminate gaps and stabilize the filling worked.

At last, we had a fresh peach pie that looked perfect, tasted of fresh peaches, and sliced neatly.

NOTES FROM THE TEST KITCHEN

BUILDING A "NO-WEAVE" LATTICE TOP
Making a lattice top for our Fresh Peach Pie can be intimidating. But it need not be if you use our simple technique: Freeze strips of dough and then arrange them in a particular order over the filling. Done properly, our approach gives the illusion of a woven lattice, with less effort.

1. Using frozen dough strips, lay 2 longest strips perpendicular to each other across center of pie to form cross. Place 4 shorter strips along edges of pie, parallel to center strips.

2. Lay 4 remaining strips between each edge strip and center strip. Trim off excess lattice ends, press edges of bottom crust and lattice strips together, and fold under.

Fresh Peach Pie

SERVES 8

If your peaches are too soft to withstand the pressure of a peeler, cut a shallow X in the bottom of the fruit, blanch them in a pot of simmering water for 15 seconds, and then shock them in a bowl of ice water before peeling. For fruit pectin we recommend both Sure-Jell for Less or No Sugar Needed Recipes and Ball RealFruit Low or No-Sugar Needed Pectin.

    3 pounds peaches, peeled, quartered, and pitted,
       each quarter cut into thirds
  ½ cup (3½ ounces) plus 3 tablespoons sugar
    1 teaspoon grated lemon zest plus 1 tablespoon juice
  ⅛ teaspoon salt
    2 tablespoons low- or no-sugar-needed fruit pectin
  ¼ teaspoon ground cinnamon
       Pinch ground nutmeg
    1 recipe Pie Dough for Lattice-Top Pie (recipe follows)
    1 tablespoon cornstarch

1. Toss peaches, ½ cup sugar, lemon zest and juice, and salt in medium bowl. Let stand at room temperature for at least 30 minutes or up to 1 hour. Combine pectin, cinnamon, nutmeg, and 2 tablespoons sugar in small bowl and set aside.

2. Remove dough from refrigerator. Before rolling out dough, let it sit on counter to soften slightly, about 10 minutes. Roll 1 disk of dough into 12-inch circle on lightly floured counter. Transfer to parchment paper–lined baking sheet. With pizza wheel, fluted pastry wheel, or paring knife, cut round into ten 1¼-inch-wide strips. Freeze strips on sheet until firm, about 30 minutes.

3. Adjust oven rack to lowest position, place rimmed baking sheet on rack, and heat oven to 425 degrees. Roll other disk of dough into 12-inch circle on lightly floured counter. Loosely roll dough around rolling pin and gently unroll it onto 9-inch pie plate, letting excess dough hang over edge. Ease dough into plate by gently lifting edge of dough with your hand while pressing into plate bottom with your other hand. Leave any dough that overhangs plate in place. Wrap dough-lined pie plate loosely in plastic wrap and refrigerate until dough is firm, about 30 minutes.

4. Meanwhile, transfer 1 cup peach mixture to small bowl and mash with fork until coarse paste forms. Drain remaining peach mixture through colander set in large bowl. Transfer peach juice to liquid measuring cup (you should have about ½ cup liquid; if liquid measures more than ½ cup, discard remainder). Return peach pieces to bowl and toss with cornstarch. Transfer peach juice to 12-inch skillet, add pectin mixture, and whisk until combined. Cook over medium heat, stirring occasionally, until slightly thickened and pectin is dissolved (liquid should become less cloudy), 3 to 5 minutes. Remove skillet from heat, add peach pieces and peach paste, and toss to combine.

5. Transfer peach mixture to dough-lined pie plate. Remove dough strips from freezer; if too stiff to be workable, let stand at room temperature until malleable and softened slightly but still very cold. Lay 2 longest strips across center of pie perpendicular to each other. Using 4 shortest strips, lay 2 strips across pie parallel to 1 center strip and 2 strips parallel to other center strip, near edges of pie; you should have 6 strips in place. Using remaining 4 strips, lay each one across pie parallel and equidistant from center and edge strips. If dough becomes too soft to work with, refrigerate pie and dough strips until dough firms up.

6. Trim overhang to ½ inch beyond lip of pie plate. Press edges of bottom crust and lattice strips together

and fold under. Folded edge should be flush with edge of pie plate. Crimp dough evenly around edge of pie using your fingers. Using spray bottle, evenly mist lattice with water and sprinkle with remaining 1 tablespoon sugar.

7. Place pie on rimmed baking sheet and bake until crust is set and begins to brown, about 25 minutes. Reduce oven temperature to 375 degrees, rotate sheet, and continue to bake until crust is deep golden brown and filling is bubbly at center, 30 to 40 minutes longer. Let pie cool on wire rack for 3 hours before serving.

Pie Dough for Lattice-Top Pie
MAKES ENOUGH FOR ONE 9-INCH PIE

- 3 **cups (15 ounces) all-purpose flour**
- 2 **tablespoons sugar**
- 1 **teaspoon salt**
- 7 **tablespoons vegetable shortening, cut into ½-inch pieces and chilled**
- 10 **tablespoons unsalted butter, cut into ¼-inch pieces and frozen for 30 minutes**
- 10–12 **tablespoons ice water**

1. Process flour, sugar, and salt in food processor until combined, about 5 seconds. Scatter shortening over top and process until mixture resembles coarse cornmeal, about 10 seconds. Scatter butter over top and pulse until mixture resembles coarse crumbs, about 10 pulses. Transfer to bowl.

2. Sprinkle 5 tablespoons ice water over flour mixture. With rubber spatula, use folding motion to evenly combine water and flour mixture. Sprinkle 5 tablespoons ice water over mixture and continue using folding motion to combine until small portion of dough holds together when squeezed in palm of your hand, adding up to 2 tablespoons remaining ice water if necessary. (Dough should feel quite moist.) Turn out dough onto clean, dry counter and gently press together into cohesive ball. Divide dough into 2 even pieces and flatten each into 4-inch disk. Wrap disks tightly in plastic wrap and refrigerate for 1 hour or up to 2 days.

Sweet American Classics

Bridget whips together the filling for lemon chiffon pie, an approach that produces the trademark fluffy, light texture.

APPLE PIE MIGHT COME TO MIND WHEN YOU THINK OF GREAT American desserts, but we'd venture to say that other sweets hold a place on the American table too, specifically lemon chiffon pie and a summertime treat, blueberry cake.

While most of us associate chiffon pie with diners, it actually is a turn-of-the-century innovation—one that didn't require baking. We wanted an easy graham cracker crust for this pie—and yes, we'd bake that. But we'd try and keep the other components as authentic as possible. We did, however, want to bump up the lemon flavor. Whipped egg whites give chiffon its fluffy texture, but they can also dilute the citrus character of the filling. We wanted that light, bright lemon flavor to be front and center, and we wanted our filling to be creamy and sliceable. Chiffon pie relies on gelatin to help set the filling, but the texture can quickly turn rubbery. We would need to get that balance just right.

Most versions of blueberry cake are more like homey snack cakes than a special finale to a meal. We wanted a dessert that was a little dressed up; we imagined a blueberry Bundt cake—a rich, buttery cake studded with juicy blueberries. Our first efforts resulted in blueberries sinking to the bottom of the pan. In other tries the blueberries bled through the cake, causing a sticky mess that refused to unmold in one piece. And we needed to find a way to boost the flavor of supermarket blueberries (while we cherish the sweet consistent flavor of wild blueberries, they're not always easy to find). Our goals were clear: infuse our cake with bright blueberry flavor and ensure a clean release so it would look as good as it tasted.

PERFECTING LEMON CHIFFON PIE

☑ **WHY THIS RECIPE WORKS:** We love the elegant simplicity of lemon chiffon pie but found the gelatin used in most recipes difficult to work with. We used a combination of cornstarch and gelatin to get a creamy pie and added a burst of lemon flavor by tucking a layer of lemon curd beneath the chiffon. Our graham cracker crust adds just a hint of flavor and is a crisp contrast to the soft and fluffy filling.

IN THE EARLY 20TH CENTURY, CHIFFON PIE WAS A breakthrough idea. Not only was the filling particularly light and silky, but it came together in no time—with nothing more than egg yolks, sugar, fruit juice or puree, and a little cream cooked into a curd and folded with sweetened whipped egg whites. Many versions didn't even require baking; instead, they were set with gelatin and chilled. Even the crust was a snap to make: Around the same time that chiffon pies became popular, crumb crusts did, too. Easier to make than pastry, their crisp, delicate texture became a common base for the billowy curd. It's no wonder the concept made its way into dozens of American cookbooks and magazines over the years and spawned dozens of flavor variations—strawberry, pumpkin, and our favorite, lemon, among them.

The dessert's popularity has waned somewhat, but to us its combination of ease and elegance is as appealing as ever. And yet we've never managed to produce a version that we'd consider perfect. Some attempts have even been complete failures, either because the filling failed to set properly and was like soup, or because it set up too much and turned out springy like a marshmallow. And the citrus flavor? With all those egg whites and the sugar, it was usually a little flat. This retro classic was due for a makeover. We moved ahead with our ideal in mind: a filling that's creamy, rich, and set but not stiff—and that packs plenty of bright lemon punch.

A classically crisp, buttery graham cracker crust seemed just fine here, so we skipped straight to the filling and sized up a handful of different recipes. The formulas were about the same, and all were quite simple: After cooking the lemon curd until it thickens, stir in a couple of teaspoons of unflavored gelatin (dissolved in a little water) and let the mixture cool. Then whip egg whites with sugar, gently but thoroughly combine the curd and whites, pour the filling into a prebaked crumb crust, and chill until set. Given the uniformity of the methods, we weren't surprised when most of the finished pies shared the same core flaw: a filling so bouncy that the most glaring example drew comparisons to marshmallow Peeps.

We knew that too much gelatin was responsible for the springiness, but we also knew that we couldn't do without at least a small amount. The outlier recipe we'd tried, from mid-20th-century pie baker Angie Earl, relied on cornstarch, not gelatin, to thicken the filling, and the results had been disastrously soupy. We tried upping the amount of cornstarch that we were adding and couldn't deny that the sturdiness of the filling improved with every extra tablespoon. But the more cornstarch we added the duller the lemon flavor—not surprising, since starch granules are known to absorb flavor molecules. We tried going back to gelatin but had no consistent luck. The problem was that gelatin is finicky. Even when we used the right amount, if we allowed the gelatin-thickened curd to firm up a bit too long, it wouldn't incorporate evenly and left streaks of curd in the chiffon. We even tried adding more eggs to the cornstarch curd, hoping that their proteins, fat, and emulsifiers would help the filling gel better. Including two egg whites helped a little, but any more egg and the chiffon tasted more like an omelet than a dessert.

We'd exhausted our options when it came to trying each of the thickeners alone, but what about using them together in moderation? Assuming that we could nail the right ratio, the gelatin would supply the chiffon with just enough structure to make it sliceable, while the cornstarch would give it a bit more body (see "For Flawless Chiffon, Two Thickeners Are Better than One"). A few days' worth of tests later, we almost had it: 1 tablespoon of cornstarch plus a mere teaspoon of gelatin produced a filling that wasn't soupy. However, it still seemed too airy and flimsy. Not wanting to dull the flavor with more cornstarch, we wondered if we could make the filling a little denser with something other than a thickener. That's when we thought of whipping: Most chiffon pie recipes call for gently

LEMON CHIFFON PIE

CRUMB CRUST DONE RIGHT

Using a measuring cup, press the crumb mixture firmly and evenly across the bottom of the pie plate. Then pack the crumbs against the side of the pie plate, using your thumb and the measuring cup simultaneously.

CREATING A SMOOTH LEMON LAYER

After spreading the lemon curd over the crust, we briefly pop the curd-lined crust in the freezer to firm it up; that way, it won't squish when topped with the chiffon.

FOR FLAWLESS CHIFFON, TWO THICKENERS ARE BETTER THAN ONE

JUST GELATIN: RUBBERY

Gelatin, a pure protein, works by forming a gel network that traps the liquid in the filling. Too much can lead to a bouncy texture—and even the ideal amount produces inconsistent results. If the gelatin-thickened curd is allowed to firm up a tad too long before being combined with the egg whites, it leaves streaks.

JUST CORNSTARCH: SOUPY

Cornstarch thickens when its starch molecules bond together and trap water, creating a solid, jellylike structure. It's more forgiving to work with than gelatin, but unless you add a glut of it, the filling will be loose. And too much cornstarch will mute the flavor of the filling.

GELATIN + CORNSTARCH: PERFECT

Using both gelatin and cornstarch in moderation produces chiffon that sets up reliably but isn't rubbery. The proteins in just 1 teaspoon of gelatin are enough to form a gel network, while a mere tablespoon of cornstarch acts as a filler that makes the network more stable without dulling the filling's lemony punch.

folding the curd into the whipped whites to preserve the filling's cloudlike consistency. We wanted to pull back on that approach, so we switched to a much more aggressive incorporation method: whipping the two components together in a stand mixer. This vigorous approach produced a filling that was less foamy and a bit more dense.

Now that we'd straightened out the structural issues, we could work on brightening up the lemon flavor and hopefully make the filling a bit richer, too.

Some of the most lemony pies we'd made early on got their citrus flavor not only from fresh-squeezed juice but also from zest and even lemon extract. Extract gave the filling an unappealing "cooked" lemon flavor, but grating some of the fruit's fragrant skin and adding it to the filling rounded out the acidity of the juice with a fresher, more complex perfume. And yet the big lemon kick that our tasters clamored for still hadn't fully come through. What the pie needed, they said, was another layer of lemon flavor.

Another layer—that wasn't a bad idea, actually. What if we reserved a portion of the potent lemon curd to line the pie shell? We took 1¼ cups of the curd base (a little more than half of the total), spread it in the bottom of the pie shell, and froze it briefly to help it set. It delivered precisely the extreme tanginess we'd been craving, not to mention an eye-catching pop of color. The only hitch was that now the ratio of curd to whipped egg whites had changed, so the texture of the filling was off. Since we were losing some of the gelatin to the curd liner, the chiffon layer now squished a bit under the knife when we sliced. It also tasted a bit lean, since the curd took some of the yolks and cream with it, too. Fortunately, there was an obvious way to solve the consistency problem: Divide the teaspoon of gelatin between the two layers. This way, both components contained just enough to be creamy yet stable.

Dairy was the obvious go-to for richness, but we could add only so much before the gelatin lost its grip on the chiffon. That ruled out liquids like heavy cream and half-and-half. But what about something more solid, like cream cheese? Four ounces, stirred into the remaining portion of the curd, enriched the chiffon nicely and also thickened it up a bit.

Creamy but sturdy, rich but still lightweight, and full of bright citrus tang, this pie was a showstopper.

Lemon Chiffon Pie

SERVES 8 TO 10

For tips on shaping the crust, see "Crumb Crust Done Right." Before cooking the curd mixture, be sure to whisk thoroughly so that no clumps of cornstarch or streaks of egg white remain. Pasteurized egg whites can be substituted for the three raw egg whites. Serve with lightly sweetened whipped cream.

CRUST

- **9** whole graham crackers
- **3** tablespoons sugar
- **⅛** teaspoon salt
- **5** tablespoons unsalted butter, melted

FILLING

- **1** teaspoon unflavored gelatin
- **4** tablespoons water
- **5** large eggs (2 whole, 3 separated)
- **1¼** cups (8¾ ounces) sugar
- **1** tablespoon cornstarch
- **⅛** teaspoon salt
- **1** tablespoon grated lemon zest plus ¾ cup juice (4 lemons)
- **¼** cup heavy cream
- **4** ounces cream cheese, cut into ½-inch pieces, softened

1. FOR THE CRUST: Adjust oven rack to lower-middle position and heat oven to 325 degrees. Process graham crackers in food processor until finely ground, about 30 seconds (you should have about 1¼ cups crumbs). Add sugar and salt and pulse to combine. Add melted butter and pulse until mixture resembles wet sand.

2. Transfer crumbs to 9-inch pie plate. Press crumbs evenly into bottom and up sides of plate. Bake until crust is lightly browned, 15 to 18 minutes. Allow crust to cool completely.

3. FOR THE FILLING: Sprinkle ½ teaspoon gelatin over 2 tablespoons water in small bowl and let sit until gelatin softens, about 5 minutes. Repeat with second small bowl, remaining ½ teaspoon gelatin, and remaining 2 table-spoons water.

4. Whisk 2 eggs and 3 yolks together in medium saucepan until thoroughly combined. Whisk in 1 cup sugar, cornstarch, and salt until well combined. Whisk in lemon zest and juice and heavy cream. Cook over medium-low heat, stirring constantly, until thickened and slightly translucent, 4 to 5 minutes (mixture should register 170 degrees). Stir in 1 water-gelatin mixture until dissolved. Remove pan from heat and let stand for 2 minutes.

5. Remove 1¼ cups curd from pan and pour through fine-mesh strainer set in bowl. Transfer strained curd to prepared pie shell (do not wash out strainer or bowl). Place filled pie shell in freezer. Add remaining water-gelatin mixture and cream cheese to remaining curd in pan and whisk to combine. (If cream cheese does not melt, briefly return pan to low heat.) Pour through strainer into now-empty bowl.

6. Using stand mixer, whip 3 egg whites on medium-low speed until foamy, about 2 minutes. Increase speed to medium-high and slowly add remaining ¼ cup sugar. Continue whipping until whites are stiff and glossy, about 4 minutes. Add curd–cream cheese mixture and whip on medium speed until few streaks remain, about 30 seconds. Remove bowl from mixer and, using spatula, scrape sides of bowl and stir mixture until no streaks remain. Remove pie shell from freezer and carefully pour chiffon over curd, allowing chiffon to mound slightly in center. Refrigerate for at least 4 hours or up to 2 days before serving.

BLUEBERRY BUNDT CAKE

✔ **WHY THIS RECIPE WORKS:** Switching from flavor-packed wild Maine blueberries to oversize, bland cultivated blueberries wreaks havoc in a cake. The berries refuse to stay suspended in the batter and burst into bland, soggy pockets in the oven. We solved these problems by pureeing the fruit, seasoning it with sugar and lemon, and bumping up its natural pectin content with low-sugar pectin for a thickened, fresh-tasting filling that could be swirled throughout the cake.

SOMEWHERE ALONG THE LINE, BLUEBERRIES GOT THE reputation of being a casual fruit, best fit for tossing into pancakes or hearty snack cakes. But one of our favorite more occasion-worthy desserts is a delicate yellow Bundt cake speckled with intensely flavored wild Maine blueberries. However, with no easy access to fresh, wild Maine blueberries, we decided that it was time to take on the challenge of baking just such a cake—one that was truly packed with fresh blueberry flavor—using widely available (and more affordable) cultivated blueberries.

While our intentions were good, our early tests were failures. In every recipe we tried, the large cultivated blueberries, rather than remaining evenly dispersed throughout like their compact wild cousins, dropped to the bottom of the pan. The few berries that did manage to stay in place burst into big, soggy pockets when subjected to the heat of the oven. Tasters found that these watery cultivated blueberries tasted incredibly bland.

We regrouped, and restarted our testing using one of the test kitchen's tried-and-true Bundt cake recipes (which uses a base of creamed butter and sugar for a light texture) and focused our efforts on wrangling the berries.

Meaning to address both flavor and texture issues in one fell swoop, we tried tossing the blueberries in various combinations of flour, cornstarch, and cornmeal, along with some sugar and lemon zest. Our hope was that the dry starches would not only absorb and trap the liquid as the berries burst but also provide some added texture to their smooth exteriors, and therefore enough drag that

the fruit would stay put. No dice. Most of the dry mixture simply sloughed off the berries as we incorporated them, leaving gummy streaks throughout. And the fruit still plummeted to the bottom of the pan like little stones.

Next we tried macerating 10 ounces of berries in sugar in a colander, hoping to draw out excess liquid before they reached the cake. But after a full hour, the fruit hadn't exuded even a drop of juice. It turns out that in addition to their generous size, commercial blueberry breeds are selected for the durability of their skins—a boon for transport but a barrier against the hygroscopic pull of sugar. We next attempted to lightly squish the blueberries with a potato masher, but alas, the juice yield barely budged. But this got us thinking: If the berries were bursting inside the cake, why not beat them to the punch and burst them before adding them to the batter?

Of course, adding plain crushed berries directly to the batter would be neither tasty nor attractive. But we could puree them and then swirl the thick mix through the batter to produce an elegant marbled cake. Pureeing was simple enough with a quick buzz in the blender. But the puree was too thin and liquidy to swirl into the cake batter on its own. We had to find a way to thicken it up.

We rounded up the usual thickening suspects: flour, cornstarch, and tapioca. We tried cooking a small portion of the puree with various amounts of all three and then stirring that into the remaining raw puree in order to retain fresh flavor. To produce a mixture that was thick enough to be successfully swirled into the batter, we needed to use a significant amount of each starch. The fallout? Dulled flavor, an artificial texture, or both.

While none of our thickening techniques had provided the texture that we were after, one positive had emerged from this barrage of testing. With the switch to pureed blueberries, we were able to bump up the flavor by adding sugar, lemon juice and zest, and a pinch of salt directly to the fruit. This stuff tasted bright and balanced. Still, if we couldn't get the puree to lace through the batter—and stay put—then this small victory would be for naught. After processing yet another batch of puree, we left the kitchen in order to brainstorm with a few fellow test cooks. Following a healthy dose of suggestions and encouragement we returned to the blueberries. To our astonishment, the puree had slightly gelled and

MARBLED BLUEBERRY BUNDT CAKE

thickened—on its own. The reason? With some research, we learned that blueberries contain a small amount of natural pectin (it's stored in their cell walls and particularly in their skins), which had been released in the blender. Our next move felt obvious: Boost the naturally present pectin with additional store-bought pectin.

We opted for pectin for low-sugar recipes, as our filling didn't have the requisite sweetness for the regular version. We tried dissolving varying amounts of pectin—along with sugar, lemon zest, and salt—in just ¼ cup of the puree on the stovetop. We stirred this sticky mixture into the remaining blueberry puree and let it sit until

slightly cooled. As we'd hoped, the extra pectin gelled the blueberry mixture just enough, and it tasted like fresh fruit. Finally satisfied with this filling, we focused on putting it all together.

The reengineered filling was so good at staying in place that we couldn't simply swirl it into the top of the cake and let it flow into the rest of the batter—it would remain stuck in place. Instead, we added it in two phases. We spooned half of the batter into our prepared Bundt pan and formed a shallow channel in the middle of it. We then added half of the filling to this depression and thoroughly swirled and folded it in with a butter knife. We repeated these steps for the second layer before baking our cake at 325 degrees for about an hour. The cake emerged from the oven lightly bronzed and smooth, with spotty hints of the lacy marbling that lay beneath. Tasters tucked into this cake and were pleased with its hits of blueberry in every bite.

EQUIPMENT CORNER

There are a lot of useless coffee-related gadgets out there; here are two that are worthwhile.

POUR-OVER COFFEE BREWER

Coffee enthusiasts love manual pour-over brewing devices because they let you control water temperature and steeping time—both key to a good cup. The Incred 'a Brew by Zevro ($24.99) has a brewing chamber that you fill with ground coffee, add 195- to 205-degree water, and let it steep. It uses a built-in wire mesh filter (similar to a French press) instead of paper filters. After steeping, place the carafe atop a mug to open the valve that releases the coffee. The tool produced 2½ cups of flavorful, full-bodied coffee with some sediment, just like from a French press. Using this product means you'll never have to worry about running out of filters—a big plus. One caveat: It won't work with mugs wider than 3½ inches in diameter.

COFFEE TEMPERATURE REGULATOR

Coffee Joulies ("JOO-lees"), small stainless-steel capsules, promise to cool your coffee quickly to the ideal drinking temperature (140 degrees) and keep it there. How do they work? The "phase change" material encapsulated within each Joulie has a melting temperature of 140 degrees. Surrounded by hotter liquid, this material absorbs heat (cooling the surrounding liquid) until it's completely melted inside the Joulie. Then it slowly releases this heat back out into the coffee, keeping the temperature stable. We tested Joulies ($49.95 for a set of five) in our favorite 16-ounce travel mug and in a 12-ounce ceramic mug. In the open mug, Joulies worked halfway: They quickly cooled coffee to 140 degrees but didn't maintain the temperature any better than coffee without Joulies. In the travel mug, the coffee quickly cooled and held steady for 2 hours. (Coffee in the travel mug without Joulies took just over 2 hours to cool to 140 degrees.) Joulies work, but only in a travel mug.

Marbled Blueberry Bundt Cake

SERVES 12

Spray the pan well in step 1 to prevent sticking. If you don't have baking spray with flour, mix 1 tablespoon melted butter and 1 tablespoon flour into a paste and brush inside the pan. For fruit pectin we recommend both Sure-Jell for Less or No Sugar Needed Recipes and Ball RealFruit Low or No-Sugar Needed Pectin. If using frozen berries, thaw them before blending in step 3. This cake can be served plain or with Lemon Glaze or Cinnamon Whipped Cream.

CAKE

  3 cups (15 ounces) all-purpose flour

1½ teaspoons baking powder

 ¾ teaspoon baking soda

  1 teaspoon salt

 ½ teaspoon ground cinnamon

 ¾ cup buttermilk

  2 teaspoons grated lemon zest plus 3 tablespoons juice

  2 teaspoons vanilla extract

  3 large eggs plus 1 large yolk, room temperature

18 tablespoons (2¼ sticks) unsalted butter, softened

  2 cups (14 ounces) sugar

FILLING

- ¾ cup (5¼ ounces) sugar
- 3 tablespoons low- or no-sugar-needed fruit pectin
  Pinch salt
- 10 ounces (2 cups) fresh or thawed frozen blueberries
- 1 teaspoon grated lemon zest plus 1 tablespoon juice

1. FOR THE CAKE: Adjust oven rack to lower-middle position and heat oven to 325 degrees. Heavily spray 12-cup nonstick Bundt pan with baking spray with flour. Whisk flour, baking powder, baking soda, salt, and cinnamon together in large bowl. Whisk buttermilk, lemon zest and juice, and vanilla together in medium bowl. Gently whisk eggs and yolk to combine in third bowl.

2. Using stand mixer fitted with paddle, beat butter and sugar on medium-high speed until pale and fluffy, about 3 minutes, scraping down bowl as needed. Reduce speed to medium and beat in half of eggs until incorporated, about 15 seconds. Repeat with remaining eggs, scraping down bowl after incorporating. Reduce speed to low and add one-third of flour mixture, followed by half of buttermilk mixture, mixing until just incorporated after each addition, about 5 seconds. Repeat using half of remaining flour mixture and all of remaining buttermilk mixture. Scrape down bowl, add remaining flour mixture, and mix at medium-low speed until batter is thoroughly combined, about 15 seconds. Remove bowl from mixer and fold batter once or twice with rubber spatula to incorporate any remaining flour. Cover bowl with plastic wrap and set aside while preparing filling (batter will inflate a bit).

3. FOR THE FILLING: Whisk sugar, pectin, and salt together in small saucepan. Process blueberries in blender until mostly smooth, about 1 minute. Transfer ¼ cup puree and lemon zest to saucepan with sugar mixture and stir to thoroughly combine. Heat sugar-blueberry mixture over medium heat until just simmering, about 3 minutes, stirring frequently to dissolve sugar and pectin. Transfer mixture to medium bowl and let cool for 5 minutes. Add remaining puree and lemon juice to cooled mixture and whisk to combine. Let sit until slightly set, about 8 minutes.

4. Spoon half of batter into prepared pan and smooth top. Using back of spoon, create ½-inch-deep channel

in center of batter. Spoon half of filling into channel. Using butter knife or small offset spatula, thoroughly swirl filling into batter (there should be no large pockets of filling remaining). Repeat swirling step with remaining batter and filling.

5. Bake until top is golden brown and skewer inserted in center comes out with no crumbs attached, 60 to 70 minutes. Let cake cool in pan on wire rack for 10 minutes, then invert cake directly onto wire rack. Let cake cool for at least 3 hours before serving.

Lemon Glaze
MAKES ABOUT 2 CUPS

- 3–4 tablespoons lemon juice (2 lemons)
- 2 cups (8 ounces) confectioners' sugar

1. While cake is baking, whisk together 3 tablespoons lemon juice and sugar until smooth, gradually adding more lemon juice as needed until glaze is thick but still pourable (mixture should leave faint trail across bottom of mixing bowl when drizzled from whisk).

2. After cake has been removed from pan and inverted onto wire rack set in baking sheet, pour half of glaze over warm cake and let cool for 1 hour. Pour remaining glaze evenly over cake and continue to let cool to room temperature, at least 2 hours.

Cinnamon Whipped Cream
MAKES ABOUT 2 CUPS

For the best texture, whip the cream until soft peaks just form. Do not overwhip.

- 1 cup heavy cream
- 2 tablespoons confectioners' sugar
- ¼ teaspoon ground cinnamon
  Pinch salt

Using stand mixer fitted with whisk, whip all ingredients on medium-low speed until foamy, about 1 minute. Increase speed to high and whip until soft peaks form, 1 to 3 minutes.

Decadent Desserts

A chocolate glaze adds a glossy sheen and sophisticated look to this irresistible chocolate tart.

WHEN WE THINK OF DECADENT DESSERTS, THOSE WITH CARAMEL AND chocolate are front and center. We wanted to develop two desserts that put the spotlight on each of these rich flavors—a creamy, comforting butterscotch pudding and a silky and sophisticated chocolate tart.

We're all familiar with butterscotch pudding from a box or those tubs of premade pudding in the dairy case. They might satisfy your sweet tooth, but not much else. They're full of preservatives and artificial flavors, and have a texture that's more caulk-like than creamy. We knew we could do far better with a homemade version. Real butterscotch pudding gets its complex flavor from simple ingredients such as brown sugar, cream, and vanilla. The best versions start with a caramelized butterscotch sauce. Preparing caramel can be tricky because sugar can burn so quickly. We needed to find a way to make this step more foolproof and fuss-free. We were also looking for a pudding with a lush and creamy texture—not gummy from too much thickener nor so loose that it wouldn't hold up on a spoon. We wanted to simplify this comfort classic so we could enjoy it anytime.

Chocolate tart fillings come in a variety of guises—from fudgy brownie to dense and intense ganache. We wanted something a bit lighter and more ethereal: a custard-style tart with deep, chocolaty flavor. We imagined layers of flavor in our tart—from a crisp, nutty crust to a creamy filling, and a thin glaze of chocolate that would give our tart a polished, glistening sheen. An approachable method for making the crust, the choice of chocolate, and a method for putting it all together were just a few of the tasks on our to-do list for this showstopper dessert.

ULTIMATE BUTTERSCOTCH PUDDING

✔ **WHY THIS RECIPE WORKS:** For butterscotch pudding with rich, bittersweet flavor, we made butterscotch sauce by cooking butter, brown and white sugar, corn syrup, lemon juice, and salt together into a dark caramel. Because making caramel can be finicky—it can go from caramelized to burnt in a matter of seconds, we used a two-step process that gave us a larger window in which to gauge the doneness of the caramel. We first brought the mixture to a rolling boil and then we reduced the heat to a low simmer where it came up to temperature slowly so we could stop the cooking at just the right moment. To turn our butterscotch into pudding, we ditched the classical (but time-consuming) tempering method in favor of a revolutionary technique that calls for pouring the boiling caramel sauce directly over the thickening agents (egg yolks and cornstarch thinned with a little milk). The result is the sophisticated bittersweet flavor of traditional butterscotch with less mess and fuss.

MOST BUTTERSCOTCH PUDDING IS SYNONYMOUS with a powdered mix or those hermetically sealed small plastic cups from the supermarket. Rarely do we take the time to cobble it together from scratch—unfortunate, since we're sacrificing flavor for convenience. Real butterscotch gets its rich, nuanced, slightly bitter character from the complex reactions that take place when brown sugar and butter are cooked together into a caramel; when it's combined with custard, the result is miles away from the painfully sweet puddings produced commercially. And yet, it comes with a price of admission: Before you even get to the point of making pudding, you've got to successfully cook that caramel, which isn't easy. With this in mind, we set ourselves a high bar: Take the scare out of making caramel, simplify the pudding-making process, and ultimately bring the flavor of true butterscotch back into the American repertoire.

We started with a recipe Ruth Wakefield (of Toll House chocolate chip cookie fame) developed in the 1936 edition of *Toll House Tried and True Recipes*—a time well before fake butterscotch came on the scene. Unfortunately, we found it easy to under- or overcook the butterscotch, resulting in pudding that was either too sweet or unpalatably bitter, respectively. The problem revolved around visual cues: We never knew whether we'd reached the critical "dark brown" (read: properly caramelized) stage of making butterscotch because the brown sugar–butter mixture is already quite dark. We needed more precision, and that meant breaking out the thermometer.

We tried again, melting butter with equal amounts of granulated and brown sugars, salt, and a little water. We boiled batches of this mixture, aiming for 300 degrees—the peak of flavor development—before adding ¼ cup of cream to halt the cooking process. But we couldn't consistently nail that temperature. The window of doneness, which lasted only a few seconds somewhere between the 6- and 7-minute mark, was simply too narrow. If it was even a couple of degrees over, the caramel burned.

We needed to slow things down, so we switched gears and tried simmering a couple of batches over a low flame. Indeed, this afforded us a much wider window (minutes, not seconds) in which to check the temperature of the mixture and add the cream. The trade-off was time: This approach took 30 minutes—triple the amount that we had been spending. But maybe we could have it both ways. In the name of compromise, we tried a hybrid method in which we boiled the butterscotch hard at first to get the caramelization going and then dropped the heat and gently simmered it to the finish line. Bingo. A 5-minute boil brought the mixture to 240 degrees, at which point we lowered the heat for another 12 to 16 minutes of simmering to climb the final 60 degrees. The method was foolproof—and surprisingly, it produced a richer-tasting butterscotch than the high-heat method did.

Curious about the pudding's better flavor, we did a little digging and discovered that the flavor of butterscotch is highly dependent on the Maillard reaction. While we normally think of Maillard in relation to browning meat, the same reaction takes place when milk

BEST BUTTERSCOTCH PUDDING

proteins in butter react with reducing sugars (fructose and glucose) to develop hundreds of new flavor compounds. This reaction depends on time and temperature: The longer the pudding cooks and the higher the temperature it cooks at, the more flavor that develops. By bringing the pudding to 240 degrees—a relatively high temperature—and then letting it slowly increase to 300 degrees, we were allowing the pudding to spend more time at higher temperatures, which translated into deeper flavor. It was a great side effect of our relatively quick, foolproof method.

Feeling confident about making the butterscotch, we wondered if there weren't other ways to nudge along the browning process and get even deeper flavor. We had been using a combination of white sugar (sucrose) and dark brown sugar (mostly sucrose, with a little glucose and fructose from the molasses). Because the Maillard reaction is fueled by simple sugars like glucose and fructose, we cast about for other sources of these sugars and made

NOTES FROM THE TEST KITCHEN

A NEW WAY TO CONSISTENTLY PERFECT CARAMEL

The rich flavor of our butterscotch pudding depends on cooking the caramel mixture to 300 degrees before adding the cream, but it's easy to over- or undercook that mixture when it's boiled from start to finish (the usual approach). Our more forgiving method: Boil the caramel over medium heat until it reaches 240 degrees, then reduce the heat to medium-low, and gently simmer it until it reaches 300 degrees. The simmer phase takes about 12 to 16 minutes—plenty of time in which to grab a thermometer and the cream.

FOR CREAMY CUSTARDS, GO STIR CRAZY

While developing our recipe for Best Butterscotch Pudding, we noticed that some batches turned out slightly grainy, while others were silky smooth. The problem, we were surprised to learn, wasn't undissolved cornstarch: It was the butter. Once the pudding cooled and the fat solidified, any bits that hadn't been thoroughly broken down came across as grainy on the tongue. Vigorously whisking the pudding—or any pudding with a generous amount of butter—breaks down the fat into tiny droplets that are too small to detect once the mixture cools. (It's the same principle as emulsifying a vinaigrette: Thoroughly whisking in the oil ensures that the fat breaks down into tiny droplets that don't "break" the dressing.)

two additions to the butterscotch mixture: corn syrup, which is loaded with glucose, and lemon juice, which, through a process called inversion, promotes the breakdown of sucrose, a complex sugar, into simple glucose and fructose molecules. As the butterscotch simmered away, more and more sucrose inverted, providing extra fuel for the flavorful reaction.

With our rich-flavored, foolproof butterscotch in place, we moved on to streamlining our pudding approach. The classic method of cooking an egg- and starch-thickened custard goes as follows: Bring the liquid (here the butterscotch caramel thinned with milk and cream) to a simmer; stir a portion of it into a mixture of egg yolks, cornstarch, and a little liquid such as milk—a process known as tempering; return everything to the pot; and bring it up to a full boil. Finally, strain the mixture into a separate bowl to remove the inevitable bits of overcooked egg, cover, and chill until set. Looking for a less fussy alternative, we paged through a number of cookbooks and stumbled upon a technique in which the liquid is brought to a full boil, immediately poured over the thickening mixture (egg yolks, cornstarch, and milk), and simply whisked until combined.

Having always known tempering as a slow, gentle method, we thought this approach sounded reckless. But for the sake of convenience, we cooked another batch of butterscotch; whisked together the yolks, cornstarch, and milk in a separate bowl; and—crossing our fingers—poured the hot butterscotch mixture over the yolk mixture and whisked vigorously. The result shocked us: Rather than a lumpy mess of curdled yolks, the pudding was smooth and glossy. Why did the mixture thicken properly—and why didn't it curdle?

It turns out that we'd misunderstood pudding making—and tempering—all along. Boiling pudding guarantees that it will thicken, but it's akin to ordering an airstrike when a single grenade will do. Why? Because the two components that thicken pudding—cornstarch and egg yolks—do so at temperatures well below the boiling point of 212 degrees. (For more information, see "Smoother Route to Pudding?")

As for why the pour-over method didn't cause the eggs to curdle, the explanation was twofold: First, the yolks were protected by the cornstarch, which absorbs water, swells, and slows down the binding of the egg proteins. Second, the pour-over approach removes the custard from direct heat, thereby eliminating any risk of curdling. (Some sources claim that the yolks must be boiled to prevent an active enzyme in them from liquefying the thickened custard, but we never encountered this problem.)

Pleased with our revamped caramel and pudding methods, we had one last tweak to make: We added 2 teaspoons of vanilla extract and 1 teaspoon of dark rum to mirror the deep caramel notes of the butterscotch.

With a dollop of lightly sweetened whipped cream on top, our butterscotch pudding was the ultimate version—simple to make yet with a flavor so complex and sophisticated that we wouldn't hesitate to serve it to company.

Best Butterscotch Pudding

SERVES 8

When taking the temperature of the caramel in step 1, tilt the pan and move the thermometer back and forth to equalize hot and cool spots. Work quickly when pouring the caramel mixture over the egg mixture in step 4 to ensure proper thickening. Serve the pudding with lightly sweetened whipped cream.

12	tablespoons unsalted butter, cut into ½-inch pieces
½	cup (3½ ounces) granulated sugar
½	cup packed (3½ ounces) dark brown sugar
¼	cup water
2	tablespoons light corn syrup
1	teaspoon lemon juice
¾	teaspoon salt
1	cup heavy cream
2¼	cups whole milk
4	large egg yolks
¼	cup cornstarch
2	teaspoons vanilla extract
1	teaspoon dark rum

1. Bring butter, granulated sugar, brown sugar, water, corn syrup, lemon juice, and salt to boil in large saucepan over medium heat, stirring occasionally to dissolve sugar and melt butter. Once mixture is at full rolling boil, cook, stirring occasionally, for 5 minutes (caramel will register about 240 degrees). Immediately reduce heat to medium-low and gently simmer (caramel should maintain steady stream of lazy bubbles—if not, adjust heat accordingly), stirring frequently, until mixture is color of dark peanut butter, 12 to 16 minutes longer (caramel will register about 300 degrees and should have slight burnt smell).

2. Remove pan from heat; carefully pour ¼ cup cream into caramel mixture and swirl to incorporate (mixture will bubble and steam); let bubbling subside. Whisk vigorously and scrape corners of pan until mixture is completely smooth, at least 30 seconds. Return pan to medium heat and gradually whisk in remaining ¾ cup cream until smooth. Whisk in 2 cups milk until mixture is smooth, making sure to scrape corners and edges of pan to remove any remaining bits of caramel.

SMOOTHER ROUTE TO PUDDING?

Pudding recipes almost always have you temper the yolks and cornstarch (i.e., add some hot dairy to the mixture to gradually raise its temperature), add everything to the remaining dairy in the pot, and stir constantly as the mixture slowly comes to a boil and thickens. Inevitably, bits of egg still overcook and need to be strained. We wondered if there was a better way.

THE EXPERIMENT

We made one batch of pudding the conventional way and a second batch in which the yolks never saw the heat of the stove: We added a little warm milk to the yolks and cornstarch, brought the remaining "dairy" (in our recipe, the butterscotch mixture) to a boil, and then dumped this hot liquid over the egg mixture and whisked briefly as the pudding thickened almost instantly.

THE RESULTS

The conventional pudding needed straining, while the "no-cook" custard was utterly smooth and perfectly thickened.

THE EXPLANATION

Boiling pudding is overkill. When cornstarch is combined with liquid, it thickens between 144 and 180 degrees, while yolks diluted by liquid coagulate between 180 and 185 degrees—significantly lower temperatures than the boiling point of 212 degrees. Whisking the hot butterscotch mixture into the yolk mixture heated the pudding to about 185 degrees—plenty hot to properly thicken it but not so hot that the yolks overcooked.

3. Meanwhile, microwave remaining ¼ cup milk until simmering, 30 to 45 seconds. Whisk egg yolks and cornstarch together in large bowl until smooth. Gradually whisk in hot milk until smooth; set aside (do not refrigerate).

4. Return saucepan to medium-high heat and bring mixture to full rolling boil, whisking frequently. Once mixture is boiling rapidly and beginning to climb toward top of pan, immediately pour into bowl with yolk mixture in 1 motion (do not add gradually). Whisk thoroughly for 10 to 15 seconds (mixture will thicken after a few seconds). Whisk in vanilla and rum. Spray piece of parchment paper with vegetable oil spray and press on surface of pudding. Refrigerate until cold and set, at least 3 hours. Whisk pudding until smooth before serving.

BEST CHOCOLATE TART

✔ **WHY THIS RECIPE WORKS:** For us, a great chocolate tart should possess deep chocolate flavor, a rich, lush texture, and a sophisticated presentation. First we made a custardy filling by melting intense dark chocolate into hot cream, adding eggs, and baking. To enrich the filling's flavor, we added some butter and a little instant espresso to echo the bittersweetness of the chocolate. Because custards tend to curdle under high heat, we baked the tart in a very low 250-degree oven for a smooth and silky texture. To make our tart a showstopper, we topped it with a simple glossy glaze of chocolate, cream, and corn syrup. A classic sweet pastry dough flavored with ground almonds made the perfect crust to complement the chocolate filling.

DESCRIPTORS LIKE "UNBELIEVABLY DECADENT" AND "death by chocolate" are de rigueur when it comes to chocolate tarts. But for us, the real draw of the dessert is its pure, uncomplicated profile: The best versions boast a flawlessly smooth, trufflelike texture; unadulterated chocolate flavor; and a sophisticated polish. With the holidays approaching, we decided that there was no better time to uncover what makes an exceptional chocolate tart.

We stocked up on high-quality bittersweet chocolate, heavy cream, eggs, and butter—the building blocks of just about every chocolate tart filling recipe we had found—and prepared to start testing. It quickly became clear that, while the filling components were more or less identical for all the recipes, the way in which those ingredients were treated separated the tarts into three unique styles. The first, a baked, egg white–aerated dessert, turned out slightly souffléed and brownielike—not quite the suave, satiny dessert that we had in mind. The other two styles started out on the same course, by calling for melting chocolate into hot cream, and then they went their separate ways. One style got a rich addition of whisked-in butter and was simply popped in the fridge to chill until set—it was essentially a very rich ganache. The other style traded butter for eggs, baked in a moderate oven for

BEST CHOCOLATE TART

about 30 minutes, and then chilled for a few hours until nicely set. Both styles had merits. Lots of butter made the ganache filling taste great—for about two bites. The custard-style tart was more velvety and less greasy—and the clear favorite among tasters.

And yet we still had plenty of testing ahead of us. Without the butter, the custard-style filling tasted flat. It also emerged from the oven with a rather drab matte finish—too underdressed, especially for a holiday table.

To nail down the basics, we tested varying ratios of chocolate and cream before landing on 9 ounces and 1¼ cups, respectively. That way, the filling was intense but not cloying, and silky without turning runny. Two whole beaten eggs (we tried one and two—the range that most recipes suggest—as well as one and two yolks) lent the filling just enough body without turning it rubbery.

Trouble was, with eggs in the mix, the tart baked up slightly curdled.

It occurred to us that perhaps the 350-degree oven we'd been using was too hot for this custard-style filling—after all, eggs curdle when overcooked. So we prepared several more tarts and staggered their baking temperatures at 25-degree intervals from 350 down to 250 degrees. The differences were astounding. The 350-degree tart was predictably stiff, but with each reduction in temperature the texture improved, and the 250-degree tart had the ethereal quality that we were after. It wasn't just curd-free; it was downright plush.

If only the filling didn't taste—and look—so dull and one-dimensional, we thought. The ganache-style filling's buttery foundation may have been too rich for more than a few bites, but dull it was not, which got us thinking: What if we strayed from the typical custard-style tart and added a moderate amount of butter? To our working recipe we compared fillings made with 8, 6, 4, and 2 tablespoons of butter and found that 4 tablespoons nicely rounded out the chocolate flavor without overdoing the richness. A touch of espresso powder, dissolved in the cream with a bit of salt, added an echo of bittersweetness that highlighted the chocolate.

As for looks, our tart needed a makeover—or at least some cover-up. In the heat of the oven, its surface formed tiny fissures and took on a matte finish. We wanted this holiday-caliber dessert to boast a glossy sheen and figured that a simple chocolate glaze would do the trick. We played with a few formulas and settled on a bittersweet chocolate ganache spiked with a little corn syrup for shine. Pouring the glaze over the baked and chilled tart created that polished look.

With the filling perfected at last, we test-drove pastry options for the crust, pitting a basic *pâte sucrée* (butter, flour, sugar, egg yolk, and heavy cream, all pulsed in the food processor) against versions dressed up with cocoa powder and toasted nuts. The cocoa pastry made for a dramatic-looking dessert (dark crust, dark filling), but a third chocolate component felt like overkill. Replacing ½ cup of the flour with sliced almonds (our tasters' choice over walnuts and pecans, although hazelnuts made a fine substitute) turned out a rich-tasting, pleasantly nubby dough—an ideal match for the lush chocolate filling. The only downside to the nut pastry: Because it contained more fat, the dough was quite tender and fragile. After some experimenting, we devised a novel technique for transferring and fitting this dough into the pan without tearing it (see "Fitting Delicate Pastry into a Tart Pan").

A dollop of lightly sweetened whipped cream plus either a sprinkle of coarse sea salt or a pile of chocolate curls were easy finishing touches producing a stunning presentation. We prepared ourselves for handing out the recipe—often. Anyone who tasted this gorgeously plush chocolate tart was going to demand to find out how to make it.

Best Chocolate Tart

SERVES 12

Toasted and skinned hazelnuts can be substituted for the almonds. Use good-quality dark chocolate containing a cacao percentage between 60 and 65 percent; our favorites are Callebaut Intense Dark Chocolate, L–60–40NV, and Ghirardelli 60% Cacao Bittersweet Chocolate. Let tart sit at room temperature before glazing in step 6. The finished tart can be garnished with chocolate curls or with a flaky coarse sea salt, such as Maldon. Serve with lightly sweetened whipped cream; if you like, flavor the whipped cream with cognac or vanilla extract.

CRUST

1 large egg yolk
2 tablespoons heavy cream
½ cup sliced almonds, toasted
¼ cup (1¾ ounces) sugar
1 cup (5 ounces) all-purpose flour
¼ teaspoon salt
6 tablespoons unsalted butter, cut into ½-inch pieces

FILLING

1¼ cups heavy cream
½ teaspoon instant espresso powder
¼ teaspoon salt
9 ounces bittersweet chocolate, chopped fine
4 tablespoons unsalted butter, cut into thin slices and softened
2 large eggs, lightly beaten, room temperature

GLAZE

3 tablespoons heavy cream
1 tablespoon light corn syrup
2 ounces bittersweet chocolate, chopped fine
1 tablespoon hot water

1. FOR THE CRUST: Beat egg yolk and cream together in small bowl. Process almonds and sugar in food processor until nuts are finely ground, 15 to 20 seconds. Add flour and salt; pulse to combine, about 10 pulses. Scatter butter

FITTING DELICATE PASTRY INTO A TART PAN

This novel method works with any tart dough, but it is especially helpful when working with higher-fat, more fragile pastry.

1. Invert tart pan (with bottom) on top of dough round. (Removable bottom will drop onto dough.) Press on tart pan to cut dough. Pick up baking sheet, carefully invert it, and set tart pan down. Remove sheet and peel off and reserve plastic wrap.

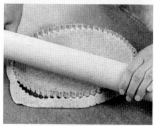

2. Roll over dough edges with rolling pin to cut (dough will slip into pan). Gently ease and press dough into bottom of pan, reserving scraps.

3. Roll dough scraps into ¾-inch rope. Line edge of tart pan with rope and gently press into fluted sides.

4. Line tart pan with reserved plastic. Using measuring cup, gently press dough to even thickness. Sides should be ¼ inch thick. Use paring knife to trim excess dough above rim of tart.

250 ISN'T A TYPO

Baking the tart at 250 degrees—about 100 degrees lower than most recipes—might sound like a mistake, but we found that heating this custard-style filling very gently is the key to producing a texture that's silky-smooth, not curdled.

over flour mixture; pulse to cut butter into flour until mixture resembles coarse meal, about 15 pulses. With processor running, add egg yolk mixture and process until dough forms ball, about 10 seconds. Transfer dough to large sheet of plastic wrap and press into 6-inch disk; wrap dough in plastic and refrigerate until firm but malleable, about 30 minutes. (Dough can be refrigerated for up to 3 days; before using, let stand at room temperature until malleable but still cool.)

2. Roll out dough between 2 large sheets of plastic into 11-inch round about ⅜ inch thick. (If dough becomes too soft and sticky to work with, slip it onto baking sheet and refrigerate until workable.) Place dough round on baking sheet and refrigerate until firm but pliable, about 15 minutes.

3. Adjust oven rack to middle position and heat oven to 375 degrees. Spray 9-inch tart pan with removable bottom with vegetable oil spray. Keeping dough on sheet, remove top layer of plastic. Invert tart pan (with bottom) on top of dough round. Press on tart pan to cut dough. Using both hands, pick up sheet and tart pan and carefully invert both, setting tart pan right side up. Remove sheet and peel off plastic; reserve plastic. Roll over edges of tart pan with rolling pin to cut dough. Gently ease and press dough into bottom of pan, reserving scraps. Roll dough scraps into ¾-inch rope (various lengths are OK). Line edge of tart pan with rope(s) and gently press into fluted sides. Line tart pan with reserved plastic and, using measuring cup, gently press and smooth dough to even thickness (sides should be about ¼ inch thick). Using paring knife, trim any excess dough above rim of tart; discard scraps. Freeze dough-lined pan until dough is firm, 20 to 30 minutes.

4. Set dough-lined pan on baking sheet. Spray 12-inch square of aluminum foil with oil spray and press foil, sprayed side down, into pan; fill with 2 cups pie weights. Bake until dough is dry and light golden brown, about 25 minutes, rotating sheet halfway through baking. Carefully remove foil and weights and continue to bake until pastry is rich golden brown and fragrant, 8 to 10 minutes longer. Let cool completely on baking sheet on wire rack.

5. **FOR THE FILLING:** Heat oven to 250 degrees. Bring cream, espresso powder, and salt to simmer in small saucepan over medium heat, stirring once or twice to dissolve espresso powder and salt. Meanwhile, place chocolate in large heatproof bowl. Pour simmering cream mixture over chocolate, cover, and let stand for 5 minutes to allow chocolate to soften. Using whisk, stir mixture slowly and gently (so as not to incorporate air) until homogeneous. Add butter and continue to whisk gently until fully incorporated. Pour beaten eggs through fine-mesh strainer into chocolate mixture; whisk slowly until mixture is homogeneous and glossy. Pour filling into tart crust and shake gently from side to side to distribute and smooth surface; pop any large bubbles with toothpick or skewer. Bake tart, on baking sheet, until outer edge of filling is just set and very faint cracks appear on surface, 30 to 35 minutes; filling will still be very wobbly. Let cool completely on baking sheet on wire rack. Refrigerate, uncovered, until filling is chilled and set, at least 3 hours or up to 18 hours.

6. **FOR THE GLAZE:** Thirty minutes before glazing, remove tart from refrigerator. Bring cream and corn syrup to simmer in small saucepan over medium heat; stir once or twice to combine. Remove pan from heat, add chocolate, and cover. Let stand for 5 minutes to allow chocolate to soften. Whisk gently (so as not to incorporate air) until mixture is smooth, then whisk in hot water until glaze is homogeneous, shiny, and pourable. Working quickly, pour glaze onto center of tart. To distribute glaze, tilt tart and allow glaze to run to edge. (Spreading glaze with spatula will leave marks on surface.) Pop any large bubbles with toothpick or skewer. Let cool completely, about 1 hour.

7. **TO SERVE:** Remove outer ring from tart pan. Insert thin-bladed metal spatula between crust and pan bottom to loosen tart; slide tart onto serving platter. Cut into wedges and serve.

A Fancy Finale

CHAPTER 26

THE RECIPE
Chocolate-Espresso
Dacquoise

*Chefs Andrea Geary and
Stephanie Pixley ready a
dacquoise for its coating of
chocolate ganache. We make
this multilayered showpiece
dessert approachable by
making a simplified meringue
layer and an easy German-
style buttercream.*

SOMETIMES ONLY A TRULY SPECTACULAR DESSERT WILL DO AS THE ending to a celebratory dinner. There are always plenty of options to pick up at a fancy bakery or patisserie, but when the rest of the meal is homemade, if we have the time, we'd like our dessert to be homemade as well. A layered confection such as a dacquoise really takes the cake in the looks department—but what about the time factor? Dacquoise is a multilayered showpiece of nutty meringue, buttercream, and sometimes chocolate ganache. The crisp meringue layers provide a wonderful contrast to the creamy buttercream and bittersweet chocolate ganache. There aren't many home recipes for this dessert—it's more often found on the menus of high-end restaurants or the aforementioned patisseries. And this is for good reason—it's not an easy dessert to pull off. We set out to break this dessert down by each component to make it approachable for even novice bakers. We envisioned a light and nutty meringue that baked up crisp; a rich, flavorful buttercream; and an easy chocolate ganache to pour over the assembled torte. We also wanted to tackle a particular challenge with this dessert—the serving. We wanted to find a way to build the torte so that it was easy to create tidy slices and so that the buttercream did not squirt out from between the layers as our knife touched the meringue. This dessert demands to look as good as it tastes. It just might be the best dessert you ever make—join us to learn how to pull it off perfectly.

CHOCOLATE-ESPRESSO DACQUOISE

INTRODUCING DACQUOISE

✔ **WHY THIS RECIPE WORKS:** We made this elaborate and impressive-looking dessert more approachable by reworking the meringue and buttercream, making them simpler and more foolproof. We swapped the traditional individually piped layers of meringue for a single sheet that was trimmed into layers after baking, and we shortened the usual 4-plus hours of oven time by increasing the oven temperature. While many recipes call for a Swiss or French buttercream made with a hot sugar syrup, we opted for a German buttercream. With equal parts pastry cream and butter, this option required no hot syrup and it enabled us to use up the egg yolks left over from the meringue.

THERE COULD BE NO MORE STUNNING FINALE TO A holiday celebration than a chocolate dacquoise. Named for Dax, a town in southwestern France where the dessert was first made, the confection is all sleek planes and clean right angles, elegantly enrobed in glossy dark chocolate studded with toasted nuts. Slicing it reveals a layered interior of light, nutty meringue sandwiched with silky buttercream. But you rarely see dacquoise anywhere but fancy patisseries or high-end restaurants—and with good reason: Making one is a project to rival all projects. The good news? Not only can you make this showpiece at home but you can have it ready long before your guests arrive. In fact, this dessert improves when it's assembled a day or two before serving, as the flavors meld and the buttercream softens the meringue.

Here's how a pastry chef makes a dacquoise: She whips egg whites with sugar to make a meringue, into which she folds finely chopped nuts. Then she pipes the meringue into several flat layers, bakes them for up to 3 hours at a very low temperature, and then leaves them in the oven to dry out completely. When the meringues are crisp, she layers them with buttercream (made from more egg whites, a hot sugar syrup, and a lot of butter). Finally, she coats the whole construction in a shiny ganache made with chocolate and warm cream.

All that is no big deal in a professional pastry shop, where there's no shortage of skilled workers, specialized equipment, big ovens, and egg whites. But for the process to be manageable at home, we would have to eliminate some of its more bothersome features: namely the fussy piping, the long baking and drying times, and that tricky sugar syrup. If possible, we would do something with all those orphaned egg yolks, too. We didn't want our dacquoise to just satisfy dinner guests; we wanted it to render them speechless.

Meringue is typically made by whipping egg whites (and perhaps an acid such as cream of tartar, which provides greater stability by preventing excess bonding and coagulation) until they begin to retain air and form soft mounds in the bowl. The sugar is then slowly added while the whipping continues, until it dissolves and the mixture thickens, forming stiff, glossy peaks when the beaters are pulled from the surface. For dacquoise, finely ground nuts are folded in at this point, and then the meringue pieces are piped and baked. Meringue made this way, though, is a bit crunchy, leading to a dacquoise that can be hard to slice (and eat) even when left to sit for a while. Our research revealed an intriguing alternative: an "automatic meringue," in which the whites and sugar were combined at the start. Not only did it sound easier than a traditional meringue but it might also produce a better texture, so we gave it a try.

The automatic meringue was indeed easy—we just dumped egg whites, cream of tartar, and sugar into the bowl of a stand mixer and let it rip. However, it took twice as long as the traditional method to reach stiff peaks, plus it baked up as dense and firm as Styrofoam. Sugar, it turns out, interferes with the unfolding and bonding of egg white proteins, so adding it too early made for a slower process and denser meringue.

Obviously that was the wrong direction. But it gave us an idea: What if we went back to the traditional method of adding sugar once soft peaks formed but withheld some of it until the end? Would that lighten up the texture? We gave it another go, this time adding just half of the sugar between the soft- and stiff-peak stages and folding in the remainder at the end with the ground nuts. Now the egg white proteins were freer to expand, forming a light, airy foam in just 4 minutes. Once baked, this meringue had a crisp, delicate texture that was the perfect foil for buttercream—and was easier to slice and eat.

With the meringue's texture nailed down, we considered its shape. We wanted a rectangular dacquoise because it would be easier to slice neatly than a round one. Reluctant to use a pastry bag to pipe the meringue, we spooned it into four piles on two baking sheets and tried using an offset spatula to coax the piles into uniform rectangles. But despite our best efforts, they were all different sizes, with rounded blobs for corners.

Then we had a brainstorm: Why not bake the meringue in one big piece? That way, we could use just one sheet (eliminating the need to bake in batches) and trim the baked meringue into even pieces with squared-off edges. We drew a 13 by 10½-inch rectangle on parchment that we then placed on a rimless baking sheet. Using the lines as a guide, we spread meringue over it in an even layer.

Most dacquoise recipes call for baking the meringue at about 200 degrees for anywhere from 1 to 3 hours and then letting it dry in the oven for several hours more. We found that even 2 hours of baking, followed by a full 3-hour rest, left our oversize meringue still chewy and impossible to cut neatly. With the temperature that low, we'd have to bake the meringue for a full 3 hours and rest it for at least as long in order to get it nice and crisp. While it was all hands-off waiting, we wanted to trim any time we could from the process.

What if we upped the heat? Although in this application we didn't need the meringue to be bright white (since it would be covered up by the buttercream), meringue baked at 300 degrees was too brown and tasted slightly burnt. With the oven at 250 degrees, we found our sweet spot: The meringue had a creamy taupe color and a firm, crisp texture after only 90 minutes of baking and the same amount of time drying.

The higher temperature sped things up, but it also caused a new problem: The surface of the meringue was now drying out faster than the bottom, forming a brittle crust that ballooned out and crumbled as soon as we took a knife to it. Though meringue and moisture are normally bitter enemies, we wondered if lightly spritzing water on the top before baking would help. This counterintuitive solution worked: Since water can't go above 212 degrees (the temperature at which it evaporates), it delayed the setting of the surface until most of the moisture had evaporated from the bottom layer, forming a meringue that remained intact and cooked evenly. We now had what looked like a plank of acoustical tile. It took some trial and error before we found the right tools and technique for dividing it into four strips. A serrated bread knife, a gentle scoring motion, and a ruler ensured that each piece was trimmed to a perfect rectangle. We had the building blocks—now for the mortar to hold it together.

In its simplest form, buttercream is just creamed butter and powdered sugar. Not wanting cloying sweetness, we ruled out that type. The trouble is, most other buttercreams rely on egg whites, which would leave us with more leftover yolks. We also wanted to avoid using a hot sugar syrup (which requires a candy thermometer to bring the syrup to precisely 240 degrees). Our salvation came in the form of a confection we'd never made before: a German buttercream, which is whipped together from butter and pastry cream, a simple custard made with egg yolks that doesn't need a thermometer.

We whisked the yolks with cornstarch, milk, and sugar over medium heat, until thickened. After cooling the pastry cream, we whipped it with an equal amount of softened butter until the mixture came together to form a velvety-smooth buttercream. It seemed a winner until we took a taste. Disappointingly, its flavor was flat and stodgy.

Dacquoise often includes a coffee-flavored element, and a few teaspoons of espresso powder mixed into the buttercream definitely improved matters. But something was still lacking. We found the missing element on the liquor shelf in the form of almond liqueur. Just an ounce gave the buttercream the sophistication it deserved and complemented the nutty meringue. We stacked the strips of meringue, spreading buttercream between each layer; thinly coated the exterior with it as well; and then let our dacquoise firm up in the fridge while we prepared its crowning glory—the shiny chocolate ganache.

To make the ganache, we poured warm cream over finely chopped bittersweet chocolate and stirred until it was smooth, adding corn syrup for enhanced shine. After it had cooled a bit, we poured the ganache over the chilled dacquoise and smoothed it over each side. For the final touch, we decorated the top of the dacquoise with toasted hazelnuts and patted some sliced almonds onto its sides.

It looked spectacular, but when we ate a slice, we knew that something was still missing. Only the outer edges of our dacquoise boasted chocolate flavor and that just wasn't enough. Next time around, we made twice as much ganache and spread some on each layer of meringue, alternating with the buttercream. Now there was crisp, nutty meringue; rich buttercream; and silky ganache in every bite.

Tasters greeted this last dacquoise with a near silence that made us wonder. Had we gotten it horribly wrong? Had the meringue glued their jaws together? No. The dessert had merely rendered them speechless.

Chocolate-Espresso Dacquoise

SERVES 10 TO 12

The components in this recipe can easily be prepared in advance. Use a rimless baking sheet or an overturned rimmed baking sheet to bake the meringue. Instant coffee may be substituted for the espresso powder. To skin the hazelnuts, simply place the warm toasted nuts in a clean dish towel and rub gently. We recommend Ghirardelli Bittersweet Chocolate Baking Bar with 60% cacao for this recipe.

MERINGUE

- ¾ cup blanched sliced almonds, toasted
- ½ cup hazelnuts, toasted and skinned
- 1 tablespoon cornstarch
- ⅛ teaspoon salt
- 1 cup (7 ounces) sugar
- 4 large egg whites, room temperature
- ¼ teaspoon cream of tartar

BUTTERCREAM

- ¾ cup whole milk
- 4 large egg yolks
- ⅓ cup (2⅓ ounces) sugar
- 1½ teaspoons cornstarch
- ¼ teaspoon salt
- 2 tablespoons amaretto or water
- 1½ tablespoons instant espresso powder
- 16 tablespoons unsalted butter, softened

GANACHE

- 6 ounces bittersweet chocolate, chopped fine
- ¾ cup heavy cream
- 2 teaspoons corn syrup

- 12 whole hazelnuts, toasted and skinned
- 1 cup blanched sliced almonds, toasted

1. FOR THE MERINGUE: Adjust oven rack to middle position and heat oven to 250 degrees. Using ruler and pencil, draw 13 by 10½-inch rectangle on piece of parchment paper. Grease baking sheet and place parchment on it, marked side down.

2. Process almonds, hazelnuts, cornstarch, and salt in food processor until nuts are finely ground, 15 to 20 seconds. Add ½ cup sugar and pulse to combine, 1 to 2 pulses.

3. Using stand mixer fitted with whisk, whip egg whites and cream of tartar on medium-low speed until foamy, about 1 minute. Increase speed to medium-high and whip whites to soft, billowy mounds, about 1 minute. With mixer running at medium-high speed, slowly add remaining ½ cup sugar and continue to whip until glossy, stiff peaks form, 2 to 3 minutes. Fold nut mixture into egg whites in 2 batches. With offset spatula, spread meringue evenly into 13 by 10½-inch rectangle on parchment, using lines on parchment as guide. Using spray bottle, evenly mist surface of meringue with water until glistening. Bake for 1½ hours. Turn off oven and allow meringue to cool in oven for 1½ hours. (Do not open oven during baking and cooling.) Remove from oven and let cool to room temperature, about 10 minutes. (Cooled meringue can be kept at room temperature, tightly wrapped in plastic wrap, for up to 2 days.)

4. FOR THE BUTTERCREAM: Heat milk in small saucepan over medium heat until just simmering. Meanwhile, whisk yolks, sugar, cornstarch, and salt in bowl until smooth. Remove milk from heat and, whisking constantly, add half of milk to yolk mixture to temper. Whisking constantly, return tempered yolk mixture to remaining milk in saucepan. Return saucepan to medium heat and cook, whisking constantly, until mixture is bubbling and thickens to consistency of warm pudding, 3 to 5 minutes. Transfer pastry cream to bowl. Cover and refrigerate until set, at least 2 hours or up to 24 hours. Before using, warm gently to room temperature in microwave at 50 percent power, stirring every 10 seconds.

5. Stir together amaretto and espresso powder; set aside. Using stand mixer fitted with paddle, beat butter at medium speed until smooth and light, 3 to 4 minutes. Add pastry cream in 3 batches, beating for 30 seconds after each addition. Add amaretto mixture and continue to beat until light and fluffy, about 5 minutes longer, scraping down bowl thoroughly halfway through mixing.

6. FOR THE GANACHE: Place chocolate in heatproof bowl. Bring cream and corn syrup to simmer in small saucepan over medium heat. Pour cream mixture over chocolate and let stand for 1 minute. Stir mixture until smooth. Set aside to cool until chocolate mounds slightly when dripped from spoon, about 5 minutes.

7. Carefully invert meringue and peel off parchment. Reinvert meringue and place on cutting board. Using serrated knife and gentle, repeated scoring motion, trim

edges of meringue to form 12 by 10-inch rectangle. Discard trimmings. With long side of rectangle parallel to counter, use ruler to mark both long edges of meringue at 3-inch intervals. Using serrated knife, score surface of meringue by drawing knife toward you from mark on top edge to corresponding mark on bottom edge. Repeat scoring until meringue is fully cut through. Repeat until you have four 10 by 3-inch rectangles. (If any rectangles break during cutting, use them as middle layers.)

8. Place 3 rectangles on wire rack set in rimmed baking sheet. Using offset spatula, spread ¼ cup ganache evenly over surface of each meringue. Refrigerate until ganache is firm, about 15 minutes. Set aside remaining ganache.

9. Using offset spatula, spread top of remaining rectangle with ½ cup buttercream; place on wire rack with ganache-coated meringues. Invert 1 ganache-coated meringue, place on top of buttercream, and press gently to level. Repeat, spreading meringue with ½ cup buttercream and topping with inverted ganache-coated meringue. Spread top with buttercream. Invert final ganache-coated meringue on top of cake. Use 1 hand to steady top of cake and spread half of remaining buttercream to lightly coat sides of cake, then use remaining buttercream to coat top of cake. Smooth until cake resembles box. Refrigerate until buttercream is firm, about 2 hours. (Once buttercream is firm, assembled cake may be wrapped tightly in plastic and refrigerated for up to 2 days.)

10. Warm remaining ganache in heatproof bowl set over barely simmering water, stirring occasionally, until mixture is very fluid but not hot. Keeping assembled cake on wire rack, pour ganache over top of cake. Using offset spatula, spread ganache in thin, even layer over top of cake, letting excess flow down sides. Spread ganache over sides in thin layer (top must be completely covered, but some small gaps on sides are OK).

11. Garnish top of cake with hazelnuts. Holding bottom of cake with 1 hand, gently press almonds onto sides with other hand. Chill on wire rack, uncovered, for at least 3 hours or up to 12 hours. Transfer to platter. Cut into slices with sharp knife that has been dipped in hot water and wiped dry before each slice. Serve.

ASSEMBLING THE DACQUOISE

Here's how to assemble the three different components of dacquoise—cooled, baked meringue; buttercream; and ganache—into a dessert that looks like it was made in a professional bakery.

1. Using serrated knife and gentle, repeated scoring motion, trim edges of cooled meringue to form 12 by 10-inch rectangle.

5. Invert one ganache-coated strip on top of buttercream-coated strip and press gently. Spread top with buttercream. Repeat twice to form 4 layers.

2. With long side of meringue parallel to counter, mark top and bottom edges at 3-inch intervals.

6. Lightly coat sides of cake with half of remaining buttercream; coat top with remaining buttercream. Smooth edges and surfaces; refrigerate until firm.

3. Repeatedly score surface by gently drawing knife from top mark to corresponding bottom mark until cut through. Repeat to make four 10 by 3-inch strips.

7. Pour ganache over top of cake and spread in thin, even layer, letting excess flow down sides. Spread thinly across sides.

4. Place 3 strips on wire rack and spread ¼ cup ganache evenly over each. Refrigerate for 15 minutes. Spread remaining strip with ½ cup buttercream.

8. Place toasted whole hazelnuts in line on top of cake and gently press sliced almonds onto sides.

CONVERSIONS & EQUIVALENCIES

SOME SAY COOKING IS A SCIENCE AND AN ART. WE would say that geography has a hand in it, too. Flour milled in the United Kingdom and elsewhere will feel and taste different from flour milled in the United States. So, while we cannot promise that the loaf of bread you bake in Canada or England will taste the same as a loaf baked in the States, we can offer guidelines for converting weights and measures. We also recommend that you rely on your instincts when making our recipes. Refer to the visual cues provided. If the bread dough hasn't "come together in a ball," as described, you may need to add more flour—even if the recipe doesn't tell you so. You be the judge.

The recipes in this book were developed using standard U.S. measures following U.S. government guidelines. The charts below offer equivalents for U.S., metric, and imperial (U.K.) measures. All conversions are approximate and have been rounded up or down to the nearest whole number. For example:

1 teaspoon = 4.929 milliliters, rounded up to 5 milliliters
1 ounce = 28.349 grams, rounded down to 28 grams

VOLUME CONVERSIONS

U.S.	METRIC
1 teaspoon	5 milliliters
2 teaspoons	10 milliliters
1 tablespoon	15 milliliters
2 tablespoons	30 milliliters
¼ cup	59 milliliters
⅓ cup	79 milliliters
½ cup	118 milliliters
¾ cup	177 milliliters
1 cup	237 milliliters
1¼ cups	296 milliliters
1½ cups	355 milliliters
2 cups	473 milliliters
2½ cups	591 milliliters
3 cups	710 milliliters
4 cups (1 quart)	0.946 liter
1.06 quarts	1 liter
4 quarts (1 gallon)	3.8 liters

WEIGHT CONVERSIONS

OUNCES	GRAMS
½	14
¾	21
1	28
1½	43
2	57
2½	71
3	85
3½	99
4	113
4½	128
5	142
6	170
7	198
8	227
9	255
10	283
12	340
16 (1 pound)	454

CONVERSIONS FOR INGREDIENTS COMMONLY USED IN BAKING

Baking is an exacting science. Because measuring by weight is far more accurate than measuring by volume, and thus more likely to achieve reliable results, in our recipes we provide ounce measures in addition to cup measures for many ingredients. Refer to the chart below to convert these measures into grams.

INGREDIENT	OUNCES	GRAMS
Flour		
1 cup all-purpose flour*	5	142
1 cup cake flour	4	113
1 cup whole-wheat flour	5½	156
Sugar		
1 cup granulated (white) sugar	7	198
1 cup packed brown sugar (light or dark)	7	198
1 cup confectioners' sugar	4	113
Cocoa Powder		
1 cup cocoa powder	3	85
Butter†		
4 tablespoons (½ stick, or ¼ cup)	2	57
8 tablespoons (1 stick, or ½ cup)	4	113
16 tablespoons (2 sticks, or 1 cup)	8	227

* U.S. all-purpose flour, the most frequently used flour in this book, does not contain leaveners, as some European flours do. These leavened flours are called self-rising or self-raising. If you are using self-rising flour, take this into consideration before adding leavening to a recipe.
† In the United States, butter is sold both salted and unsalted. We generally recommend unsalted butter. If you are using salted butter, take this into consideration before adding salt to a recipe.

OVEN TEMPERATURES

FAHRENHEIT	CELSIUS	GAS MARK (imperial)
225	105	¼
250	120	½
275	135	1
300	150	2
325	165	3
350	180	4
375	190	5
400	200	6
425	220	7
450	230	8
475	245	9

CONVERTING TEMPERATURES FROM AN INSTANT-READ THERMOMETER

We include doneness temperatures in many of our recipes, such as those for poultry, meat, and bread. We recommend an instant-read thermometer for the job. Refer to the table above to convert Fahrenheit degrees to Celsius. Or, for temperatures not represented in the chart, use this simple formula:

Subtract 32 degrees from the Fahrenheit reading, then divide the result by 1.8 to find the Celsius reading.

EXAMPLE:

"Roast until chicken thigh registers 175 degrees."
To convert:

$175°$ F − 32 = $143°$
$143°$ ÷ 1.8 = $79.44°$C, rounded down to $79°$C

INDEX